Proceedings of the

Workshop on
nd Design

Proceedings of the

8th International Workshop on Software Specification and Design

March 22 – 23, 1996   Schloss Velen, Germany

Sponsored by

The IEEE Computer Society Technical Council on Software Engineering

In cooperation with

The Association for Computing Machinery (SIGSOFT)

IEEE Computer Society Press
Los Alamitos, California

Washington   •   Brussels   •   Tokyo

IEEE Computer Society Press
10662 Los Vaqueros Circle
P.O. Box 3014
Los Alamitos, CA 90720-1264

IEEE Computer Society Press Order Number PR07361
ISBN 0-8186-7361-3
ISSN 1063-6765

Additional copies may be ordered from:

IEEE Computer Society Press
Customer Service Center
10662 Los Vaqueros Circle
P.O. Box 3014
Los Alamitos, CA 90720-1264
Tel: +1-714-821-8380
Fax: +1-714-821-4641
Email: cs.books@computer.org

IEEE Computer Society
13, Avenue de l'Aquilon
B-1200 Brussels
BELGIUM
Tel: +32-2-770-2198
Fax: +32-2-770-8505
euro.ofc@computer.org

IEEE Computer Society
Ooshima Building
2-19-1 Minami-Aoyama
Minato-ku, Tokyo 107
JAPAN
Tel: +81-3-3408-3118
Fax: +81-3-3408-3553
tokyo.ofc@computer.org

Editorial production and cover layout by Mary E. Kavanaugh
Printed in the United States of America by KNI, Inc.

The Institute of Electrical and Electronics Engineers, Inc.

Table of Contents

Position Papers

Message from the Chairs

It is our pleasure to welcome you to the 8th International Workshop on Software Specification and Design (IWSSD-8), which for the first time is being held in Germany. It has become traditional to associate the workshop with a major international conference on Software Engineering, and this year is no exception. IWSSD-8 is being held in conjunction with the 18th International Conference on Software Engineering (ICSE-18), which takes place in Berlin directly following IWSSD-8. A remote location, separate from ICSE-18, was selected for IWSSD-8 to provide the true spirit of a workshop, and so facilitate and encourage participants to continue discussions and interactions outside of the formal workshop sessions. We hope that participants will enjoy the venue, Schloss Velen, a renovated fairy tale castle, as well as enjoy the surrounding area of Westphalia, which is close to a number of old German university towns, such as Münster, Paderborn, and Osnabrück.

In order to foster informed and fruitful discussions, the workshop is an invitation-only event of limited size. Based on formal submissions, approximately 80 people were selected and invited. From the submissions, the Program Committee carefully reviewed, discussed, and selected the papers that appear here. Papers are either full-size research contributions or shorter position statements; the two kinds of papers have been grouped separately in these proceedings. Each submission was read by at least three reviewers. For the position papers, we particularly tried to be receptive to new and interesting research ideas and provide a forum for their presentation and discussion.

Like its predecessors, IWSSD-8 maintains the principle that the accepted papers should serve as background material for the workshop. Therefore, the workshop does not include formal paper presentations, but rather provides an opportunity to engage in real work, with intensive discussions focused around major themes. Each theme is discussed in a separate working group directed by a Working Group Chair who organizes their group members so as to discuss the research issues of that particular theme.

This year the themes selected were Software Architecture, Design Engineering, Requirements Engineering, and Concurrency/Distribution. The theme discussions are based on a common case study, namely the London Ambulance Service (LAS), which is briefly summarized in the first paper appearing in these proceedings. The case study will be presented in a plenary session at the beginning of the workshop and the findings of the different working groups will be presented and discussed at the end of the workshop, again in a plenary session. In order to make best use of the time available, working group members were asked to prepare for the workshop by familiarizing themselves with the case study and the major issues in their area relevant to that case study. We believe that this format makes it both attractive and rewarding for people to attend, and is a major reason for the success of this workshop series.

As in the past, we plan to publish a workshop "Succeedings" in a future issue of ACM SIGSoft Notes. These will contain summaries of the discussions and results from each working group, as well as a summary of the workshop as a whole.

We gratefully acknowledge the work of the Program Committee and the Working Group Chairs — Daniel Jackson, Gerald Karam, Debra Richardson, and Kevin Ryan — who contributed a great deal of effort to the preparation of the workshop. We thank Anthony Finkelstein for suggesting the LAS case study and making the material available on-line, and thank the Communications Directorate, South West Thames Regional Health Authority, for allowing us to use the material. We thank the members of the IWSSD Steering Committee — Axel van Lamsweerde, Martin Feather, Jean-Pierre Finance, Carlo Ghezzi, Catalin Roman (Chair), and Jack Wileden — for their support, guidance, and continuing commitment to the IWSSD series. Finally, we acknowledge the help of all our staff, particularly our assistants Susanne Hueppmeier at Paderborn and Laura Vidal at Colorado, and the IEEE Computer Society for again sponsoring this event.

Wilhelm Schäfer
General Chair
wilhelm@uni-paderborn.de

Jeff Kramer
Program Co-Chair
jk@doc.ic.ac.uk

Alexander Wolf
Program Co-Chair
alw@cs.colorado.edu

Program and Organizing Committee

General Chair

Wilhelm Schäfer

Universität Paderborn, Germany

wilhelm@uni-paderborn.de

Program Co-Chairs

Jeff Kramer

Imperial College, London

jk@doc.ic.ac.uk

Alexander Wolf

University of Colorado, Boulder

alw@cs.colorado.edu

Program Committee

U. Buy – *USA*

P. Cunha – *Brazil*

F. Cristian – *USA*

M. Feather – *USA*

A. Fekete – *Australia*

S. Fickas – *USA*

A. Finkelstein – *United Kingdom*

D. Garlan – *USA*

C. Ghezzi – *Italy*

M. Goedicke – *Germany*

C. Heitmeyer – *USA*

P. Inverardi – *Italy*

D. Jackson – *USA*

S. Jähnichen – *Germany*

G. Karam – *Canada*

R. Kurki-Suonio – *Finland*

A. van Lamsweerde – *Belgium*

T. Maibaum – *United Kingdom*

D. Richardson – *USA*

D. Rosenblum – *USA*

K. Ryan – *Ireland*

M. Saeki – *Japan*

P. Zave – *USA*

Proceedings of the 8th International

CASE STUDY

Workshop on Software Specification and Design

A Comedy of Errors:
The London Ambulance Service Case Study

Anthony Finkelstein and John Dowell
School of Informatics, City University, London

A Comedy of Errors: the London Ambulance Service case study

Anthony Finkelstein & John Dowell
School of Informatics, City University, UK
{acwf@soi.city.ac.uk, johnd@soi.city.ac.uk}

Abstract

This paper provides an introduction to the IWSSD-8 case study - the "Report of the Inquiry Into the London Ambulance Service". The paper gives an overview of the case study and provides a brief summary. It considers how the case study can be used to orient discussion at the workshop and provide a bridge between the various contributions.

Introduction

The International Workshop on Software Specification & Design has established a tradition of using "case studies" to focus and provide coherence to its intensive working sessions. These case studies, supplied in advance to participants in the various tracks, have proved a fruitful way of working. Evidence of this can be seen most clearly in the "succeedings" or workshop reports which have followed previous workshops. It was decided for IWSSD-8 that, in order to provide common ground between the tracks, a single shared "case study" should be used, with each track drawing on it in a manner appropriate to their own interests and concerns. After some discussion we settled on the "Report of the Inquiry Into the London Ambulance Service" which is interesting in its own right, reflects aspects of requirements architecture, design, concurrency and distribution, and raises significant issues on the relation between these aspects.

The report is available by ftp, details of how to obtain it can be found at the bottom of the paper. Subsequent comments in this paper assume that you have access to the report. References in this paper are to report paragraph numbers.

Overview & Summary

Like most computing professionals in the UK we were aware of the failure, using this term broadly, of the computer aided despatch (CAD) system deployed by the London Ambulance Service (LAS) in, or shortly after,

October 1992. We suspect, as London residents, we were more immediately aware of it than most. At any rate, both of us read the items that appeared in the newspapers with considerable interest and concern.

Neither of us can remember when we first saw a copy of the report, probably in summer 1993, but both remember clearly our initial reactions - a mixture of horror and, we must confess, a certain macabre enjoyment. If not a comedy of errors it is at least a compounding of them. It seemed, on first reading, as if everything had gone wrong - every component of good engineering practice had been ignored, every guideline of software engineering disregarded, basic management principles neglected, even the dictates of common sense overlooked. Subsequent readings have rather changed our understanding of the failure which now emerges as an example of "systemic failure" or "normal accident" of the type identified by Perrow (1984). This having been said it is evident that at the heart of the failure are breakdowns in specification and design common to many software development projects and that the context in which they occurred is far from atypical. Therein lies its particular interest and challenge from our standpoint.

The failure, and the subsequent reaction to it must be understood in a broad political setting. The National Health Service (NHS), the government supported "free-at-the-point-of-use" system of health care provision in the UK, was undergoing considerable changes - in particular the move towards more decentralised and directly financially accountable management. These changes were combined with a lack of prior investment, significant ongoing resource pressures and a reallocation of NHS priorities drawing money away from London. A further feature of the political environment was a strong focus on the "effectiveness" or "performance" of public services. The mix of these changes with a combative political scene and fraught labour relations gave a particular significance and weight to the failure and lead to the establishment of the inquiry which reported in February 1993.

For orientation a short sketch of the report follows. There have been a number of other analyses of the LAS CAD system failure of which Mellor (1994) is probably the most useful.

The LAS despatch system is responsible for: receiving calls; despatching ambulances based on an understanding of the nature of the calls and the availability of resources; and, monitoring progress of the response to the call. A computer-aided despatching system was to be developed and would include an automatic vehicle locating system (AVLS) and mobile data terminals (MDTs) to support automatic communication with ambulances. This system was to supplant the existing manual system.

Immediately following the system being made operational the call traffic load increased (but not it should be noted to exceptional levels). The AVLS could not keep track of the location and status of units. This lead to an incorrect database so that (a) units were being despatched non-optimally (b) multiple units were being assigned to some calls. As a consequence of this there were a large number of exception messages and the system slowed down as the queue of messages grew. Un-responded exception messages generated repeated messages and the lists scrolled off the top of the screens so that awaiting attention and exception messages were lost from view. Ambulance crews were frustrated and, under pressure, were slow in notifying the status of their unit. They could not (or would not) use their MDTs and used incorrect sequences to enter the status information. The public were repeating their calls because of the delay in response. The AVLS no longer knew which units were available and the resource proposal software was taking a long time to perform its searches

The entire system descended into chaos (one ambulance arrived to find the patient dead and taken away by undertakers, another ambulance answered a 'stroke' call after 11 hours - 5 hours after the patient had made their own way to hospital). The CAD system was partly removed and aspects of its function (notably despatch decisions) were performed manually. This part-manual system seized up completely 8 days later. The back-up server did not work since it had not been fully tested. Operators used tape recordings of calls then reverted to a totally manual system. The Chief Executive of the LAS resigned.

A summary of this form cannot do justice to the range of problems identified by the inquiry. Key points which emerged were: the software was incomplete and effectively untested; the implementation approach was 'high risk'; inappropriate and unjustified assumptions were made during the specification process; there was a lack of consultation with users and clients in the development process with knock-on consequences for their "ownership" of the resulting system; the poor fit of the system with the organisational structure of the ambulance service. Subsidiary to these points but nevertheless important were the poorly designed user interfaces; lack of robustness; poor performance and straightforward bugs or errors. Though outside the scope of IWSSD there is a very strong message in the report about the attempt to change working practices through the specification, design and implementation of a computer system.

The report is exceptionally easy to read. It is divided into 6 parts: summary conclusions and recommendations on the part of the inquiry team; the background to the inquiry itself, including an orientation to the LAS and CAD; an account of the development of the CAD system; a discussion of the major system problems and breakdowns (failure in the narrow sense); a strategy for the future of CAD within the LAS; an analysis of the management and operation of the LAS. Another way to view the report is as having two facets - record and recommendation - and two targets - system and organisational context. The recommendations are less important for our purposes than the record though they are, for the most part, sensible and interesting. The discussion of the system is obviously our principal concern but the context is vital if it is to be properly understood. The report is best read in its entirety even if only pieces are to be used.

Inevitably the serious reader will experience some frustration with the report and will want access to parts of the underlying data and related source documents which are not readily available. These lacunae are the price that is paid for dealing with "real" cases - the flip side of the contextual richness of the material.

Using the Report

The report is not typical of specification and design case studies or "exemplars". It is not itself a specification or problem statement (like the lift, central heating system, package router or library system), though it contains significant fragments of such documents. Nor is it a complete account of the system development process, though again, it contains significant fragments of such an account. The particular role of the report, as a postmortem study, does however open some possibilities for analysis which "classical" exemplars do not.

The most obvious use of the report is simply to extract relevant specification-like fragments and use them, in isolation, to demonstrate specification and design techniques. An instance of this might be to model the manual despatch process, a typical office information system with the added complications of safety criticality and real-time constraints, see 3001 et seq. This has the clear merit of demonstrating the techniques in a real system. A variant of this is to rework some of the models presented in the report such as the communications structure, a sort of system architecture crudely presented in diag 3.1 and associated text.

A more challenging approach is to identify specific problems highlighted by the report and demonstrate, convincingly, that these problems would be avoided by particular specification and design techniques. An example, chosen almost at random, is the false assumption of "near perfect information of vehicle location and crew/vehicle status" on which the developers relied and which is documented in 4008. A related, though significantly more difficult, task is to demonstrate these techniques would work in the context described in the report. In other words that the specification and design techniques are robust with respect to the process, management and organisation which frame them. That is that they possess what psychologists term "ecological validity".

Less work is required to identify problems which lie outside the current state of the art in specification and design. The interplay between procurement and specification processes is a good example, see 3029 et seq. This can be combined with the use of the report to rebalance concerns within the field as a whole. There is, on the face of it, clear blue water between the primary concerns of the report, which line up neatly with those commonly expressed by industrial managers, and those which constitute the main targets of specification and design research. This suggests, we put it no stronger than that, the need for a reappraisal of research priorities.

Somewhat obliquely the report raises questions about how inquiries into system failures ought to be conducted what information should be recorded and how, in general, we can learn from our experience.

Our preference is to treat the report as a whole and to look at recurring themes. An illustration of this is how performance concerns bind together requirements, architecture, usability and testing. Another interesting example is how system integration and the reliability of behaviour and service provision by "bought-in" components continually emerges as a problem. We leave the identification of further themes as an exercise for the reader. This gestalt approach links well to the concept of systemic failure to which the LAS CAD so closely conforms.

Conclusion

Software engineers, and more specifically those concerned with specification and design, have become enamoured of what might be termed a "lachrymose theory" of software engineering - a fixation on errors and bugs. Software engineering can often be said to define itself by reference to problems and failures. The use of the LAS as a case study is not intended to reinforce this. However, "breakdowns" are important as it is only through an understanding of failed systems that we can formulate a view of what a successful system would be and, perhaps, the role of specification and design in this context.

How to Obtain the Report

We would like to thank the Communications Directorate of South West Thames Regional Health Authority for permission to scan and distribute this document electronically. The original printed version is available as ISBN 0-905133-70-6. The electronic version is available as:

Flavour 1: includes scanned images, 529K compressed
ftp://ftp.cs.city.ac.uk/pub/requirements/lascase0.9.ps.gz
ftp://ftp.cs.colorado.edu/users/iwssd8/lascase0.9.ps.gz

Flavour 2: without scanned images, 83K compressed
ftp://ftp.cs.city.ac.uk/pub/requirements/lasnodiags0.9.ps.gz
ftp://ftp.cs.colorado.edu/users/iwssd8/lasnodiags0.9.ps.gz

References

Mellor, P. (1994); CAD: computer-aided disaster; High Integrity Systems; 1, 2, pp101-156.

Perrow, C. (1984); Normal Accidents: living with high-risk technology; Basic Books, New York.

FULL PAPERS

A Case Study in Architectural Modeling: The AEGIS System*

Robert Allen   David Garlan

Computer Science Department

Carnegie Mellon University

Pittsburgh, PA 15213

Abstract

Software architecture is receiving increasingly attention as a critical design level for software systems. However, the current practice of architectural description is largely informal and ad hoc, with the consequence that architectural documents serve as a poor communication mechanism, are difficult to analyze, and may have very little relationship to the implemented system. In an attempt to address these problems several researchers have experimented with formalisms for architectural specification and modelling. One such formalism is WRIGHT. *In this paper we show how* WRIGHT *can be used to provide insight into an architectural design by modelling a prototype implementation of part of the AEGIS Weapons System.*

1 Introduction

A critical aspect of any complex software system is its architecture. At an architectural level of design a system is typically described as a composition of high-level, interacting components. Components represent a system's main computational elements and data stores: clients, servers, filters, databases, etc. Interactions between these elements range from the simple and generic (e.g., procedure call, pipes, shared data access) to the complex and domain-specific (e.g., implicit invocation mechanisms, client-server protocols, database protocols).

The description of a system at an architectural level of design is important for several reasons. Perhaps the most significant is that an architectural description makes a complex system intellectually tractable by characterizing it at a high level of abstraction. In particular, the architectural design exposes the top-level design decisions and permits a designer to reason about satisfaction of system requirements in terms of assignment of functionality to design elements.

For example, for a system in which data throughput is a key issue, an appropriate architectural design would allow the software architect to make system-wide estimates based on values of the throughputs for the individual components. Other issues relevant to this level of design include organization of a system as a composition of components; global control structures; protocols for communication, synchronization, and data access; assignment of functionality to design elements; physical distribution; scaling and performance; dimensions of evolution; and selection among design alternatives.

Unfortunately, the current state of the practice is to use informal, diagrammatic notations (such as box-and-line diagrams) and idiomatic characterizations (such as "client-server organization," "layered system," or "blackboard architecture"). The meanings of such diagrams and phrases, if they are given meanings at all, are typically established by informal convention among a small set of developers. (E.g., "in this diagram a line means a pipe.") This relative informality leads to architectural designs that are inherently ambiguous, difficult to analyze, and hard to mechanize.

To address these problems several researchers are investigating the application of formalisms for architectural specification and modelling. The general thrust of these efforts is to investigate the applicability of existing formal models (sometimes with new surface syntax) to the problem of characterizing and reasoning about software architectures.

An important challenge for this research community is to evaluate these languages and to understand their respective strengths and weaknesses. In the past, software specification languages faced similar needs. One mechanism for comparison has been the use of benchmark problems. Examples from the formal specification community include the library problem, the lift problem, the package router, etc.

What are the comparable problems for architecture? One candidate problem is the "AEGIS Weapons System." AEGIS is a large software system used to control ships for the US Navy. In 1994 a part of the system was used by the ARPA Prototech community as a vehicle to demonstrate their prototyping languages. While (architecturally speaking) the constructed system was relatively simple – less than a dozen architectural components – during the course of construction, it raised a surprisingly number of thorny architectural problems for the system implementors and integrators. The challenge for architectural specification languages, then becomes: could these problems have been detected and/or resolved through appropriate descriptive

*The research reported here was sponsored by the Wright Laboratory, Aeronautical Systems Center, Air Force Materiel Command, USAF, and the Advanced Research Projects Agency (ARPA) under grant F33615-93-1-1330; by National Science Foundation Grant CCR-9357792. Views and conclusions contained in this document are those of the authors and should not be interpreted as representing the official policies, either expressed or implied, of Wright Laboratory, the US Department of Defense, the United States Government, the National Science Foundation. The US Government is authorized to reproduce and distribute reprints for Government purposes, notwithstanding any copyright notation thereon.

formalisms?

In this paper we pick up the gauntlet. Specifically, we look at ways in which the WRIGHT architectural specification language can be used to characterize and reason about the AEGIS architecture. We begin with a brief characterization of related work. Next we outline AEGIS and the challenges that it represents. We then provide a naive architectural description of the architecture, and show how architectural formalism helps expose and resolve some of the architectural problems that arose in the course of implementing the system. We finish by providing a revised, more accurate description of the final system.

2 Related work

Our approach to architectural specification is based on the use of CSP to model the behavior of the components and their interactions in an architectural design. A number of other formalisms have been proposed for modelling architectures of software systems. Inverardi and Wolf have used the Chemical Abstract Machine [BB92] as a formal basis for architectural description [IW95]. Architectural elements are represented by "molecules" and architectural interaction by "reactions." Reactions operate as a set of rewrite rules, which determine how the computations proceed over time. We understand that this formalism has been applied to the AEGIS problem.

In their work on architectures for distributed systems, Magee and Kramer have used the π-calculus to model the dynamic aspects of architectures described in the Darwin language [MK95]. Their work can be viewed as a good example of formalization for a particular style (embodied in Darwin) using a semantic model different than the one we use in this paper.

In their investigations of architectural refinement, Moriconi and his colleagues have characterized styles as theories in first order predicate logic and with Lamport's TLA Actions [MQR95]. The latter treatment is consistent with our approach, although it is based on a somewhat different formal model, and is more concerned with understanding the relationship between different architectural styles than with the expressiveness of an architectural formalism for a given system.

Rapide [L+95] is a module description language, whose interface model is based on partially ordered event sets and event patterns. Rapide's main advantage is that it can be executed to produce event traces that can be examined for violation of interaction invariants. This is in contrast to Wright, which provides a stronger basis for static analysis. Rapide has been used to model the AEGIS System, and in fact was one of the original prototyping languages applied to the problem.

In earlier work the authors and other colleagues have used Z to model architectural style [AG92, GN91, AAG93]. While this work demonstrated that many properties of architecture can be handled in a set-theoretic context, we also found that Z was a poorly matched to the problem of capturing the dynamic behavior of architectural systems. It was this insight (among other things) that led us to develop WRIGHT.

Currently, it is difficult to compare these different formalisms, except in a very abstract way. In fact, it is an open and challenging research problem in itself to determine which of the proposed formalisms are most appropriate

for architectural specification. However, one of the ways in which this evaluation can take place is through the use of shared case studies. It is the purpose of this paper to contribute to this process: by exhibiting a case study of a non-trivial system, one that others are also investigating, we hope to provide a more concrete basis for comparison and discussion by the architecture community.

The use of model problems for software architecture is not without precedent. Shaw and her colleagues have devised a set of "challenge problems" for architectures, including "compiler", "ATM", "KWIC", "cruise control", "sea buoy", and others [S+94]. This list is an evolving and one and we expect that through efforts like this paper, AEGIS will be added to the list.

3 The AEGIS "Problem"

The problem was first posed by Bob Balzer at an ARPA program meeting in Fall 1994. It was later re-presented as a challenge problem at the 1995 Dagstuhl Workshop on Software Architecture [GPT95].

The AEGIS Weapons System is a large, complex software system that controls many of the defense functions of modern US Navy ships. As described in one DoD report:

> The AEGIS Weapons Systems (AWS) is an extensive array of sensors and weapons designed to defend a battle group against air, surface and subsurface threats. These weapons are controlled through a large number of control consoles, which provide a wide variety of tactical decision aids to the crew. To manage complexity, the crew can preset conditions under which automated or semi-automated responses occur. This capability is generally referred to as doctrine.

The motivation for using AEGIS as a challenge problem arose through a demonstration exercise of the ARPA Prototyping Technology Program in 1993. Engineers on the real AEGIS system provided a design for a part of the system that takes monitored sensor data about moving objects near the ship, and decides what actions to take. To do this the system must resolve the "tracks" of moving objects against its geometrical model of the ship and nearby entities.

An informal description of the proposed architecture of the system is shown in Figure 1. The system consists of seven modules. The Experment Control module provides simulated input from the operator and sensors. Tracking data is sent to the Track Server, which maintains a record of the currently-monitored moving objects (missiles, other planes, submarines, etc.) within its tracking region. The Doctrine Authoring module receives input describing rules of engagement and activation. The GeoServer module takes doctrine information (from the Doctrine Authoring module), and track information (from the Track Server) and based on its own geometric models, determines which tracks intersect which geometric regions. This information (together with track and doctrine information) is fed to the Doctrine Reasoning module, which determines what action should take place. For the purposes of the prototype these actions, as well as other status information is displayed to the user via a Display Server module. The arrows in the figure indicate the direction of information flow.

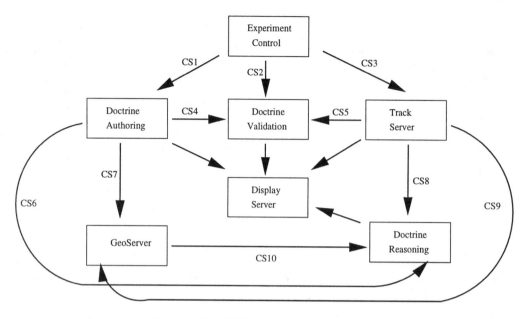

Figure 1: The AEGIS Prototype Architecture

In the Prototech demonstration, each of the research teams in the program was assigned the task of implementing one or more modules of the system. The modules were to be integrated into a running system that could then be demonstrated for the program sponsors. To make this integration possible the teams had to agree on the nature of the architectural connection that they would use. For implementation reasons (they were building on top of Unix with sockets) they initially agreed to use a uniform client-server organization, in which clients requested data from the servers. Thus information would be "pulled" from the top to the bottom of the figure: i.e., clients at the tip of the arrows, and the servers at the tails. Components that have both incoming and outgoing arrows, would act both as a client and a server.

Putting aside internal details of the individual modules, this sounds like a relatively straightforward task. Unfortunately, it turned out to be anything but trivial. First, there were some serious misconceptions about the meaning of client-server interactions. Which party initiated the connection? Was it reestablished after each request? Was the data transferred synchronously? Moreover, there turned out to be restrictions induced by implementation constraints of the modules making it infeasible for certain modules to act both as clients and as servers. Furthermore, the basic design did not account for some advanced monitoring capabilities of the inter-module communication. The net result was that (according to one of the participants) the final integration was something of a nightmare, and the resulting system considerably more complex than had been originally envisioned.

In the remainder of this paper we use the WRIGHT architectural specification language to expose some of these problems. While space does not allow us to treat all of the issues, we will focus on a few key problems – primarily those relating to potential deadlock. We start by characterizing the naive architectural design. Then we show how it

must be modified to characterize the "as-built" system.

4 The WRIGHT Notation

Before presenting the AEGIS specification, we provide a brief overview of the WRIGHT notation. (We will assume rudimentary familiarity with CSP [Hoa85].) Details of the semantic model and the supporting toolset can be found elsewhere [AG94b, AG94a].[1]

WRIGHT describes the architecture of a system as a collection of components interacting via instances of connector types. A simple Client-Server system description is shown in Figure 2. This example shows the three elements of a system description: style declaration, instance declarations, and attachments. The instance declarations and attachments together define a system configuration.

An *architectural style* is a family of systems with a common vocabulary and rules for configuration. A simple style definition is illustrated in Figure 3. This style defines the vocabulary for the system example of Figure 2. (Although not illustrated in this paper a style can also define topological constraints on systems that use the style.)

In WRIGHT, the description of a component has two important parts, the *interface* and the *computation*. An interface consists of a number of *ports*. Each port defines the set of possible interactions in which the component may participate.

A connector represents an interaction among a collection of components. For example, a pipe represents a sequential flow of data between two filters. A WRIGHT description of a connector consists of a set of *roles* and the *glue*. Each role defines the behavior of one participant in the interaction. A

---

[1]The version of WRIGHT used in this paper differs in minor ways from previously published papers. In particular, this version distinguishes input and output events, and introduces a quantification operator and conditional process expression. These differences are elaborated in this section.

```
System SimpleExample
Style ClientServer
Instances
    s: Server
    c: Client
    cs: C-S-connector
Attachments
    s.provide as cs.server;
    c.request as cs.client
end SimpleExample.
```

Figure 2: A Simple Client-Server System

```
Style ClientServer
    Component Server
        Port Provide [provide protocol]
        Computation [Server specification]
    Component Client
        Port Request [request protocol]
        Computation [Client specification]
    Connector C-S-connector
        Role Client [client protocol]
        Role Server [server protocol]
        Glue [glue protocol]
end ClientServer.
```

Figure 3: A Simple Client-Server Style

pipe has two roles, the source of data and the recipient. The glue defines how the roles will interact with each other.

Each part of a WRIGHT description – port, role, computation, and glue – is defined using a variant of CSP. For example, a simple client role might be defined as:

$$\textbf{Role Client} = (\overline{request} \rightarrow result?x \rightarrow Client) \sqcap \S$$

A participant in an interaction repeatedly makes a request and receives a result, or chooses to terminate successfully.

As is partially evident from this example, WRIGHT extends CSP in some minor syntactic ways. First, it distinguishes between *initiating* an event and *observing* an event. An event that is initiated by a process is written with an overbar: The specification of the Client's Request port would use the event $\overline{request}$ to indicate that it initiates a request. The Server's Provide port, on the other hand, waits for some other component to initiate a request (it *observes* the event), so in its specification this event would be written without an overbar: request.

Second, a special event in WRIGHT is $\sqrt{}$, which indicates the successful termination of a computation. Because this event is not a communication event, it is not considered either to be initiated or observed. Typically, use of $\sqrt{}$ occurs only in the process that halts immediately after indicating termination: $\S = \sqrt{} \rightarrow STOP$.

Third, to permit parameterization of connector and component types, WRIGHT uses a quantification operator: $\forall x : S \langle op \rangle P(x)$. This operator constructs a new process based on a process expression and the set S, combining its parts by the operator $\langle op \rangle$. For example,

$\forall i : \{1, 2, 3\} \, [] \, P_i = P_1 \, [] \, P_2 \, [] \, P_3$. A special case is $\forall x : S ; P(x)$, which is some unspecified sequencing of the processes: $\forall x : S ; P(x) = \forall x : S \sqcap (P(x) ; \forall y : S \setminus \{x\} ; P(y))$.

The final extension is the use of "conditional processes," which we will illustrate in the next section.

As discussed in [AG94b], descriptions of connectors can be used to determine whether the glue constrains the roles enough to guarantee critical properties such as local absence of deadlock. These descriptions can also be used to determine whether a configuration is properly constructed, *e.g.,* whether the interfaces of a component are appropriate for use in a particular role. But these issues are beyond the scope of this paper.

The global behavior of a WRIGHT architecture *system instance* is constructed from the processes introduced by the component and connector types in the style definition. For each component instance, the process specifying the component type's **Computation** is relabelled with the component instances name and placed in parallel (CSP operator ∥) with the other component instances. The connector instances influence the components' communication pathways by appearing as similarly relabelled **Glue** processes.

In addition to relabelling the glue processes so that different instances of the same connector have distinct event names, the connector instances' events are also renamed so that the attachments represent a communication pathway. For example, the attachment 's.provide as cs.server,' shown in figure 2, would mean that each event with the prefix cs.server (for example cs.server.e) would be renamed to have the prefix s.provide (for example s.provide.e). The net effect of this renaming is that a connector instance that has its roles attached to a particular set of ports synchronizes the events of those ports in the global system behavior. In figure 2, this means that the glue of C-S-connector will synchronize the roles s.provide and c.request, just as we would expect from the attachment and instance declarations.

5 The Naive Specification

As noted earlier, the simple model of the AEGIS system uses a client-server model; a client initiates a data request from a server, which fills the requests of each of its clients as they arrive. But this simple, informal, description brushes a lot of important information under the rug, and leaves us without enough details even to begin a more detailed design. The abstraction doesn't resolve issues such as what protocols are used to make the data request and reply, how termination is signalled, and whether servers must handle multiple requests simultaneously. By characterizing this "naive" architectural description in WRIGHT, we will see how these issues come to the fore.

In WRIGHT we begin an architectural description by characterizing the architectural "style" from which the system is developed. We will develop each of the elements of the architecture as a type, either of port or role, component, or connector. Each of the type definitions will provide a building block from which the particular system instance can be developed.

The smallest building block in a system is a protocol fragment, used to describe either the interface of a component or the constraints on a participant in an interaction protocol (connector). These protocol fragment patterns are introduced as **Process** types.

9

Process ClientPullT = $\overline{\text{open}}$ →Operate ⊓ §
 where Operate = $\overline{\text{request}}$→result?x→Operate
    ⊓ Close
   Close = $\overline{\text{close}}$→§

Process ServerPushT = open →Operate [] §
 where Operate = request→$\overline{\text{result!x}}$→Operate
    [] Close
   Close = close→§

Component Client(numServers : 1..) =
 Port Service$_{1..\text{numServers}}$ = ClientPullT
 Computation = (∀ x :1..numServers ;
          $\overline{\text{Service}_x.\text{open}}$) ; UseOrExit
 where UseOrExit = UseService ⊓ Exit
   UseService = ∀ x :1..numServers
        ⊓ $\overline{\text{Service}_x.\text{request}}$
         →Service$_x$.result?y
         →UseOrExit
  Exit = (∀ x : 1..numServers ; $\overline{\text{Service}_x.\text{close}}$) ;
   §

The ClientPullT is the basic type used for the ports of a client component (and for the role in a connector which will be played by such a component). As we will see in the component and connector declarations, the ClientPullT process indicates that a client will begin by establishing the connection with the open event. After opening the connection, an operational phase is begun, in which the client repeatedly chooses to request data. The client expects to receive exactly one result for each request. At any time, the client may choose to close the connection, after which the interaction ceases (as indicated by the § process).

The ServerPushT process is the complement of the ClientPullT. The server expects another party to open the connection (it *observes* this event, as indicated by the absence of an overbar). Then, it will repeatedly provide responses to requests until it recognizes a close event, after which it is free to terminate.

In combination (or even singly), these processes would seem to be adequate to define the client-server interaction; each initiated event in one process corresponds to an observed event in the other. The ClientServer connector specification confirms this relation between events; each line of the **Glue** specification indicates the correspondence between a pair of events – when the client initiates an open, the server will observe an open, and so on. This is a very common case in architectural connectors, and many descriptive notations specialize their connector descriptions to it (*e.g.,* [L+95, YS94]). As we will see later, however, there are other cases where there may be more complex relationships, involving partial visibility of events or run-time mechanisms (that are not part of the abstract computation) that require a more complex **Glue**. WRIGHT requires that even the "trivial" glue be spelled out in full, although it could easily be generated automatically.

Connector ClientServer =
 Role Client = ClientPullT
 Role Server = ServerPushT
 Glue = Client.open →$\overline{\text{Server.open}}$→**Glue**
  [] Client.close→$\overline{\text{Server.close}}$→**Glue**
  [] Client.request→$\overline{\text{Server.request}}$→**Glue**
  [] Server.result?x→$\overline{\text{Client.result!x}}$→**Glue**
  [] §

In a client-server system such as AEGIS, there are three kinds of components: those that act as clients, those that act as servers, and those that combine the two functions. Components of each of these kinds can have different numbers of interfaces (client or server interfaces), and so we represent them by parameterized types.

The Client component type is straightforward. It has complete control over its actions at any time, as long as it obeys the ClientPullT protocol on each of its ports. For simplicity, we assume that it begins by opening each of its connections, and finishes by closing each of them. During the middle phase, the process UseService selects from among its connections to request a new data item. The choice is entirely up to the client, as indicated by the use of non-deterministic choice.

The picture for a server is considerably more complicated (see figure 4). A Server component provides data services to one or more clients. With each client, the server uses the ServerPushT protocol. At any point in the protocol, each client is in one of three states: "Open" (represented by the set O), "Closed" (represented by the set C), or "not yet Open" (all others).

The **Computation** specification shows many of the difficult issues that arise in specifying this architectural style. What mechanisms are available for the server to locate new connections that should be opened? To receive a client's request? When can a newly closed client connection be recognized, and what action should be taken? As a component *type*, the Server specification provides a generic answer to these questions.

The **Computation** shown in figure 4 describes a server that can handle at most one client request at a time. This is indicated by the non-deterministic (or internal) choice among versions of the process ReadFromClient. The server may also choose to wait for an open request from any of a set of clients. This interaction pattern, of selecting a single client for a request or a set of clients for an open, is characteristic of the Unix socket mechanism, which was selected as an implementation base. We can see the consequences of this choice, while abstracting other implementation details, in its effects on the server component type.

Because of the blocking open and request protocol, as well as the requirement that the server eventually handle all requests, the server must keep track of the statuses of the different clients. Some have not yet opened, and the server can wait for them to open; some have opened but not closed, and server can expect either a request or a close from them; and some have closed, and the server must not expect any further action from them. The open and the closed clients are represented by the state variables O and C respectively (those that have never opened are members of the set $(1..\text{numClients}) \setminus (O \cup C)$). Given these different statuses, there are four distinct cases for the server, requiring different choices of action: The least constrained case is when there are both open and unopened clients; in this case, the server is free to make any choice of action. If every client has already opened, the server must not wait

Component Server(numClients : 1..) =
  Port $\text{Client}_{1..numClients}$ = ServerPushT
  Computation = $\text{WaitForClient}_{\{\},\{\}}$
    where $\text{WaitForClient}_{O,C}$ = $\forall x : ((1..numClients) \setminus (O \cup C)) \; [] \; \text{Client}_x.\text{open} \rightarrow \text{DecideNextAction}_{O \cup \{x\},C}$
      $\text{DecideNextAction}_{O,C}$ = $\text{WaitForClient}_{O,C} \sqcap \forall x : O \sqcap \text{ReadFromClient}_{x,O,C}$
        $O \neq \{\} \wedge O \cup C \neq (1..numClients)$
      $\text{DecideNextAction}_{O,C}$ = $\forall x : O \sqcap \text{ReadFromClient}_{x,O,C}$
        $O \neq \{\} \wedge O \cup C = (1..numClients)$
      $\text{DecideNextAction}_{\{\},C}$ = $\text{WaitForClient}_{\{\},C}$
        $C \neq (1..numClients)$
      $\text{DecideNextAction}_{\{\},(1..NumClients)}$ = §
      $\text{ReadFromClient}_{x,O,C}$ = $\text{Client}_x.\text{request} \rightarrow \overline{\text{Client}_x.\text{result!}y} \rightarrow \text{DecideNextAction}_{O,C}$
        $[] \; \text{Client}_x.\text{close} \rightarrow \text{DecideNextAction}_{O \setminus \{x\}, C \cup \{x\}}$

Figure 4: **Component** Server

for a client to open. If no client is open, then the server does not have the option of waiting for a request. Once every client has closed, the only possible action by the server is to terminate.

These various cases are handled by the use of conditional process definitions:

$$\mathsf{P}_V = \mathsf{Q}$$
$$p(V)$$

defines a process P over variables V only when the boolean expression $p(V)$ is true.

The component type MixedComp (figure 5) combines the properties of a Client and a Server. It must deal with open, close, and request events from its clients, but it also has the option of requesting a service from one of its servers at any time.

Now that we have described the basic vocabulary of the naive AEGIS style, we can show the configuration of the testbed system:[2]

Configuration Testbed
Style Aegis
Instances
  ExperimentControl : Server(3)
  DoctrineAuthoring : MixedComp(1,3)
  DoctrineValidation : Client(3)
  TrackServer : MixedComp(1,3)
  GeoServer : MixedComp(2,1)
  DoctrineReasoning : Client(3)
  $\text{CS}_{1..10}$: ClientServer
Attachments
  ExperimentControl.Client **as** CS_1.Server
  DoctrineAuthoring.Service **as** CS_1.Client
  ExperimentControl.Client **as** CS_2.Server
  DoctrineValidation.Service **as** CS_2.Client
  ExperimentControl.Client **as** CS_3.Server
  TrackServer.Service **as** CS_3.Client
  DoctrineAuthoring.Client **as** CS_4.Server
  DoctrineValidation.Service **as** CS_4.Client

[2]For reasons that will become clearer later this initial description excludes the DisplayServer. In the next section we include it in the specification.

  TrackServer.Client **as** CS_5.Server
  DoctrineValidation.Service **as** CS_5.Client
  DoctrineAuthoring.Client **as** CS_6.Server
  DoctrineReasoning.Service **as** CS_6.Client
  DoctrineAuthoring.Client **as** CS_7.Server
  GeoServer.Service **as** CS_7.Client
  TrackServer.Client **as** CS_8.Server
  DoctrineReasoning.Service **as** CS_9.Client
  TrackServer.Client **as** CS_9.Server
  GeoServer.Service **as** CS_9.Client
  GeoServer.Client **as** CS_{10}.Server
  DoctrineReasoning.Service **as** CS_{10}.Client
end Testbed.

6 Analyzing and Changing the Specification

The WRIGHT specification described in the previous section is a reasonable and useful description of the architecture of the AEGIS system as it was initially envisioned. The protocol described in the ClientServer connector and the computation patterns covered by the connectors Client, Server, and MixedComp describe the high level design of the system, exposing the computation model and the requirements on the run-time infrastructure for the proposed system.

The specification also exposes a number of shortcomings of the initial design, shortcomings which led to a major reworking of the system and that seriously complicated the final product. The system as it was eventually constructed bore little resemblance to the simple client-server system described above. In this section, we look at some of the issues that arose in the AEGIS design, show how they are exposed by the preceding WRIGHT description, and further show how the solutions found by the AEGIS team can be expressed in WRIGHT, thus ensuring that the architectural description matches the system as built.

6.1 Issue: Direction of Data Flow

One of the issues that is exposed by the formal description of the AEGIS system is that of dataflow. The AEGIS system contains a server, the Display Server that does not supply data, but instead receives it. The protocols described above for the ClientServer connector, which simply encode the default interpretation of client-server interaction, does

Component MixedComp(numServers : 1..; numClients : 1..) =
  Port Service$_{1..\texttt{numServers}}$ = ClientPullT
  Port Client$_{1..\texttt{numClients}}$ = ServerPushT
  Computation = OpenServices ; WaitForClient$_{\{\},\{\}}$
    where WaitForClient$_{O,C}$ = $\forall\, x$: $((1..\texttt{numClients}) \setminus (O \cup C))\; \square$ Client$_x$.open$\rightarrow$ DecideNextAction$_{O \cup \{x\}, C}$
      DecideNextAction$_{O,C}$ = WaitForClient$_{O,C} \sqcap \forall\, x$: $O \sqcap$ ReadFromClient$_{x,O,C}$
        $\sqcap$ (UseService ; DecideNextAction$_{O,C}$)
       $O \neq \{\} \wedge O \cup C \neq (1..\texttt{numClients})$
      DecideNextAction$_{O,C}$ = $\forall\, x$: $O \sqcap$ ReadFromClient$_{x,O,C} \sqcap$ (UseService ; DecideNextAction$_{O,C}$)
       $O \neq \{\} \wedge O \cup C = (1..\texttt{numClients})$
      DecideNextAction$_{\{\},C}$ = WaitForClient$_{\{\},C} \sqcap$ (UseService ; DecideNextAction$_{\{\},C}$)
       $C \neq (1..\texttt{numClients})$
      DecideNextAction$_{\{\},(1..\texttt{NumClients})}$ = (UseService ; DecideNextAction$_{\{\},(1..\texttt{numClients})}$) $\sqcap$ Exit
      ReadFromClient$_{x,O,C}$ = Client$_x$.request$\rightarrow$(OptionalUseService ; $\overline{\text{Client}_x.\text{result!y}}\rightarrow$DecideNextAction$_{O,C}$)
        $\square$ Client$_x$.close$\rightarrow\overline{\text{DecideNextAction}}_{O\setminus\{x\}, C\cup\{x\}}$
      UseService = $\forall\, x$: $(1..\texttt{numServers}) \sqcap \overline{\text{Service}_x.\text{request}}\rightarrow$Service$_x$.result?y$\rightarrow\S$
      OptionalUseService = (UseService ; OptionalUseService) $\sqcap\; \S$
      OpenServices = $\forall\, x$: $\overline{(1..\texttt{numServers})}$; $\overline{\text{Service}_x.\text{open}}\rightarrow\S$
      Exit = $\forall\, x$: $(1..\texttt{numServers})$; $\overline{\text{Service}_x.\text{close}}\rightarrow\S$

Figure 5: **Component** MixedComp

not handle this situation. Thus, interactions with the Display Server require a second connector, ClientServerPush, along with corresponding new port/role declarations. (The term Push is used to indicate that the client *pushes* data toward the server, rather than pulling it from the server.)

Process ClientPushT = $\overline{\text{open}}\rightarrow$Operate $\sqcap\; \S$
    where Operate = $\overline{\text{request!x}}\rightarrow$result$\rightarrow$Operate
        $\sqcap$ Close
      Close = $\overline{\text{close}}\rightarrow\S$

Process ServerPullT = Open $\rightarrow$Operate $\square\; \S$
    where Operate = request?x$\rightarrow\overline{\text{result}}\rightarrow$Operate
        $\square$ Close
      Close = close$\rightarrow\S$

Connector ClientServerPush =
  Role Client = ClientPushT
  Role Server = ServerPullT
  Glue = Client.open $\rightarrow\overline{\text{Server.open}}\rightarrow$**Glue**
    $\square$ Client.close$\rightarrow\overline{\text{Server.close}}\rightarrow$**Glue**
    $\square$ Client.request?x$\rightarrow\overline{\text{Server.request!x}}\rightarrow$**Glue**
    $\square$ Server.result$\rightarrow\overline{\text{Client.result}}\rightarrow$**Glue**
    $\square\; \S$

6.2 Issue: Potential for Deadlock in Servers

A more serious issue is the potential for deadlock in a system that uses the Server component as described above. Deadlock can arise because the server must, in effect, *guess* which of the clients will be the next one to make a request. A server does not deadlock on its own: If the clients are able to fulfill their obligation to either request or close, then no problems occur. Deadlock can be a problem, however, when more than one client and server are involved. Consider a simplified system topology with two servers, S1 and S2, and two clients C1 and C2, in which both clients interact with both servers. (One such pattern occurs in the system with components DoctrineAuthoring, TrackServer, GeoServer, and DoctrineReasoning.) What happens if client C1 plans to make a request first to S1 and then S2, while client C2 makes a request first to S2 and then S1? If S1 and S2 both guess wrong about which component will make the first request (*i.e.* S1 guesses C2 and S2 guesses C1), then the system will deadlock. Neither service can proceed before the other, since each is waiting for the other client, which is itself waiting for the other server. The problem of guessing which client will be next is exposed in the specification as a non-deterministic choice over the set of request events in the Server (and MixedComp) specification. This indicates that the servers are free to handle any of their clients, excluding the other clients while doing so.

6.2.1 Using Dynamic Connections

The AEGIS designers took three approaches to solving this problem. The first takes advantage of the fact that it is possible to make a deterministic choice over the set of open events. The protocols are changed so that an open event precedes *every* client request:[3]

Process DynamicClientPullT = $\overline{\text{open}}\rightarrow\overline{\text{request}}$
            $\rightarrow$result?x$\rightarrow\overline{\text{close}}$
            $\rightarrow$DynamicClientPullT
        $\sqcap\; \S$
Process DynamicServerPushT = open $\rightarrow\overline{\text{request}}$
            $\rightarrow\overline{\text{result!x}}\rightarrow$close
            $\rightarrow$DynamicServerPushT
        $\square\; \S$

---

[3]Similar definitions for DynamicClientPushT and DynamicServerPullT, not shown. Also, connectors DClientServer and DClientServerPush are straightforward but omitted for brevity.

These protocols can be used to make a DynamicServer that waits for open events rather than request events:

Component DynamicServer (numClients : 1..) =
  Port Client$_{1..numClients}$ = DServerPushT
  Computation = WaitForClient [] §
  where WaitForClient = $\forall i$:1..numClients
           [] Client$_i$.open
               $\rightarrow$Client$_i$.request
               $\rightarrow\overline{\text{Client}_i\text{.result!x}}$
               $\rightarrow$Client$_i$.close$\rightarrow$**Computation**

This problem can also arise with the service request portion of a MixedComp, and this is solved by *serverizing* a mixed computation. That is, instead of using a ClientPullT to wait for data, the component uses a ServerPullT port to receive notification when data is available.

Component DynamicServerized (numServers : 0..;
                           numClients : 0..) =
  Port Service$_{1..numServers}$ = DServerPullT
  Port Client$_{1..numClients}$ = DServerPushT
  Computation = WaitForService [] WaitForClient [] §
  where WaitForService =
        $\forall i$:1..numServers
          [] Service$_i$.open$\rightarrow$Service$_i$.request?x
            $\rightarrow\overline{\text{Service}_i\text{.result}}\rightarrow$Service$_i$.close
            $\rightarrow$**Computation**
    WaitForClient =
        $\forall i$: 1..numClients [] Client$_i$.open
                    $\rightarrow$Client$_i$.request
                    $\rightarrow\overline{\text{Client}_i\text{.result!x}}$
                    $\rightarrow$Client$_i$.close
                    $\rightarrow$**Computation**

6.2.2 Avoiding Unnecessary Synchronizations

A second approach to avoiding a server blocking on a request is to permit the server to provide the data asynchronously, in anticipation of a request. This is achieved through the use of an OpenLoopBuffer connection (figure 6), which guarantees that the source of data will never block waiting for the target to become ready. The buffer stores data until the target requests it, or blocks the target until the source makes new data available. (Such a connection is essentially a pipe.)

Notice how the WRIGHT **Glue** mechanism permits this interaction to be described *without modifying the component interfaces*. This connector can replace a ClientServer connector without modifying the data target, or a ClientServerPush connector without modifying the data source.

6.2.3 Multi-threading Components

The third and final approach to avoiding server deadlocks is perhaps the most flexible: to alter the server's implementation mechanism so that it can handle multiple connections at once. If we use a multi-threaded implementation (easily

represented in CSP using the || operator), a single component type can use each of the possible interface protocols (see figure 7).[4]

This solution is used for two of the components, TrackServer and ExperimentControl. The instance declarations for these are as follows:

TrackServer : ThreadedMixedComp (3,0,1,0,1,0,0,0)
ExperimentControl : ThreadedMixedComp (1,0,0,0,0,0,0,2)

TrackServer has three static push server ports, one dynamic push server port, and one static pull client port. ExperimentControl has one static push server port and two dynamic push client ports.

6.3 Issue: Instrumenting Communication

Another issue that is not dealt with in the initial specification is that the AEGIS testbed is an experimental system. As such, there is a requirement that the interactions of the system be monitored. This monitoring must not, of course, alter the components as designed, or the data collected would be invalid. This results in the need for instrumented connectors. WRIGHT can represent these easily by adding a new Listener role to each connector specification, and altering the **Glue** to copy data to the new participant. For example, an instrumented ClientServer connector could be described as follows:

Connector InstrumentedClientServer =
  Role Client = ClientPullT
  Role Server = ServerPushT
  Role Listener = data?x $\rightarrow$Listener [] §
  Glue = Client.open $\rightarrow\overline{\text{Server.open}}\rightarrow$**Glue**
      [] Client.close$\rightarrow\overline{\text{Server.close}}\rightarrow$**Glue**
      [] Client.request$\rightarrow\overline{\text{Server.request}}\rightarrow$**Glue**
      [] Server.result?x$\rightarrow\overline{\text{Client.result!x}}$
          $\rightarrow\overline{\text{Listener.data!x}}\rightarrow$**Glue**
      [] §

The same Listener can also be added to any of the other connectors. For example, InstrumentedDClientServerPush:

Connector InstrumentedDClientServerPush =
  Role Client = DClientPushT
  Role Server = DServerPullT
  Role Listener = data?x $\rightarrow$Listener [] §
  Glue = Client.open $\rightarrow\overline{\text{Server.open}}\rightarrow$**Glue**
      [] Client.request?x $\rightarrow\overline{\text{Server.request!x}}$
          $\rightarrow\overline{\text{Listener.data!x}}\rightarrow$**Glue**
      [] Server.result $\rightarrow\overline{\text{Client.result}}\rightarrow$**Glue**
      [] Client.close $\rightarrow\overline{\text{Server.close}}\rightarrow$**Glue**
      [] §

7 The Updated AEGIS System

We can now give the full, new configuration:

Configuration Testbed2
Style Aegis

---

[4]While CSP makes this look like the simplest solution of all, depending on the implementation base it may require a complex implementation.

Connector OpenLoopBuffer =
    Role Source = ClientPushT
    Role Target = ClientPullT
    Glue = OpenPhase ; $\text{Operate}_{()}$
        where OpenPhase = Source.open $\rightarrow$ $\overline{\text{Target.open}}$ $\rightarrow$ § $\Box$ Target.open $\rightarrow$ $\overline{\text{Source.open}}$ $\rightarrow$ §
            $\text{Operate}_{()}$ = Source.request?x $\rightarrow$ $\overline{\text{Source.result}}$ $\rightarrow$ $\text{Operate}_{\langle x \rangle}$
                $\Box$ Target.request $\rightarrow$ WaitForData
            $\text{Operate}_{S+\langle x \rangle}$ = Source.request?y $\rightarrow$ $\overline{\text{Source.result}}$ $\rightarrow$ $\text{Operate}_{\langle y \rangle + S + \langle x \rangle}$
                $\Box$ Target.request $\rightarrow$ $\overline{\text{Target.result!x}}$ $\rightarrow$ Operate_{S}
            WaitForData = Source.request?x $\rightarrow$ $\overline{\text{Target.result!x}}$ $\rightarrow$ $\overline{\text{Source.result}}$ $\rightarrow$ $\text{Operate}_{()}$

Figure 6: An Open Loop Buffer

Component ThreadedMixedComp (numPushServers :0..; numPullServers : 0 .. ;
                                numDPushServers :0..; numDPullServers :0..;
                                numPullClients : 0..; numPushClients : 0..;
                                numDPullClients : 0..; numDPushClients : 0..;
) =
    Port $\text{PushServer}_{1..numPushServers}$ = ServerPushT
    Port $\text{PullServer}_{1..numPullServers}$ = ServerPullT
    Port $\text{DPushServer}_{1..numDPushServers}$ = DServerPushT
    Port $\text{DPullServer}_{1..numDPullServers}$ = DServerPullT
    Port $\text{PushClient}_{1..numPushClients}$ = ClientPushT
    Port $\text{PullClient}_{1..numPullClients}$ = ClientPullT
    Port $\text{DPushClient}_{1..numDPushClients}$ = DClientPushT
    Port $\text{DPullClient}_{1..numDPullClients}$ = DClientPullT
    Computation = $\forall i : 1..numPushServers$ $\|$ PushServer_i:ServerPushT
      $\|$ $\forall i : 1..numPullServers$ $\|$ PullServer_i:ServerPullT
      $\|$ $\forall i : 1..numDPushServers$ $\|$ DPushServer_i:DServerPushT
      $\|$ $\forall i : 1..numDPullServers$ $\|$ DPullServer_i:DServerPullT
      $\|$ $\forall i : 1..numPushClients$ $\|$ PushClient_i:ClientPushT
      $\|$ $\forall i : 1..numPullClients$ $\|$ PullClient_i:ClientPullT
      $\|$ $\forall i : 1..numDPushClients$ $\|$ DPushClient_i:DClientPushT
      $\|$ $\forall i : 1..numDPullClients$ $\|$ DPullClient_i:DClientPullT

Figure 7: A Multi-threaded Solution

Instances
    ExperimentControl : ThreadedMixedComp (1,0,0,0,0,0,0,2)
    DoctrineAuthoring : DynamicSeverized(1,3)
    DoctrineValidation : DoctrineValidationT
    TrackServer : ThreadedMixedComp (3,0,1,0,1,0,0,0)
    GeoServer : GeoServerT
    DoctrineReasoning : DoctrineReasoningT
    DisplayServer : DisplayServerT
    $\text{CS}_{1..4}$: ClientServer
    $\text{DCS}_{1..5}$: DClientServer
    $\text{DCSPush}_{1..4}$: DClientServerPush
    OpenLoop : OpenLoopBuffer

Attachments
    ExperimentControl.DClientPush as DCSPush_1.Client
    DoctrineAuthoring.Service as DCSPush_1.Server
    ExperimentControl.DClientPush as DCSPush_2.Client
    DoctrineValidation.ExCtrl as DCSPush_2.Server
    ExperimentControl.ServerPush as CS_1.Server
    TrackServer.ClientPull as CS_1.Client

    DoctrineAuthoring.Client as DCS_1.Server
    DoctrineValidation.DoctAuth as DCS_1.Client
    TrackServer.ServerPush as DCS_2.Server
    DoctrineValidation.TrSrv as DCS_2.Client
    DoctrineAuthoring.Client as DCS_3.Server
    DoctrineReasoning.DoctAuth as DCS_3.Client
    DoctrineAuthoring.Client as DCS_4.Server
    GeoServer.DoctAuth as DCS_4.Client
    TrackServer.ServerPush as CS_2.Server
    DoctrineReasoning.TrSrv as CS_2.Client
    TrackServer.ServerPush as CS_3.Server
    GeoServer.TrSrv as CS_3.Client
    GeoServer.DoctReas as OpenLoop.Source
    DoctrineReasoning.GeoSrv as OpenLoop.Target
    DoctrineAuthoring.Client as DCS_5.Server
    DisplayServer.DoctAuth as DCS_5.Client
    TrackServer.ServerPush as CS_4.Server
    DisplayServer.TrSrv as CS_4.Client
    DisplayServer.DoctVal as DCSPush_3.Server

DoctriveValidation.DispSrv **as** DCSPush$_3$.Client
DisplayServer.DoctReas **as** DCSPush$_4$.Server
DoctrineReasoning.DispSrv **as** DCSPush$_4$.Client
end Testbed2.

8 Evaluation

We have seen that WRIGHT can be used to provide a formal specification of the style used by the AEGIS prototype implementors. As we have illustrated, this specification illuminates many of the issues left unresolved in a less formal treatment.

The primary benefit of this specification has been its precision and its attention to detail. We note, however, that although we have been quite specific about the protocols of interaction, the specification has abstracted considerably from the actual functional behavior of the components in the system.

A secondary benefit of the treatment that we have given is the ability to reason about the architectural style within which AEGIS was developed. Although space did not permit it here, arguments about absence of deadlock and about substitutability of one connector type for another can be made in a rigorous fashion. These results become general rules that can be applied to all instances of the style. Hence the architectural level specification becomes cost effective through amortization of its results across a wide variety of systems.

Although the specifications shown in this paper are complex, they provide a basis for precise reasoning about the system and may be used, in other instances of this same style, as a basis for more concise descriptions of functioning systems. In effect, they act to give meaning to the informal descriptions such as shown in figure 1, and as building blocks for a family of precise architectural specifications.

On the negative side, this specification highlights some of the weaknesses of WRIGHT. The most glaring is the fact that the process structure of a WRIGHT description is (like CSP) static: new components and connections cannot be created on the fly. We were able to circumvent the problems in the case of the dynamic connectors, by simulating the opening and closing of a connection, and also by the use of parameterized components. But for an architecture with more dynamic behavior – e.g., new components are created while the system is running – this kind of model would not suffice. However, in exchange for this limitation, we get all of the benefits of CSP: its algebraic rules, its simple treatment of refinement, and its capability for reasoning about deadlock.

WRIGHT is not, however, intended to stand alone as the only architectural representation of a fully functioning system. Other formalisms will be more appropriate for the exploration of issues such as run-time performance, user- and machine-interfaces, allocation to hardware, and configuration maintenance. The software architect must confront many issues in developing the system, and so we would expect many tools to be deployed.

In addition, the structuring of WRIGHT is not uniquely tied to the CSP mechanisms described in this paper. We are exploring, in a different case study, ways that we can use WRIGHT-like descriptions with Z as the semantic base to provide a data-oriented view of a system's architecture.

In the broader scheme of things, it will be interesting to compare our specification with others of the same system. Through such comparisons we can begin to understand what are the tradeoffs in expressiveness and reasoning capability of alternative formal models.

References

[AAG93] G. Abowd, R. Allen, and D. Garlan. Using style to understand descriptions of software architecture. In *Proc. of SIGSOFT'93: Foundations of Software Eng.*, Software Eng. Notes 18(5). ACM Press, Dec 1993.

[AG92] R. Allen and D. Garlan. A formal approach to software architectures. In Jan van Leeuwen, editor, *Proc. of IFIP'92*. Elsevier Science Publishers B.V., Sept 1992.

[AG94a] R. Allen and D. Garlan. Formal connectors. Technical Report CMU-CS-94-115, Carnegie Mellon University, Mar 1994.

[AG94b] R. Allen and D. Garlan. Formalizing architectural connection. In *Proc. of the 16th International Conf on Software Eng.*, May 1994.

[BB92] G. Berry and G. Boudol. The chemical abstract machine. *Theoretical Computer Science*, (96), 1992.

[GN91] D. Garlan and D. Notkin. Formalizing design spaces: Implicit invocation mechanisms. In *VDM'91: Formal Software Development Methods*. Springer-Verlag, LNCS 551, Oct 1991.

[GPT95] David Garlan, Frances Newberry Paulisch, and Walter F. Tichy, editors. *Summary of the Dagstuhl Workshop on Software Architecture*, Feb 1995. Reprinted in ACM Software Eng. Notes, July 1995.

[Hoa85] C.A.R. Hoare. *Communicating Sequential Processes*. Prentice Hall, 1985.

[IW95] P. Inverardi and A. Wolf. Formal specification and analysis of software architectures using the chemical, abstract machine model. *IEEE Trans. on Software Eng.*, 21(4), Apr 1995.

[L$^+$95] D. Luckham et al. Specification and analysis of system architecture using Rapide. *IEEE Trans. on Software Eng.*, 21(4), Apr 1995.

[MK95] J. Magee and J. Kramer. Modelling distributed software architectures. In *Proc. of the 1st International Workshop on Architectures for Software Systems*. Carnegie Mellon University Technical Report CMU-CS-95-151, Apr 1995.

[MQR95] M. Moriconi, X. Qian, and R. Riemenschneider. Correct architecture refinement. *IEEE Trans. on Software Eng.*, 21(4), Apr 1995.

[S$^+$94] M. Shaw et al. Candidate model problems in software architecture. Draft Publication, 1994.

[YS94] D. M. Yellin and R. E. Strom. Interfaces, protocols, and the semi-automatic construction of software adaptors. *Proc. of OOPSLA'94*, Oct 1994.

A Survey of Architecture Description Languages

Paul C. Clements
Software Engineering Institute
Carnegie Mellon University
Pittsburgh, PA 1521

Abstract

Architecture Description Languages (ADLs) are emerging as viable tools for formally representing the architectures of systems. While growing in number, they vary widely in terms of the abstractions they support and analysis capabilities they provide. Further, many languages not originally designed as ADLs serve reasonably well at representing and analyzing software architectures. This paper summarizes a taxonomic survey of ADLs that is in progress. The survey characterizes ADLs in terms of (a) the classes of systems they support; (b) the inherent properties of the languages themselves; and (c) the process and technology support they provide to represent, refine, analyze, and build systems from an architecture. Preliminary results allow us to draw conclusions about what constitutes an ADL, and how contemporary ADLs differ from each other.

1. Introduction

Architecture description languages (ADLs) are formal languages that can be used to represent the architecture of a software-intensive system. As architecture becomes a dominating theme in large system development and acquisition, methods for unambiguously specifying an architecture will become indispensable.

By *architecture*, we mean the components that comprise a system, the behavioral specifications for those components, and the patterns and mechanisms for interactions among them. Note that a single system is usually composed of more than one type of component: modules, tasks, functions, etc. An architecture can choose the type of component most appropriate or informative to show, or it can include multiple views of the same system, each illustrating different componentry.

To date, architectures have largely been represented by informal circle-and-line drawings in which the nature of the components, their properties, the semantics of the connections, and the behavior of the system as a whole are poorly (if at all) defined. Even though such figures often give an intuitive picture of the system's construction, they usually fail to answer such questions as:

- What are the components? Are they modules that exist only at design-time, but are compiled together before run time? Are they tasks or processes threaded together from different modules, assembled at compile-time, and form run time units? Or are they something as nebulous as "functional areas," as in data flow diagrams, or something else entirely?

- What do the components do? How do they behave? What other components do they rely on?

- What do the connections mean? Do they mean "sends data to," "sends control to," "calls," "is a part of," some combination of these, or something else? What are the mechanisms used to fulfill these relations?

ADLs result from a linguistic approach to the formal representation of architectures, and as such they address the shortcomings of informal representations. Further, as will be shown, sophisticated ADLs allow early analysis and feasibility testing of the design decisions.

ADLs trace their roots to module interconnection languages of the 1970s. ADLs today are in a maturing phase but several exist. Current examples include Rapide [12], UniCon [18], ArTek [19], Wright [1], and Meta-H [21].

This paper describes a survey of contemporary ADLs that is currently in progress. Using the techniques of domain analysis, a questionnaire was produced that characterizes an individual ADL in terms of the systems and architectures it can support, the analysis or automated development it can facilitate or provide, and intrinsic qualities about the ADL itself. The questionnaire has been applied to over a dozen ADLs to date and the resulting data allows ADLs to be compared and contrasted. The data also provides insight into the question of when a language is an ADL as opposed to some other kind of language, such as a requirements, programming, or modelling language.

2. Architecture and ADLs

An architecture plays several roles in project development, all of them important, and all of them facilitated by a formal representation of the architecture, such as with an ADL. A formal architecture representation is more likely to be maintained and followed than an informal one, can more readily be consulted and treated as authoritative, and can more easily be transferred to other projects as a core asset. Roles include:

- Basis for communication: Project team members, managers, and customers all turn to the architecture as the basis for understanding the system, its development, and how it works during execution.

- Project blueprint: The choice of architectural components is institutionalized in the developing organization's team structure, work assignments, management units, schedule and work breakdown structures, integration plans, test plans, and maintenance processes. Once it is made, an architectural decision has an extremely long lifetime and survives even outside of the software that it describes.

- Blueprint for product line development. An architecture may be re-used on other systems for which it is appropriate. If managed carefully, an entire product family may be produced using a single architecture. In this case, the importance of an appropriate architecture is magnified across all the projects it will serve.

- Embodiment of earliest design decisions: The architecture represents the first mapping from requirements to computational components. The selection of components and connections, as well as the allocation of functionality to each component, is a codification of the earliest design decisions about a project. All downstream design decisions must be consistent with the architectural choices. As such, architectural decisions are the hardest to change, and have the most far-reaching consequences.

- First approach to achieving quality attributes: An architecture can either allow or preclude the achievement of most of a system's targeted quality attributes. Modifiability, for example, depends extensively on the system's modularization, which reflects the encapsulation strategies. Reusability of components depends on how strongly coupled they are with other components in the system. Performance depends largely upon the volume and complexity of the inter-component communication and coordination, especially if the components are physically distributed processes. Thus, an architecture embodies decisions about quality priorities and tradeoffs, and represents the earliest opportunity for evaluating those decisions and tradeoffs.

Some ADLs provide an opportunity for architecture-level analysis, such as automatic simulation generation, schedulability analysis, and the like. However, even in the absence of automated analysis capabilities, other evaluative strategies can be applied to the architecture [5]. Thus, these early design decisions and quality attribute tradeoffs can be tested before they are too expensive to change.

3. ADLs and their relationship to other languages

How do ADLs differ from programing languages, requirements languages, modelling languages, and the like? Given a language for expressing properties or behaviors of a system, what are the criteria for deciding if it is an ADL or not? Unfortunately, it isn't clear.

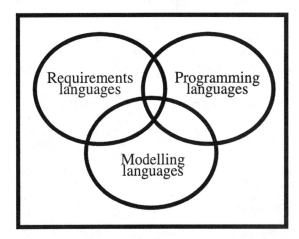

Figure 1: Requirements languages, programming languages, and modelling languages have aspects in common with ADLs.

In principle, ADLs differ from requirements languages because the latter describe problem spaces whereas the former are rooted in the solution space. In practice, requirements are often divided into behavioral chunks for ease of presentation, and languages for representing those behaviors are sometimes well-suited to representing architectural components, even though that was not the original goal of the language. For example, Modechart [10], a requirements language similar to Statechart [7], exhibited stronger analytical capabilities than any other ADL in our survey because of the presence of a model-checking verifier. Modechart was considered to be an ADL because its componentry (state machines) could be *interpreted* as architectural components. But Modechart was not designed to be an ADL, and so it is easy to produce artifacts in Modechart that do not, under any reasonable semantic interpretation, correspond to an architectural view of a system.

In principle, ADLs differ from programming languages because the latter bind all architectural abstractions to specific point solutions whereas ADLs intentionally suppress or vary such binding. In practice, architecture is embodied and recoverable from code, and many languages provide architecture-level views of the system. For example, Ada offers the ability to view a system just in terms of its package specifications, which are the interfaces to components. However, Ada offers little or no architecture-level analytical capabilities, nor does it provide architecture-level insight into how the components are "wired" together.

In principle, ADLs differ from modelling languages because the latter are more concerned with the behaviors of the whole rather than of the parts, whereas ADLs concentrate on representation of components. In practice, many modelling languages allow the representation of cooperating components and can represent architectures reasonably well.

Two leading ADL researchers offer their desiderata for ADLs. Shaw lists the following as important properties that ADLs should exhibit [18]:

- ability to represent components (primitive or composite) along with property assertions, interfaces and implementations;

- ability to represent connectors, along with protocols, property assertions, and implementations

- abstraction and encapsulation

- types and type checking

- ability to accommodate analysis tools openly

Luckham lists the following as requirements for an ADL [13]:

- component abstraction

- communication abstraction

- communication integrity (limiting communication to those components connected to each other architecturally)

- ability to model dynamic architectures

- ability to reason about causality and time

- hierarchical refinement support

- relativity, the mapping of behaviors to (possibly different) architectures, as a first step towards checking conformance.

These lists illustrate the different points of view about what constitutes an ADL. There is no clear line between ADLs and non-ADLs. Languages can, however, be dis-criminated from one another according to how much architectural information they represent, and our survey has attempted to capture this. Languages that were born as ADLs show a clear advantage in this area over languages built for some other purpose and later co-opted to represent architectures. In Section 6, we will re-visit this issue in light of the survey results.

4. The ADL survey

This section outlines the purpose, form, content, and methodology of the ADL survey.

4.1: Purpose

Our survey of ADLs was intended to provide information to three communities:

- architects, who must choose an ADL. Our survey is intended to highlight the capabilities and qualities of ADLs presently available. It is not a score card or even an evaluation; ADLs are not better or worse than each other. Rather, they feature different capabilities and qualities, and the best choice is use specific.

- technology sponsors, who fund development of ADLs and ADL tools. Our survey is intended to allow them to spot and re-direct duplicative work.

- ADL creators. Our survey is intended to allow creators to identify capability areas that have, to date, been largely passed over by ADLs.

4.2: Form

Drawing from previous efforts to survey ADLs [20] as well as other kinds of specification languages [2], we crafted a *feature analysis* of ADLs. Feature analysis is a tool of certain domain analysis methods such as the Feature-Oriented Domain Analysis (FODA) method [11]; it proceeds by cataloguing user-visible system features in a structured fashion. In our survey, the domain consisted of the set of languages that might be considered ADLs; "user-visible" means apparent to a user of the language.

The feature analysis took the form of a survey questionnaire; the questionnaire is the manifestation of a framework of important features that a particular ADL may or may not have. An ADL in the survey is characterized by answering a series of questions about its capabilities, features, and usage history. A set of completed questionnaires thus provides a basis for comparing and contrasting the ADLs with each other, and ADLs with languages that would not be considered ADLs.

Features are structured into the following three categories: system-oriented features, language-oriented features, and process-oriented features.

System-oriented features

System-oriented features are related to the application system derived from the architecture description. For example, certain ADLs may not be able to express real-time constraints about a system's architectural components, while others can. All features in this category are attributes of an end system; however, they reflect on the ability of the ADL to express or describe those attributes at the architectural level.

Specific questions from the survey include[1]:

Applicability: How suitable is the ADL for representing a particular type of application system?
- **Architectural styles: How well does the ADL allow description of architectural styles, such as those enumerated in [6]? Styles include pipe and filter, blackboard, etc.**
- **System class: What broad classes of systems can have their architectures represented with the ADL? Classes include: hard real-time, soft real-time, embedded, distributed, dynamic architectures, imported component systems, other.**
- **Domains: What application domains is the ADL designed specifically to support, if any, and how and to what degree?**

Language-oriented features

Language-oriented features are features of the ADL itself, independent of the system(s) it is being used to develop. These attributes include the kind of information usually found in a language reference manual. An example is how formally specified the ADL's syntax and semantics are and what architectural abstractions are embodied by the ADL.

Language-oriented questions include:

Language definition quality
- **Formality: How formally are the ADL's syntax and semantics defined?**
- **Completeness: How well is completeness defined for an architecture descriptions? How does the ADL treat an incomplete architecture description?**

---

1. For brevity, a great deal of clarifying elaboration has been omitted, as has the explanation of the response scales. For instance, the question, "How does the ADL treat an incomplete architecture description?" is instantiated in the actual questionnaire as several detailed questions dealing with the operations that can be performed on an incomplete description, whether built-in or user-defined completeness rules exist or prevail, whether the language features a wildcard or incompleteness token, etc. We ask the reader's indulgence to believe that the subjective-sounding questions presented in this paper are backed up in the actual questionnaire with detailed sub-questions that address each issue much more objectively.

- **Consistency: Is self-consistency defined for an architecture description? Is it defined between two different architecture description, or between an architecture description and some other rendering of the system such as a requirements specification or coded implementation? Are the consistency rules built-in or user-defined?**

Scope of language: How much non-architecture information can the ADL represent?

Design History: How well does the ADL provide for recording architectural design information?

Views: How well does the ADL support different views that highlight different aspects/perspectives of the architecture?
- **Syntactic view list: Which syntactic views are supported? Graphical, textual, etc.**
- **Semantic view list: Which semantic views are supported? Data flow, control flow, process view, etc.**
- **Inter-view cross reference: Does the ADL provide for translating among views?**
- **Architectural content of views: Does the ADL provide views that show mostly architectural information?**

Readability
- **Embedded comments**
- **Presentation control**

Characteristics of intended users
- **Target users: domain engineer, application engineer, systems analyst, software manager?**
- **Expertise required: domain expertise, software design expertise, programming language expertise?**

Modifiability of software architecture description
- **Ease of change: How well does the ADL support ease of change of the architecture and its representation?**
- **Scalability: the degree to which the ADL can represent large and/or complex systems. Hierarchies? Cross-referencing? Subset capability? Composition? Multiple instantiation of templates?**

Variability: How well does the ADL represent the variations in the application systems that can be derived from an architecture?

Expressive power of the ADL.
- **Powerful primitives featured**
- **Extensibility**
- **What abstractions does the ADL support or provide? Are the abstractions architectural, behavioral, or implementation based?**

Process-oriented features

Process-oriented features are features of a process related to using the ADL to create, validate, analyze, and refine an architecture description, and build an application system from it. Included are attributes that measure or describe how or to what extent an ADL allows predictive evaluation of the application system based on architecture-level information.

The survey draws a distinction between the language, the analysis that can be performed on architectural information representable by the language, and the tools that actually exist to perform such analysis. However, just as no one would use Ada without an Ada compiler, it is not likely that anyone would adopt an ADL for a project without also adopting any editing, refinement, analysis, or system-building tools that come with it. Thus, in a survey designed to help practitioners choose an ADL, we view an ADL as the language plus its supporting toolset, the sum of which practitioners will use as the basis for selection, usage, and after-the-fact evaluation.

The survey measures whether or not the ADL contains enough information to make an architecture analyzable, independently of whether or not tools actually exist that exploit that capability. For example, an ADL may allow enough timing information to be given to support schedulability analysis. A rate monotonic analysis schedule analyzer (if it exists for the ADL) would be an example of a tool that exploits such information.

The analysis areas are primarily drawn from IEEE Std 1061, "Software Quality Metrics Methodology" [9]. Many of these attributes are not addressed by any existing ADLs.

Process-oriented questions delve into:

Architecture creation support: textual editor, graphical editor, import tool?

Architecture validation support: syntax checker, semantics checker, completeness checker, consistency checker?

Architecture refinement support: browser, search tool, incremental refinement tool, version control, architecture comparison?

Architecture analysis support: What support is provided by the ADL for analyzing architecture-level information in order to predict or project qualities of the end system?

- **Analyzing for time and resource economy: schedulability, throughput, other time economies, memory utilization, other resource economics?**
- **Analyzing for functionality: completeness, correctness, security, interoperability?**
- **Analyzing for maintainability: correctability, expandability, testability?**
- **Analyzing for portability: hardware independence, software independence?**
- **Analyzing for reliability: error tolerance, degraded operation capability, availability?**
- **Analyzing for usability: understandability, ease of learning, operability?**

Application building: building a compilable (or executable) software system from a specific system design.

- **System composition: the composition or integration of components' bodies, in order to produce a compilable or executable software system for: single processor target, distributed homogeneous system, distributed heterogeneous system, components written in more than one language?**
- **Application generation support: component code generation, wrapper code generation, test case generation, documentation generation?**

Tool Maturity, availability, and support.

Process support: Does a user's manual exist? Does a training course exist?

5. Gathering data

The questionnaire has been circulated to the proprietors of over a dozen ADLs to date. Table 1 contains the list of those who have responded and had their results validated to date. Other surveys in progress include those for Rapide [12], Gestalt [17], ACME [4], and FR [8].

In order to gain confidence in the questionnaire, we applied it to some languages, such as Modechart, that would not be considered mainstream ADLs. The intent was to observe how these "cusp" languages scored in order to try to understand qualities that distinguish ADLs from non-ADLs.

Table 1: ADLs surveyed (alphabetical order)

ADL	Source	Citation
ArTek	Teknowledge	[19]
CODE	Univ. of Texas at Austin	[15]
Demeter	Northeastern Univ.	[16]
Modechart	Univ. of Texas at Austin	[10]
PSDL/ CAPS	Naval Postgrad. School	[14]
Resolve	Ohio State Univ.	[3]
UniCon	Carnegie Mellon Univ.	[18]
Wright	Carnegie Mellon Univ.	[1]

The intent of the questionnaire was to make as many of the questions as possible objective, in the sense that two independent observers would be highly likely to respond the same way to the question. Where subjectivity was called for (e.g., "how well does the language support architecture representations that are easy to change?") we asked the respondent to provide specific language features and usage scenarios that justified the answer. Nevertheless, it has been necessary to conduct a validation interview for each questionnaire in order to add credibility to the responses.

6. Conclusions

This section will present the results of the survey to date and postulate some conclusions about ADLs in general.

6.1: Survey results

Table 3 distills many of the detailed questions down into summary statements about the languages' capabilities. Table 2 explains the answer symbols in Table 3. Table 3 serves as a quick-reference guide for readers interested in finding a language for a particular application. The intent is that the quick-reference guide would provide a reader with a small set of candidate languages mostly likely to suit his or her purpose. For complete details and final selection, the full surveys of the languages (not reproduced in this paper) should be consulted.

To create the quick-reference guide, the full surveys were distilled using the following heuristics:

- If it was possible to combine a set of questions into a general one about the language's capability without loss of significant detail, this was done. The rating of a language's general capability is either the arithmetic average of its ratings on the component questions (if the rating scale is ordered, such as High/Medium/Low), or the answer that appeared most often in the component questions (if the rating scale is unordered). If the component questions were Yes/No, then the summary rating reflects the ratio of Yes answers.

- Questions on which all languages scored the same or nearly the same tended to be suppressed, since they did not serve as useful discriminators among the languages.

Shading information is used in the cells to augment the textual content. The lighter the shading, the more capable the language rated on the particular issue.

6.2: ADLs versus other languages

Languages that are generally considered "mainstream" ADLs shared the following aspects:

- The abstractions they provided to the user were architectural in nature. All represented components and connections (although Rapide represents connections only by specifying communication behaviors among components).

- Most of the views provided by the ADLs contained predominantly architectural information. This is in contrast to a programming language or a requirements language that tends to show other kinds of information.

- Analysis provided by the language relies on architecture-level information. Rapide's discrete event simulator, for instance, uses behavioral information about each component to generate partially ordered event sets. UniCon's interface to the rate monotonic analyzer uses black-box performance information about each component in order to compute schedulability. This is in contrast to a performance analyzer that identifies bottlenecks based on implementation information (i.e., code).

6.3: Discriminators

The following areas uncovered interesting differences among the ADLs we surveyed:

- ADLs differed markedly in their ability to handle real-time constructs at the architectural level. Roughly half claimed to deal with hard-real-time constructs such as deadlines; only a small number dealt with soft-real-time constructs such as tasking priorities.

- ADLs varied in their ability to support the specification of particular architectural styles. All ADLs could represent pipe-and-filter architectures, either directly or indirectly. Other styles did not fare as well. All provided hierarchical structuring of components, and could represent objects, but only a few could handle object-oriented class inheritance. Only two handled dynamic architectures.

- The set of surveyed ADLs split evenly on their ability to let a user define new types of components and connectors, define new statements in the ADL, and represent non-architectural information (such as requirements, or test cases) using the ADL. Extensibility and scope were good discriminators.

- While all languages provided built-in internal consistency and completeness rules for artifacts rendered in those languages, only a few allowed the user to define what was meant by consistency, and only a few dealt with consistency between different artifacts (e.g., between an architecture and component designs).

- ADLs varied widely in their ability to support analysis. Rapide features a discrete-event simulator based on partially-ordered sets of event behaviors. Modechart features a model-checking verifier that takes as input a logical assertion and reports whether the system description guarantees, prohibits, or is merely compatible with that assertion. UniCon interfaces directly to a rate monotonic schedule analyzer. A more general analysis capability (such as in the case of a verifier) showed up in the questionnaire as the ability to analyze for many different quality attributes. For instance, a simulator could be used to analyze for usability by letting users observe the simulated behavior to see if it meets their expectations.

- ADLs differed in their ability to handle variability, or different instantiations of the same architecture. All supported component variability through simple rewrite capability, but few supported maintaining different instantiations of the same architecture simultaneously.

- When offering more than one architectural view, ADLs varied widely in their ability to translate among those views. View interchangeability is a strong discriminator among the ADLs we surveyed.

6.4: Commonalities

The following commonalities were noticed:

- All of the ADLs surveyed had a graphical syntax; all but one also had a textual form. Every language but one featured a formal syntax, and the vast majority featured formally-defined semantics.

- Every language claimed to be able to model distributed systems.

- ADLs tended not to provide much support for capturing design rationale and/or history, other than through generic or general-purpose annotation mechanisms.

- All of the ADLs claimed to handle data flow and control flow as interconnection mechanisms. Modechart was the weakest in this regard, because of its ability to deal only with state predicates (such as "data sent") instead of actual data values.

- All ADLs provided help with creation and validation an refinement of architectures, even if validation was only done in the context of the language's own rules for completeness or legality.

- All featured the ability to represent hierarchical levels of detail, and handle multiple instantiations of a template as a quick way to perform copying substructures during creation.

- All ADLs support the application engineer, and most support the domain engineer, even if only indirectly. Most support the systems analyst by providing upfront analytical capabilities. None claimed to directly support project management.

- Finally, a glaring commonality was the lack of indepth experience and real-world application that ADLs currently offer. It is to be hoped that as the benefits of architecture become better understood, that the benefits of formal representations will be equally prized, and ADLs will come into their own as viable technologies for complex system development.

6.5: What constitutes an ADL?

After surveying a broad selection of languages, all of which have some claim to being ADLs, what can we conclude about what makes a language an ADL? The following seems to be a minimal set of requirements for a language to be an ADL:

- An ADL must support the tasks of architecture creation, refinement, and validation. It must embody rules about what constitutes a complete or consistent architecture.

- An ADL must provide the ability to represent (even if indirectly) most of the common architectural styles enumerated in [6].

- An ADL must have the ability to provide views of the system that express architectural information, but at the same time suppress implementation or non-architectural information.

- If the language can express implementation-level information, then it must contain capabilities for matching more than one implementation to the architecture-level views of the system. That is, it must support specification of families of implementations that all satisfy a common architecture.

- An ADL must support either an analytical capability, based on architecture-level information, or a capability for quickly generating prototype implementations.

6.6: Future trends

Communicating an architecture to a stakeholder becomes a matter of representing it in an unambiguous, readable form that contains the information appropriate to that stakeholder. Current trends in ADL development seems to be focusing on enhancing the analysis and system-generation capabilities of the languages. Architecture is, after all, only a means to an end, and information that developers can infer about the end system is more valuable than information about just the architecture. Being able to quickly develop a system or manage qualities of the final product are the real payoff of ADLs. While development of architecture languages is proceeding apace, there is less attention being paid to the following areas:

- **Infrastructures to support ADL development.** Most ADLs share a set of common concepts. Building tools to support an ADL involves solving a common set of problems. Development of an ADL development environment would facilitate the rapid production of ADLs and supporting tools, thus allowing good ideas to come to market faster. Garlan's Aesop/ACME work represents an early and important contribution to this area [4].

- **Integration of ADL information with other life-cycle products.** As ADLs mature, they will take a more prominent role in the litany of life-cycle products (such as detailed design documents, test cases, etc.). Encouragement should be given to early consideration of the relationship that an architecture description will bear to these other documents. For example, what test cases might be generated for a system based on a description of its components and interconnection mechanisms? What kind of and how much executable code can be automatically generated? How can traceability of architecture to requirements be established? This work could culminate in the complete integration of architecture descriptions into the development environment, giving rise to a sort of "architectorium." This can be thought of as an exploration environment in which architectures are drafted, validated via mapping to requirements, their implications explored via analysis or rapid prototyping, alternatives suggested in an expert-system-like fashion, and project infrastructures necessary for development (e.g., work schedule templates, component-based configuration control libraries, test plans, etc.) are generated.

It is to be hoped researchers will be spurred to provide ADLs that address gaps in current capability, particularly in analysis and program family support.

7. Acknowledgments

Paul Kogut of Loral is a co-creator of the ADL feature analysis and a co-author of the SEI report describing it. Many of the insights in this paper are his. Thanks are due to the many ADL creators who patiently filled out our questionnaire, and allowed us to come visit and discuss the survey results in depth. This work would not have been possible without them. Special thanks go to Allan Terry, J. C. Browne, Karl Lieberherr, David Garlan, Bruce Weide, Luqi, Mary Shaw, and their respective, usually overworked, ADL-building teams.

The SEI is sponsored by the U.S. Department of Defense.

Table 2: Answer key for Table 3

Symbol	Meaning
Y	Yes
N	No
H	High capability: language provides explicit features to support this capability
M	Medium: language provides generic features through which this capability may be indirectly achieved
L	Low: language provides little support
T	Tool specifically developed for the ADL supports this capability
E	External tool provides this capability
P	Language provides enough information to support the capability, but no tool support currently exists.

23

Table 3: ADL survey results

Attributes	ARTEK	CODE	DEMETER	MODECHART	PSDL/CAPS	RESOLVE	UNICON	WRIGHT
Applicability								
Ability to represent styles	M	M	M	M	H	M	M	H
Ability to handle real-time issues	M		M	H	H	L	H	L
Ability to handle distributed system issues	H	H	H	H	H	M	M	M
Ability to handle dynamic architectures	L	H	H	L	M	L	?	L
Language definition quality								
Attention to completeness of arch. spec.	M	L	H	M	M	L	M	H
Attention to consistency of arch. spec.	L	L	M	L	M	H	L	H
Scope of language; intended users								
Requirements	H	L	?	H	H	M	L	L
Detailed design/algorithms	L	M	H	M	H	M	L	L
Code	M	L	H	L	L	H	H	L
Domain engineer	Y	Y	Y	N	Y	N	Y	Y
Application engineer	Y	Y	Y	Y	Y	Y	Y	Y
Systems analyst	Y	N	Y	Y	Y	Y	N	Y
Capturing design history	?	L	?	L	?	?	?	?
Views								
Textual	Y	N	Y	Y	Y	Y	Y	Y
Graphical	Y	Y	Y	Y	Y	N	Y	N
Semantic view richness	L	M	H	H	H	L	?	L
Inter-view cross reference	M	L	L	M	M	L	M	L
Support for Variability	M	L	H	L	H	H	L	H
Expressive power, extensibility	H	L	M	M	H	H	M	M
Support for architecture creation	T	T	P	T	T	E	T	
Support for architecture validation	T	T	E	T	T	P	T	E
Support for architecture refinement	T	P	P	T	T	P	P	P
Support for architecture analysis	E		P	T	T	P		
Support for application building		T	P		P			
Tool Maturity								
Available as COTS?	N	N	?	N	N	N	N	N
Age (years)	3	?	10	7	5	?	2	3
Number of sites in use	11	?	?	4	12	4	1	1
Customer support available	Y	Y	N	N	N	Y	N	N

8. References

1. Allen, R., & Garlan, D. "Beyond Definition/Use: Architectural Interconnection," *Proceedings, Workshop on Interface Definition Languages,* Portland Oregon, 20 January 1994.

2. Clements, P., Gasarch, C., & Jeffords, R. "Evaluation Criteria for Real-Time Specification Languages," Naval Research Laboratory Memorandum Report 6935, February 1992.

3. Edwards, S., Heym, W., Long, T., Sitarman, M., & Weide, B.; "Specifying Components in RESOLVE," Software Engineering Notes, vol. 19, no. 4, October 1994.

4. Garlan, D., Allen, R., & Ockerbloom, J. "Exploiting Style in Architectural Design Environments," *Proceedings of SIGSOFT '94: Foundations of Software Engineering,* December 1994, ACM Press.

5. R. Kazman, L. Bass, G. Abowd, & M. Webb, "SAAM: A Method for Analyzing the Properties Software Architectures". In *Proceedings of the 16th International Conference on Software Engineering,* (Sorrento, Italy), May 1994, pp. 81-90.

6. Garlan, D. & Shaw, M. *An Introduction to Software Architecture.* (CMU/SEI-93-TR-33). Pittsburgh, Pa.: Software Engineering Institute, Carnegie Mellon University, December 1993. Also in Ambriola, V.; and Tortora, G. (eds.), Advances in Software Engineering and Knowledge Engineering, Volume I. Singapore: World Scientific Publishing, 1993.

7. Harel, D., Lachover, H., Naamad, A., Pnueli, A., Politi, M., Sherman, R., & Shtul-Trauring, A.; "STATEMATE: a working environment for the development of complex reactive systems" Proceedings of the 10th International Conference on Software Engineering Singapore, April 1988;

8. Hartman, J. & Chandrasekaran, B., "Functional Representation and Understanding of Software: Technology and Application," *Proceedings, 1995 Dual-Use Technologies and Applications Conference,* 1995.

9. IEEE Std 610.12, *IEEE Standard Glossary of Software Engineering Terminology,* September 1990.

10. Jahanian, F. & Mok, A. "Modechart: A Specification Language for Real-Time Systems," *IEEE Transactions on Software Engineering,* vol. 20, no. 12, December 1994, pp. 933-947.

11. Kang, K., Cohen, S., Hess, J., Novak, W., & Peterson, A.. *Feature-Oriented Domain Analysis (FODA) Feasibility Study* (CMU/SEI-90-TR-21, ADA235785). Pittsburgh, PA: Software Engineering Institute, Carnegie Mellon University, Nov. 1990.

12. Luckham, D., Kenney, J., Augustin, L., Vera. J., Bryan, D., & Mann, W. "Specification and Analysis of System Architecture Using Rapide," Stanford University technical report, 1993.

13. Luckham, D. & Vera, J. "An Event-Based Architecture Definition Language," *IEEE Transactions on Software Engineering,* vol. 21, no. 9, September 1995.

14. Luqi, Shing, M., Barnes, P., & Hughes, G. "Prototyping Hard Real-Time Ada Systems in a Classroom Environment," *Proceedings of the Seventh Annual Ada Software Engineering Education and Training (ASEET) Symposium,* Monterey, 12-14 January 1993.

15. Newton, P. & Browne, J. "The CODE 2.0 Graphical Parallel Programming Language," *Proceedings, ACM International Conference on Supercomputing,* July 1992.

16. Palsberg, J., Xiao, C., & Lieberherr, K. "Efficient Implementation of Adaptive Software (Summary of Demeter Theory)", Northeastern University, Boxton, 10 January 1995.

17. Schwanke, R., "Industrial Software Architecture with Gestalt," technical report, Siemens Corporate Research, Princeton NJ.

18. Shaw, DeLine, Klein, Ross, Young, & Zelesnik "Abstractions for Software Architectures and Tools to Support Them," Carnegie Mellon University, unpublished report Feb. 1994

19. Terry, Hayes-Roth, Erman, Coleman, Devito, Papanagopoulos, & Hayes-Roth "Overview of Teknowledge's DSSA Program," *ACM SIGSOFT Software Engineering Notes,* October 1994.

20. Vestal, S. *A Cursory Overview and Comparison of Four Architectural Description Languages,* technical report, Honeywell, Feb. 1993

21. Vestal, S. "Mode Changes in a Real-Time Architecture Description Language," Proceedings, Proc. International Workshop on Configurable Distributed Systems: Honeywell Technology Center and the University of Maryland.

Tool Specification with GTSL*

Wolfgang Emmerich

Dept. of Computer Science, City University London,
Northampton Square, London EC1V 0HB, UK

Abstract

The definition of software development methods encompasses the definition of syntax and static semantics of formal languages. These languages determine documents to be produced during the application of a method. Developers demand language-based tools that provide document production support, check syntax and static semantics of documents and thus implement methods. Method integration must determine inter-document consistency constraints between documents produced in the various tasks. Tools must, therefore, be integrated to implement the required method integration and check or even preserve inter-document consistency. The focus of this paper is on the specification of such integrated tools and outlines the main concepts of the object-oriented tool specification language GTSL.

1 Introduction

A software process that develops and maintains a software system performs a number of different *tasks*. Examples are *requirements analysis* tasks where the requirements of future customers of a software system are elicited or *architectural design* tasks where the different components of software systems and relationships among them are identified. The suggestion of the Waterfall model [21] that these tasks be performed in mutual exclusion has been proved infeasible [3]. Instead the tasks are often carried out in an incremental and intertwined manner [23, 12].

Tasks are performed using *development methods*, like *structured analysis* [6] for requirements analysis or object-oriented methods (for instance the Booch methodology [4]) for architectural design. Method definitions have to determine formal graphical or textual *languages*. Examples are data flow diagrams or class hierarchies. These languages then determine *document types* and the purpose of each task of a software process is to create, analyse and maintain *documents* of the types identified. Hence, the definition of a method encompasses the precise definition of *document types*. Document types are defined in terms of the syntax and static semantics of the underlying formal languages.

Apart from static semantic constraints of the formal languages, there are also consistency constraints between different documents. These *inter-document consistency constraints* are not confined to documents of the same type but frequently exist between documents of different types. A need for *method integration* arises whose aim is to define the consistency constraints that documents must obey. An important factor for the quality of a software system is then whether these constraints have been defined properly and are respected by the documents produced during the process.

A particular mix of methods that is appropriate in one process need not be appropriate for another. A process developing a real-time application, for instance, should use a requirements definition language that can express response time constraints, but such a language might be unnecessarily complicated for a banking application, where response time constraints need not be expressed. This means that it is impossible to find **the** mix of methods that could be used in arbitrary software processes. Therefore, method integration must become part of process modelling and deserves appropriate attention.

Development methods are implemented by tools that software developers can use to apply the method. To implement method integration then requires tools to be integrated. The main contribution of this paper is the presentation of the *GOODSTEP[1] tool specification language (GTSL)*, an object-oriented language dedicated to the specification of integrated tools. The language is executable and the GTSL compiler GENESIS generates tools from GTSL specifications.

The rest of this paper will be structured as follows.

---

*This work has been partly funded by the CEC as part of ESPRIT-III project 6115 (GOODSTEP) and was done while the author was at University of Dortmund, Germany.

[1]GOODSTEP's aim is to enhance a general object-oriented database for software engineering processes.

26

In the next section, we discuss the need for method and tool customisation in more detail. Section 3 suggests a representation for documents as a basis for the specification of tools and document types and relates it to the literature. In Section 4 we present the main concepts of GTSL. We conclude the paper in Section 5 with work that remains to be done.

2 Method and Tool Customisation

As an illustrating example that we will use throughout this paper consider Figure 1. It displays four different documents of four different types. Starting from the bottom left, there are in clock-wise order an entity relationship diagram, an architectural definition that identifies different types of modules as components of a software system[2], a module interface definition that identifies exported types and operations as well as an import interface, and a module implementation that implements the exported types and operations of a module in the C programming language. The integration of the underlying methods requires a number of inter-document consistency constraints to be defined between the respective document types. Entities of the entity relationship diagram, for instance, must be refined in terms of abstract data type modules in the architecture diagram. Modules in these diagrams, in turn, must be refined by a module interface definition, that defines the export and import interface in detail. Each arrow of the architecture diagram should appear as an entry in the import interface of a module interface definition. Operations and types that have been identified in the export interface must be implemented in the C document. Therefore, parameter lists and result types in the interface design and in the C document should match. Moreover, import interfaces are refined by preprocessor #include statements. Conversely, there should be no such statements when the design does not include the respective entry in the import interface, otherwise there would be dependencies among source code components that are not properly reflected in the design.

The need arises to assist software developers in the production of documents that meet inter-document consistency constraints such as those outlined above, and thus to implement the methods and their integration. Users[3] require a *tool* for each document type. Such a tool should support the methods and offer commands to edit documents of that type. It should be supportive in achieving syntactic and static semantic correctness of documents, browsing of semantically related documents and most importantly, it must check for inter-document consistency. This requires that tools be aware of the syntactic structure of documents. We denote different syntactic units of documents as *increments* because users can modify these units incrementally. The granularity of increments can range from complete documents to single identifiers. The example of Figure 1 displays the user interfaces of tools contained in the *Groupie* environment [11]. They are used to edit, analyse and check documents of the types identified above.

To implement method integration, tools have to check for inter-document consistency constraint violations. Different strategies can be considered how a tool should react to a constraint violation. It might tolerate a violation and only visualise an inconsistency to the user when it has been introduced. This visualisation might be achieved by the use of colours or by underlining. In the example of Figure 1, a parameter list increment in the C implementation is underlined because it does not match the parameter list determined in the interface design. Detailed error messages should be provided on demand. Alternatively, a tool might follow an intolerant approach and reject the execution of commands that would violate an inter-document consistency constraint. A tool might even automatically correct erroneous increments. Upon a change of one increment, it can, for instance, automatically modify related increments in other documents in such a way that consistency is retained. We refer to these automatic modifications of related increments as *change propagations*.

Most software processes are conducted by multiple rather than single developers. This implies that we also have to consider the concurrent use of tools by multiple users. Different *versions* of documents must be managed to facilitate independent document development. The methods defined in terms of document types, therefore, also have to identify the granularity for version management. Versions are then used to allow users to edit documents in *isolation* for a certain period of time. However, due to inter-document consistency constraints, the development cannot be performed in complete isolation. At some point in time, the documents produced by one developer must become consistent with documents produced by other developers. Users must then share their document versions. In the above example a requirements engineer might use the entity relationship tool to define an information model of a software system, while a designer

---

[2]The detailed notion is of no concern here and we refer to [11].

[3]The software developers that use tools are referred to as *users* hereafter.

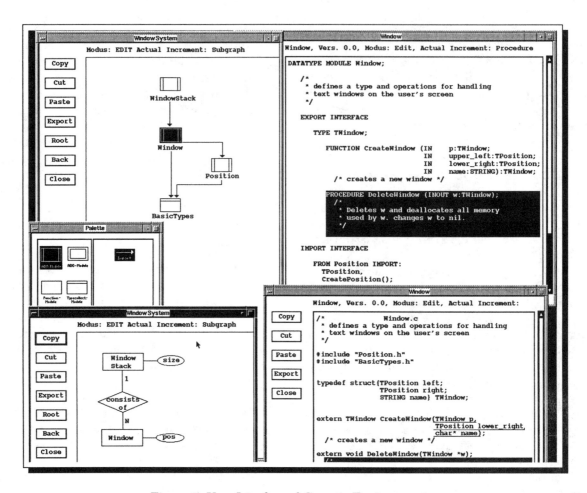

Figure 1: User Interface of Groupie Environment

is defining its architecture. Their document versions should become consistent with each other before implementation begins, otherwise significant effort might be wasted during implementation if, for instance, wrong names are used or it turns out that an implemented module is obsolete. They, therefore, have to edit the corresponding versions of the entity relationship and the architecture diagram concurrently.

To reach a state of consistency, users want to see the impact of concurrent document updates as soon as possible. Tight cooperation requires updates to a document version to be done in such a way that all tools concurrently displaying a document version are informed of the update as soon as possible. They should then redisplay the document version in order to reflect the update as well. In the above example of inconsistent parameter lists, a designer might remove the inconsistency by deleting the additional parameter. If a programmer is concurrently accessing the version of the implementation document that corresponds to the interface, he or she should see, as soon as possible,

that the inconsistency has been resolved and requires no further attention. The shared and cooperative updates of document versions must, therefore, not be disabled by exclusive locking of complete documents by long transactions but transactions must be short and locking must be done with a more fine-grained granularity.

3 Document Representation

Before we can identify concepts of a higher-level specification language for the definition of methods and their integration, we have to understand how documents should be represented. During this discussion we compare our considerations to related work. The common internal representation for documents manipulated by tools is an *abstract syntax tree* of some form [20, 8, 13]. Nodes in the abstract syntax tree often have additional attributes whose values represent semantic information such as references to a string ta-

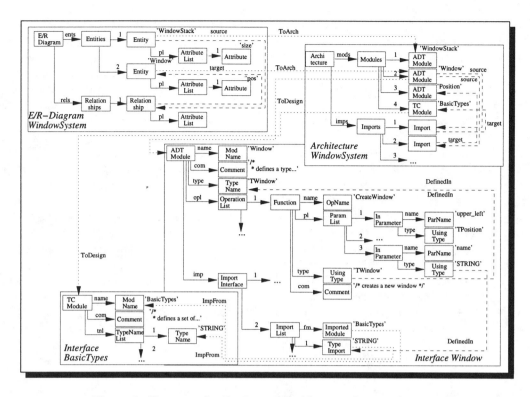

Figure 2: Excerpt of a Project-wide Abstract Syntax Graph

ble, symbol tables or type information. Operations, like insertion of a new parameter list place holder can be implemented as subtree replacements. After free textual input, the abstract syntax tree can be established with parsing techniques well-known from compiler construction [1].

Static semantic checking of a document that is represented as an abstract syntax tree can be done by *attribute evaluations* along parent/child paths in the document's attributed abstract syntax tree [17, 20]. The evaluation paths are computed at tool construction time based on attribute dependencies. If inter-document consistency checks are implemented by attribute evaluations, inter-document consistency constraints must be checked at an artificial root node, which has sub-trees for each document. With respect to concurrent tool execution many concurrency control conflicts arise at these root nodes and decrease tools' performance. Therefore, techniques based on the introduction of additional, non-syntactic paths for more direct attribute propagation have been developed [15, 18, 14]. They generalise the concept of abstract syntax trees to *abstract syntax graphs*. Such non-syntactic paths implement *semantic relationships* that connect syntactically disjoint parts of possibly different documents even of different types. They can be used for consistency checking, change-propagation when the

document is changed and even for implementing static semantic analysis and browsing facilities. To handle these semantic relationships in a consistent way, the obvious strategy is to view the set of documents making up a project as a single *project-wide abstract syntax graph*.

In such a graph, we distinguish between *aggregation edges*, which implement syntactic relationships, from *reference edges*, which arise from semantic relationships. A document is then represented by the subgraph whose node-set is the closure of nodes reachable by aggregation edges from a document root node. Nodes that cannot have outgoing aggregation edges are called *terminal nodes*, for their origin lies in terminal symbols of the underlying grammar. Those nodes that may have outgoing aggregation edges are called *non-terminal nodes* accordingly.

As an example, consider Figure 2. It outlines how the different abstract syntax trees representing documents of Figure 1 are integrated to a project-wide abstract syntax graph. The refinement of entities defined in the entity relationship diagram in terms of modules of the architecture is reflected by inter-document reference edges (drawn as dotted arrows) labelled ToArch. Likewise, the refinement of modules of the architecture definition in terms of module interface documents is stored by means of reference edges labelled ToDesign.

Intra-document reference edges (drawn with dashed arrows) labelled `DefinedIn` represent the use/declare relationship between type increments of a module interface document. The parameter type of function `CreateWindow` with the attribute `STRING` (given in quotes), for instance, has an outgoing reference edge to the node where it is declared, that is to the `TypeImport` node with attribute `STRING`. This node represents an import that is itself connected via an inter-document reference edge labelled `ImpFrom` to another node contained in the subgraph of module `BasicTypes` where the type is exported.

Graph grammars have been suggested in [12] to specify the structure of such abstract syntax graphs. Productions of the grammar can then be considered as available operations to modify abstract syntax graphs. Graph grammars, however, do not appropriately specify concurrency constraints, lexical syntax, external document representations and dialogues between users and tools during command execution. Moreover, graph grammars do not impose a particular structuring paradigm and specifications of graphs that occur in practice tend to become so complex that they can hardly be managed appropriately.

4   GTSL

On the basis of the above concepts, we can now focus on the question how document types and tools are defined appropriately. We propose GTSL for that purpose. The language allows tool builders to define *static* and *dynamic properties* of syntax graphs as well as mappings between syntax graphs and *external document representations*. The static properties that are to be defined are the various node types, their attributes and the edges that may start at or lead to nodes. Dynamic properties are, firstly, the available tool commands and their definition on the basis of syntax graph access and modification operations and, secondly, the dependencies between attribute values and reference edges that define static semantics and inter-document consistency constraints. The mappings to external document representations must define the appearance of abstract syntax graphs at the user interface of tools or in printed tool output.

For the definition of a project-wide abstract syntax graph, as many node types must be defined as there are productions in the underlying language grammars. The specification of document types and tools, therefore, becomes rather complex for methods and languages that occur in software engineering practice. The specification language must incorporate structur-

ing facilities to keep this complexity manageable. The overall specification of a project-wide abstract syntax graph should, therefore, be decomposed into the specifications of the various subgraphs that represent different document types and each of these subgraph specifications should be decomposed into specifications for the node types that occur in the subgraph. GTSL supports this decomposition in an object-oriented way. Tools are specified in terms of *configurations* of *increment classes*. Import/Export relationships between tool configurations make the dependencies between different tool specifications explicit and simplify customisation and reuse. Increment classes determine node types of the project-wide syntax graphs and configurations determine the increment classes that belong to a tool.

The complexity of specifying a tool is significantly reduced if tool builders can reuse already existing tool specification components. GTSL, therefore, allows the tool builder to identify similarities among different increment classes and to specify the common structure and behaviour of increments in one class and reuse it in similar classes. The object-oriented paradigm is exploited and similarities are expressed by inheritance. Definitions inherited from super classes can be customised by redefining them. Reuse is then further supported since GTSL comes with a library of predefined classes defining, for instance version management, common tool commands, symbol tables or standard scoping rules.

Due to the heterogeneity of the different static and behavioural concerns, it is impossible to find a unique formalism that is appropriate for their specification. Instead, we separate the different concerns and offer the most appropriate formalism for each of them. We integrate these different formalisms into a domain-specific *multi-paradigm language* that uses rule-based, object-oriented and imperative concepts.

Following the principle of information hiding [19], the definition of a class is divided into a public *class interface* and a private *class specification*. The class interfaces and specifications are, in turn, structured into different sections that offer different paradigms to specify the various concerns.

The node types in an abstract syntax graph definition play different roles. *Terminal classes*, which define leaf nodes of the abstract syntax tree, must not have commands to expand child increments, whereas *non-terminal classes*, which define inner syntax tree nodes, require these commands. Non-terminal classes must also specify the unparsing scheme that defines the external representation of their instances. *Abstract classes* define common properties of classes that are inherited by its subclasses. We call instances of non-terminal classes *non-terminal increments* and instances of terminal classes *terminal increments*. We refer to them as *increments*, if their position in the syntax tree is not important. Besides increment classes, we additionally support *non-syntactic* classes that will be used for the declaration of non-atomic attribute types, such as error lists or symbol tables. Instances of these classes are referred to as *attributes*. If the distinction between attributes and increments is not important, we will denote instances of classes as *objects*.

4.1 Specification of Static Properties

Abstract Syntax: Aggregation edges starting from nodes of a type are defined within an *abstract syntax section* in the increment class interfaces that specifies the type. The abstract syntax section is available for abstract and non-terminal increment classes. If a child is defined in an abstract class it is inherited by all subclasses. Children are specified in the abstract syntax section with the name and a formal type that restricts child increments to instances of the formal type or subtypes thereof, which are induced by the inheritance hierarchy. Multi-valued aggregation edges are defined by the LIST type constructor. Below there are several examples of abstract syntax sections for node types displayed in Figure 2. Note, how ADTModule reuses definitions inherited from Module.

```
ABSTRACT INCREMENT INTERFACE Module;
   INHERIT DocumentVersion, ScopingBlock; ...
   ABSTRACT SYNTAX
     name:ModName;
     com:Comment;
   END ABSTRACT SYNTAX; ...

NONTERMINAL INCREMENT INTERFACE ADTModule;
   INHERIT Module; ...
   ABSTRACT SYNTAX
     type:TypeName;
     opl:OperationList;
     imp:ImportInterface;
   END ABSTRACT SYNTAX; ...

NONTERMINAL INCREMENT INTERFACE OperationList;
   INHERIT Increment; ...
   ABSTRACT SYNTAX
     ol:LIST OF Operation;
   END ABSTRACT SYNTAX; ...
```

The distinction between different types of classes enables us to exclude a number of potential specification errors. It does not make sense, for instance, to have a terminal increment class that inherits from an abstract class, which, in turn, defines abstract syntax children. In that case the terminal class would inherit these children and no longer be terminal.

Attributes: Node attributes are declared within the attribute section of increment classes. An attribute definition declares a *name* and a *type* of an attribute. Non-syntactic classes can also be used to impose a particular behaviour on attribute types. We do not address non-syntactic classes any further here. They provide the expressive power of an object-oriented language including multiple inheritance, construction of types and encapsulation with methods.

As an example, consider the following example from the Groupie interface editor definition. It defines an attribute DefinedNames whose type is of class SymbolTable. It is used to maintain associations between names and increments.

```
ABSTRACT INCREMENT INTERFACE ScopingBlock; ...
   ATTRIBUTES
     DefinedNames:SymbolTable;
   END ATTRIBUTES; ...
```

Semantic Relationships: Reference edges are defined as pairs of unidirectional *links* in the *semantic relationship* sections of the two increment classes that are connected by the edge. The *explicit link* denotes the direction from the source to the target increment class. The *implicit link* denotes the reverse direction. Both kinds of links can be single- and multi-valued so as to allow for 1:1, 1:n and m:n relationships.

Relationships are created and deleted during static semantics and inter-document consistency analysis. Creation of a relationship is specified by assigning an expression that denotes an increment to an explicit link. The implicit link is established by including the source increment in the set that stores the implicit link. A relationship is deleted by assigning the undefined value NIL to the explicit link of the relationship. As an example, consider the relationships DefinedIn/UsedBy between UsingType and TypeDecl.

```
TERMINAL INCREMENT INTERFACE UsingType;
 INHERIT UsingName;
 SEMANTIC RELATIONSHIPS
  DefinedIn: TypeDecl
 END SEMANTIC RELATIONSHIPS; ...

ABSTRACT INCREMENT INTERFACE TypeDecl;
 INHERIT DefiningName;
 SEMANTIC RELATIONSHIPS
  IMPLICIT UsedBy:SET OF UsingType.DefinedIn;
 END SEMANTIC RELATIONSHIPS; ...
```

Increment class UsingType defines an explicit link DefinedIn to an abstract increment TypeDecl. Using that link, a UsingType increment can refer to the increment where its type is declared. If TypeName and TypeImport are declared as subclasses of TypeDecl,

31

polymorphism can be exploited to have `DefinedIn` edges to the two classes as they occur in Figure 2. `UsedBy` then refers to the set of increments that use the type declarations.

4.2 Specification of Dynamic Properties

Semantic Rules: Attributes and semantic relationships are concepts that can be used for defining data structures for static semantics and inter-document consistency constraints. Changes of attribute values and the creation or deletion of semantic relationships will be defined in tool command definitions. These changes, however, usually require a number of follow-on activities in order to check static semantic constraints for related increments.

If tool builders have to use imperative concepts to define static semantics and inter-document consistency constraints they would have to find valid execution orders to perform the required follow-on actions for all potential attribute and semantic relationship changes. We strongly consider this to be at the wrong level of abstraction. Tool builders require instead a declarative concept for defining the correctness of the various static semantic and inter-document consistency constraints. This concept should, in particular, relieve them from worrying about the order in which evaluations are performed. The new concept should also support our structuring paradigm and be defined in terms of increment classes. In addition, the concept must enable the efficient evaluation of static semantic constraints to be carried out as this has to be done online, i.e. during the execution of user commands. We introduce *semantic rules* for that purpose.

Each semantic rule consists of a list of statements called *action* that is bound to a *condition*. The condition is specified after the `ON` clause and the action is defined between `ACTION` and `END ACTION` keywords. Temporal predicates may be used to specify conditions, namely `CHANGED` and `DELETED`. A `CHANGED` predicate becomes `TRUE` if its argument has been created or changed since the last execution of the semantic rule. The `DELETED` expression becomes `TRUE` if its argument is about to be removed. Arguments of a `CHANGED` or `DELETED` expression may be attributes or semantic relationships of any other increments. Path expressions are used to determine attributes or semantic relationships of remote increments. A name of an attribute may only occur as the last name in a path expression. Compound conditions can be built by using the `OR` operator. An `EXISTS` operator is used in the usual sense of first-order logic to specify that the rule has to be executed as soon as some other condition holds for an el-

ement in a multi-valued syntax child or a multi-valued semantic relationship.

As an example we now consider a solution to a problem that occurs during static semantics specification, namely the *name analysis problem* [16]. We solve it with three abstract classes, i.e. `ScopingBlock`, `DefiningName` and `UsingName`. The classes are independent of a particular target language and can thus be reused to define name analysis in multiple tools. `ScopingBlock` serves as super class for increment classes that start a new block. `DefiningName` serves as a super class for classes whose increments contribute to the declaration of new names. Finally, `UsingName` serves as a super class for all applied occurrences of names. The attribute `DefinedNames` in class `ScopingBlock` is used to maintain associations between names and references to increments where the respective names are declared. We then have to define that an association is included for those and only those increments that declare names. Hence associations are entered into the table when definitions are created, the table is updated when the increment name is changed and associations are deleted when the declaration is deleted. This is defined in the semantic rules below.

```
INCREMENT SPECIFICATION ScopingBlock;
 INITIALIZATION
  DefinedNames := NEW DuplicateSymbolTable;
 END INITIALIZATION;
 SEMANTIC RULES
  ON EXISTS(name:DefiningName IN IncludedNames):
          CHANGED(name.value);
  ACTION
   DefinedNames.associate(name,name.value);
  END ACTION;
  ON EXISTS(name:DefiningName IN IncludedNames):
          DELETED(name);
  ACTION
   DefinedNames.deassociate(name,name.value);
  END ACTION;
 END SEMANTIC RULES;
END INCREMENT SPECIFICATION ScopingBlock.
```

In these two rules, `IncludedNames` denotes the implicit link of a semantic relationship between class `DefiningName` and `ScopingBlock`. We can assume that it is established during construction of defining name increments. The first rule then fires whenever a new declaring increment is created or its value is being changed. Then the symbol table is updated to include the association between the new value and the increment declaring the value. If a name in the scope is deleted, the respective association is removed from the table by the second rule. Then the symbol table can be accessed from semantic rules in class `DefiningName` to check for uniqueness of names and from class `UsingName` to check for existence of applied occurrences of names.

Interactions: The steps of a software development method are implemented by the commands that the tool offers. The command definition must determine the names of commands, preconditions for their applicability and the particular dialogues between tool and user, if any. In GTSL commands are defined as *interactions*. The definition of an interaction encompasses an internal and an external name, a selection context, a precondition and an action. The external name appears in context sensitive menus or is used to invoke a command from a command-line. The internal name is used to determine the redefinition of an inherited interaction. The selection context defines which increment must be selected so that the interaction is applicable. It is actually included in a context-sensitive menu if the precondition that follows the `ON` clause evaluates to `TRUE`. The action is a list of GTSL statements that is executed as soon as the user chooses the command from the menu. The interaction displayed below is considered to be offered if the selected increment is a type name.

```
INCREMENT SPECIFICATION TypeName; ...
 INTERACTIONS
  INTERACTION ChangeType
  NAME "Change Type"
  SELECTED IS SELF
  ON (SELF.expanded)
  VAR t:TEXT;
    err:TEXT_SET;
  BEGIN       // start a new transaction
   t:=NEW TEXT(value);  // read-lock SELF
   IF (t.LINE_EDIT("Enter New Type!")) THEN
    IF SELF.scan(t.CONTENTS()) THEN
     FOREACH i:TypeImport IN ExpTo DO
       i.react_to_change(t.CONTENTS())
     ENDDO;
     FOREACH i:UsingType IN UsedBy DO
       i.react_to_change(t.CONTENTS())
     ENDDO;
     value:=t.CONTENTS() // write-lock SELF
    ELSE    // read-lock SELF
     err:=NEW TEXT_SET(SELF.get_errors());
     err.DISPLAY;
    ENDIF
   ENDIF
  // release all locks, changes persist
  END ChangeType;
```

It is actually offered if the type has already been expanded. If this is the case and the user has requested a menu, the string `Change Type` will become a menu item. If the user chooses this item, the action is executed and the user will be prompted to edit the type identifier in a line edit window. The default character string in this line edit window is the value of the old type identifier. If the dialogue is completed, the `LINE_EDIT` method returns `TRUE` and the method `scan` is executed. The method implementation is generated from a regular expression that is provided for terminal increment classes. It returns `TRUE` if the identifier is lexically correct, otherwise it returns `FALSE`. If the identifier is correct semantic relationships of a type name will be exploited to propagate the change to dependent increments such as parameter types or type imports in order to retain consistency. Then the new lexical value is stored in attribute `value`. If the identifier is wrong an appropriate error message will be displayed.

Multiple users cannot concurrently execute commands in a totally unrestricted way. This is due to the *lost update* and *inconsistent analysis* problems, known from concurrency control in database systems [5]. As an example of the inconsistent analysis problem, consider the following scenario. A designer uses the above interaction to change the name of an exported type. A concurrently working designer creates an import statement referring to the old type. During that, the included type name is searched in the symbol table `DefinedNames` of the module where the type is being changed. An inconsistent analysis problem occurs if this search is performed after the other tool has done the change propagation and before the association was changed in the table. Then the import statement will not be displayed as inconsistent although the imported type does not exist anymore. The construction of an example for lost updates is straight-forward.

Now we have encountered the dilemma that we cannot lock document versions exclusively while they are being edited without hampering cooperation. On the other hand, we must restrict concurrency to avoid the lost update and inconsistent analysis problems. The dilemma is solved by decreasing granularity with respect to both the subject that performs locking and the objects that are being locked. This means that tool sessions are considered as sequences of command executions, each of which is executed in isolation from concurrent commands. Isolation is achieved by locking objects in a traditional way. Locking is inferred from the use of objects and relationships and need not be specified explicitly. An object is locked in shared mode when the object is read and in exclusive mode when it is updated. While shared locks are compatible to each other, any other combination reveals a concurrency control conflict. To decrease the probability of concurrency control conflicts, commands do not lock the complete representation of a document version, but only those nodes that are being accessed or updated during the execution of the command. In the examples that encounter lost updates or inconsistent analysis problems, we would then obtain a concurrency control conflict. Tools react to these conflicts by delaying the execution of one command to await completion of the conflicting command, that is until conflicting locks have been released. This is appropriate because command execution requires only a few hundred milliseconds, which users will hardly recognise as delays.

Apart from the *isolation* property sketched above, interactions have further transaction properties. They are *atomic*, i.e. they are either performed completely or not at all. Once completed, the effect of an interaction is *durable*, i.e. all changes that were made during the interaction persist even if the tool is stopped accidentally by a hardware or software failure. Due to atomicity, tools then recover to the state of the last completed command execution.

4.3 External Document Representation

The external document representation is determined in terms of unparsing schemes. Unparsing schemes are defined for non-terminal increment classes only. They cannot be defined for abstract increment classes. In that case abstract syntax children that might be added in subclasses would not be reflected. Neither are unparsing schemes required for terminal increment classes. For terminal increments the layout computation only needs to output the terminal increment's lexical value. As an example for a textual document representation consider the unparsing schemes of classes OperationList and ADTModule below.

```
NONTERMINAL INCREMENT INTERFACE OperationList;
 UNPARSING SCHEME
  ol DELIMITED BY (NL),(NL) END
  END UNPARSING SCHEME; ...
NONTERMINAL INCREMENT INTERFACE ADTModule; ...
 UNPARSING SCHEME
  "DATATYPE",WS,"MODULE",WS,name,";",(NL),(NL),
  ("   "),com,(NL),(NL),
  ("   "),"EXPORT",WS,"INTERFACE",(NL),(NL),
  ("      "),"TYPE",WS,type,";",(NL),(NL),
  ("         "),opl,(NL),
  ("   "),imp,(NL),(NL),
  "END",WS,"MODULE",WS,name,".",(NL)
  END UNPARSING SCHEME; ...
```

5 Summary and Further Work

We have discussed the need for method definition and integration. Method definitions have to identify document types. Method integration must define

inter-document consistency constraints. The application of methods should be supported by tools whose integration implements method integration. We then have discussed why documents should be represented as project-wide abstract syntax graphs. Then we have outlined GTSL as a specification language capable to define these project-wide abstract syntax graphs as well as commands that are offered by tools to modify these graphs. The implementation of the GTSL compiler GENESIS generates ASG schemas for the O_2 database system [2] as discussed in [9]. Standard database transactions are exploited to implement interactions.

GTSL has been evaluated within the GOODSTEP project for the construction of an SEE for British Airways. An account on this evaluation is given in a companion paper [10]. One of the results of this evaluation was that often document types, such as module interface definitions and the corresponding implementations have a similar structure and documents should, therefore, not be stored redundantly. To improve efficiency and reduce the number of required change propagations these documents should be considered as different views of the same conceptual syntax graph. An extension of GTSL with language concepts to define different views has been done and it is now being implemented on the basis of a view mechanism for object-oriented databases [22].

Different document versions can be managed on the basis of the version manager of the O_2 database system [7]. The problem of configuration management has not yet been sufficiently addressed. Semantic relationships with other document versions are established during editing as determined by the semantic rules. They are, however, only created with those other versions of documents that have either been selected explicitly or are the default version. In that way a user accesses exactly one configuration at a time. What is not yet supported is the explicit construction of a configuration. To facilitate this, tools would have to compute the set of document versions that are consistent with each other. This obviously interferes with evaluation of semantic rules and it is not yet clear to us when the required evaluations can best be done.

Acknowledgements

I thank a number of my students, namely Werner Beckmann, Jörg Brunsman, Boris Gesell, Jens Jahnke, Matthias Kurth, Ralph Mertingk, Wiebke Reimer and Mike Wagener who contributed to the implementation of the GTSL compiler. I thank Uwe Kastens, Carlo Ghezzi and Wilhelm Schäfer for the discussions we had about GTSL. The presentation was improved by the valuable comments I got from Jun Han, Willi Hasselbring, Jim Welsh and the anonymous referees on earlier drafts of this paper.

References

[1] A. V. Aho, R. Sethi, and J. D. Ullmann. *Compilers – Principles, Techniques and Tools*. Addison Wesley, 1986.

[2] F. Bancilhon, C. Delobel, and P. Kanellakis. *Building an Object-Oriented Database System: the Story of O_2*. Morgan Kaufmann, 1992.

[3] B. W. Boehm. A Spiral Model of Software Development and Enhancement. *IEEE Computer*, pages 61–72, May 1988.

[4] G. Booch. *Object Oriented Design with Applications*. Benjamin/Cummings, 1991.

[5] C. J. Date. *Introduction to Database Systems, Vol. 1*. Addison Wesley, 1986.

[6] T. de Marco. *Structured Analysis and System Specification*. Yourdan, 1978.

[7] C. Delobel and J. Madec. Version Management in O_2. Technical report, O_2-Technology, 1993.

[8] V. Donzeau-Gouge, G. Kahn, B. Lang, and M. Mélèse. Document structure and modularity in Mentor. *ACM SIGSOFT Software Engineering Notes*, 9(3):141–148, 1984.

[9] W. Emmerich. *Tool Construction for process-centred Software Development Environments based on Object Database Systems*. PhD thesis, University of Paderborn, Germany, 1995.

[10] W. Emmerich, J. Arlow, J. Madec, and M. Phoenix. Construction of the British Airways SEE with the O_2 ODBMS. Technical report, City University London, Dept. of Computer Science, 1996. To appear.

[11] W. Emmerich and W. Schäfer. Groupie — An Environment supporting Group-Oriented Architecture Development. Technical Report 71, University of Dortmund, Dept. of Computer Science, Chair for Software Technology, 1994.

[12] G. Engels, C. Lewerentz, M. Nagl, W. Schäfer, and A. Schürr. Building Integrated Software Development Environments — Part 1: Tool Specification. *ACM Transactions on Software Engineering and Methodology*, 1(2):135–167, 1992.

[13] A. N. Habermann and D. Notkin. Gandalf: Software Development Environments. *IEEE Transactions on Software Engineering*, 12(12):1117–1127, 1986.

[14] R. Hoover. *Incremental graph evaluation*. PhD thesis, Cornell University, Dept. of Computer Science, Ithaca, NY, 1987.

[15] G. F. Johnson and C. N. Fisher. Non-syntactic attribute flow in language based editors. In *Proc. of the 9th Annual ACM Symposium on Principles of Programming Languages*, pages 185–195. ACM Press, 1982.

[16] U. Kastens and W. M. Waite. An abstract data type for name analysis. *Acta Informatica*, 28:539–558, 1991.

[17] D. E. Knuth. Semantics of Context-Free Languages. *Mathematical Systems Theory*, 2(2):127–145, 1968.

[18] M. Nagl. An Incremental and Integrated Software Development Environment. *Computer Physics Communications*, 38:245–276, 1985.

[19] D. C. Parnas. A Technique for the Software Module Specification with Examples. *Communications of the ACM*, 15(5):330–336, 1972.

[20] T. W. Reps and T. Teitelbaum. The Synthesizer Generator. *ACM SIGSOFT Software Engineering Notes*, 9(3):42–48, 1984.

[21] W. W. Royce. Managing the Development of Large Software Systems. In *Proc. WESCON*, 1970.

[22] C. Santos, S. Abiteboul, and C. Delobel. Virtual Schemas and Bases. In M. Jarke, J. Bubenko, and K. Jefferey, editors, *Proc. of the 4th Int. Conf. on Extending Database Technology, Cambridge, UK*, volume 779 of *Lecture Notes in Computer Science*, pages 81–94. Springer, 1994.

[23] A. L. Wolf, L. A. Clarke, and J. C. Wileden. The AdaPIC Tool Set: Supporting Interface Control and Analysis Throughout the Software Development Process. *IEEE Transactions on Software Engineering*, 15(3):250–263, 1989.

ACME/PRIME: Requirements Acquisition for Process-Driven Systems

Mark Feblowitz, Sol Greenspan, Howard Reubenstein, Robert Walford†

GTE Laboratories Incorporated
Computer and Intelligent Systems Lab
40 Sylvan Road
Waltham, Massachusetts USA 02254
{feblowitz, greenspan, hbr}@gte.com

Abstract

This paper discusses a requirements gathering methodology and tool support for a class of systems we term service-oriented systems. The requirements acquisition methodology that our tools support is, not surprisingly, a process centered methodology, since the processes of the system map to the services provided by our organization. The ACME/PRIME tool to support this methodology is built upon a conceptual modeling platform (ACME) that traces its roots to RML. The paper will discuss our approach to one of the fundamental problems of requirements engineering, i.e., dealing with over and under specification of requirements. We will also provide some lessons learned from deploying the ACME/PRIME tool in our corporate requirements office.

1. Introduction

This paper discusses a requirements gathering methodology and tool support for a class of systems we term service-oriented systems [1]. Service-oriented systems are responsible for supporting and executing the daily transactions that allow a business to provide service(s) to its customers. Central to these systems are the business processes that define how an enterprise will conduct its business to provide the services. Requirements engineering for these systems involves, roughly, two main tasks. First, business processes that satisfy the service requirements must be analyzed and designed. Second, the systems capabilities leading to a system specification (or set of integrated, existing and new, system components) that will correctly implement the processes must also be designed.

A key problem that we confronted in developing and applying the methodology corresponds to one of the fundamental problems of requirements engineering, namely, dealing with over and under specification of requirements. Requirements were initially elicited from subject matter experts (SMEs) who provided fragments of relevant knowledge that were in some ways underspecified and in other ways overspecified. A typical requirements engineering approach might have advocated that the elicitation from SMEs should result in the expression of complete and consistent requirements. However, the approach that was devised and used was designed to accommodate the initial and evolving knowledge of the SMEs, who were not trained in systems analysis or formal specification techniques. Subsequently, the methodology prescribes how to systematically resolve the under and over specification until a suitably complete and consistent requirements specification was produced. Among our goals was to acquire enough requirements information, and in such a form, that validation of the specifications could be performed through simulation of service scenarios.

Our solution was embodied in the methodology called PRIME (Process Implementation MEthodology) developed within our telephone operations company [2]. To achieve both the modeling and simulation goals, tool support turned out to be essential and was implemented on a conceptual modeling platform, ACME (A Conceptual Modeling Environment [3]), taking advantage of ACME's knowledge representation and reasoning facilities. The methodology and tools were used on several systems requirements projects that arose in the context of corporate business process re-engineering efforts. In each case, one or more business processes were modeled and specifications were derived by following the approach and using the tools.

ACME was developed as an evolving prototype from 1990 to 1995, was implemented on Intellicorp's Knowledge Engineering Environment (KEE) and deployed on Sun workstations. ACME/PRIME was built on ACME in 1994 and used for seven large business process re-engineering projects during 1994-5 to support the PRIME methodology. The capabilities demonstrated during that period were ported to a network of PCs for a megaproject that integrated several of the prior modeling projects.

The paper describes the essential elements of the approach to eliminating over and under specification. It also reports experience in accommodating the differing capabilities of the various stakeholders involved in this

---

† R. Walford works for GTE Telephone Operations in Tampa, Florida.

overall system design process and how aspects of the tool design helped achieve the goals of the methodology. This paper is not a study of requirements processes in general (as, for example, in [4]) but rather is a study of one requirements process and experience gained in extensive usage of its methods and tools.

2. Business Process Centered Requirements Modeling

Recently our company undertook a series of internal business process re-engineering (BPR) efforts managed by a "requirements office" whose role is to provide the people, methodology and tools to facilitate requirements projects leading to systems (re)development. These efforts required modeling of the company's business processes (e.g., customer subscription services, facilities repair, and billing) that are performed by a combination of automated systems and human agents. The problem faced by the requirements office was to gather information from experts in the business functional areas and create valid specifications to hand off to the system procurement process.

The PRIME methodology, employed by the requirements office, is centered around modeling of business processes and starts with requirements gathering sessions with subject matter experts (SMEs) who provide, among other inputs, *process maps* which represent a combination of the current and desired business processes for performing tasks. The process maps (illustrated in the next section) need to be validated to provide confidence in the correctness of the elicited information. These maps also need to be made more precise to provide input for the ensuing phases of process development that will result in deployed systems and procedures for performing the tasks. The second phase of requirements gathering, termed *logical design*, involves making some information more precise, eliciting additional detailed information, and discarding information deemed to be artifacts of overspecification. Motivated by the promise of simulation, modelers add (just) enough information to be able to drive an execution of the model to simulate business scenarios.

The emphasis on process modeling during requirements acquisition represents a paradigm shift in how projects are organized in corporations that employ information technology. Previously, projects were typically system-centered or data-centered rather than business process centered, and a requirements project would focus on specifying system functionality and interfaces to other systems. Business process centered projects, in contrast, involve the modeling and analysis of business processes that cut across systems (and typically across organizations). A business process centered approach in the projects we supported appeared to have the following impacts on the requirements process:

- A different population of stakeholders plays the most prominent role in the requirements gathering sessions, namely the SMEs who are involved in the daily operations of the company and are concerned that the business needs will be met by any new systems that result from the requirements effort. The experts in a particular system play a less prominent role initially.

- Process modeling takes precedence over system functional decomposition. Thus, the emphasis of the specifier is on describing the work to be done, and not the system functions that do the work.

- With a process-centered approach, data is considered secondary as well. The user of the methodology does not engage in explicit data modeling. In fact, data models (actually, object models) are automatically generated from the data items that are associated with process actions.

- Validation takes on a different meaning, one that is more related to business objectives than to system functionality. A "valid" specification (i.e., the result of the logical design activity) is one that exhibits the desired behavior when subjected to business scenarios (captured in the process maps) in which service is being provided to customers. This definition of validation differs substantially from a focus on I/O functional behavior.

3. The Requirements Acquisition Problem

The methodology and problem described above involves the design of a combined software and human agent solution to the creation of a business process implementation. While there are some unique aspects to solving this kind of problem, there are significant overlaps with the general problems of software requirements acquisition.

In particular, we are faced with a recurring problem in requirements acquisition. The SMEs provide initial process descriptions that are overspecified in certain respects and underspecified in others. The PRIME methodology combined with the ACME/PRIME tool support allows us to correct both the over and underspecification of the initial process models. The overspecification is corrected primarily as a property of the methodology (with automation support from ACME/PRIME) which requires a partitioning of the process model (and redesign of individual components). The underspecification is remedied primarily via a simulation component provided by ACME/PRIME. Not unexpectedly, the simulator requires input of well specified process descriptions (in this case descriptions of process component descriptions termed "actions"). Motivated by the promise of simulation, and assisted by some automatic data model completion, the process modelers have been able to provide action descriptions with an appropriate level of detail.

Over and underspecification of requirements descriptions is a long standing problem that has been dealt with in a number of efforts that attempt to bridge the gap between informal and formal descriptions (e.g., [5,6,7]). More typically, overspecification is dealt with at its limits, e.g., when overspecification leads to inconsistency. Underspecification is usually dealt with as a problem of completeness. We will discuss our solution to these problems more precisely in the next sections.

4. Acquiring the Process Requirements

In this section, we introduce the process model acquisition problem in more detail and the acquisition of a simulable process representation.

4.1 Process Maps

The initial reengineering phase begins with acquiring process descriptions from the business subject matter experts. These descriptions are called process maps and a fragment of one is show in Figure 1.

The semantics of the process map diagram are quite simple. Each box is a process step described by text. Links represent sequential flow of control. Paths through the process map represent process threads, i.e., sequences of steps elicited from the SMEs. Process steps on the process map are assigned to a role (as shown by organization of the steps into rows). Each role is a placeholder for an agent or agents who will be assigned to perform the process steps. Step and role identification, step sequencing, and role assignment comprise the business process design decisions that are made during business process modeling.

While the process map notation is relatively simple, its level of representation was found to match the level of detail that the SMEs are/were able and willing to provide. Our decision was to accommodate the natural level of information transfer rather than attempt to coerce it (e.g., by prescribing a formal specification language that would be beyond their training and inclination). It is therefore interesting to reflect on what is and what is not represented in a process map.

What is represented: The process map captures elicited scenarios from the SMEs. In our experience with requirements processes, one of the most common forms of valuable input is a set of scenarios that are experienced or anticipated by operations people in the field. Usually, these scenarios are described by semi-structured text. The graphical language of the process maps captures a set of interrelated scenarios.

What is not represented: The process map should not be misunderstood as a process design, however. There is no sense in which the process map is a designed artifact. The process map is deficient as a specification model in the following respects:

-    The scenarios captured are only a subset of the scenarios that could happen. A designed process should explain how all possible scenarios are handled, including responses to known exceptions and responses to unexpected situations.   In this sense, the process maps are an underspecification. The SMEs did not consider it their job to think of all possible situations and scenarios, nor is it feasible or practical to capture all possible situations using such a language.

-    Process maps capture only sequential process steps. Sequences of steps described by the SMEs are overspecifications of the process threads. Concurrency is not expressible.

-    The conditions under which actions occur are only informally stated. The level of detail that the SMEs could include in their elicitation sessions had to be kept shallow in order to allow them to finish in the available time. This underspecification needs to elaborated with additional details in the context of a more precise modeling notation.

-    The SMEs did not use abstraction in the form of decomposition, specialization, or generalization. A related tendency was to not be concerned with naming conventions beyond a very local context. The need for careful naming and abstraction has to do with issues of model sharing, context and reuse, and management of system complexity, which were not of concern to the SMEs during their elicitation sessions. Other participants in the requirements process needed to be concerned with abstraction at later stages. The absence of abstraction mechanisms did, however, act to reduce the number of "religious" debates over naming and partitioning, but the downside was that reusable/sharable descriptions were hard to come by, causing replication of many similar process threads.

The level of information that the SMEs were able to provide presented us with a harsh reality. Since they were not thinking about the design of a complete, coherent process and since they were not using abstraction to successively refine the definitions of processes (i.e., processes were defined at a single level with a descriptive string), we acquired from them a substantially underspecified process description. Furthermore, since they were using a simple sequential control flow semantics, we also acquired a process that was overspecified in terms of control flow dependencies.

4.2 Dialogs and Actions

Given the process maps, the PRIME methodology moves to an activity called "logical design" in an attempt to derive a better defined process description, in a form suitable for transfer to system developers. Whereas the initial process mapping was performed by SMEs with little or no systems engineering expertise, logical design is done by modelers who think more in terms of abstraction and other systems engineering concepts. The initial part of the logical design step involves breaking the process maps into units that the methodology refers to as "dialogs." A dialog is a set of steps that can be performed by one agent (usually a human/workstation pair) in an unbroken span of time. The intuition is to break down the process into what begins to look like assignable work tasks.

Once the process map is segmented into dialogs (a dialog will consist of one or more process steps), the (re)design of each dialog begins. The behavior of a dialog is respecified by looking at the steps of the dialog and proposing a set of actions that can be used to do the work implied by the step descriptions.

An example of a dialog that models the previous fragment of the process map, along with its associated action list is shown in Figure 2.

Actions are defined with launch conditions, request and response variables (see Figure 3). Launch conditions represent prerequisite conditions to enable the action to be executed. An action execution corresponds to launching a transaction (against a database or other system object) with the request and response variables as inputs to and outputs from the transaction. The (operational) semantics of dialogs are defined with the goals of simulation in mind. For each dialog in the process map, its steps and links, which constitute overspecified step to step sequential control, are replaced with actions, which predominantly express information flow dependencies that are a more accurate reflection of the true process behavior requirements.

Since the emphasis in PRIME is on process modeling, an additional interesting aspect of action modeling is the inference of the application data model. The initial process map does not include a data model. At the logical design step, the request variables, response variables and the variables appearing in launch conditions are specified for each action. ACME/PRIME automatically creates object classes corresponding to the variable types and associates appropriate properties to these classes. Data (object) modeling is therefore not an activity in which the process modelers are explicitly engaged, but a data (object) model is created incrementally as actions are specified, and kept consistent as action definitions are added and modified.

Because the two forms of process description (process maps with steps/links versus dialogs consisting of actions) are separate and because the transformation between them is predominantly manual, there is a great likelihood that the two descriptions will diverge. This is a problem inherent in any attempt to transition from informal to formal descriptions. It is somewhat remedied by the fact that the informal description has been partitioned (into dialogs), with the partitions then being associated with the more formal and simulable description, thus narrowing the scope of any changes to be propagated.

4.3 Simulation

The detail required in creating action descriptions is motivated by a desire for a more semantically meaningful validation capability. The basic semantics of the simulation engine are similar to the basic control loop in rule-based expert systems: the launch conditions of each action are evaluated, for each action whose launch conditions are satisfied the action is run, the results of running the action are recorded and the execution continues until no actions have their launch criteria satisfied. To reduce the need for numerous guard conditions in the launch condition expressions, an action only fires once within the context of any dialog.

The action modeler's initial focus is on the identification of the actions, and the specification of their launch conditions. Specification of the detailed behavior of the "transaction" – the body of the action – is deferred by stubbing out the transactions, but the inputs to and outputs from the stubbed transactions are specified. A simple form of simulation is provided, whereby the simulation tool user emulates the expected (stubbed) behavior of each action, manually transforming inputs to outputs and watching how the simulation proceeds. During simulation the actions that are running are presented to the user, who inspects both the launch conditions that triggered the action and the action's request variables (input data); the user then provides values for the response variables (output data) and marks the action as complete. Upon action completion, the response variables are used to update the simulation state, and the launch conditions of the remaining, unfired actions are queried to determine which of them are to be run. This proceeds until no actions are running and no launch conditions are satisfied.

An example of a validation scenario is shown in Figure 4. The Dialog Execution Graph shows actions occurring across successive time steps of the dialog simulation. In the current (rightmost) time interval, several actions have fired and are candidates for completion. The tool user decides which actions should complete and with what effect on the dialog state and which actions should continue. The dialog state is represented by objects in the "cluster store," as depicted in the window on the right side of the figure. The cluster store is the set of all objects referenced in all actions of this dialog (a model of shared task memory).

Logical designers use the simulation to trace through scenarios and observe the set of actions that are invoked, looking for actions that are invoked inappropriately, actions that do not fire as expected, and process threads that are not addressed in the action definitions. Action descriptions are modified, launch conditions respecified, and the scenarios rerun until the modeler is confident in the resulting specification.

Although the action modeler can simulate various scenarios to gain confidence that the specification adequately describes the process and adequately covers the expected scenarios, there are no other mechanisms to evaluate or guarantee correctness or completeness. In fact, given the aforementioned execution semantics, there are numerous specification difficulties and pitfalls, e.g., non-determinism and potential race conditions, and little practical tool support to identify and eliminate these problems. At this level of specification, however, this style of validation seemed appropriate and adequate, since the goal of the modelers was simply to specify action logic to cover as many scenarios as possible, and to defer addressing these difficulties until a later design phase.

After the logical designer is satisfied that the set of actions adequately represents the behavior described by the original process map segment, the SME is brought in to walk through various scenarios and see what the logical design simulation does. Because the over- and under-specification has been removed from the model, the SME must adapt to this new form of representation. This often results in both the discovery of new scenarios that the SME had not anticipated, and also in interesting debates over whether one action really does or does not have to follow some other action, and the accompanying discovery of forgotten or unexpressed data or temporal ordering dependencies. This may necessitate revisiting earlier logical phases, and may even require that the initial process maps be modified.

As mentioned earlier, ordering dependencies between actions are not explicitly defined, but can be determined for a given scenario ex post facto by examining the satisfaction of launch conditions. The language that was developed for expressing launch conditions was empirically determined by studying a set of a few hundred actions definitions that had been manually specified. The logic for expressing launch criteria is therefore expressive enough to capture the types of conditions that arise in practice (for the set of projects done) but not as expressive as a more general formalism (such as first-order logic). It is, however, machine processible, i.e., truth values can be determined during simulation from the data in the cluster store.

Each simulated scenario is captured as a replayable scenario trace. Once the logical designers and the SMEs are satisfied with the logical design model, the model and replayable simulation traces are passed along to the procurement phase; and together are used as executable specification to help the subsequent designers and implementers understand the intended system behavior.

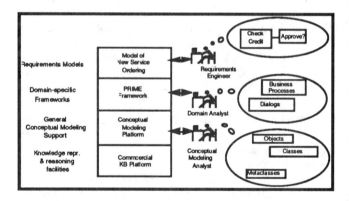

Figure 5: Architecture of ACME

5. The Underlying Technology

The practice of the PRIME methodology was made practical by tool support provided by ACME/PRIME. When the methodology was piloted, there was difficulty dealing with manual recording and revising of models, checking of models for syntactic and logical consistency, and validation through simulation (by humans engaged in role playing). The need for tool support was clear. Compromising the methodology by adapting it to existing (commercial off-the-shelf) tools was not an option; tools were needed that could: a) capture, analyze and simulate models in the PRIME framework, b) be developed quickly,

c) flexibly adapt to changes in the methodology that resulted from feedback/experience using PRIME in the field. We believe that the reason these needs could be met by ACME/PRIME was due to specific architectural and representational decisions in the design of ACME.

ACME/PRIME is built upon A Conceptual Modeling Environment (ACME) which provides an implementation of the Requirements Modeling Language [8, 9] (see [10] for related work) in an environment that supports class definition and rule-based programming. Conceptual modeling allows one to devise a modeling framework appropriate to some systems domain in order to give a structured description of requirements information. The uniform organization of all model objects into object categories organized according to classification and generalization/specialization was an important factor in the tool construction.

Figure 5 gives a schematic overview of the layered structure of ACME. Note that there are several "users" of ACME, the "end-user" being the Requirements Engineer. There is also a Domain Analyst, who defines modeling frameworks. In our case, the crafting of (successive versions of) the PRIME framework was performed by the ACME implementers; some metamodeling facilities have been developed to make this easier, but not easy enough for the end-users.

One of our representational decisions was to encode RML's basic language axioms in the rule-based mechanism of the underlying knowledge-based systems implementation (i.e., KEE). This technique resulted in enforcement of the language axioms through background firing of rules, so that essentially no other code needed to be written to enforce consistency. This systematic way of implementing the conceptual modeling platform was clean and reliable although it contributed to runtime overhead.

A second representation decision was to represent the embedded modeling framework (i.e., PRIME) by defining metaclasses with metaproperties, whose methods defined the semantics of the embedded framework. Generic object editors, associated with the ACME meta-level objects, were specialized for PRIME objects. Thus, defining new framework constructs quickly resulted in an acquisition system for models in that framework.

These decisions were important because the PRIME methodology was something of a moving target throughout the ACME/PRIME development. Thus, instead of hard coding the methodology into ACME/PRIME, we modeled its concepts (e.g., dialogs, actions, launch conditions) using the conceptual modeling platform and attached appropriate methods to the classes in the PRIME ontology. Changes to the methodology were accommodated by changing the metamodel that represented the ontology of the modeling framework. Only some relatively primitive tools were available for the metamodeler at this stage in ACME's development, so the ACME developers rather than the ACME/PRIME users were responsible for making such changes to the PRIME modeling framework. There was also significant, but not overwhelming overhead in the execution performance of the modeling and simulation facilities due to the dynamic metamodeling capabilities. However, during the use of ACME/PRIME, the need for the tool to accommodate changes to the methodology was much stronger than were the disadvantages of doing so.

A third decision in the design of ACME was to use the truth-maintenance system of the underlying knowledge-based system, in combination with the conceptual modeling language axioms, for automatic model maintenance. Thus, the structure of models was represented as justified beliefs, e.g., beliefs that depend on the existence of an object or property. The consequence was that the insertion and removal of objects composing a model structure automatically generated the insertion/remove of dependent parts, again, without the need for other explicit (procedural) code to maintain model integrity/consistency. Again, there was a tradeoff between the reduction in complexity of the implementation versus the overhead for executing the reasoning mechanism.

6. Summary and Conclusion

This paper has discussed the application of a requirements engineering methodology and tool in the context of service oriented system development. We believe BPR efforts will continue to drive the need for development of process-oriented modeling support. Modeling the business processes as part of the requirements acquisition process was key to the validation of business requirements and greatly increased the likelihood that the systems contracted for will meet the real business requirements. However, the business process information elicited from business subject matter experts, and captured as process models, needed to accommodate information that was both under- and over-specified. Since, ultimately, substantially more precise and complete behavioral specifications were needed as input to software developers, a means of dealing with the under and over specification had to be devised, the solution being deployed as part of the PRIME methodology.

The transition from the process maps to the logical design of dialogs is an instance of elaborating a description along the dimensions indicated in NATURE [11], namely:

1) making the information more formal, which PRIME does by defining dialog action semantics;

2) adding more information, which is done by filling in properties, e.g., launch conditions, of action definitions; and

3) attributing more agreement to the them, which is done by validating the models in the presence of the subject matter experts.

Performing the methodology—both the capture of information as requirements models and the simulation of scenarios against dialog/action models—turned out to be achievable only with tool support. As the application of PRIME on several requirements projects motivated changes and improvements to the methodology, it became extremely important that the tool support was implemented in a systematic way, based on conceptual modeling principles and with a modifiable metamodel.

The architectural and representational decisions made in the design of ACME are expected to be useful in the implementation of other tools in a suite of tools that are at various stages of development and consideration.

7. References

[1] Greenspan, S., and M. Feblowitz, "Requirements Engineering Using the SOS Paradigm," Proc. of IEEE International Symposium on Requirements Engineering, San Diego, 1993, pp. 260-265.

[2] R. B. Walford, PRIME—Process Implementation Methodology: A New Paradigm for the Development and Implementation of Software, book in preparation, 1996.

[3] Greenspan, S., M. Feblowitz, C. Shekaran, and J. Tremlett, "Addressing Requirements Issues Within a Conceptual Modeling Environment," Proc. of the 6th Int. Workshop on Soft. Spec. and Design, October, 1991.

[4] Rolland, C., G. Grosz, "A General Framework for Describing the Requirements Engineering Process," Int'l Conf. on Systems, Man and Cybernetics, October 1994.

[5] Meyer, B., "On Formalism in Specifications," IEEE Software, Jan. 1985, pp. 6-26.

[6] Balzer, R., N. Goldman, and D. Wile, "Informality in Program Specifications," IEEE Trans. on Software Engineering, March 1978, pp. 94-103.

[7] Reubenstein, H., and R. Waters, "The Requirements Apprentice: Automated Assistance for Requirements Acquisition," IEEE Trans. on Software Engineering,, March 1991, pp. 226-240.

[8] Borgida, A., Greenspan, S. and Mylopoulos, J., "Knowledge Representation as a Basis for Requirements Specification," IEEE Computer 18(4), April 1985. Reprinted in Rich, C. and Waters, R., Readings in Artificial Intelligence and Software Engineering, Morgan-Kaufmann, 1987.

[9] Greenspan, S., A. Borgida, and J. Mylopoulos, "A Requirements Modeling Language and Its Logic," Information Systems, 11(1), pp. 9-23, 1986. Also appears in Knowledge Base Management Systems, M. Brodie and J. Mylopoulos, Eds., Springer-Verlag, 1986.

[10] Greenspan, S., Mylopoulos, J. and Borgida, A., "On Formal Requirements Modeling Languages: RML Revisited," Proc. 16th Int. Conf. on SE, Sorrento, 1994.

[11] Pohl, K., "The Three Dimensions of Requirements Engineering," Proc CAISE'93 Conf., Springer-Verlag, 1993.

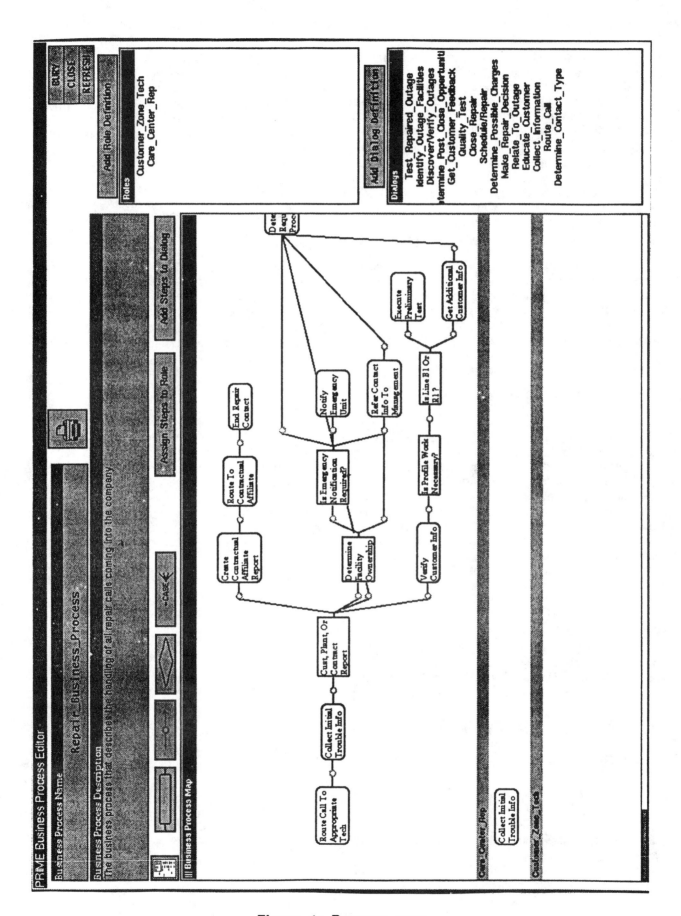

Figure 1: Process map

42

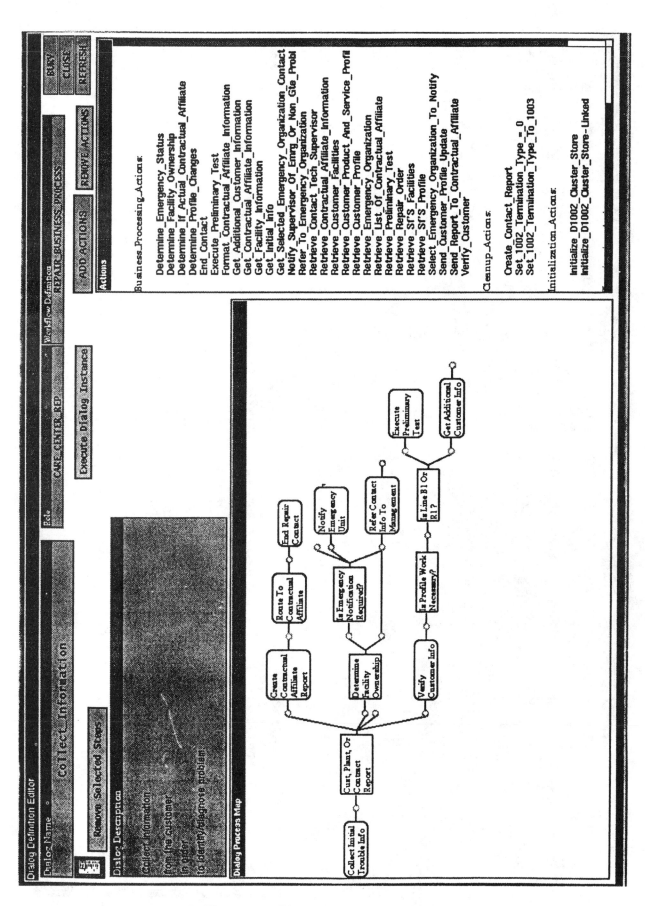

Figure 2: Dialog and its actions

43

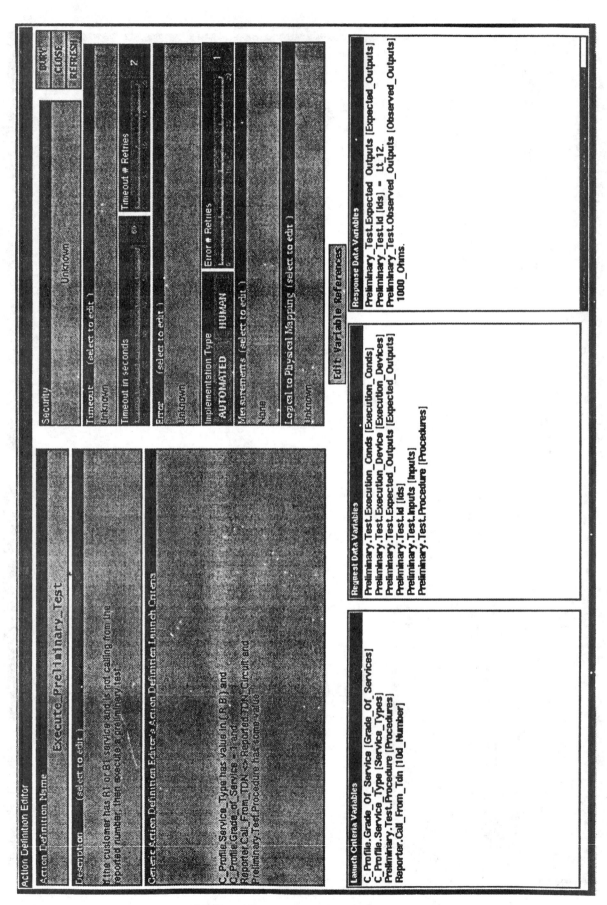

Figure 3: Action with launch conditions

44

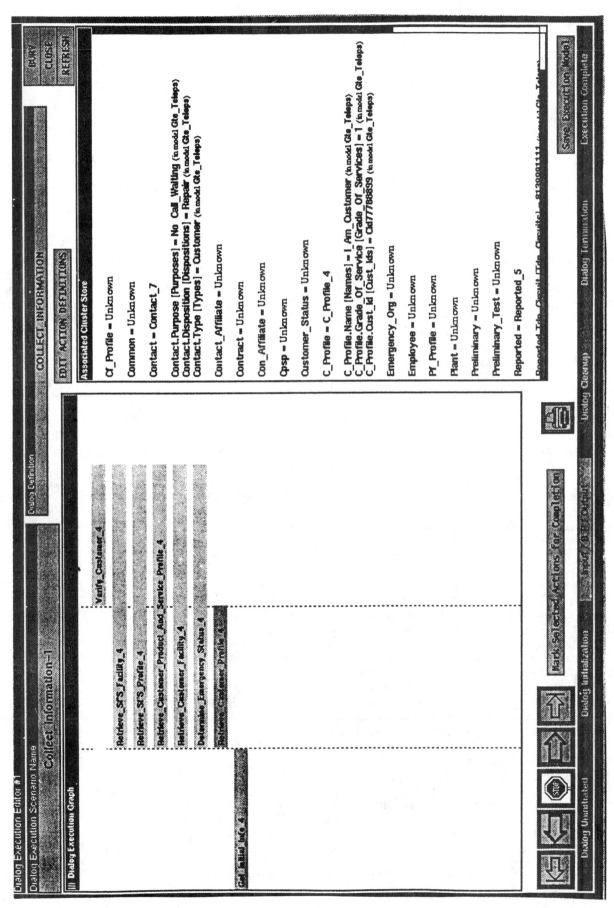

Figure 4: **Simulation of a dialog**

A Mathematical Toolbox for the Software Architect[†]

José Luiz Fiadeiro
Department of Informatics
Faculty of Sciences, University of Lisbon
Campo Grande, 1700 Lisboa, PORTUGAL
llf@di.fc.ul.pt

Tom Maibaum
Department of Computing
Imperial College of Science, Technology and Medicine
180 Queen's Gate, London SW7 2BZ, UK
tsem@doc.ic.ac.uk

Abstract

It is suggested that Category Theory provides the right level of mathematical abstraction to address languages for describing software architectures. Contrarily to most other formalisations of SA concepts, Category Theory does not promote any particular formalism for component and connector description but provides instead the very semantics of the concepts that are related to the gross modularisation of complex systems like "interconnection", "configuration", "instantiation" and "composition". Two examples, a category of programs for a parallel program design language and a category of temporal logic specifications, together with comparisons with other work, namely by Allen and Garlan, and Moriconi and Qian, are adduced to justify this claim.

1. Introduction

In a particularly stimulating panel introduction, Garlan and Perry present an overview of current research issues in Software Architecture (SA) [11]. They characterise SA to be "emerging as a significant and different design level that requires its own notations, theories, and tools".

The purpose of this paper is to introduce some of the mathematical techniques that we think are useful for the toolbox of the software architect. Our aim is not to cover any specific language or approach but to illustrate how work developed in related fields of Computing is directly relevant to the concerns of SA. The specific tools that we have in mind are based on Category Theory, a fairly recent mathematical theory (as far as Mathematics is concerned), and have been developed since the early 70's by J.Goguen for formalising aspects of General Systems Theory (e.g. [15]), namely the process of building complex systems as interconnections of simpler components!

Our main objective is to show that, as a mathematical notion, Category Theory (CT) captures much of the "spirit" and "practice" that one can recognise in the literature on SA. First of all, one of the "myths" of Software Engineering, is that the use of diagrammatic notation is not formal, that it is at best semi-formal. Well, CT is all about chasing diagrams! In fact, one of the basic principles summarised in [13] is that complex systems can be usefully identified with diagrams, system components and connectors corresponding to nodes, and interconnections being established through the edges of the diagrams. The subtlety here is that the word "diagram" in CT has a formal meaning and, at the same time, carries all the intuitions that come from practice. This does not imply, however, that all we have done with diagrams is CT! It just means that we can keep the same "language" and do "maths" that are not particularly distant from intuition.

Secondly, and contrarily to most other formalisations of SA concepts that we have seen, CT is not another semantic domain in which to formalise the description of components and connectors (like, say, the use of CSP in [2] or first-order logic in [20]) but the very semantics of "interconnection", "configuration", "instantiation" and "composition", that which is related to the gross modularisation of complex systems. CT does this at a very abstract level because what it proposes is a toolbox that can be applied to whatever formalism is chosen for capturing the behaviour of components (as long as that formalism satisfies some structural properties). Indeed, contrarily to Set Theory, CT focuses on relationships between objects (morphisms) rather that the representations of these objects. The focus on morphisms is paramount for SA because it determines the nature of the interconnections that can be established between the objects. Hence, the choice of a particular category can be seen to reflect the choice of a particular "architectural style".

Thirdly, CT provides techniques for manipulating and reasoning about diagrams, namely for establishing hierarchies of system complexity, allowing systems to be used as components of even more complex systems (i.e. to use diagrams as objects), and for inferring properties of systems from their configurations. Indeed, as pointed out in [2], descriptive power is not sufficient: the underlying theory should also make it possible to analyse architectural descriptions, namely support reasoning about compositions of components and connectors.

The message that we would like to convey is that there is a universality in the way that SA can be approached through CT. This universality facilitates the comparison

---

[†] This work was partially supported by the Esprit BRA 8035 (MODELAGE), the HCM Scientific Network CHRX-CT92-0054 (MEDICIS) and JNICT under contract 2/2.1/MAT/46/94 (ESCOLA).

46

between different styles and supports the integration of different approaches.

These are the aspects that we shall illustrate in the paper. In order to do so, we need to choose a particular category, which implies choosing a particular representation model for system behaviour. The category we chose corresponds to a language, COMMUNITY, conceived for parallel program design in a style similar to UNITY [4] but that we have adapted to the style required for SAs. In fact, as explained in the paper, it turns out that these are the very adaptations that were necessary for the definition of a category, thus providing further evidence of the close fit between CT and SA. This category was already briefly introduced in [8] in order to illustrate how different specification formalisms can be combined. The results presented in that paper will be used as further evidence of the adequacy of CT, namely in what concerns mapping between architectures in different levels of abstraction, one of them being programs in COMMUNITY, the other temporal logic specifications similar to those used in [20]. The style of the paper is not "mathematical", making appeal more to the intuition than formality. All the results can be found in [9].

We should again stress that much of the work that we shall present is inspired by the work of J. Goguen and can derived from the general principles enunciated in the Categorical Manifesto [13]. The only disadvantage of previous papers on the subject is that they are based on mathematical models of system behaviour, namely sheaf-theoretic ones, which are seldom part of the day-to-day vocabulary of the software architect (or, for that matter, the software engineer). More recent applications of these ideas to Software Engineering can be found in [12], namely in the context of module interconnection languages. Our intention with this paper is to present the subject in terms that are more directly related to SA, in particular by addressing concurrent and reactive behaviour, and, in this way, contribute to the promotion of what we believe is a very useful toolbox for Software Engineering in general, and SA in particular.

2. A parallel program design language

In order to illustrate the application of CT to SA practice, we use a parallel program design language, COMMUNITY, that we introduced in [8]. This is a language for parallel program design in the style of IP (Interacting Processes) [10], UNITY [4] and Action Systems [3]. A complete account of the categorical formalisation of this language is given in [9].

A COMMUNITY program P has the following structure:

$$P \equiv \begin{array}{ll} data & \Sigma \\ read & R \\ var & V \\ init & I \\ do & \underset{g\in\Gamma}{[\![}\, g : [B(g) \rightarrow \underset{a\in D(g)}{\|}\, a := F(g,a)] \\ where \end{array}$$

- Σ represents the data types that the program uses; if we intend to use COMMUNITY to actually develop programs in a given environment, then Σ represents the data types available in that environment and, hence, is fixed for every program (and is thus omitted); however, to support more abstract levels of program design, it may be helpful to work with specifications of these data types, in which case Σ can be given through a signature (S,Ω) in the usual algebraic sense [6], i.e. S is a set (of sort symbols) and Ω is an $S^*\times S$-indexed family (of function symbols), together with a set of (first-order) axioms over (S,Ω) defining the properties of the operations.
- R is the set of external attributes, i.e. the attributes that the program needs to read from its environment;
- V is the set of local attributes (the program "variables");
- A is the union (assumed disjoint) of R and V, the set of attributes of the program; attributes are typed – every attribute $a\in A$ has an associated sort s; A_s will denote the set of attributes of sort s;
- Γ is the set of *action names*; each action name has an associated statement (see below) and can act as a *rendez-vous* point for program synchronisation;
- I is a condition on the local attributes – the initialisation condition;
- for every action $g\in\Gamma$, $B(g)$ is a condition on the attributes – the *guard* of the action;
- for every action $g\in\Gamma$, $D(g)\subseteq V$ is the set of attributes that action g can change; we also denote by $D(a)$, where $a\in V$, the set of actions that can change a;
- for every action $g\in\Gamma$ and local attribute $a\in D(g)$, $F(g,a)$ is an expression that has the same type as a.

We call the triple (V,R,Γ) the *signature* θ_P of the program P. We shall also use the notation $\theta=(A=V\oplus R,\Gamma)$, or just $\theta=(A,\Gamma)$, in contexts where the distinction between local and external attributes is not meaningful. We denote the quadruple (I,F,D,B) by Δ_P so that every program P is defined by the pair (θ_P,Δ_P).

The language of expressions and conditions over a signature $\theta=(A=V\oplus R,\Gamma)$ is defined as follows. Expressions of sort $s\in S$:

$$t_s ::= a \mid c \mid f(t_{1_{s_1}},\ldots,t_{n_{s_n}})$$

for $a\in A_s$, $c\in\Omega_{<>,s}$ and $f\in\Omega_{<s_1,\ldots,s_n>,s}$. Conditions:

$$\phi ::= (t_{1_s}=_s t_{2_s}) \mid (\phi_1\supset\phi_2) \mid (\neg\phi)$$

As an illustration, the following program is capable of successively reading (action r) the value of x, stopping (action t) whenever it consecutively reads the same value, unless the first value it reads is 0:

$$\Delta_r \equiv \begin{array}{ll} read & x{:}int \\ var & xo{:}int;\ xd{:}bool \\ init & xd{=}false \wedge xo{=}0 \\ do & t : [\neg xd \wedge xo{=}x \rightarrow xd := true] \\ {[\!]} & r : [\neg xd \rightarrow xo := x] \end{array}$$

For simplicity, we have omitted the data declarations. This simplification will be made throughout the paper except where it is necessary to illustrate a particular point.

3. Configuration of complex systems

SA is a world populated by components, connectors, configurations, etc. With the help of the program design language introduced in the previous section, we will attempt to illustrate how CT can assist in interconnecting components, quite independently of the nature of these components.

A category consists of a collection of objects, a collection of morphisms for every pair of objects (f: a→b denotes a morphism f whose source is the object a and whose target is the object b) and a law of composition (denoted by ;) satisfying the following properties:

- if f: a→b and g: b→c then f;g: a→c
- ; is associative – f;(g;h) = (f;g);h whenever the compositions are well defined
- for every object a there is a distinguished morphism (the identity of a) id_a: a→a that satisfies the following property: for every f: a→b, id_a;f=f and for every g: b→a, g;id_b=g.

Interconnections in CT are achieved through morphisms. There is some overloading in the use of morphisms as both a way of interconnecting objects and expressing relationships between objects. This overloading also explains why the "categorical" approach to interconnection is based on "sharing".

The first intuition about morphisms can be given in terms of the relationship that exists between an object and a system of which it is a component. Because programs in COMMUNITY are structured in terms of signatures, we shall explain first what signature morphisms are. The role of signatures is, in fact, primordial in SA as we, we hope, this paper will make clear.

Given $\theta_1=(A_1=V_1\oplus R_1,\Gamma_1)$ and $\theta_2=(A_2=V_2\oplus R_2,\Gamma_2)$, a *signature morphism* σ from θ_1 to θ_2 consists of a pair $(\sigma_\alpha: A_1 \to A_2, \sigma_\gamma: \Gamma_1 \to \Gamma_2)$ of (total) functions such that $\sigma(V_1)\subseteq V_2$. That is to say, a signature morphism maps attributes to attributes and actions to actions but it can only map local attributes to local attributes. External attributes, however, can be mapped to local ones (as what is external at the level of a program may be local at the level of a system that contains that program).

This constraint already illustrates one of the ways a category can capture an architectural style in the sense of [11]. Relationships between components impose accessibility constraints on their attributes and, thus, restrict the way components can be interconnected.

Signature morphisms relate the syntax of programs. Morphisms between programs are more semantical relationships: a *program morphism* $\sigma:(\theta_1,\Delta_1)\to(\theta_2,\Delta_2)$ is a signature morphism $\sigma: \theta_1\to\theta_2$ such that

1. For all $a_1\in V_1$, $D_2(\sigma(a_1))=\sigma(D_1(a_1))$.
2. For all $g_1\in\Gamma_1, a_1\in V_1$,

$\vDash_{\theta_2} B_2(\sigma(g)) \supset \sigma(F_1(g_1,a_1))=F_2(\sigma(g_1),\sigma(a_1))$.

3. $\vDash_{\theta_2} (I_2 \supset \sigma(I_1))$.
4. $\vDash_{\theta_2} (B_2(\sigma(g)) \supset \sigma(B_1(g)))$ for every $g\in\Gamma_1$.

In this definition, $\vDash$ stands for the consequence relation of the logic associated with the language of expressions and conditions introduced in section 2. See [9] for details.

This notion of program morphism captures what is called in [10,18] *regulative superposition*. Requirement 1 corresponds to the locality condition: the set of actions that can change local attributes of the source program (those that belong to $\sigma(V_1)$) remains unchanged, i.e. no new actions can change the attributes of the source program. Requirement 2 corresponds to the preservation of the functionality of the base program: the effects of its actions are preserved, i.e. the translation $\sigma(F_1(g_1,a_1))$ of the effects of action g_1 over attribute a_1 is the same as the effects $F_2(\sigma(g_1),\sigma(a_1))$ of the image of g_1 over the image of a_1 in the target program. Requirement 3 implies that every properly initialised computation for (θ_2,Δ_2) is also properly initialised for (θ_1,Δ_1). Requirement 4 corresponds to the strengthening of the guards (or, more accurately, to the non-weakening of the guards): the guard $B_2(\sigma(g))$ of the image of every action g must imply the translation of the guard of that action in the source program. It implies that safe computations for (θ_2,Δ_2) are also safe for (θ_1,Δ_1).

Notice that morphisms also act as translations between the languages of terms and propositions associated with the signatures. Formally, given a morphism $\sigma:\theta_1\to\theta_2$, we define for $a\in A_s$, $c\in\Omega_{<>,s}$, and $f\in\Omega_{<s_1,...,s_n>,s}$:

$\sigma(t) ::= \sigma(a) \mid \sigma(c) \mid f(\sigma(t_1),...,\sigma(t_n))$

$\sigma(\phi) ::= (\sigma(t_1)\vDash\sigma(t_2)) \mid (\sigma(\phi_1)\supset\sigma(\phi_2)) \mid \neg\sigma(\phi)$

As an example of a superposition morphism consider the following programs (for simplicity, we shall denote a program (θ,Δ) just by Δ and omit most declarations in the *data* part of the signature):

$$\Delta_a \equiv \begin{array}{ll} data & \eta:int,int\to int \\ var & y:int \\ read & z:int \\ init & y>0 \\ do & k : [true \to y := \eta(y,z)] \end{array}$$

$$\Delta_b \equiv \begin{array}{ll} data & \phi,\psi:int,int\to int \\ var & a,b:int \\ init & a>0 \wedge b>0 \\ do & f : [true \to a := \phi(a,b)] \\ {[]} & g : [true \to b := \psi(a,b)] \end{array}$$

All the conditions of a program morphism are satisfied by the mapping i:$<\eta\mapsto\phi, y\mapsto a, z\mapsto b, k\mapsto f>$, meaning that Δ_b is a (regular) superposition of Δ_a.

This is the view that characterises morphisms as relationships between components. However, morphisms are also the mechanisms via which components can be interconnected. As an example, consider the program Δ_a above. It corresponds to a component that updates the value of the attribute y by reading the value of z from the environment and computing the value of the function η applied to the current value of y and the value of z that was read.

Suppose that we want to determine situations in which the value of y remains invariant after such an assignment. Having already developed a program that can do exactly that, namely Δ_r as defined in the previous section, all we need to do is interconnect Δ_r and Δ_a. The required interconnection has to identify the external attribute x of Δ_r with the local attribute y of Δ_a and synchronise the action r of Δ_r with the action k of Δ_a.

Such an interconnection is achieved in CT by identifying the object that is shared between the two components that we want to interconnect, and the morphisms that express how that object is part of the given ones. In the example at hand, this interconnection is expressed by the following *configuration diagram:*

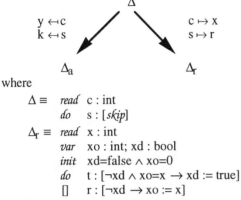

where

$$\Delta \equiv \quad read \quad c : int$$
$$do \quad s : [skip]$$

$$\Delta_r \equiv \quad read \quad x : int$$
$$var \quad xo : int; \ xd : bool$$
$$init \quad xd=false \wedge xo=0$$
$$do \quad t : [\neg xd \wedge xo=x \rightarrow xd := true]$$
$$[] \quad r : [\neg xd \rightarrow xo := x]$$

and Δ_a is as before.

Using the always suggestive analogy with *hardware*, the middle object (program) Δ acts as an interconnection *cable* between the two given devices (a complex cable for that matter, as it is required to connect two different pairs of ports), the morphisms establishing the *ports* to which the cable is connected: as required, y and x, and r and k are connected to each other.

Notice that the established interconnection is, primarily, a relationship between the signatures (languages) of the two components. This is an essential characteristic of the categorical approach and one in which COMMUNITY differs, for instance, from IP [10]. Indeed, in languages like IP, action names as interaction (rendez-vous) points are global so that interconnections are established within programs by direct reference to the global locations. Such approaches do not promote reuse as they rely on some "engineering omniscience" that precludes any form of separation between the activities of programming components and interconnecting them. Locality of names is intrinsic to CT and it forces interconnections to be explicitly established outside the programs. Hence, the categorical framework is much more apt to support the complete separation between the structural language that describes the software architecture and the language in which the components are themselves programmed or specified, as advocated in configuration languages like those of the CONIC-family [19].

The use of a set-theoretic binding of names would, of course, be sufficient for achieving the same result, but it would not provide the right level of abstraction to discuss the interconnection. The advantage of CT in this respect is that it makes such bindings and renamings "logical", i.e. it does not require the "architect" to program them. This is why we claim CT to be at the right level of abstraction to discuss SA in general, and interconnections in particular.

It still remains to define the actual semantics of the interconnection, i.e. to determine the exact behaviour of the system that has this configuration. CT provides for the composition of the component behaviours given their interconnections through so-called universal constructions, namely colimits. The colimit of a (configuration) diagram returns a new object that represents the overall system behaviour, and morphisms that establish how the components are part of the system. This approach has been proposed by J.Goguen in several occasions, the following motto summarising the general principle: "given a category of widgets, the operation of putting a system of widgets together to form a super-widget corresponds to taking a colimit of the diagram of widgets that shows how to interconnect them" (see [13] in particular).

Because of its shape, the colimit of the above configuration diagram is called a pushout. It computes the program

$$\Delta_s \equiv \quad read \quad z : int$$
$$var \quad y, yo : int; \ yd : bool$$
$$init \quad y>0 \wedge yd=false \wedge yo=0$$
$$do \quad kr : [\neg yd \rightarrow y := \eta(y,z) \parallel yo := y]$$
$$[] \quad kt : [\neg yd \wedge yo=y \rightarrow yd := true]$$

together with the morphisms $\langle y \mapsto y, \ z \mapsto z, \ k \mapsto kr \rangle: \Delta_a \rightarrow \Delta_s$ and $\langle x \mapsto y, \ xo \mapsto yo, \ xd \mapsto yd, \ r \mapsto kr, \ t \mapsto kt \rangle: \Delta_r \rightarrow \Delta_s$. Colimits are computed up to isomorphism, i.e. up to renaming of the features in the signature. That is why the morphisms are necessary: they keep track of the way the component features were renamed in the resulting system. Some constraints, however, apply. Features that, through the interconnections, are identified have to be given the same name: this was the case of (y,x) and (k,r) that were renamed y and kr, respectively. Features that happen to have the same names in different components but that are not identified through the interconnections have to be given different names. That is, no accidental interference must result from the naming of features. Indeed, as already discussed, names in CT are local. As long as these constraints are met, renamings can be performed to suit the developer (like the renamings applied to the features of Δ_r).

Because they are the image of the same action of the channel (Δ), the two commands k and r are "merged" into kr, meaning that the two components are required to synchronise in order to perform these actions. This operation of "merging" two actions operates as follows: the resulting joint action performs, synchronously, the assignments of the component actions, and is guarded by the conjunction of the guards of the components. That is, the joint action is the synchronisation of the component actions.

Moreover, Δ_r is able to read the attribute y of Δ_a. This is achieved, as already discussed, by connecting, via Δ and the morphisms, the attribute which in Δ_r was declared to be external with the local attribute y of Δ_a. This is, in fact, an adaptation of an example used in [10]. By reading y, the regulator Δ_r detects a pair of values of y and z such that $y=\eta(y,z)$. When this pair is detected, and because k and r are now synchronised, the base program Δ_a can no longer assign to y. Indeed, according to the properties of pushouts, the guard of the joint action is given by the conjunction of the synchronised actions – ($\neg yd \wedge yo=y$).

The proof that pushouts of program morphisms work as illustrated can be found in [9]. Therein, it is also shown how colimits provide a semantics for the use of superposition as a generalised parallel composition operator, as suggested in [10].

Notice how close this approach is to the formalisation of architectural connections proposed in [2]. The main technical difference is that where we have used COMMUNITY, they use CSP. Their notion of a connector description can be identified with that of a configuration diagram for "roles" and "glue" whose behaviour is described by a CSP program. The meaning of a connector description which in [2] is given by the parallel composition of the roles and glue, corresponds to the colimit of the configuration diagram. Indeed, the categorical approach proposed by Goguen is abstract enough to be applicable to a whole range of formalisms, thus providing a neat separation between the support for configuration, which is, in a sense, universal, and the actual choice of formalism for describing the behaviour of the systems being configured. One of the actual advantages of the categorical approach is in the universality of the approach which allows for different configuration languages to be compared, and for different architectural styles to be formally related. We shall return to these points later in the paper.

To further explore the comparison with [2], we should point out that, whereas the example above was presented as an exercise in connecting two previously built components, there is a sense in which what we have built is a connector type that can be instantiated. What we have in mind is the use of Δ_a and Δ_r as "roles" that can be fulfilled by components with more complex behaviour.

In CT, instantiation is also formalised via morphisms. Depending on the category, morphisms can capture notions of "simulation" (e.g. between abstract machines) or "refinement" (e.g. of CSP programs as required in [2]). For instance, the morphism between Δ_a and Δ_b used as an illustration at the beginning of this section, can be used to "apply" the fixpoint detector to Δ_b:

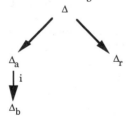

Indeed, the morphism i identifies in Δ_b the attribute over which the fixpoint is to be computed, together with the action that updates that attribute and the external attribute that needs to be read (which in this case is instantiated to a local attribute, as allowed by the notion of morphism).

The program returned by the colimit is (again up to isomorphism):

$$\Delta_t \equiv \begin{array}{ll} var & \text{a, b, ao : int; ad : bool} \\ init & \text{a>0} \wedge \text{b>0} \wedge \text{ad=false} \wedge \text{ao=0} \\ do & \text{fr : }[\neg ad \rightarrow a := \varphi(a,b) \parallel ao := a] \\ {[]} & \text{g : }[\text{true} \rightarrow b := \psi(a,b)] \\ {[]} & \text{ft : }[\neg ad \wedge ao=a \rightarrow ad := \text{true}] \end{array}$$

Similarly to the mechanism of instantiation proposed in [2], the resulting system should correspond to the substitution of Δ_a (the formal role) by Δ_b. Because morphisms compose, the instantiation gives rise to the configuration diagram

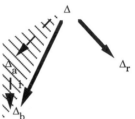

where the morphism $\Delta \rightarrow \Delta_b$ is the composition of $\Delta \rightarrow \Delta_a$ with the instantiation morphism i. The pushout of this diagram is the same as that for the previous one. Moreover, the properties of the colimit construction imply that there is a unique morphism $\Delta_s \rightarrow \Delta_t$ (where Δ_s is the program built from the pushout of Δ_a and Δ_r interconnected through Δ as before) such that the composition $\Delta_a \rightarrow \Delta_s \rightarrow \Delta_t$ is the same as $\Delta_a \rightarrow \Delta_b \rightarrow \Delta_t$ meaning that Δ_t "refines" or "simulates" Δ_s in the same way that Δ_b refines Δ_a. That is, Δ_b is indeed replacing Δ_a (the formal role).

The reader may have noticed that there is another possible morphism between Δ_a and Δ_b, namely the mapping $j:<\eta \mapsto \psi, y \mapsto b, z \mapsto a, k \mapsto g>$! This instantiation allows us to detect fixpoints of the attribute b of Δ_b. Hence, if we wanted to build a system that detects fixpoints for a and fixpoints for b we might choose the following configuration diagram:

Notice that we now have a diagram where different nodes are labelled with the same component. In CT, nodes act as instances and their labels as types. Hence, the configured system contains two instances of each of the roles and of the connector. In a non-diagrammatic configuration language, this would be achieved by declaring two instances of the same component.

Colimits in categories based on sets, like that of programs, compute amalgamated sums, i.e. they take disjoint unions and identify those features that, through the interconnections, were declared to be the same. Therefore, names have to be properly disambiguated. CT does not deal directly with disambiguation. The actual choice of names can be left to an implementation, possibly assisted by the architect who certainly will want to provide his own renaming, subject to the restrictions that we have already mentioned. The program that results from the colimit is, therefore, given up to isomorphism by:

$$\Delta_{t'} \equiv var \text{ a, b, ao, bo : int; ad, bd : bool}$$
$$init \text{ a>0} \wedge \text{b>0} \wedge \text{ad=false} \wedge \text{bd=false}$$
$$\wedge \text{ao=0} \wedge \text{bo=0}$$
$$do \quad \text{fr} : [\neg\text{ad} \rightarrow \text{a} := \varphi(\text{a,b}) \parallel \text{ao} := \text{a}]$$
$$[] \quad \text{gr} : [\neg\text{bd} \rightarrow \text{b} := \psi(\text{a,b}) \parallel \text{bo} := \text{b}]$$
$$[] \quad \text{ft} : [\neg\text{ad} \wedge \text{ao=a} \rightarrow \text{ad} := \text{true}]$$
$$[] \quad \text{gt} : [\neg\text{bd} \wedge \text{bo=b} \rightarrow \text{bd} := \text{true}]$$

This program now detects both situations in which b=ψ(a,b) and situations in which a=φ(a,b). However, it does not necessarily detect a situation in which *both* a=φ(a,b) and b=ψ(a,b). In order to achieve that, we need to synchronise *ft* and *gt*. This can be done by interconnecting the two instances of Δ_r via a communication channel:

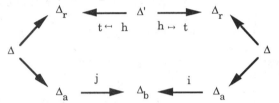

where $\Delta' \equiv do$ h:[*skip*] is the cable (a simple one, with just one "wire").

The colimit of the configuration diagram provides a program isomorphic to:

$$var \text{ a, b, ao, bo : int; ad, bd : bool}$$
$$init \text{ a>0} \wedge \text{b>0} \wedge \text{ad=false} \wedge \text{bd=false} \wedge \text{ao=0} \wedge \text{bo=0}$$
$$do \text{ fr} : [\neg\text{ad} \rightarrow \text{a} := \varphi(\text{a,b}) \parallel \text{ao} := \text{a}]$$
$$[] \text{ gr} : [\neg\text{bd} \rightarrow \text{b} := \psi(\text{a,b}) \parallel \text{bo} := \text{b}]$$
$$[] \text{ stop} : [\neg\text{ad} \wedge \text{ao=a} \wedge \neg\text{bd} \wedge \text{bo=b}$$
$$\rightarrow \text{ad} := \text{true} \parallel \text{bd} := \text{true}]$$

This program now terminates when it detects a situation in which (a,b)=(φ(a,b),ψ(a,b)).

We illustrated the process of constructing a configuration diagram and of applying operations to such diagrams on a flat structure. However, CT allows diagrams to be treated as objects themselves, giving rise to hierarchies of diagrams and operations for manipulating diagrams. This suggests that formalisms like graph grammars [5] can be usefully employed for giving semantics to specific configuration languages in a way similar to their application in [21] to inheritance and reuse. Unfortunately, there is no space left to illustrate these points in the paper.

4. Mapping between architectures

As already mentioned, the categorical framework that we outlined in the previous section applies to other component description formalisms besides COMMUNITY. The use of CSP as in [2] is a possibility (although, to our knowledge, no attempt has been made to marry CSP and CT). Another one is the use of logic as in [20]: the notions that are used in [20] like interpretation mappings, name mappings, style mappings, etc, have all been formalised in CT and

generalised to arbitrary logics in what are called institutions [14].

In fact, one of the main applications of the categorical framework has been to abstract data type specification, using theories in a given logic (or institution) instead of programs. There is a considerable amount of work on developing specification techniques that are independent of the underlying institution and that are formalised over CT using techniques similar to the ones illustrated in section 3 [22]. In this section, we will show how the choice of a specification logic like temporal logic instead of COMMUNITY programs leads to more abstract software architectures, and how these can be instantiated in lower level ones, such as programs in COMMUNITY.

Adapting from [7], we can assign a temporal language to every signature (in the sense of section 2) as follows:

$$t_s ::= a \mid c \mid f(t_{1_{s_1}},...,t_{n_{s_n}}) \mid \mathbf{X}t_s$$

for $a \in A_s$, $c \in \Omega_{<>,s}$ and $f \in \Omega_{<s_1,...,s_n>,s}$.

$$\phi ::= (t_{1_s} =_s t_{2_s}) \mid g \mid (\phi_1 \supset \phi_2) \mid (\neg\phi) \mid \mathbf{beg} \mid \mathbf{X}\phi \mid \phi_1 \mathbf{U}\phi_2$$

for $g \in \Gamma$. The special operators are **beg** (denoting the initial state), **X** (**X**φ holds in a state when φ holds in the next state), and **U** (φ**U**ψ holds when ψ will hold sometime in the future and φ holds between the next instant and then).

The specificational counterpart of a program is a theory presentation, i.e. a pair (θ, Φ) where θ is a signature (as before) and Φ is a set of temporal propositions. Morphisms $\sigma: (\tau_1, \Phi_1) \rightarrow (\tau_2, \Phi_2)$ between theory presentations are signature morphism $\sigma: \theta_1 \rightarrow \theta_2$ such that $\Phi_2 \vdash_{\theta_2} \sigma(\phi)$ for every $\phi \in \Phi_1$ where by $\vdash_\theta$ we mean the usual consequence relation for linear, discrete temporal logic over the temporal language of θ [e.g. 16]. Notice that signature morphisms also induce a translation between temporal languages as follows

$$\sigma(t_s) ::= \sigma(a) \mid c \mid f(\sigma(t_{s_1}),...,\sigma(t_{s_n})) \mid \mathbf{X}\sigma(t_s)$$
$$\sigma(\phi) ::= (\sigma(t_{1_s}) \models_s \sigma(t_{2_s})) \mid \sigma(p) \mid (\sigma(\phi_1) \supset \sigma(\phi_2)) \mid$$
$$\neg\sigma(\phi) \mid \mathbf{beg} \mid \mathbf{X}\sigma(\phi) \mid (\sigma(\phi_1)\mathbf{U}\sigma(\phi_2)).$$

As an example of an abstract architecture, we shall describe a producer-consumer-buffer style of interconnection. Consider the following abstract specifications:

$$\Phi_p \equiv actions \quad \text{prod, put}$$
$$axioms$$
$$\mathbf{beg} \supset (\neg\text{put}) \wedge (\text{prod} \vee (\neg\text{put})\mathbf{W}\text{prod})$$
$$\text{prod} \supset (\neg\text{prod})\mathbf{U}\text{put}$$
$$\text{put} \supset (\neg\text{put})\mathbf{W}\text{prod}$$
$$\text{prod} \supset (\neg\text{put})$$

$$\Phi_c \equiv actions \quad \text{cons, get}$$
$$axioms$$
$$\mathbf{beg} \supset (\neg\text{cons}) \wedge (\text{get} \vee (\neg\text{cons})\mathbf{W}\text{get})$$
$$\text{cons} \supset (\neg\text{cons})\mathbf{W}\text{get}$$
$$\text{get} \supset (\neg\text{get})\mathbf{U}\text{cons}$$
$$\text{cons} \supset (\neg\text{get})$$

The theory presentation Φ_p specifies the behaviour of a producer: a producer cannot do a *put* until it does the first *produce*. Then, each time it does a *produce*, it cannot do any other *produce* until it has done a *put*, and vice-versa for *put*. Finally, a producer cannot do both a *produce* and a *put* during the same state transition. The temporal operator

W (weak until) works like **U** except that a **W**b does not require b to occur, allowing for a to hold forever. The specification Φ_c of the consumer is similar.

A producer and a consumer can be interconnected by a buffer. The signature of the buffer will have two actions *sto* and *del* that will be used as ports for interconnection with the producer and the consumer:

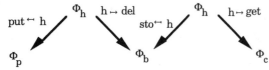

In this diagram, Φ_h is a simple channel specification (like Δ' in section 3): just one action h for establishing the synchronisation, and no axioms.

The axioms of Φ_b define the discipline of interaction between the producer and the consumer. The simplest is a direct synchronisation: sto ≡ del. But we could just as well specify an arbitrarily delay: sto⊃(¬sto)**U**del. Or else, define a queue with a given discipline.

For simplicity, we shall take the synchronised discipline. In this case, the configuration diagram can be simplified to a direct connection between the producer and the buffer:

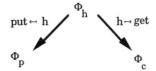

The colimit of this diagram returns a new theory presentation specifying the joint behaviour of the components of the system:

$\Phi_s \equiv$ *actions*   prod, trade, cons
  axioms
   beg ⊃ (¬trade) ∧ (prod ∨ (¬trade)**W**prod)
   prod ⊃ (¬prod)**U**trade
   trade ⊃ (¬trade)**W**prod
   prod ⊃ (¬trade)
   beg ⊃ (¬cons) ∧ (trade ∨ (¬cons)**W**trade)
   cons ⊃ (¬cons)**W**trade
   trade ⊃ (¬trade)**U**cons
   cons ⊃ (¬trade)

That is to say, the joint behaviour has to satisfy the properties of both components and the interconnection specified via the channel (synchronisation of *put* and *get* which are identified in the action *trade*). The set of axioms of the composite specification is, therefore, the union of the translations of the axioms of the components. Because the union of sets of formulae has the same logical value as their conjunction, the categorical approach complies with the "composition as conjunction" idea also used in [1] for parallel composition of reactive systems and also, in a related sense, in [25]. Once again, the idea that the semantics of a connector description is given by the parallel composition of the roles and glue [2] is recovered in another category.

However, we should stress that our approach is more "structured" in the sense that formulae are not being considered individually as units of construction but are organ-

ised into modules (theories) that have a meaning in terms of the structure of the system – hence the use of morphisms for establishing interconnections through the language of these theories, something that cannot be achieved at the level of individual formulae. The explicit handling of language through signatures, namely the use of morphisms to keep track of components within complex systems, and its use for formalising component interconnection is an important asset of the categorical approach.

Category Theory also provides us with the means to establish relationships between different architectural levels: functors. Functors map the objects and morphisms of one category to corresponding objects and morphisms of another category. The fact that morphisms, and not only objects, get related is very important because it means that it is the architectural "styles" that are being related and not just their objects.

In the sequel, we will show how a functor can be defined between the category of COMMUNITY programs and the category of temporal specifications, and how this functor allows us to instantiate an abstract architecture like the one defined in terms of a producer and a consumer with programs in COMMUNITY.

Because COMMUNITY programs and temporal specifications are defined over the same notion of signature (see [8,9] for examples where the signatures are not the same), all that needs to be done is translate programs into axioms and prove that program morphisms defined theorem-preserving mappings.

Consider the following translation of a program (θ,Δ) to the theory presentation $Spec(\theta,\Delta)$ consisting of:

- the proposition (**beg** ⊃ I);
- for every action g∈ Γ and every a∈ D(g), the proposition (g ⊃ **X**a=F(g,a));
- for every action g∈ Γ, the proposition (g ⊃ B(g)).
- for very attribute a∈ V, the proposition
  $(\mathbf{X}a = a)\mathbf{W}(\bigvee_{g\in D(a)} g)$

These (non-logical) axioms do capture the semantics of the program: the first axiom establishes that I is an initialisation condition; the second set of axioms formalises the assignment – if g is about to occur, the next value of attribute a is the current value of F(g,a); the third establishes B(g) as a necessary condition for the occurrence of g; and the last axiom (the locality axiom) captures locality of attributes: local attributes remain invariant until one of the actions in their domain occurs [7].

In order to prove that this translation extends to morphisms and, hence, defines a functor, it is sufficient to see that, given a program morphism σ: $(\theta,\Delta)\rightarrow(\theta',\Delta')$, the conditions laid down for program morphisms together with the axioms of $Spec(\theta',\Delta')$ imply the axioms of $Spec(\theta,\Delta)$. It is easy to see that this is so: for instance, the condition (σ(g) ⊃ σ(B(g))) (the translation of (g ⊃ B(g))∈ $Spec(\theta,\Delta)$) is trivially derived from the axiom (σ(g) ⊃ B'(σ(g))) of $Spec(\theta',\Delta')$ and the condition (B'(σ(g)) ⊃ σ(B(g))) required on σ to be a program morphism (vide section 3).

Notice that if a different notion of program morphism had been chosen, *Spec* might not be a functor, i.e. it might not map the program morphisms (of this new category) to specification morphisms. Indeed, the "semantics" of the programming language is more encoded in the morphisms than in the objects. For instance, if guards had been allowed to be weakened, then *Spec* as defined above would not be a functor because the property ($g \supset B(g)$) would not necessarily be preserved by program morphisms.

A notion of instantiation can now be defined between "abstract" and "concrete" architectures. We call a *realisation* of a specification S a pair $\langle \sigma, P \rangle$ where P is a program and σ is a specification morphism $S \rightarrow Spec(P)$. This notion of realisation is a generalisation of the *satisfaction* or *refinement* relation between programs and specifications.

Traditionally, we say that a program P refines a specification S, $P \vDash S$, if every computation of P is a model of S. This notion of refinement requires that the program and the specification share the same "signature" and is equivalent to saying that $S \subseteq Spec(P)$. Realisations generalise this notion by allowing the program and the specification to be over different signatures. More concretely, the program is allowed to have features that are not relevant to the specification. Hence the morphism from S to *Spec*(P) corresponds to the way in which P realises S, i.e., intuitively, it records the *design decisions* that lead from S to P.

Realisations can themselves be organised into a category. A morphism $\mu: \langle \sigma, P \rangle \rightarrow \langle \sigma', P' \rangle$ between realisations of S is a morphism $\mu: P \rightarrow P'$ between the corresponding programs such that $\sigma' = \sigma; \mu$ (the composition of σ and μ). This condition means that a realisation morphism is, essentially, a translation (or simulation) between the underlying programs that preserves the way the specification is being implemented, i.e. respects the design decisions. Hence, what we get in this way are categories of design decisions, which seems to be the right level of abstraction at which to discuss software engineering notions such as compositionality and reusability.

And it is, indeed, at this level that we can discuss the instantiation of software architectures. We call a realisation of an abstract configuration

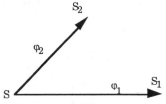

an interconnection of realisations of the components such that $\eta; \mu_i = \varphi_i; \eta_i$, i.e. such that the programs are interconnected in a way that is consistent with the interconnections of the specifications. (We should point out that we have committed a slight abuse in mixing programs and specifications in the same diagram. To be correct, we should have labelled the nodes of the bottom triangle with the translations of the programs into their specifications, but the abuse is justified not only because it simplifies the diagram but because the morphisms are the same.)

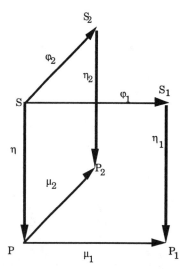

For this process of interconnection to be "correct", we would expect that the complex system that results from the program configuration be a realisation of the specification that results from the abstract configuration diagram. That is, we would expect that by picking instantiations of the roles (in a generalisation of the previous sense to objects in different categories) interconnected as specified by the abstract architecture, we obtain a system that satisfies the properties that can be inferred at the abstract level.

This is a very important property because it allows the properties of the abstract architecture to be analysed independently of their actual use. This point was argued in more detail in [8] and meets the requirement put forward in [2] for the ability to understand the behaviour of connectors independently of the specific context (instantiations) in which they will be used.

This property is, indeed, valid provided that we are working with a functor between programs and specifications. Diagrammatically, the property tells us that we can compute the colimits at both the abstract and the concrete levels with the certainty that there is a unique way (a unique morphism η') in which the concrete system will be a realisation of its abstract specification.

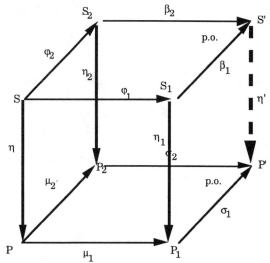

We should stress that this property holds for any categories and functor between them, showing that functors are, indeed, indicators of very strong structural relationships between architectures.

5. Concluding remarks

In this paper, we have shown how (elementary) concepts of Category Theory can be used to formalise key notions of Software Architecture independently of the formalism chosen for describing the behaviour of components, thus providing a semantic domain for SA that complements the choice of a computational model. As illustrated by the proposed category of COMMUNITY programs, the categorical "style" favours the choice of formalisms in which the process of interconnecting components in configurations of complex systems is "separated" from their internal description, thus supporting a "philosophy" of software development very close to the one advocated in [17,19]. Indeed, the goal of this paper was to show that CT provides the right level of mathematical abstraction to address languages for describing software architectures, reiterating the point made earlier by Goguen in [12] for module interconnection languages.

In addition to other works on the application of CT to Computing Science in general, and Software Engineering in particular, we made use of logics and languages for parallel program design to illustrate complex system configuration and the definition of connectors in the sense of [2]. Full definitions of the categorical formalisations of these logics and languages can be found elsewhere [7,8,9]. But the approach can be applied to other domains, notably mathematical models of behaviour such as sheaves [24] and other models for concurrency [23]. A challenge that we would like to undertake is the actual formalisation of the CSP-based approach proposed by [2].

An important contribution of CT to SA that we attempted to illustrate is the formalisation of mappings between different levels of SA, namely a generalisation of the notion of role instantiation by components that are at a lower architectural level. It was shown how the existence of a functor between two such levels ensures compositionality (the ability to reason about compositions at the abstract level, independently of the instantiations that can later be made). However, compositionality cannot always be achieved [1] meaning that it is not always easy to find a functor. For instance, in the example developed in section 4, the functor provided therein does not cater for liveness properties (the use of the strong until operator). The weakening of the functorial relationship is a line of research that we are currently pursuing, namely in conjunction with the detection of emergence of behaviour in abstract architectures.

References

[1] M.Abadi and L.Lamport, "Composing Specifications", *ACM TOPLAS* 15(1), 1993, 73-132.

[2] R.Allen and D.Garlan, "Formalising Architectural Connection", in *Proc. 16th ICSE*, 1994, 71-80.

[3] R.Back and R.Kurki-Suonio, "Distributed Cooperation with Action Systems", *ACM TOPLAS* 10(4), 1988, 513-554.

[4] K.Chandy and J.Misra, *Parallel Program Design – A Foundation*, Addison-Wesley 1988.

[5] H.Ehrig, "Introduction to the Algebraic Theory of Graph Grammars (A Survey)", in *Graph Grammars and Their Application to Computer Science and Biology*, LNCS 73, Springer, 1-69.

[6] H.Ehrig and G.Mahr, *Fundamentals of Algebraic Specification 1: Equations and Initial Semantics*, Springer-Verlag 1985.

[7] J.Fiadeiro and T.Maibaum, "Temporal Theories as Modularisation Units for Concurrent System Specification", *Formal Aspects of Computing* 4(3), 1992, 239-272.

[8] J.Fiadeiro and T.Maibaum, "Interconnecting Formalisms: Supporting Modularity, Reuse and Incrementality", in G.E.Kaiser (ed) *Proc. Third Symposium on the Foundations of Software Engineering*, ACM Press 1995, 72-80.

[9] J.Fiadeiro and T.Maibaum, *Categorical Semantics of Parallel Program Design*, Technical Report, FCUL and Imperial College, 1995.

[10] N.Francez and I.Forman, "Superimposition for Interacting Processes", in *CONCUR'90*, LNCS 458, Springer-Verlag 1990, 230-245.

[11] D.Garlan and D.Perry, "Software Architecture: Practice, Potential, and Pitfalls", in *Proc. 16th ICSE*, 1994, 363-364.

[12] J.Goguen, "Reusing and Interconnecting Software Components", *IEEE Computer* 19(2), 1986, 16-28.

[13] J.Goguen, "A Categorical Manifesto", *Mathematical Structures in Computer Science* 1(1), 1991, 49-67.

[14] J.Goguen and R.Burstall, "Institutions: Abstract Model Theory for Specification and Programming", *Journal of the ACM* 39(1), 1992, 95-146.

[15] J.Goguen and S.Ginali, "A Categorical Approach to General Systems Theory", in G.Klir (ed) *Applied General Systems Research*, Plenum 1978, 257-270.

[16] R.Goldblatt, *Logics of Time and Computation*, CSLI 1987.

[17] J.Kramer, "Exoskeletal Software", in *Proc. 16th ICSE*, 1994, 366.

[18] R.Kurki-Suonio and H.-M.Järvinen, "Action System Approach to the Specification and Design of Distributed Systems", in *Proc. 5th Int. Workshop on Software Specification and Design*, 1989, 34-40

[19] J.Magee, J.Kramer and M.Sloman, "Constructing Distributed Systems in Conic", *IEEE TOSE* 15 (6), 1989.

[20] M.Moriconi and X.Qian, "Correctness and Composition of Software Architectures", *Proc. Second Symposium on the Foundations of Software Engineering*, ACM Press 1994, 164-174.

[21] C.Paredes, J.Fiadeiro and J.F.Costa, "Object Specification: Modeling Behaviour through Rules", in *Proc. OOPSLA'93 Workshop on Specification of Behavioral Semantics in Object-Oriented Information Modelling*, H.Kilov and B.Harvey (eds), 115-123, 1993

[22] D.Sannella and A.Tarlecki, "Building Specifications in an Arbitrary Institution", *Information and Control* 76, 1988, 165-210.

[23] V.Sassone, M.Nielsen and G.Winskel, "A Classification of Models for Concurrency", in E.Best (ed) *CONCUR'93*, LNCS 715, Springer-Verlag 1993, 82-96.

[24] D.Wolfram and J.Goguen, "A Sheaf Semantics for FOOPS Expressions", in M.Tokoro, O.Nierstrasz and P.Wegner (eds), *Object-Based Concurrent Computing*, LNCS 612, Springer Verlag 1991, 81-98.

[25] P.Zave and M.Jackson, "Conjunction as Composition", *ACM TOSEM* 2(4), 1993, 371-411.

Towards a Formal Specification Method for Graphical User Interfaces Using Modularized Graph Grammars

M. Goedicke

Dept. of Math. and CS
University of Essen
D - 45 117 Essen
goedicke@informatik.uni-essen.de

B.E. Sucrow

Dept. of Math. and CS
University of Essen
D - 45 117 Essen
sucrow@informatik.uni-essen.de

Abstract

Well designed graphical user interfaces offer a high potential to increase the productivity of human users. The necessary condition for such a good performance is that the user interface represents the semantics of the underlying application in a clear and comprehensible way. This means, especially, that not only syntactical layout but also semantic consistency conditions between the various interaction objects have to be presented in a graphical user interface appropriately. This is usually termed semantic feedback.

Many representation schemes have been proposed to express the properties of graphical man-machine interfaces. However, many of them concentrate on control flow design and do not easily scale up to realistic problems. In this contribution we propose a graph and graph grammar based approach which addresses the problem of semantic consistency of dialogs in graphical user interfaces. The main emphasis here lies on an appropriate specification of the consistency conditions between the various graphical interaction objects of a man - machine interface. We also propose a modularization technique in order to cope with large systems. We show the expressiveness and modularization features of our approach which is based on an analysis of the relationships between the various grafical interaction objects and conclude our paper with remarks on future work.

1 Introduction

Modern graphical user interfaces allow direct manipulation which increases the productivity of their users dramatically. This statement, however, applies only if the user interface is not in the way i.e. it is a consistent and user-friendly problem oriented representation of the application's state and applicable operations.

This consistency problem has many aspects. One is that the graphic representation and manipulation capabilities are usable and problem specific. Once such concepts for representing a given problem using graphical user interfaces are tackled two design problems in specifying these graphic concepts appear. One is the problem that the various graphic presentations have to be consistent with each other especially when several different ones are used at the same time. These consistency conditions reflect the aspect of *semantic feedback* which is very important in the context of graphical user interfaces.

The second aspect of the problem lies in the used formal specification method. Existing methods either are not expressive enough or are powerful but offer highly incomprehensible specifications. Therefore, specification methods of the latter case, although powerful, do not easily scale up to interactive systems of realistic size. The problem here is to find a suitable modularization technique for specifying complex interactive systems by a powerful specification method in an comprehensible manner.

In this contribution we address these two problems: the problem of specifying graphical user interfaces which use different consistent views and the one of representing a suitable formal method for specifying graphical user interfaces in a powerful but also concise way. We propose to use graphs and graph grammars to specify static and dynamic properties of graphical user interfaces. In addition we present an idea of a modularization technique by classifying sets of possible user interactions where the latter are described by graph grammar rules.

Below we discuss briefly related work and why existing specification formalisms are not sufficient. Then we describe our approach. We first present our idea of specifying graphical user interfaces using graph grammars. Further, we introduce our approach of modularizing graph grammars. These grammars are modularized according to a classification of user interactions.

Finally, we demonstrate our approach using a simple *HTML*-editor and conclude with a brief evaluation and plans for further work.

2 Related Work

Methods and techniques for specifying dialogs and dialog behaviour of graphical user interfaces is a wide

Proceedings of IWSSD-8

and complicated research area. A variety of such description techniques can be found in the literature. Keil-Slawik, for example, writes in [8] that traditionally three fundamental techniques exist for modelling user interfaces: grammars for linear languages, finite automata and nets. Grammars are mainly suitable for describing command oriented linear languages. However, they are poor for describing error cases and they only allow the description of the static component of the interaction but not its dynamics. Finite automata are mainly suitable for specifying state transitions thus offering sequentiality. Such an approach, however, allows only the description of context free behaviour which is very untypical for a human being. Nets offer the advantage for modelling processes especially in the form of Petri nets. But for all three classes of specification techniques mentioned above experiences with realistic examples have shown that specifications become very large hence complex and incomprehensible.

In [7] it is also shown that state transition diagrams form the basis of a variety of description techniques for user interfaces. As pure sequential techniques they are only suitable for mask and menue dialogs. Describing user interfaces using statecharts permits modelling parallel dialogs but does not show the context between such parallel subdialogs. Dialog nets ([6]), a special form of Petri nets, overcome this problem with the features of modal subdialogs, a clear net structure and hierarchy.

Our experience shows, however, that dialog net specifications of graphical user interfaces result quickly in very complex descriptions of even simple user interfaces hence do not help much in understanding user interface definitions. It seems that all the above mentioned techniques are not expressive enough (as for example the Dialog nets) as specification methods on one hand **or** they result into too complex descriptions (as for example the grammars for linear languages) on the other hand so that they are not helpful as specification methods for graphical user interfaces.

Graph grammar descriptions have also been used in other approaches dealing with user interfaces. For example, in [1] a customized user interface design environment is generated. First, a conceptual framework for task-oriented user interface specification is specified as a visual language. The specification is then applied to a visual language generator so that a visual syntax-directed editor for the specification language is generated. In this approach the visual language is specified with graph transformation systems. Specification and representation of user interfaces based on end user tasks using attributed graphs and related graph rewriting systems can also been seen in [3]. In our approach, however, we propose using graph grammars for specifying graphical user interfaces of specific interactive systems with special consideration of the consistency conditions between the various graphic presentations of the underlying data of these systems.

Ideas to decompose graph grammars in several smaller components can be found in [2] and [9]. In [2] a conceptual framework for a module concept for graph transformations is discussed and in [9] a structuring method for building up large systems of graph rewrite rules from small pieces is proposed for enhancing the usefulness of graph rewriting. As opposed to these two theoretical approaches we propose a modularization technique for graph grammars by classifying certain graph rewrite rules which specify specific user interactions of an interactive system.

3 The Graph Grammar Specification Method

Our idea of describing the graphical user interface of an interactive system is inspired by the observation that a graphical user interface – similar to any heavily state based system – can be characterized by

- *dialog states,*

- *dialog states transistions.*

A dialog state is like a snapshot of the highly dynamic interactive system, and therefore is a static element. A dialog state transition is a possibly complex transformation of a dialog state into another one, possibly caused by an interaction between the interactive system and the user, and therefore represents a potential dynamics of the system.

In particular, a dialog state describes the *appearance* of the user interface objects in a particular situation on the display. For example, actual geometric coordinates and colours of the windows are given, as well as ressource values like the actual content of a text field. Because a dialog state is only representing static properties it is necessary to capture the relationships between user interface objects related to the desired dynamics of the interactive system. This is expressed by describing a dialog state transition which transforms one dialog state into a new one if and when a certain event occurs. It is therefore necessary to express in a description of a dialog state transition how the various user interface objects involved may change.

3.1 Using Graph Grammars for Specifying Graphical User Interfaces

Based on the above observations our idea is to represent dialog states as graphs and dialog state transitions as transformations between such graphs. The reason for this idea is that graphs are in general a powerful mechanism for describing problems of various kinds. The technique of graph grammars will be the mathematical formalism here for specifying dialogs of graphical user interfaces.

The important question at this point is how to organize these graphs and graph transformations in order to obtain useful user interface descriptions. The crucial point is to find a suitable and useful **structure** for the graphs representing dialog states. The various user interface objects constituting the graphical user interface and the underlying data of an interactive system can have various kinds of relationships to each other. This fact should be reflected in the formal description of the graphical user interface, i.e. in the structure of the graphs representing the dialog states which also implies this reflection in the relevant graph transformations.

In the following we describe more precisely the kinds of relationships between graphical user interface objects, what graph structure these relationships imply on the graphs representing dialog states and finally, what this means for the structure of the graph rewrite rules.

Up to now we have classified three kinds of relationships between graphical user interface objects:

- *widget hierarchy*,
- *semantics specific*,
- *application specific*.

While the meaning of the first item is obvious the second one resembles the relationship between objects representing the same data of the underlying application possibly also at the same time. This kind of relationship is very important for the consideration of the consistency conditions between graphical user interface objects reflecting the aspect of semantic feedback. The third item resembles the relationship between objects and certain data of the underlying application represented by these objects. The first two items refer to the man machine interface while the last item refers to the relationship between the graphical user interface representation of the data and operations managed by the entire application. We investigate this area more deeply in [5] where the main emphasis lies in investigating the various interdependencies possibly existing between the functional kernel of an interactive system and its man machine interface with the goal of finding suitable software components within an architectural structure for the system.

We concentrate here on the relationships of the two first items, more precisely,

- the first item refers to the syntactical appearance while
- the second item refers to the semantics of the graphic elements which appear on the screen.

Dialog States modelled through Directed Attributed Graphs A directed graph whith attributes at its nodes as well as at its edges is suitable for representing a dialog state. Therefore we define informally:

A dialog state of a graphical user interface of an interactive system is formally specified by a directed graph with attributes at its nodes as well as at its edges. The nodes represent graphical user interface objects, attributes attached to the nodes specify ressource values of the resp. objects. The edges of

the graph represent the specific relationships between the objects. They can be labelled with the attribut **wh** *indicating the widget hierarchy, with the attribut* **appl** *indicating the application specific relationship or labelled* **sem** *indicating the semantic specific relationship between graphical user interface objects.*

Examples for parts of dialog states with the three kinds of relationships between user interface objects are the following: An user interface object could be a modal subwindow of a primary window which reflects the widget hierarchy between these two user interface objects. Two graphical objects acting as user interface objects in a canvas of a window could represent two nodes of a binary search tree (part of the underlying application) represented in this canvas. These two objects clearly are subject to an application specific relationship. Finally, two windows could represent the same data of the underlying application at the same time in a different way, so that a semantic specific relationship is reflected in this case.

Dialog State Transitions modelled through Graph Rewrite Rules A graph rewrite rule is suitable for modifying graphs of the kind described above and therefore to describe dialog state transitions. Therefore we define informally:

A dialog state transition of one dialog state into another one is formally specified by a graph rewrite rule.

For example, a button could be pressed which implies that a window has to be closed. This new state is represented by a graph which looks like the graph for the first state except that the value for the visibility ressource of the closed window (represented by a node) has changed.

In summary, our approach to specify dialogs for graphical user interfaces using graph grammars can be characterized in the following way: A highly interactive software system becomes evident to the user through its highly interactive graphical user interface. The appearance and the behaviour of its dialogs may be specified through graphs and graph rewrite rules of a certain structure, respectively. Thus, the interaction part of an interactive system is specified by a so called *graph grammar* or *graph rewriting system*.

Below we first give (in)formal definitions of the graph grammar formalism which will be used to define the notions of dialog states and dialog state transitions. Then we present some simple examples demonstrating the aforementioned ideas to specify graphical user interfaces using graph grammars.

3.2 Some Definitions

In this subsection we give a very brief account of the formal definitions for the graph grammar formalism used in this paper. Sometimes the definitions will be only semi-formal and incomplete due to lack of space. We therefore refer to [4] and [10] (see also [11], [12]) for a detailed and complete description.

If $Attr_V$ and $Attr_E$ are two sets of attributes which will be used to label nodes and edges of graphs, then we define:

Definition An $(Attr_V, Attr_E)$-*graph* M is a system $M = (V_M, E_M, s_M, t_M, l_M, m_M)$, where
V_M set of nodes,
E_M set of edges,
$s_M : E_M \to V_M$ source function of edges,
$t_M : E_M \to V_M$ target function of edges,
$l_M : V_M \to Attr_V$ node labelling,
$m_M : E_M \to Attr_E$ edge labelling.
M represents a *directed node and edge labelled graph*.

For describing modifications of graphs by graph rewrite rules we need the definition of a match between two graphs:

Definition A *graph match* g of a $(Attr_V, Attr_E)$-graph M in a $(Attr_V, Attr_E)$-graph N is given by a 4-tupel $g = (g_V, g_E, p_V, p_E)$, where
$g_V : V_M \to V_N$ and $g_E : E_M \to E_N$ mappings,
$p_V : (Attr_V \times Attr_V) \to \{true, false\}$ node attribute match predicate,
$p_E : (Attr_E \times Attr_E) \to \{true, false\}$ edge attribute match predicate.

Remark: For the induced match $g(M)$ it has to be assured on the one hand that g_V and g_E map consistently the source and target of each edge in graph M onto nodes in the target graph N such that the graph structure of M - i.e. without considering labels - is mapped onto a proper subgraph of N. On the other hand the label of a graph element (node or edge) in M and the label of the corresponding picture of that graph element in graph N (under the mapping g_V or g_E respectively) have to be *compatible* with respect to the predicates p_V or p_E respectively.

Modifications of graphs are described by graph rewrite rules:

Definition A *graph rewrite rule* $r = (L, R, K)$ is a tripel of graphs, where graph L is the left hand side of the rule, graph R is the right hand side of the rule and graph K is the so called glueing graph. K takes care that no dangling edges appear in the new graph after applying r to the old graph (see also the definition below). Hence, K identifies some anchor elements which have to remain unchanged by the modification and is a subgraph of L and R as well.

Definition A *modification of a graph* M into a new graph N by applying a graph rewrite rule $r = (L, R, K)$ is realized by the following two principal steps:
1) a graph match is chosen between the graph L and the graph M to be modified,
2) the induced match of graph L is removed in graph M and graph R is added. The connection of graph R to the remaining part of graph M is given by the glueing graph K (see above).

At this point we have all necessary bits and pieces to define:

Definition A *graph grammar* is a system $G = (Attr_V, Attr_E, P, P_r, Z)$, where
$Attr_V, Attr_E$ are node and edge attributes respectively,
P is a set of graph rewrite rules,
P_r is a set of attribute match predicates required for a graph match,
Z is the start graph (Z is a $(Attr_V, Attr_E)$-graph).

For the sake of simplicity a graph grammar G will be described in the following by $G = (S, P)$, where S denotes the start graph, P the set of graph rewrite rules.

Definition A *graph grammar language* $\mathcal{L}(G)$ is the set of all graphs generated by a graph grammar G.

3.3 First Example introducing edges labelled *wh* and *appl*

Suppose, one can start a system opening a window representing a simple binary search tree. One can delete the single leaf of that tree by clicking with the mouse on that leaf, and one can finish the system by clicking with the mouse in the background of the window. These three possible user interactions are listed below together with a graphical presentation of the resp. resulting dialog states.

User Interactions:

- Start (I_{Start}) of the system $\hookrightarrow$ state S_{Start}:

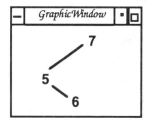

- Mouse-Click (I_6) on leaf with value 6 in state $S_{Start} \hookrightarrow$ state S_6:

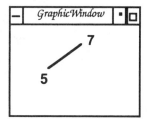

- Mouse-Click (I_{Stop}) into the background of the window in state $S_6 \hookrightarrow$ state S_{Stop}.

It follows a graphical presentation of the graphs specifying the dialog states described above, where the *empty* graph is named by $G_\emptyset$ and graphically indicated by $\emptyset$. Note, that nodes 5 and 6 of the binary search tree in state S_{Start} are subwidgets of the widget *GraphicWindow* in the same manner as is the root 7 and therefore also should have be connected to the node called *GraphicWindow* by edges labelled *wh* in the graph. These edges, however, are irrelevant for the graph rewriting rules and are not considered further.

Graphs:

- States before starting and after finishing the system $\hookrightarrow$ graph $G_\emptyset$: $\emptyset$
- Graphs specifying the state $S_{Start} \hookrightarrow$ graph $G_{S_{Start}}$ and the state $S_6 \hookrightarrow$ graph G_{S_6}:

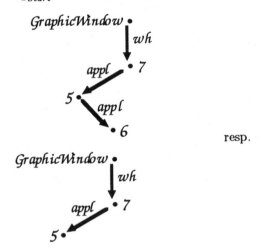

resp.

Finally, the graph rewrite rules specifying the three user interactions described above are shown below. They are presented graphically in the form $L ::= R$.

Graph Rewrite Rules:

- Graph Rewrite Rule for User Interaction I_{Start}: $P_{I_{Start}} = (G_\emptyset, G_{S_{Start}}, G_\emptyset)$

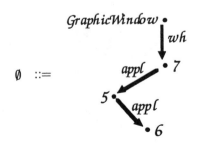

- Graph Rewrite Rule for User Interaction I_6: $P_{I_6} = (G_{S_{Start}}, G_{S_6}, G_{S_6})$

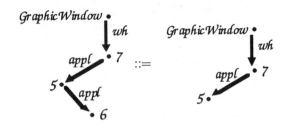

- Graph Rewrite Rule for User Interaction I_{Stop}: $P_{I_{Stop}} = (G_{S_6}, G_\emptyset, G_\emptyset)$

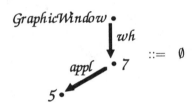

The graphical description above shows that the interactive system can be specified formally by the graph grammar language

$$\mathcal{L}(GG) = \{G_\emptyset, G_{S_{Start}}, G_{S_6}\} \quad \text{with}$$

Graph Grammar $\quad GG = \{G_\emptyset, P_{BST}\} \quad$ where

- $G_\emptyset$ the starting graph,
- $P_{BST} = \{P_{I_{Start}}, P_{I_6}, P_{I_{Stop}}\}$ set of the rewrite rules.

This example demonstrates nicely that the formal method of graph grammars is very well suited for specifying graphical user interfaces in a powerful but also in a succinct manner.

Semantics specific relationships between graphical user interface objects (c.f. subsections 3.1 and 3.4) still are not considered in the example above. It will be shown in the next subsection how specification of *semantic feedback* as an important aspect of graphical user interfaces of highly interactive systems is possible with additional features. These features will finally suggest also an elegant idea for modularizing complex user interface specifications (c.f. section 4).

3.4 Extended Example introducing edges labelled *sem*

Suppose now a more complex system, where starting the system means opening two windows representing the *same* data of the underlying application in *different* forms, graphically and textually. User interactions in either of the two windows *have* to be reflected in the resp. other one at the same time. This property is usually termed *semantic feedback* and of course has to be considered in the formal specification of a graphical user interface, too.

The state S_1 after starting the system is represented by the graph G_{S_1}, which has additional attributes *v_exists* and *v_works* attached to the node labelled 5 (which will be explained later). The label *sem* at an edge means that there exists a semantic relationship between the two connected nodes. In the figure below the node labelled 5 of the tree is represented in **both** windows.

State S_1 specified through graph G_{S_1}:

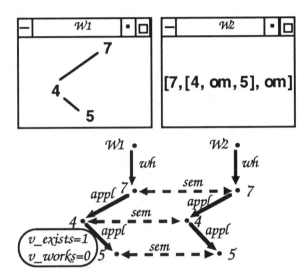

To point out the problem of specifying the semantic feedback one specific user interaction will be considered in the following.

User Interaction I_5: Mouse-Click on node with value 5 in window $W1$ in state S_1 will cause two effects:

- Changing the value 5 to 6 in $W1$ (direct effect of the user interaction),
- Changing the value 5 to 6 in $W2$ (effect of semantic feedback).

This will cause another state S_2 of the system:

State S_2 specified through graph G_{S_2}:

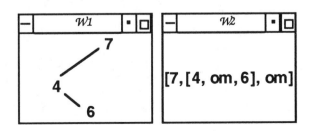

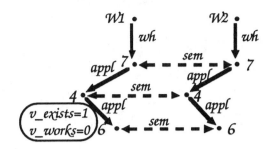

In order to specify the immediate semantic feedback of an user interaction one has to take care with regard to the specifying graph grammar that in certain situations special graph rewrite rules **must not** be applied, or in other words, specific graph rewrite rules **have to** be applied. This is since we use a declarative approach to graph rewriting as opposed to programmed ones (c.f. [14]). In the above case the user interaction could be specified using two graph rewrite rules, in fact according to the two effects described above:

- $P_{S_1} = (G_{S_1}, FG_{S_1}, G_\emptyset)$ (direct effect of the user interaction),

- $FP_{S_1} = (FG_{S_1}, G_{S_2}, G_\emptyset)$ (effect of semantic feedback),

where the resulting intermediate graph FG_{S_1} is shown below:

Graph FG_{S_1}:

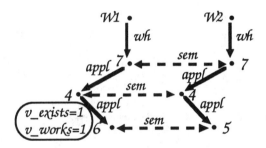

Very important in this situation is, as already mentioned above, that the application of the graph rewrite rule FP_{S_1} has to be applied immediately after the application of the rule P_{S_1}, specifying the semantic feedback in this way. This can be achieved by making application of rules dependent on predicates over attributes as those, for example, attached to the node with value 5: the attribute *v_exists* specifies the existing number of edges with label *sem* outgoing from the relevant node, the attribute *v_works* specifies the same but is used for decreasing this number during application of rules of the kind $FP_{-}...$. This ensures, for example in the case above, that the graph rewrite rule FP_{S_1} will be applied immediately after the rule P_{S_1} because *v_works* > 0 holds (implied by the previous application of P_{S_1}, see also graphs G_{S_1} and FG_{S_1}

above), but also not longer because it decreases this attribute by 1 during application as part of its effect.

The problem of specifying semantic feedback is solved as described above. Moreover, this approach suggests an elegant idea for modularizing specifications of graphical user interfaces becomming too complex: a suitable classification of graph rewrite rules as discussed above gives cause to separate a graph grammar specifying a system into several smaller graph grammars according to this classification (c.f. section 4).

It should be noted at this point that the problem described above could be solved also by one single graph rewrite rule specifying the two effects of the user interaction together in one (monolithic) step. Such an approach, however, would not allow to achieve flexible user interface specifications because of a low granularity of the resulting graph grammar specifications (granularity of the rules). Also, it would not be possible to modularize such *monolithic* graph grammar specifications in an elegant form as mentioned above.

Our idea of classifying graph rewrite rules according to natural properties of graphical user interface objects will be used for the purpose of modularizing graph grammar specifications of graphical user interfaces in the next section and a non-trivial example will be used for demonstration und discussion.

4 The Modularization of Graph Grammars

The idea of specifying graphical user interfaces with modularized graph grammars will be investigated in this section using the example of an system similar to the *HTML Pro 1.07*-editor for the Macintosh system.

The *HTML Pro 1.07*-editor is a WYSIWYG editor allowing to create HTML-documents which are in plain (ASCII) text format where HTML is a markup language used by the world wide web[1]. HTML uses markup tags to tell the web browser how to display the text. For example, the `<Title>`-tag and corresponding `</Title>`-tag specify the title of a document, the `<H1>`-tag and corresponding `</H1>`-tag specify text in a specific font and size and the `<P>`-tag specifies a paragraph separator.

If one starts the editor two windows appear, one for the HTML source text, the other for displaying the related formatted text. Both windows are empty, the text cursor in the upper left corner of each of the windows and the window for the formatted text is active. One alternatively can click in the resp. inactive window with the mouse which changes only the activity attribut of the two windows but never their contents. This is the first interesting observation, that the above mentioned actions keep the contents of the windows always invariant. Now, this classification of the two actions leads to the first small *graph grammar module* $GGM_{ContInv} = (S, P)$ with starting graph S and

[1] *c.f. A Beginners's Guide to HTML*, National Center for Supercomputing Applications / pubs@ncsa.uiuc.edu

set of graph rewrite rules $P = \{P_{Source}, P_{Html}\}$ for specifying a part of the graphical user interface of the editor. P_{Source} and P_{Html} specify the interactions of clicking with the mouse in the inactive window *Source* resp. *Html*. Labels *wh* at the edges are omitted in the following for reason of clearness.

Starting Graph S:

Graph Rewrite Rule $P_{Source} \in P$: Clicking in the inactive window *Source* is specified by $P_{Source} = (L_{Source}, R_{Source}, K_{Source})$ with

L_{Source}:

R_{Source}:

K_{Source}:

Screen
•

Graph Rewrite Rule $P_{Html} \in P$: Clicking in the inactive window *Html* is specified by $P_{Html} = (L_{Html}, R_{Html}, K_{Html})$ with

$$L_{Html} = R_{Source},$$
$$R_{Html} = L_{Source},$$
$$K_{Html} = K_{Source}.$$

With this first step of modularization one can imagine how the specification of the graphical user interface of the editor does look like at this point although several parts of the system are not yet considered as, for example, the contents of the windows. The interaction part described above can now be specified formally by the graph grammar language (c.f. picture below).

$$\mathcal{L}(GGM_{ContInv}) = \{L_{Source}, R_{Source}\} \quad \text{with}$$

Graph Grammar $GGM_{ContInv} = \{S, P\}$ where

- S the starting graph,
- $P = \{P_{Source}, P_{Html}\}$ set of the rewrite rules.

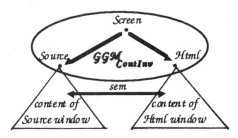

The interaction part of the editor specified by the graph grammar $GGM_{ContInv}$ keeps the other parts (specified by the subgraphs of the nodes *Source* resp. *Html*, c.f. picture above) invariant as was explained above. Therefore, it can be seen as a *module* belonging to the entire system. Hence, $GGM_{ContInv}$ represents a *graph grammar module* of the entire specification in this sense.

Considering the other parts of the editor yields the second interesting observation. Several user interactions possible in the window *Source* keep the content of the window *Html* invariant. A graph grammar specifying this interaction part of the editor could be a candidat for another graph grammar module of the entire specification. This aspect will be considered more concretely in the following.

The content of the window *Source* consists of text which either represents formatting commands in the form of markup tags as mentioned above or pure application text. All user interactions by which markup tags will be typed into this window or by which markup tags will appear by triggering menu items keep the window *Html* invariant. In this latter window neither text will appear during such actions nor the cursor position will change. Hence, describing user interactions of that kind could belong to a graph grammar module $GGM_{HtmlInv}$ specifying a part of the interaction part of the window *Source* as is shown in the picture below. Obviously, $GGM_{HtmlInv}$ never will specify the graphical user interface of the window *Source* entirely because of the existence of additional user interactions having effects on the window *Html* as will be discussed in connenction with a further classification of user interactions below.

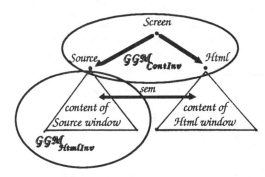

We will conclude with a third classification of user interactions which will yield a third interesting graph grammar module contributing to the specification of the editor. It should be noted here that the editor will not be specified by graph grammar modules **completely** in this paper. Rather, this example is used here to demonstrate our idea of modularization technique for graph grammar specifications.

As is obvious there exist several possible user interactions in the window *Source* as well as in the window *Html* which imply an immediate feedback in the resp. other window. Typing application text in one of the windows belongs to these user interactions as well as clicking somewhere in the windows with the mouse (changing the cursor position). Such user interactions are involved in the interaction part comprising the window *Source* as well as the window *Html*. Hence, their specification contributes to a graph grammar module $GGM_{SourceHtml}$ specifying this interaction part of the editor as can be seen in the picture below.

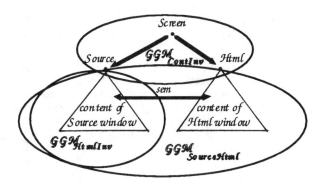

If GGM_{Editor} will be the graph grammar module specifying the editor entirely, then we can establish at this point the relationship

$$GGM_{Editor} \supset$$

$$GGM_{ContInv} \cup GGM_{HtmlInv} \cup GGM_{SourceHtml},$$

where $\supset$ and $\cup$ denote set relationships wrt. the corresponding elements of a graph grammar. Proceeding in this way the graph grammar module GGM_{Editor} composed of several smaller graph grammar modules can be completed yielding the entire specification of the editor, finally.

5 Conclusion and Further Work

We presented in our discussion above a new approach to specify graphical user interfaces using graph grammar based descriptions and a proper modularization technique. Two fundamental aspects have been addressed: the problem of specifying graphical user interfaces which use different consistent views and the one of representing a suitable formal method for specifying graphical user interfaces in a powerful but also succinct way.

We first discussed related approaches which mainly lack suitable abstraction facilities. Based on an analysis of various existing relationships between graphical user interface objects of an interactive system we proposed to use graphs and graph rewrite rules to specify properties of the (graphic) state and potential dynamics, respectively. For the resulting graph grammar specifications we finally presented a modularization technique by classifying sets of possible user interactions.

The main advantages of our approach are:

- A powerful specification method. Graph grammars represent an highly expressive formalism for specifying graphical user interfaces of complex interactive systems.

- A flexible and problem-adequate specification method. Graphical user interface objects of an interactive system together with their various possible relationships yield a structure which can be specified by graph grammars in a flexible and problem-adequate manner (as discussed and demonstrated in detail in section 3). Especially, the consideration of such important aspects like the immediate semantic feedback can be expressed conveniently.

- An comprehensible specification method. A suitable modularization decomposes a graph grammar in several smaller graph grammar modules. This allows the consideration of several small graph grammars with regard to the resp. subproblems instead of the consideration of the entire complex graph grammar specifying the entire system.

Our main question which will be adressed first in the future research is to find suitable classifications of user interactions. We are interested in finding out whether there possibly exist other classifications than the one discussed above and whether these could lead to other, perhaps more suitable modularizations of graph grammar specifications.

Another important topic not considered here is the specification of the coupling of internal and external events to the application of graph rewrite rules. Up to now we define the semantics of a specification by the set of all graphs which may be derived applying graph rewrite rules of the related graph grammar. This does not specify when a certain event is actually processed.

At the level of representing graphs and graph rewrite rules we are also looking into appropriate tool support. Recently a graph grammar machine was finished based on the definition in [4]. This allows the textual specification of graphs and graph rewrite rules. A useful high level notation for expressing semantic relations between elements of a graphical user interface is possible and enhances the specification process. Currently, also work is going on to expand the still *textual* graph grammar machine for allowing also *graphical* specifications of graph grammars and graph rewrite systems.

Based on our experiences we also investigate practical and general module concepts for graph grammars ([13]).

Acknowledgements

We would like to thank the anonymous reviewers for many helpful comments and hints on the draft version of this paper.

References

[1] F. Arefi, M. Milani, and C. Stary. Towards Customized User Interface Design Environments. *Journal of Visual Languages and Computing*, pages 146–151, 1991.

[2] H. Ehrig and G. Engels. Pragmatic and Semantic Aspects of a Modul Concept for Graph Transformation Systems. Research Report, Technical University of Berlin and University of Leiden, Departments of Computer Science, 1995.

[3] R. Freund, B. Haberstroh, and C. Stary. Applying Graph Grammars for Task-Oriented User Interface Development. In W. et. al., editor, *Proceedings IEEE Conference on Computing and Information ICCI'92*, pages 389–392, 1992.

[4] M. Goedicke. On the Structure of Software Description Languages: A Component Oriented View. Research Report 473/1993, University of Dortmund, Dept. of Computer Science, Dortmund, May 1993. Habilitation.

[5] M. Goedicke and B. Sucrow. Flexible Architecture of Interactive Systems. In P. Phalanque and D. Benyon, editors, *Critical Issues in User Interface Design*. Springer, 1996.

[6] C. Janssen. Dialognetze zur Beschreibung von Dialogabläufen in graphisch-interaktiven Systemen. In K.-H. Rödiger, editor, *Software-Ergonomie '93*, volume 39 of *German Chapter of the ACM*, pages 67–76, Stuttgart, 1993. Teubner. Fachtagung vom 15. bis 17.3.1993 in Bremen.

[7] C. Janssen, A. Weisbecker, and J. Ziegler. Generierung graphischer Benutzungsschnittstellen aus Datenmodellen und Dialognetz-Spezifikationen. In H. Züllighoven, W. Altmann, and E.-E. Doberkat, editors, *Requirements Engineering '93: Prototyping*, volume 41 of *German Chapter of the ACM*, pages 335–347, Stuttgart, 1993. Teubner.

[8] R. Keil-Slawik. KONSTRUKTIVES DESIGN – Ein ökologischer Ansatz zur Gestaltung Interaktiver Systeme. Research Report 90-14, Technical University of Berlin, Dept. of Computer Science, Berlin, March 1990. Preliminary version of the habilitation.

[9] H.-J. Kreowski and S. Kuske. On the interleaving semantics of transformation units- A step into GRACE. Research Report, University of Bremen, Dept. of Computer Science and Mathematics, 1995.

[10] H.-J. Kreowski and G. Rozenberg. On structured Graph Grammars. Technical Report 1/85, Dept. of Mathematics and Computer Science, 1985.

[11] H.-J. Kreowski and G. Rozenberg. On structured Graph Grammars. I. *Journal of Information Sciences*, 52:185–210, 1990.

[12] H.-J. Kreowski and G. Rozenberg. On structured Graph Grammars. II. *Journal of Information Sciences*, 52:221–246, 1990.

[13] T. Meyer. Definition and Implementation of Abstract Graph Types for Modularization of Graph Grammar Systems. Master's thesis, University of Essen, December 1995. in German.

[14] A. Schürr. PROGRES: A VHL-Language Based on Graph Grammars. In H. Ehrig, H.-J. Kreowski, and G. Rozenberg, editors, *Proc. 4th Int. Workshop on Graph Grammars and Their Application to Computer Science*, LNCS 532, pages 641–659. Springer, 1991.

Relating CHAM Descriptions of Software Architectures

Paola Inverardi

Dip. di Matematica Pura ed Applicata
Universitá di L'Aquila
L'Aquila, ITALY 67010

Daniel Yankelevich

Dep. de Computación
Universidad de Buenos Aires
Buenos Aires, Argentina

Abstract

In this paper we propose an approach to compare descriptions of software architectures based on the CHAM formalism. The need to compare descriptions of the same system at different level of abstraction often arises tipically when the software practice uses a stepwise refinement approach. Differently from other approaches presented in the literature our framework allows for expressing correct *refinement both of the static structure and of the dynamic behaviour of an architecture. Statically we rely on a suitable definition of partial morphism between the signatures of the two architectures. Dinamically we propose a notion of structure preserving simulation which allows the behaviours of the two CHAM descriptions to be (preorderly) related. In both definitions an important role is played by the* membrane *construct which allows for expressing non-functional constraints on the architecture to be refined. The main idea is to use the* membranes *to denote basic software co mponents of the architecture that can be further decomposed during a refinement process but that cannot be destroyed even if the behaviour of the overall system is preserved. One point in favour of our approach is that we do not constrain too much the further development since we only require the membrane structure to be preserved.*

1 Introduction

In this paper we propose an approach to compare descriptions of software architectures based on the Chemical Abstract Machine (CHAM) formalism as introduced in [10].

A CHAM description of a software architecture consists of a syntactic description of the static components of the architecture (the *molecule*) and of a set of reaction rules which describe how the system dinamically evolves through reaction steps.

The need to compare descriptions of the same system at different level of abstraction often arises tipically when the software practice uses a stepwise refinement approach.

Differently from other proposals presented in the literature [13, 14, 4] based on a logic approach, our framework allows for expressing *correct* refinement both of the static structure and of the dynamic behaviour of an architecture. Statically, we rely on a suitable definition of partial morphism between the signatures of the two architectures. Dinamically we propose a notion of structure preserving simulation inspired by [2, 3, 12] which allows the behaviours of two CHAM descriptions to be (preorderly) related. Therefore we have two level of refinements, the static and the dynamic one, and two different ways of relating them. Clearly these are not independent but suitably related. In both definitions an important role is played by the *membrane* construct which allows for expressing extra–functional constraints on the architecture to be refined. By extra–functional requirements we mean all those requirements that are meaningful for the customer but have no impact on the functional behaviour of the system. For example, requirements on the topology of the system architecture due to hardware or physical constraints or fault-tolerance requirements which may result in the need of replicating resources. From our perspective, the key issue here is in the ability of expressing these properties in the same formalism used for the specification of the functional/behavioural ones [5].

Besides expressing these properties it is then important to define a way to ensure that they are preserved by a refinement step. This is not an obvious point since they are not behavioural properties.

The main idea is thus to use the CHAM concept of

Proceedings of IWSSD-8

membrane to denote basic software components of the architecture that can be further decomposed during a refinement process but that cannot be destroyed even if the behaviour of the overall system is preserved. One point in favour of this approach is that we introduce a certain degree of expressivity in the description formalism without constraining too much the further development. In this way it is possible to modify the static and dynamic structure by adding both components and connectors as long as the membrane constituents and the dynamic behaviour of the original architecture is preserved. Moreover, since a CHAM description naturally gives rise to a transition system [15], the checking of the dynamic correctness of the refinement can be completely automated [8, 9] provided that the transition system is finite state. This last condition is not difficult to require (and obtain) due to the high level of abstraction of software architecture descriptions.

2 CHAM Concepts for Software Architectures

In this section we briefly summarize the most relevant concepts the CHAM model is based on. We also report on the use of the membrane concept as introduced in [10] and we refer to that paper and to the original paper [1] for more details.

A Chemical Abstract Machine is specified by defining *molecules* $m, m', \ldots$ defined as terms of a syntactic algebra that derive from a set of constants and a set of operations and *solutions* $S, S', \ldots$ of molecules. Molecules constitute the basic elements of a CHAM, while solutions are multisets of molecules interpreted as defining the *states* of a CHAM. A CHAM specification contains *transformation rules* $T, T', \ldots$ that define a *transformation relation* $S \longrightarrow S'$ dictating the way solutions can evolve (i.e., states can change) in the CHAM.

The transformation rules can be of two kinds: general *laws* that are valid for all CHAMs and specific *rules* that depend on the particular CHAM being specified. The specific rules must be elementary rewriting rules that do not involve any premises. In contrast, the general laws are permitted such premises.

Any solution can be considered as a single molecule with respect to other solutions by means of an encapsulation construct called a *membrane*. More importantly, a membrane allows the effects of a transformation to be localized to within that membrane. In other words, the solutions inside a membrane can freely evolve independently of other solutions. A re-

versible operator called an *airlock* is used to selectively extract molecules from a solution and place the rest of that solution within a membrane. The reversibility of the airlock allows molecules to be "reabsorbed" into the original solution. Finally, membranes are semipermeable, allowing certain molecules to enter and leave the membrane.

Solutions can be built from other solutions by combining them through the multiset union operator. For example, given solutions $S = m_1, \ldots, m_n$ and $S' = m'_1, \ldots, m'_k$, $S \uplus S' = m_1, \ldots, m_n, m'_1, \ldots, m'_k$ is another solution.

A solution enclosed in $\{\!| \cdot |\!\}$ denotes a membrane. The reversible airlock operator applied to solution $S = m_1, \ldots, m_n$ to extract m_i from S is denoted

$$S' = m_i \triangleleft \{\!| m_1, \ldots, m_{i-1}, m_{i+1}, \ldots, m_n |\!\}$$

CHAMs obey four general laws.

The Reaction Law. An instance of the right-hand side of a rule can replace the corresponding instance of its left-hand side. Thus, given the rule

$$M_1, M_2, \ldots, M_k \longrightarrow M'_1, M'_2, \ldots, M'_l$$

if $m_1, m_2, \ldots, m_k$, and $m'_1, m'_2, \ldots, m'_l$ are instances of the $M_{1 \ldots k}$ and $M'_{1 \ldots l}$ by a common substitution, then we can apply the rule and obtain the following solution transformation.

$$m_1, m_2, \ldots, m_k \longrightarrow m'_1, m'_2, \ldots, m'_l$$

The Chemical Law. Reactions can be performed freely within any solution, as follows.

$$\frac{S \longrightarrow S'}{S \uplus S'' \longrightarrow S' \uplus S''}$$

In words, when a subsolution evolves, the supersolution in which it is contained is also considered to have evolved.

The Membrane Law. A subsolution can evolve freely within any context.

$$\frac{S \longrightarrow S'}{\{\!| \mathcal{C}[S] |\!\} \longrightarrow \{\!| \mathcal{C}[S'] |\!\}}$$

The Airlock Law. A molecule can always be extracted from, and reabsorbed into, a solution at the same time that its identity as an individual molecule is preserved.

$$m \uplus S \longleftrightarrow m \triangleleft \{\!| S |\!\}$$

At any given point, a CHAM can apply as many rules as possible to a solution, provided that their premises do not conflict—that is, no molecule is involved in more than one rule. In this way it is possible to model parallel behaviors by performing parallel transformations. When more than one rule can apply to the same molecule or set of molecules then we have nondeterminism, in which case the CHAM makes a nondeterministic choice as to which transformation to perform.

In [10] it is proposed to use the membrane construct for expressing further refinements of molecules. Therefore, in order to properly model the behaviour of the membranes in a solution two new reactions rules have been defined that we will take as part of the general rules: The goal of this rules is to define the interaction between the membranes and their external environment. What we need to do is to make the membranes semi-permeable to allow the appropriate reactions to take place.

This requires a two step process. The first step makes use of the Airlock Law to extract a molecule of interest out of the membrane. The second step associates the communication capability of that molecule with the membrane as a whole. For that, we must introduce a new transformation rule T_{m1}.

$$T_{m1} \equiv \{|m \diamond m_1 \lhd \{|m_2, \ldots, m_k|\}|\} \longrightarrow$$
$$m \diamond \{|m_1 \lhd \{|m_2, \ldots, m_k|\}|\}$$

where $m, m_1, \ldots, m_k \in M$.

Once the appropriate reaction has taken place, the Airlock Law can be used to reabsorb the remaining molecule back into the main solution so that the processing can continue. Analogously, a molecule can be reabsorbed into the membrane if no reaction is possible.

In this way, we use generic rules that allow all molecules within a membrane to be offered to the environment, not just a select few.

3 A Formal Definition of Refinements

The formal definition and analysis of how different architectures are related involves the study of relationships between CHAMS. A formal study of the relations may reveal details that are hidden in an informal view and, moreover, may contribute to the foundations of the architectural analysis of systems. We claim that a formal definition of what means to refine and to relate architectures must be done prior to construct refinement techniques and tools. Moreover, we claim that

this formal study must be carried on in relation with concrete examples and case studies.

The CHAM model differs from other operational models [11, 7] in that reactions are not labelled, and thus present no information to the external environment. In this approach, the information is included in the solutions, not in the reactions.

Hence, in order to relate CHAMs we must relate solutions i.e. states; and a way of analyzing the information contained in the states must be given. Given two CHAMs, one more abstract and one more concrete, the more concrete one may include different molecules and transitions, because it introduces more details. Moreover, the overall architecture may be slightly different: a procedure call in the abstract level may be implemented in a handshaking with wait protocol in the concrete one. In some cases this may correspond to very clear requirements: a system designed for a centralized configuration may be adapted to work on a distributed network.

In what follows, $C(S)$ will denote the CHAM C with initial solution S.

Definition 1 *Let $C(S)$ and $C'(S')$ be two CHAMs. Let $T_\Sigma, T_{\Sigma'}$ be the term algebras of molecules of $C(S)$ and $C'(S')$ respectively. We call abstraction mapping a (partial) morphism $I : T_{\Sigma'} \to T_{\Sigma \cup \{*_s\}}$ where $*_s$ is a distinguished element for each sort s of T_Σ.*

By abuse of notation, we will say that $I : C'(S') \to C(S)$.

The intended meaning of $T_{\Sigma \cup \{*_s\}}$ is that of a conservative extension of T_Σ where the $*$ element is an absorbing element. That is $T_{\Sigma \cup \{*_s\}}$ is the initial algebra on $\Sigma \cup \{*_s\}$ equipped with the absorbing laws for $*_s$. These axioms can straightforwardly be turned into reaction laws in the corresponding CHAM.

We allow the mapping to be partial (some non-relevant molecules may not have a counterpart). Intuitively, this means that the concrete architecture may introduce more details and more elements to implement what is described in the abstract level. For instance, if the language used in a particular implementation supports only coroutines and not concurrency, a small scheduler may be included, which has no counterpart in the abstract description.

The following definition characterizes the abstraction homomorphisms which preserve refinements.

Definition 2 *Let $C(S)$ and $C'(S')$ be two CHAMs. Then, $I : C'(S') \to C(S)$ is a refinement preserving mapping if and only if I is an abstraction mapping that verifies the following conditions:*

1. $\forall a,b \in T_{\Sigma'}$ $I(a) = I(b) \Rightarrow \neg\exists m_1, m_2$ *membranes such that* $m_1 \neq m_2 \wedge a \in m_1 \wedge b \in m_2$.

2. $\forall$ *membrane* $m \in S$ $\exists$ *a membrane* $m' \in S'$ *such that* $I(m') \subseteq m$ *and*

3. $S \subseteq I(S')$.

The first condition ensures that if two molecules in the refined CHAM *come* from expanding the same molecule then they cannot be part of two different membranes. That is expansion through the refinement preserves the membrane boundaries.

The second condition says that the refinement cannot *forget* the membrane information. The third condition simply requires the two solutions as a whole to be related through the mapping.

Now, we are ready to formalize the notion of *dynamic* refinement.

Definition 3 *Let* $C(S)$ *and* $C'(S')$ *be two CHAMs. The CHAM* $C'(S')$ *is a* dynamic refinement *of* $C(S)$, *written* $C(S) \leadsto C'(S')$ *iff there exists a refinement preserving mapping* $I : C'(S') \to C(S)$ *and* $\forall$ *reactions* $S \to S_1$ *in* C, *there exists a derivation* $S' \to S_1'$ *in* C' *and* I *is a refinement preserving mapping for* $C(S_1), C'(S_1')$.

This definition is actually quite simple, it corresponds to a simulation: any derivation in C can be simulated by a corresponding one in C'.

It is clear that every CHAM $C(S)$ has an associated transition system, that results from taking all the states and derivations defined by it. Following the definitions above, it is possible to perform verification of refinements, using the associated transition systems. Moreover, if the associated transition systems are finite, the verification can be done automatically. This is the case, in general, in software architectures: the information contained in the description gives rise to a finite (usually large) set of possible interactions. If the associated transition system is not finite, it might imply that the information included in the CHAM is not relevant from an architectural point of view. This rule of thumb may be of help for the analysis of an architectural description. These methods of analysis can be used together with the more standard analysis of CHAMs using rewriting techniques.

4 Analysis of a Refinement

In this section we discuss our approach by means of the rule-based system example [6]. We first give the CHAM specification of the simpler architecture and then of the sophisticated one. We will then show that these two descriptions are actually equivalent with respect to the notion introduced in the previous section, thus assuring that all the relevant properties are preserved trough the refinement. This is an interesting example because it exhibits a modified structure in the refined architecture which also add new connectors with respect to the initial architecture. This can often happen and we believe it is important to allow it as long as the global behaviour of the original system is preserved.

4.1 The rule-based system: A simple Architecture

We begin with the simple architecture. As discussed above, a chemical abstract machine is specified by defining molecules, solutions, and transformation rules. In order to define molecules, we must define an algebra of molecules or, in other words, a syntax by which molecules can be built. Both architectures have the same syntax which starts with a set of constants P representing the processing elements, and two infix operators "$\diamond$" and $+$ that we use to express the status of a processing element. The connecting elements for the simple architecture are given by a third set C consisting of two kind of operations, i_E, o_E that act on the channels that are uniquely identified by numbers. The syntax Σ_{sim} of molecules M in the simple architecture is then

$$M ::= P \mid C \diamond M$$

$$P ::= \mathbf{WM} \mid \mathbf{RI} \mid \mathbf{KB} \mid \mathbf{RDS}$$

$$C ::= i\_E \mid o\_E \mid C + C$$
$$E ::= 0 \mid 1 \mid 2 \mid 3 \mid 4 \mid 5 \mid 6$$

We take as the set of syntactic elements the initial algebra in the class of all the Σ_{sim} algebras.

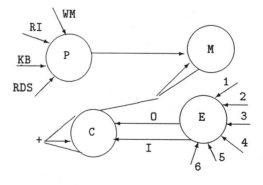

Figure 1: Signature of the Simplified CHAM

Let us provide some intuition behind this syntax. We use the operations i_E and o_E to represent data-element communication ports, where i is for input and o is for output . Finally, the infix operator "$\diamond$" is used to express the state of a processing element with respect to its input/output behavior, the $+$ operator specifies that both communications have to be performed and the order is not relevant.

The next step in specifying the architecture is to define an initial solution S_1. This solution is a subset of all possible molecules that can be constructed under Σ_{sim} and corresponds to the initial, static configuration of a system conforming to the architecture. Transformation rules applied to the solution define how the system dynamically evolves from its initial configuration.

$$S_1 = i\_0 \diamond (o\_1 + o\_2 + i\_3) \diamond \mathbf{WM},$$
$$o\_4 \diamond \mathbf{KB},$$
$$(i\_1 + i\_4) \diamond o\_5 \diamond \mathbf{RDS},$$
$$(i\_2 + i\_5) \diamond (o\_3 + o\_6) \diamond \mathbf{RI},$$

The final step is to define the transformation rules which describe the evolution of the system.

$$T_1 \equiv a + b \longrightarrow b + a$$
$$T_1' \equiv (a + b) + c \longrightarrow a + (b + c)$$
$$T_2 \equiv a + b \longrightarrow a \diamond b$$
$$T_3 \equiv \mathbf{KB} \longrightarrow o\_4 \diamond \mathbf{KB}$$
$$T_4 \equiv i\_X \diamond m_1, o\_X \diamond m_2 \longrightarrow m_1, m_2$$

4.2 The rule-based system: A sophisticated Architecture

In this section we present a more complex architecture for the rule based system.

Basically it represents a refinement of the structure of the system. In particular the Rule Interpreter molecule and the Rule and Data Selection molecule have been replaced with a set of interacting molecules as shown in figure 4. Moreover two other connections have been set up in between the Rule Interpreter and the Knowledge Base and the Rule and Data element Selection, respectively.

The syntax of this new architecture can be obtained by suitably enriching Σ_{sim}.

The syntax Σ_{soph} of molecules M in the sophisticated architecture is then

$$M \quad ::= P \mid C \diamond M$$

$$P \quad ::= \mathbf{WM} \mid RI \mid \mathbf{KB} \mid RDS$$

$$RI \quad ::= \mathbf{IN} \mid \mathbf{SCH} \mid \mathbf{ES} \mid \mathbf{CP}$$
$$RDS ::= \mathbf{RFC} \mid \mathbf{DFN} \mid \mathbf{AG} \mid \mathbf{MR}$$
$$C \quad ::= i\_E \mid o\_E \mid C + C$$
$$E \quad ::= 0 \mid 1 \mid 2 \mid 3 \mid 4 \mid 5 \mid 6 \mid 7 \mid 8 \mid 1.1 \mid 1.2 \mid 1.3$$
$$\mid 1.4 \mid 2.1 \mid 2.2 \mid 2.3 \mid 2.4 \mid 2.5$$

Let us now consider the initial solution: We introduce here the membrane construct in order to identify all those molecules that make part of the same substructure. That is all those molecules that correspond to the refinement of RI and RDS , respectively.

Let S_1'' be the initial solution for the sophisticated architecture, defined as follows.

$$S_1'' = i\_0 \diamond (o\_1 + o\_2 + i\_3) \diamond \mathbf{WM},$$
$$(o\_7 + o\_4) \diamond \mathbf{KB}, S_1^{RDS}, S_1^{RI}$$

where S_1^{RDS} is the initial solution for the refined version of the Rule and Data element Selection component and S_1^{RI} is the initial solution for the Rule Interpreter component.

$$S_1^{RDS} = \{\!| i\_4 \diamond o\_1.1 \diamond \mathbf{RFC},$$
$$(i\_1.1 + i\_1) \diamond o\_1.2 \diamond \mathbf{DFN},$$
$$(i\_1.4 + i\_1.2) \diamond o\_1.3 \diamond \mathbf{RFC},$$
$$(i\_8 + i\_1.3) \diamond o\_5 \diamond \mathbf{AG}, o\_1.4 \diamond \mathbf{MR} |\!\}$$

$$S_1^{RI} = \{\!| (i\_2 + o\_3 + i\_2.3 + o\_2.1 + i\_2.2) \diamond$$
$$(o\_6 + o\_7 + o\_8) \diamond \mathbf{I},$$
$$(i\_5 + i\_2.5 + i\_2.4) \diamond o\_2.3 \diamond \mathbf{SCH}$$
$$i\_2.1 \diamond (o\_2.2 + o\_2.4) \diamond \mathbf{ES}, o\_2.5 \diamond \mathbf{CP} |\!\}$$

Note that, in this second architecture two new connections are possible. Namely, the connection between the Interpreter, inside the membrane corresponding to the Rule Interpreter and the Knowledge base, and again the Interpreter and the Agenda, inside the membrane corresponding to the Rule and Data selection membrane.

As far as reaction rules are concerned, the sophisticated CHAM maintains exactly the same ones of the simplified CHAM Of course, in this case, since membranes are present in the initial solutions also the two general laws presented in Section 2 for dealing with membranes become part of the description.

4.3 Relating the two CHAM descriptions

According to what defined in the previous section, we want now to show that the sophisticated architecture of the interpreter is indeed a refinement of the

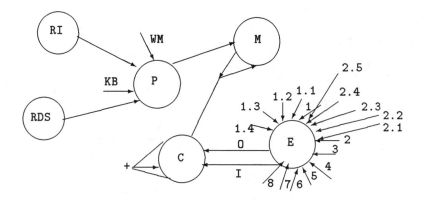

Figure 2: Signature of the Sophisticated CHAM

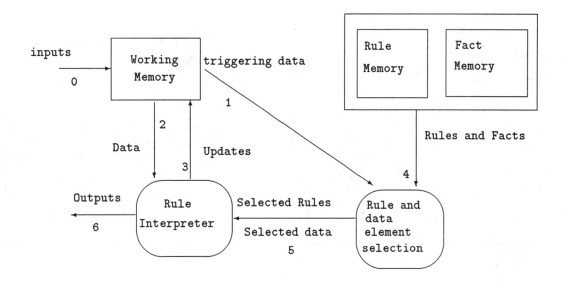

Figure 3: Simplified Interpreter Architecture

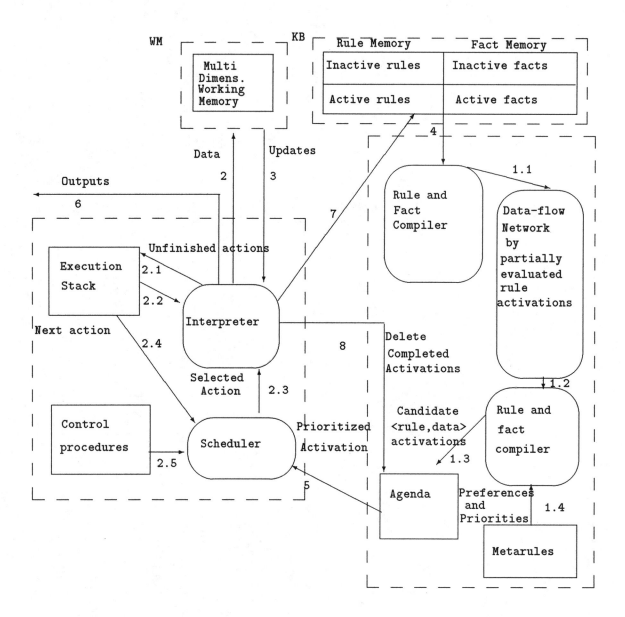

Figure 4: Sophisticated Interpreter Architecture

simple one. In order to do this we must proceed in two steps: first we have to show that a suitable morphism exists between the two sets of molecules, and we will do this by providing a mapping between the two initial algebras. This determines a correspondence between the static descriptions of the two architectures.

Then, we can prove that there exists a correspondence also between the dynamic behaviours of the two architectures by showing that for each derivation of the first CHAM there exists an *equivalent* derivation in the second one, according to Definition 3.

Let $I : T_{\Sigma_{soph}} \to T_{\Sigma_{sim} \cup \{*_s\}}$ be the following partial abstraction mapping:

1. $\forall t \in \text{RI } I(t) = \mathbf{RI}$

2. $\forall t \in \text{RDS } I(t) = \mathbf{RDS}$

3. $\forall t \in P, C, M \qquad\qquad I(t) = t.$

4. Let $t = \mathbf{7}\ t_1 = \mathbf{8} \in E$ then $I(t) = I(t_1) = *_E$ and for $t = \{1, 2, \ldots, 6\} \in E, I(t) = t.$

Note that the mapping is partial because we do not define the mapping for the new channels introduced by the sophisticated architecture, inside the membranes for local interactions i.e. $1.1, 1.2, 1.3, 1.4, 2.1, 2.2, 2.3, 2.4, 2.5.$

It is straightforward to see that the above defined mapping is indeed an abstraction morphism and furthermore it is a *refinement* abstraction morphism according to Definition 2.

Proposition 1 *The abstraction mapping $I : T_{\Sigma_{soph}} \to T_{\Sigma_{sim} \cup \{*_s\}}$ defined above is a refinement preserving mapping.*

Proof 1 *According to Definition 2, we have to check three conditions: The first one is easily verified since all the molecule in the sophisticated architecture which come from the expansion of $\mathbf{RI}$ and $\mathbf{RDS}$, respectively, are included into two different membranes. The second condition does not apply in our case since in $T_{\Sigma_{sim}}$ there are no membranes, and the third is straightforwardly verified since $T_{\Sigma_{soph}}$ is a syntactic extension of $T_{\Sigma_{sim}}$.*

The next step is to show that also the dynamic behaviour of the simplified CHAM is preserved under the refinement into the sophisticated one. In order to do this, according to Definition 3, we have to show that, given the above defined mapping $I : T_{\Sigma_{soph}} \to T_{\Sigma_{sim} \cup \{*_s\}}$, and the initial solutions $S_1, S"_1$ then for any reaction $S_1 \to S_2$ in the simplified CHAM

there exists a reaction $S"_1 \to S"_2$ in the sophisticated CHAM and I is a preserving mapping for $C_{\Sigma_{soph}}(S"_2), C_{\Sigma_{sim}}(S_2).$

Note that in order to start the reaction we have actually to enrich the initial solution with a molecule which represents the initial data. Therefore, we assume that the two initial solutions also contain an instance of the molecule $o\_0 \diamond \mathbf{Init}$.

Proposition 2 *The sophisticated CHAM $C_{\Sigma_{soph}}(S"_1)$ is a dynamic refinement of the simplified CHAM $C_{\Sigma_{sim}}(S_1).$*

Proof 2 *We will not give a complete account of the proof, but only sketch the main arguments used along it. The proof is by induction on the length n in the rule derivation of the simplified CHAM. Let us consider the reaction steps that can be performed by the simplified CHAM starting from the initial solution S_1 augmented with the initial data molecule. For our purposes the only interesting reactions are those which involve the molecules $\mathbf{RDS}, \mathbf{RI}$. Thus we have to show that whenever a reaction occurs in the simplified Cham with respect to $\mathbf{RDS}, \mathbf{RI}$ respectively, the same can be performed in the sophisticated Cham and the reached solutions are still related by the mapping. Let us consider reactions which involve $\mathbf{RDS}$. Suppose to have the sequence $S_1 \to S_2 \to \cdots \to S_n \to S_{n+1}$ and consider only $S_n \to S_{n+1}$ where S_n contains an instance of the molecules $o\_1 \diamond (o\_2 + i\_3) \diamond \mathbf{WM}$ and $i\_1 \diamond i\_4 \diamond o\_5 \diamond \mathbf{RDS}$. The transformation can be only performed by applying T_4.*

By inductive hypothesis there is in the sophisticated CHAM a simulating derivation, such that it contains a solution S'_m which is related through the mapping I to S_n. Therefore it must contain the same instance of the molecule $o\_1 \diamond (o\_2 + i\_3) \diamond \mathbf{WM}$ and, inside the membrane, an instance of a molecule which exhibits the potential communication i_1. Then we have only to apply the proper reactions inside the membrane in order to extract from the membrane the connector i_1, to simulate the wanted reaction.

In this way we can prove that also the dynamic behaviour of the two CHAMS is correctly preserved through the refinement.

5   Conclusions

In this paper we have presented an approach to formally relate CHAM descriptions of a software architecture at different level of abstractions. Given the chosen description formalism it has been possible to suitably relate both the static and the dynamic descriptions of the software architectures. Another point we would like to stress is that the CHAM formalism naturally provides a concept which can be used to express extra–functional requirements on the structure under description. The membrane concept nicely capture the idea of localizing building blocks at a very early stage of design whose internal refinement can be performed later on in the development process. Our definition of correct refinement takes the membrane concept into account and allows for mantaining the membrane structure also with respect to dynamics. In this way we do not consider acceptable any CHAM which simulates the dynamic behaviour of the one under refinement, but only those ones which also preserve the membrane structure. For example, let us imagine to describe the software architecture of a system which for fault tolerance problem needs the redundant presence of two identical components. This can be expressed at a very early stage of design. When this architecture is refined we want to be able to express that the redundancy has to be mantained, even if there exist behaviourally equivalent descriptions which do not exhibit this redundancy. Moreover, our approach does not constraint too much the notion of refining. The case study presented in the previous section can be treated in our framework as a refinement, as one would reasonably expect. This is not the case in other logic based approaches like [13, 14] which would instead not permit the existence of the two new connections $7, 8$ in order to establish a refinement relation between the two architectures.

Future work include the treatment of other case studies and the attempt to automatize the correctness proofs as much as possible. Furthermore, following the studies carried on in other fields of verification of properties of complex systems, like for process algebras, it is possible to investigate a larger set of *simulation* based relations which can be tailored on the particular architectural style or design constraint.

References

[1] G. Berry and G. Boudol. The Chemical Abstract Machine. *Theoretical Computer Science*, 96:217–248, 1992.

[2] G. Boudol, I. Castellani, M. Hennessy, and A. Kiehn. Observing Localities. *Theoretical Computer Science*, 114:31–61, 1993.

[3] G. Boudol, I. Castellani, M. Hennessy, and A. Kiehn. A Theory of Processes with Localities. *Formal Aspects of Computing*, 6:165–200, 1994.

[4] E. Brinksma, B. Jonsson, and F. Orava. Refining Interfaces of Communicating Systems. In *TAPSOFT '91: Proceedings of the 3th International Joint Conference CAAP/FASE*, number 494 in Lecture Notes in Computer Science, pages 297–312. Springer-Verlag, April 1991.

[5] W. Tichy D. Garlan and F. Paulisch. Summary of the Dagsthul Workshop on Software Architecture. *SIGSOFT Software Engineering Notes*, July 1995.

[6] D. Garlan and M. Shaw. An Introduction on Software Architecture. In *Advances in Software Engineering and Knowledge Engineering*, 1993.

[7] C.A.R. Hoare. *Communicating Sequential Processes*. Prentice-Hall, Englewood Cliffs, New Jersey, 1985.

[8] P. Inverardi and C. Priami. Automatic Verification of Distributed Systems: The Process Algebra Approach. *Formal Methods in System Design*, 1996. To appear.

[9] P. Inverardi, C. Priami, and D. Yankelevich. Automatizing distributed Reasoning on Distributed Concurrent Systems. *Formal Aspects of Computing*, 6:676–695, 1994.

[10] P. Inverardi and A.L. Wolf. Formal Specifications and Analysis of Software Architectures Using the Chemical Abstract Machine Model. *IEEE Transactions on Software Engineering*, 21(4):100–114, April 1995.

[11] R. Milner. *Communication and Concurrency*. Prentice-Hall, Englewood Cliffs, New Jersey, 1989.

[12] U. Montanari and D. Yankelevich. A Parametric Approach to Localities. In *Proceedings of the 19th ICALP Conference*, number 623 in Lecture Notes in Computer Science, pages 617–628. Springer-Verlag, July 1992.

[13] M. Moriconi and Xiaolei Qian. Correctness and Composition of Software Architectures. *SIGSOFT Software Engineering Notes*, 19(5):164–174, December 1994.

[14] M. Moriconi, Xiaolei Qian, and R.A. Riemenschneider. Correct Architectures Refinement. *IEEE Transactions on Software Engineering*, 21(4):356–372, April 1995.

[15] G. Plotkin. A Structural Approach to Operational Semantics. Technical Report DAIMI FN–19, University of Aarhus, 1981.

Specification and Verification of Real-Time Properties Using LOTOS and SQTL

Abderrahmane Lakas

Gordon S. Blair

Amanda Chetwynd

Computing Department
Lancaster University
Lancaster LA1 4YR, UK.

Computing Department
Lancaster University
Lancaster LA1 4YR, UK.

Computing Department
Lancaster University
Lancaster LA1 4YR, UK.

Abstract

In this paper we present a new approach to the formal specification of distributed real-time systems using the formal description technique LOTOS together with a real-time temporal logic SQTL. This approach characterized by a separation of concerns, aims to construct abstractly a model from the a functional specification according to real-time constraints. The functional behaviour is described in LOTOS without regard for the time critical constraints. The specification is then extended with precise real-time properties written in SQTL. We present a method to generate a timing event scheduler from the properties in order to monitor the functional behaviour. The model of event schedulers is based on timed automata and intended to be used for an automata-based verification technique.

1 Introduction

Over the past few years there have been several formal techniques used for the design and verification of distributed systems. The most popular ones are process algebras, Petri nets and finite state machines based techniques. More recently, the rise of multimedia applications and real-time systems required the definition of new techniques including both qualitative and real-time analysis. Indeed, time critical properties have become the main issue in such applications and therfore verification is not complete until these properties are satisfied.

Due to the fact that the qualitative and the quantitative description of systems are of different natures, we opted for a methodology that uses two description techniques: one for the functional behaviour and one for the quantitative information. Our work focuses on the use of the LOTOS specification language [7] for the formal description of functional behaviour, and a stochastic temporal logic for the specification of timing constraints. LOTOS has been proved to be a powerful formal description technique with a well de-

fined semantics. Considerable research has been carried out on the verification of LOTOS specifications. The verification techniques are mainly based either on bisimulation relations [13] or on simulation techniques as in [9]. We also consider SQTL as a linear real-time temporal logic used for the description of timing properties. The purpose of this language is not only to specify the temporal ordering between the events occurring during the system's life but also to specify the time interval between these events. A wide range of real-time temporal logics has been defined in the last few years. We can nonexhaustively cite [1], [11] and [17]. The temporal logic we present in this work is an extension of QTL [5] to include probabilistic and stochastic features. For example, QTL is commonly used to express *bounded responsiveness* properties of the standard form:

$$\Box \, (send \rightarrow \Diamond_{\leq d} \, receive)$$

which states that every time an action *send* happens, the action *receive* will occur within d time-units. SQTL extends this capability to enable the expression of *stochastically bounded responsiveness* properties such as:

$$\Box \, (send \rightarrow \Diamond_{Exp,\lambda} \, receive)$$

where *receive* will now occur within a delay randomly determined with respect to an exponential distribution with an average rate of $\frac{1}{\lambda}$. A previous paper [12] describes the use of this stochastic information for simulation and performance analysis. This paper focuses on more formal verification using SQTL.

Two kinds of timing properties are expressed in SQTL. Firstly, *real-time assumptions* are used to impose real-time constraints over the underlying LOTOS behaviour. The combination of LOTOS and these assumptions allows us to build up a real-time model based on timed automata[2]. The events specified

Proceedings of IWSSD-8

by LOTOS are then scheduled according to the real-time assumptions. Secondly, *real-time requirements* are used to express the desired real-time properties of the timed model. The verification problem now consists of checking the conformity of our real-time model in respect to the requirements. Due to the decidability problem related to real-time logics in general[3], the language used for the description of the requirements is reduced to a fragment of SQTL.

Our approach is motivated by the desire to maintain a separation between functional concerns and real-time concerns. This approach, first adopted in [4], is used in order to tackle complex systems in a simpler way. This mainly allows us to reuse the qualitatively validated specification and extend it with the time constraint requirements for further timing analysis. Also, with this approach, there is no need to change the functional specification when timing constraints are changed. Furthermore, it is easier for the designer to tune the whole system by adding more time constraints.

The paper is structured as follows. In section 2 we give a short description of the language LOTOS and its syntax and semantics. Then we introduce, in section 3, the real-time temporal logic SQTL. After giving its syntax and semantics, we present an overview of the main properties expressible in SQTL. In this section we focus on the integration of real-time issues in the logic. In section 5, we define the real-time event scheduler model and view the way the SQTL formulae are translated into real-time event schedulers. We also show how LOTOS systems are composed with event schedulers in order to build real-time systems. In section 6, we present an example of a real-time stream protocol illustrating the generation of a real-time system from its functional behaviour and real-time assumptions. In section 7, we discuss our main approach to the verification of real-time systems in respect to real-time requirements. Finally, we end with a conclusion in section 8.

2 Background on LOTOS
2.1 Syntax

The specification language LOTOS [7] is a process algebra based on CCS [16]. Its terms are called behaviour expressions which are composed with a few operators. The set of LOTOS behaviour expressions is defined as follows:

- **stop** is the unsuccessful termination. The process executing this action is locked,

- **exit** is the successful termination. This action also permits the control, when a termination is

reached, to pass from one process to another,

- $g; B$ the process can execute an action offered on the gate g and then behaves like B

- $B \backslash G$ the process behaves like B except for actions belonging to G; in this case, these actions are hidden from the environment,

- $B_1 [] B_2$ the process has a non-deterministic choice to behave either like B_1 or like B_2. When one alternative is selected, the other one is discarded,

- $B_1 [> B_2$ the process behaves like B_1 but at any time it could start executing B_2. When it does so, the alternative B_1 is discarded,

- $B_1 \gg B_2$ the process behaves like B_1 and when B_1 terminates successfully, it behaves like B_2,

- $B_1 |[G]| B_2$ the process in this case corresponds to the concurrent behaviour of B_1 and B_2. If the actions are executed on gates from G then B_1 and B_2 synchronize their execution, otherwise the two sides progress in an interleaving fashion.

Action:	$\dfrac{}{g; B \xrightarrow{g} B}$	$\dfrac{}{\text{exit} \xrightarrow{\delta} \text{stop}}$
Hidding:	$\dfrac{B \xrightarrow{g} B' \ , \ g \notin G}{B \backslash G \xrightarrow{g} B' \backslash G}$	$\dfrac{B \xrightarrow{g} B' \ , \ g \in G}{B \backslash G \xrightarrow{i} B' \backslash G}$
Choice:	$\dfrac{B_1 \xrightarrow{g} B_1'}{B_1 [] B_2 \xrightarrow{g} B_1'}$	$\dfrac{B_2 \xrightarrow{g} B_2'}{B_1 [] B_2 \xrightarrow{g} B_2'}$
Enabling:	$\dfrac{B_1 \xrightarrow{g} B_1'}{B_1 \gg B_2 \xrightarrow{g} B_1' \gg B_2}$	$\dfrac{B_1 \xrightarrow{\delta} B_1'}{B_1 \gg B_2 \xrightarrow{\delta} B_2}$
Disabling:	$\dfrac{B_1 \xrightarrow{g} B_1'}{B_1 [> B_2 \xrightarrow{g} B_1' [> B_2}$	$\dfrac{B_1 \xrightarrow{\delta} B_1'}{B_1 [> B_2 \xrightarrow{\delta} B_1'}$
	$\dfrac{B_2 \xrightarrow{g} B_2'}{B_1 [> B_2 \xrightarrow{g} B_2'}$	
Parallel:	$\dfrac{B_1 \xrightarrow{g} B_1' \ , \ g \notin G}{B_1 |[G]| B_2 \xrightarrow{g} B_1' |[G]| B_2}$	$\dfrac{B_2 \xrightarrow{g} B_2' \ , \ g \notin G}{B_1 |[G]| B_2 \xrightarrow{g} B_1 |[G]| B_2'}$
	$\dfrac{B_2 \xrightarrow{g} B_2' \ , \ B_1 \xrightarrow{g} B_1' \ , \ g \in G}{B_1 |[G]| B_2 \xrightarrow{g} B_1' |[G]| B_2'}$	

Table 1: The operational semantics of LOTOS

2.2 Semantics

A LOTOS specification is interpreted as a *Labelled Transition System*. A transition $B \xrightarrow{a} B'$ indicates that the system behaving as B, executes an action a and moves to B'. The following presents the structure of a labelled transition system which represent the LOTOS semantics.

Definition 2.1 *A labelled transition system over the set Act is defined by the tuple* $LTS = \langle S, \rightarrow, s_0 \rangle$ *where:*

- S *is a finite set of states,*

- $s_0 \in S$ *is the initial, state*

- $\rightarrow \subseteq S \times Act \times S$ *is a transition relation:*
  $\rightarrow = \{\xrightarrow{a} | a \in Act, \exists(s, s') \in S \times S, s \xrightarrow{a} s'\}.$

The set of transitions that a LOTOS system may execute is derived from the inference rules defined in table 1. In order to calculate the associated LTS of a LOTOS system, we define the function $Der(B)$ as the smallest set satisfying the following properties:

- $B \in Der(B)$

- if $B' \in Der(B)$ and $\exists a \in Act, B' \xrightarrow{a} B''$ then $B'' \in Der(B)$

Der is finite since we assume that the finiteness conditions holds for the specifications that we consider. A specification is considered finite when the processes are guarded and regular [14]. This condition allows us to calculate the labelled transition system corresponding to a LOTOS process. Given a behaviour expression B then $LTS(B) = \langle S, \rightarrow, s_0 \rangle$ where:

- $S = Der(B)$ and $s_0 = B$

- $\rightarrow = \{\xrightarrow{a} | a \in Act(B), \exists s, s' \in Der(B), s \xrightarrow{a} s'\}$

3 Stochastic and Real-Time Temporal Logic

In our research, we use a linear time temporal logic featuring boolean connectives and temporal operators. Formulae are interpreted on infinite sequences of states $s_0 s_1 ...$ For the sake of simplicity, we consider here a minimal version of SQTL with a constant operator *True*, the negation $\neg$ and the disjunction $\vee$. Other classical boolean connectives can be derived as well: $\psi_1 \wedge \psi_2 \equiv \neg(\neg\psi_1 \vee \neg\psi_2)$ and $\psi_1 \rightarrow \psi_2 \equiv \neg\psi_1 \vee \psi_2$. The temporal operators consist of two dual classes of operators: future operators and past operators:

- Future operators: $\bigcirc\psi$ (read *next*) which means that ψ will hold in the next state, and $\psi_1 \, \mathcal{U} \, \psi_2$ (read *until*) which means that ψ_1 will hold at every state from now on until at some state in the future ψ_2 holds.

- Past operators: $\ominus\psi$ (read *previous*) which means that ψ has held in the previous state, and $\mathcal{S}$ (read *since*) which means that ψ_2 has held at some state in the past and since that state ψ_1 has continuously held until now.

Other temporal operators can be derived for convenient use like:

$$\Diamond\, p \equiv True \, \mathcal{U} \, p \qquad \ominus p \equiv True \, \mathcal{S} \, p$$
$$\Box\, p \equiv \neg\Diamond\,\neg p \qquad \boxminus p \equiv \neg\ominus\,\neg p$$

where $\Diamond\, \psi$ means that statement ψ will *eventually* hold at some state in the future, $\Box\, \psi$ means that *henceforth*, ψ will hold at every state in the future, $\ominus\psi$ means that *once*, at some state in the past, ψ has held, and $\boxminus\psi$ means that ψ *has-always-been* held in the past.

In order to quantify the time distance between events, the states are now extended with dates and the modalities with quantitative information on the temporal distance between these states.

The first extension, in common with other real-time logics, is to allow the expression of quantitative modalities such as:

$$\psi_1 \, \mathcal{U}_{\leq d} \, \psi_2$$

where d is a time constant that bounds the time during which ψ_1 will hold and at the end of which ψ_2 will hold. This formulation is equivalent to

$$\bigvee_{0 \leq \delta \leq d} \psi_1 \, \mathcal{U}_{=\delta} \, \psi_2$$

or in more compact and more general form $\psi_1 \, \mathcal{U}_{[l,u]} \, \psi_2$. The time interval between events can also be stochastically distributed as in:

$$\psi_1 \, \mathcal{U}_{=Exp,\lambda} \, \psi_2$$

where (Exp, λ) means that the time interval d is now randomized according to an exponential distribution with a mean interval of $\frac{1}{\lambda}$, i.e, d is following an exponential distribution whose probability density function is $f(d) = \frac{1}{\lambda}.e^{-\frac{1}{\lambda} \cdot d}$ with $d \geq 0$ and $\int_0^\infty f(x)\, dx = 1$.

The temporal logic expressing only qualitative properties represents then a subset of quantified temporal logic where time distance between the situations is undefined, i.e:

$$\Box\, \psi \equiv \Box_{<\infty} \quad \Diamond\, \psi \equiv \Diamond_{<\infty} \quad \psi_1 \, \mathcal{U} \, \psi_2 \equiv \psi_1 \, \mathcal{U}_{<\infty} \, \psi_2$$

We also define a "*probabilistic or*" which is an *exclusive or* quantified by a probability such that $\psi_1 \overset{p}{\vee} \psi_2$ with $p \in [0,1]$ and standing for either ψ_1 holds with probability p or ψ_2 holds with probability $1 - p$.

3.1 Formal presentation

3.1.1 Syntax

The complete syntax of SQTL is then defined by the following rule:

$$\psi \quad := \quad a \quad | \quad True \quad | \quad \neg\psi$$
$$| \quad \psi \vee \psi \quad | \quad \psi \overset{p}{\vee} \psi$$
$$| \quad \bigcirc_{\prec Q}\psi \quad | \quad \ominus_{\prec Q}\psi$$
$$| \quad \psi\, \mathcal{U}_{\prec Q}\, \psi \quad | \quad \psi\, \mathcal{S}_{\prec Q}\, \psi$$

where $\prec \in \{=, <, \leq\}$ and Q a quantification that could be any constant value or an exponential distribution and $p \in [0, 1]$

3.1.2 Semantics

We define a *time sequence* $\vec{\tau} = \tau_0\tau_1...\tau_i...$ as a finite or infinite sequence of positive values $\tau_i \in \mathbb{R}_{\geq 0}$ such that $\vec{\tau}$ increases *monotonically* and *progressively* [2]; that is $\forall i \geq 0 : \tau_i \leq \tau_{i+1}$. Let $\mathcal{D}$ be the domain of time delays ranging over positive reals $\mathbb{R}_{\geq 0}$. An *interval sequence* over $\mathcal{D}$ is a finite or infinite sequence $\vec{I} = I_0I_1...I_n...$ such that for some time sequence $\tau = \tau_0\tau_1...\tau_i...$ we have $I_i = \tau_{i+1} - \tau_i$. We say that an interval sequence is following a stochastic distribution X with parameter λ if the interval values of $\vec{I}$ are also values of (X, λ). We then denote by $\mathcal{D}_{X,\lambda} \subseteq \mathcal{D}$ the interval sequence generated by the distribution X of parameter λ.

Let $\mathcal{P}$ be the finite set of atomic propositions. A *state* is a subset of $\mathcal{P}$. We then denote by $S = 2^{\mathcal{P}}$ the set of all possible states. We define the *timed state* as a pair (s, τ) of state $s \in S$ and a time $\tau \in \mathbb{R}_{\geq 0}$. A *computation* is then a possibly infinite sequence of timed states:

$$\sigma = (s_0, \tau_0), (s_1\tau_1), ..., (s_i\tau_i), ...$$

where $s_i \in S, \tau_i \in \mathbb{R}_{\geq 0}$.

The *evaluation* $I : (S, \mathbb{R}_{\geq 0}) \to 2^{\mathcal{P}}$ is a mapping of each *timed state* (s, τ) where $s \in S$ and $\tau \in \mathbb{R}_{\geq 0}$, to the set of propositions $I(s, \tau) \subseteq \mathcal{P}$ that are true in s at τ. Then, we define the *satisfaction relation* $\models$ between a temporal formula ψ, a computation σ and the time position τ in the computation as follows:

$$(\sigma, \tau_i) \models True$$
$(\sigma, \tau_i) \models a$	iff	$a \in I(\sigma, \tau_i)$
$(\sigma, \tau_i) \models \neg\psi$	iff	$(\sigma, \tau_i) \not\models \psi$
$(\sigma, \tau_i) \models \psi_1 \vee \psi_2$	iff	$(\sigma, \tau_i) \models \psi_1$ or $(\sigma, \tau_i) \models \psi_2$

$(\sigma, \tau_i) \models \psi_1 \overset{p}{\vee} \psi_2$ iff $(\sigma, \tau_i) \models \psi_1$ with probability p and $(\sigma, \tau_i) \models \psi_2$ with probability $1 - p$

$(\sigma, \tau_i) \models \bigcirc_{X,\lambda}\psi$ iff $\exists I \in \mathcal{D}_{X,\lambda}, (\sigma, \tau_{i+1}) \models \psi$ and $\tau_{i+1} = \tau_i + I$

$(\sigma, \tau_i) \models \psi_1\, \mathcal{U}_{X,\lambda}\, \psi_2$ iff $\exists I \in \mathcal{D}_{X,\lambda}$ such that $(\sigma, \tau_i+I) \models \psi_2$ and $\forall I' \in \mathcal{D}$ with $0 \leq I' < I$: $(\sigma, \tau_i + I') \models \psi_1$

When the time intervals are reduced to constant values, the prefix X is replaced by a constant and λ is omitted.

4 Using LOTOS with SQTL

A LOTOS system is seen as a black box interacting with its environment through action synchronizations. A synchronization holds when both the system and its environment agree to synchronize. By introducing real-time assumptions, these synchronizations are now constrained and forced to happen at appropriate times. In addition to the ordering causality between events provided by LOTOS, we provide an extension with time causality. This extension leads to three consequences: event dating, reduced non-determinism and timed synchronization.

- Dated events: The introduction of quantified temporal logic allows us to deduce the time delays between LOTOS events from the timed states. Indeed, derivations like $B \overset{a}{\to} B'$ are now extended with time such that $(B, \tau) \overset{a}{\to} (B', \tau')$ with τ and τ' represent the time-stamps associated with states B and B' such that $\delta = \tau' - \tau$ indicate the amount of time that a should wait before it happens. Thus, we write $B \overset{a,\delta}{\longrightarrow} B'$. The state/time association should be made according to the the introduced real-time assumptions.

- Reduced non-determinism: The introduction of real-time assumptions reduces the non-determinist alternatives in LOTOS in a different way. Firstly, events are made deterministic by stating when they should occur. Consider the following expression:

$$B = a; B_1 \;[\,]\; b; B_2$$

If action a and action b are scheduled to happen after respectively δ_1 and δ_2 time-units, then the chosen action is enabled as soon as the associated delay has passed. This property, called the *maximal progress property*, guarantees maximal progress of time. Consequently, $a; B_1 \; [\;] \; b; B_2 \xrightarrow{a,\delta_1} B_1$ if a is enabled and $\delta_1 > \delta_2$ otherwise $a; B_1 \; [\;] \; b; B_2 \xrightarrow{b,\delta_2} B_2$ if b is enabled. Secondly, the non-determinism can also explicitly be reduced using probability quantification using the "*exclusive or*" operator. For instance, the formula:

$$\Box \, (send \to \Diamond \, (error \overset{0.1}{\vee} receive))$$

reduces the non-determinism in the LOTOS expression $send; (error[\,]receive)$ using a probabilistic distribution $\{0.1, 0.9\}$. This construction is similar to the probabilistic choice introduced in timed LOTOS [15]: $send; (error[\,]_p receive)$.

- Timed synchronization: The synchronization through the parallel operator $|[...]|$ in LOTOS is now explicitly or implicitly timed by specifying the time at which it takes place. As actions are constrained with deadlines, their synchronization are assumed to have the same constraints. In addition to the semantics of synchronization in LOTOS we assume that synchronization fails when the synchronized actions have no compatible deadlines. In the expression:

$$a; B_1 \, |[a]| \, a; B_2$$

the synchronization will occur after the same delay δ as the one action a must wait for, i.e: $a; B_1 |[a]| a; B_2 \xrightarrow{a,\delta} B_1 |[a]| B_2$. However, due to the maximal progress property, when the deadline constraint is bounded by an interval, the participating agents should engage in the synchronization as soon as they are ready.

5 Event Schedulers
5.1 The Event Scheduler Model

The aim of this section is to build up an automaton-based model from the timing properties which will be able to schedule the functional behaviour according to the specified real-time assumptions. In other words, every action enabled to happen in the labelled transition system is submitted to the event scheduler which will decide, according to the timing properties, if this action is going to happen, and, if so, will indicate when it will happen.

The resulting model of the event scheduler and the LTS is represented by a *timed labelled transition system* where each labelled transition $\xrightarrow{a}$ in the LTS

is associated with a fixed delay which is either determined from a probabilistic distribution or from a bounded interval, such that we have transitions which are extended to $\xrightarrow{(a,\delta)}$. Based on the model of timed automata[1] [2] and probabilistic automata [18], the event scheduler is seen as a labelled transition system $A = \langle S, \Sigma, E, s_0 \rangle$ extended with timers, time constraints, an updating function, and a probability distribution over the elements of Σ. The timers are set to *deadline* values and decreased with the elapsing of time. The transitions are chosen in accordance with the constraints stated over the reading of the timers and the probability distribution associated with the transitions.

Definition 5.1 *An event scheduler is represented by the tuple $Sch = \langle S, \Sigma, T, E, P, R, \Pi, s_0 \rangle$ where:*

- S *is a finite set of states*

- $s_0 \in S$ *is the initial state.*

- Σ *is a finite set of events*

- $E \subseteq S \times S$ *is a finite set of edges.* $(s_1, s_2) \in E \Rightarrow \exists a \in \Sigma: s_1 \xrightarrow{a} s_2$.

- T *is a finite set of timers. The timers are initially set to a deadline value. The value of every timer coupled with the current state represents a generalized state $(s, [T_i]_i)$ where $s \in S$ and $[T_i]_i$ denotes the current reading of all timers $T_i \in T$. The reading of every timer changes automatically with the progress of time. It is decreased with the elapsed delay: $(s, [T_i]) \xrightarrow{(a,\epsilon)} (s', [T_i \leftarrow T_i - \epsilon])$.*

- $P: E \to \mathcal{C}_T$ *is a function associating with each edge in E a timing constraint from $\mathcal{C}_T$. A transition $s_1 \xrightarrow{a} s_2$ is enabled if the constraint $P(s_1, a, s_2)$ holds. $\mathcal{C}_T$ is constructed from algebraic relation $\prec \in \{=, <, \leq\}$ with the standard form*

$$\mu = \bigwedge [\tau_l \prec T_i \prec \tau_u]$$

where τ_l, τ_u are values representing respectively the lower and upper bound of the timer T_i. Then we say that a value ϵ satisfies a constraint μ and write $\epsilon \models \mu$ if ϵ is a possible solution to μ.

- $R: E \to \mathcal{V}$ *is reset function associating a deadline value from $\mathcal{D}^*$ with each edge in E. $\mathcal{V}: 2^T \to \mathcal{D}^*$ is*

---

[1] The main difference between this model and the timed automata [2] resides in the use of timers rather than clocks that increase indefinitely. The reset function is extended to any positive deadline value rather than a zero-initialization.

a partial function when applied on timers $T' \subseteq T$, it resets the elements of T' to corresponding values $\nu \in \mathcal{D}^*$. $\mathcal{D}^*$ denotes either the set $\mathcal{D}$ of fixed intervals or the set $\mathcal{D}_{X,\lambda}$ of stochastic intervals. When the reset is not defined, the timer is automatically reset according to the time elapsed:

- $\Pi : E \rightarrow [0,1]$ *is a probability distribution associating a probability with each edge in E such that $\forall (s, s_i) \in E : \sum\limits_{s_i \in S} \Pi(s, s_i) = 1$. When the probabilities of outcoming edges of some state are not specified, the choice is resolved as a non-determinism.*

We denote by $s_1 \xrightarrow{\mu, a, \nu} s_2$ the full transition which moves the event scheduler from a state s_1 to the state s_2 by executing the action a. The action is fired after a delay ϵ determined according to the timing constraint μ; i.e, $\epsilon \models \mu$. The re-initialization of the timers is then carried out according to ν. Timers not affected by the re-initialization are automatically decreased with the elapsing time; i.e, ϵ. The event scheduler behaviour is formally defined by the following rules:

$$\frac{Sch \xrightarrow{\mu, a} Sch' \text{ and } \epsilon \models \mu}{(Sch, [T_i]) \xrightarrow{a} (Sch, [T_i \leftarrow T_i - \epsilon])}$$

$$\frac{Sch \xrightarrow{\mu, a} Sch' \text{ and } \epsilon \models \mu \text{ and } Sch \xrightarrow{\nu} Sch'}{(Sch, [T_i]) \xrightarrow{a} (Sch, [T_i \leftarrow \nu(T_i)])}$$

5.2 Translating Real-Time Constraints to Event Schedulers

In order to give an operational interpretation of the event scheduler, we define a *derivative* of a formula at some state as the formula that holds in the next state. Intuitively, given a timed state sequence σ, if for some formula ψ, $(\sigma, \tau_i) \models \psi$ then the derivative $D_\alpha[\![\psi]\!]$ is such that $(\sigma, \tau_{i+1}) \models D_\alpha[\![\psi]\!]$ with $\alpha \in I(\sigma, \tau_{i+1})$.

The event scheduler is then interpreted as a finite state machine where states are defined as a pair $(\psi, [T_i])$ representing the state and the corresponding timer values at which ψ holds. The transitions from state to state indicate the move in the interpretation of the current formula: $(\psi, [T_i]) \xrightarrow{\alpha} (D_\alpha[\![\psi]\!], [T_i'])$. The values $[T_i]$ and $[T_i']$ correspond respectively to the previous and actual reading of the timers. The state $(\psi, [T_i])$ represents also a projection of the timed state (σ, τ_i) where $\psi \in I(\sigma, \tau_i)$ and $[T_i]$ are the reading of timers at time τ_i. We also denote by $D_{\alpha, \mu}[\![\psi]\!]$ the derivative of ψ with α with a condition that the constraint $\mu \in \mathcal{C}_C$ holds. When μ is omitted D_α stands for $D_{\alpha, True}$.

This approach allows us to build an event scheduler that permits only appropriate behaviours since the input real-time properties are satisfied by construction.

The event scheduler moves from state to state according to the initial property. In first stage, we inductively deduce the derivative of a formula according to its structure:

$$
\begin{aligned}
D_\alpha[\![True]\!] &= True \\
D_\alpha[\![a]\!] &= True \text{ if } a = \alpha, \ False \text{ if not} \\
D_\alpha[\![\neg\psi]\!] &= \neg D_{\alpha, \mu}[\![\psi]\!] \\
D_\alpha[\![\psi_1 \vee \psi_2]\!] &= D_\alpha[\![\psi_1]\!] \vee D_\alpha[\![\psi_2]\!] \\
D_{\alpha, T=0}[\![\bigcirc_{=\delta}\psi]\!] &= \psi \text{ where initially } T \leftarrow \delta \\
D_\alpha[\![\psi_1 \, \mathcal{U}_{=\delta} \, \psi_2]\!] &= D_{\alpha, T=0}[\![\psi_2]\!] \vee \\
&\quad [D_{\alpha, T \geq 0}[\![\psi_1]\!] \wedge (\psi_1 \, \mathcal{U}_{=T} \, \psi_2)] \\
&\quad \text{where initially } T \leftarrow \delta
\end{aligned}
$$

The following function D^* denotes the transitive closure of D as defined by the following properties:

- $\psi \in D^*[\![\psi]\!]$

- if $\phi \in D^*$ then $\forall a \in \Sigma : D_a[\![\phi]\!] \in \psi$

The set D^* corresponds to the set of states, each representing the state of the formula interpretation and the current time. It is easy to see that the size of the transitive closure is exponential in the size of the formula. However, it is not necessary to worry about the size of D^* since most formulae are not understandable when their size is over 3.

The set of timers is built inductively from the structure of the formula. Every temporal operator with a real-time modality corresponds to a timer. The number of timers is then bounded by the number of temporal operators: $|T| \leq |\psi|$. If we denote by $T(\psi)$ the set of timers needed to collect the time quantification over the formula ψ, then we have:

$$
\begin{aligned}
T[\![True]\!] &= \emptyset \\
T[\![a]\!] &= \emptyset \\
T[\![\neg\psi]\!] &= T[\![\psi]\!] \\
T[\![\psi_1 \vee \psi_2]\!] &= T[\![\psi_1]\!] \cup T[\![\psi_2]\!] \\
T[\![\bigcirc_Q \psi]\!] &= \{T_Q\} \cup T[\![\psi]\!] \\
T[\![\psi_1 \, \mathcal{U}_Q \, \psi_2]\!] &= \{T_Q\} \cup T[\![\psi_1]\!] \cup T[\![\psi_2]\!] \\
&\wedge \ (T_Q, Q) \in Res(\bigcirc_Q \psi) \\
&\wedge \ (T_Q, Q) \in Res(\psi_1 \, \mathcal{U}_Q \, \psi_2)
\end{aligned}
$$

The (T_Q, Q) association corresponds to the initial value Q of the timer T_Q. Intuitively, the timer T_Q is set to the value Q when we start interpreting the temporal operator with the quantification Q. $Res(\psi)$ is the set of all such associations. The translation of a formula ψ to an event scheduler is then obtained by $Sch_\psi = \langle S, \Sigma, E, s_0, T, P, R, \Pi \rangle$ where:

- $S = D^*[\![\psi]\!]$ and $s_0 = \psi$

- $E = \{(s, a, s') | (s, s) \in S^2 \text{ such that } a \in \Sigma, s' = D_{a,\mu}[\![\psi]\!] \text{ and } \mu \in \mathcal{C}_T\}$

- $P = \{(s, \mu, s') | s, s \in S \text{ and } s' = D_{a,\mu}[\![\psi]\!], a \in \Sigma\}$

- $T = T(\psi)$

- $R = \{(s, \nu, s') | s, s' \in S \ s.t \ \exists a \in \Sigma, s \xrightarrow{a} s' \text{ and } \nu = (t, Q) \text{ and } \nu \in Res(s), t \in T\}$

- $\Pi = \{(s, \pi, s') | s, s' \in S \ s.t \ \forall s' \text{ such that } s \xrightarrow{a} s' \text{ and } s \xrightarrow{\pi_i} s' : \sum \pi_i = 1\}$

As an example, consider the formula:

$$\Box \, (send \rightarrow \Diamond_{\leq Exp,30} \, receive)$$

expressing the stochastic bounded responsiveness property: *every time a sending event occurs, the reception will occur within a time exponentially distributed with parameter* 30. Figure 1 illustrates the associated two-states event scheduler. The state 0 (initial state of this event scheduler) corresponds to the starting state of the interpretation process of the formula. The event scheduler moves to the second state 1, when a *send* event occurs. The timer is then set to a value randomly determined with respect to the exponential distribution with parameter 30. Then, at this stage, all the events are allowed to happen so long the timer reading is positive. Events denoted by "*" represent any events other than the atomic propositions composing the formula; i.e, $\{send, receive\}$. However, when *receive* occurs, the event scheduler returns to the initial state.

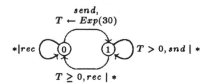

Figure 1: Stochastic bounded responsiveness

5.3 Composing LOTOS with Event Schedulers

As explained previously, the aim of this approach is to provide a model able to be executed according both to the functional description and the timing properties. The functional specification is provided by the generated LTS and the timing properties are represented by the event scheduler. The behaviour of the event scheduler is to synchronize with the LTS for each step and to monitor their actions. Informally, every

possible transition of the LTS is submitted to the event scheduler which will first check if its associated label is also a label of a possible transition within the event scheduler. If so, the event scheduler will check, according to the current date, if its prefixing predicate holds and chose a delay such that the predicate holds. The LTS transition is then enabled for this label with the associated delay. The formal semantics of the composition of the LOTOS associated LTS and the SQTL event scheduler is defined by the following rules:

$$\frac{B \xrightarrow{\alpha} B' \ , \ Sch \xrightarrow{\mu,\beta,\nu} Sch' \ \wedge \ \epsilon \models \mu \ \wedge \ \beta \in \{\alpha, *\}}{(B, Sch, [T_i]_i) \xrightarrow{\beta} (B', Sch', [T_i \leftarrow \nu'(T_i)]_i)}$$

where

$$\nu'(T_i) = \begin{cases} \nu(T_i) & if \ Sch \xrightarrow{\nu} Sch' \text{ and } T_i \in \nu \\ T_i - \epsilon & otherwise \end{cases}$$

6 The Multimedia Stream Example

As an illustration of the approach presented above, we present the case of a multimedia stream (first introduced in [6]). In this, example we consider a structure linking a multimedia data source and a data sink. The data source and the data sink are assumed to be communicating asynchronously over an unreliable channel. The functional description is given by LOTOS as follows:

```
specification stream [start,play,error]:noexit
behaviour
    start;( hide src, snk, loss in
        ( ( source[src] ||| sink[snk,play,error])
        |[src,snk]|
        channel[src,snk,loss] ))
where
    process source[src]:noexit:=
        src; source[src]
    endproc (* source *)
    process sink[snk,play,error]:noexit:=
        snk;(    play;sink[snk,play,error]
            [] error;stop )
    endproc (* sink *)
    process channel[src,snk,loss]:noexit:=
        src;(    snk; channel[src,snk,loss]
            [] loss;channel[src,snk,loss] )
    endproc (* channel *)
endspec (* stream *)
```

The above functional description is now extended with real time assumptions. These constraints are described with SQTL formulae. Each formula is assumed to describe a local property for each component of the functional specification.

P_1 : The data source arrivals are modeled as a Poisson process with an average rate of one frame every

$50ms$. This implies that the waiting time I between successive src events follows an exponential distribution with a probability density function $X(I) = 0.02.e^{0.02.I}$ with $I \geq 0$.

$$\Box\,[src_i \rightarrow (\Diamond_{<e,0.02}\,\neg src_{i+1} \wedge \Diamond_{=e,0.02}\,src_{i+1})]$$

P_2 : The next constraint states that successfully transmitted frames arrive at the data sink between $80ms$ and $90ms$ after their transmission.

This property represents the channel latency. It fixes the occurrence time of snk within $[80ms, 90ms]$ after a src. A jitter of $10ms$ is then permitted. However, some frame loss is permitted; a rate of 10% of the sent frames are lost.

$$\Box\,[src_i \rightarrow (\bigcirc loss_i \overset{0.1}{\vee} \Diamond_{[80,90]}\,snk_i)]$$

P_3 : The next property contributes to making the decision on which of play and err events to enable when a frame arrives in the data sink. The choice is now decided in a deterministic way by looking at the arrival time of snk. If the arrival rate at the data sink is not within $[15, 20]$ frames per second, then an error should be reported.

$$\Box\,[snk_i \wedge (\Diamondblack_{\leq 1000} snk_{i-21} \vee \Diamondblack_{\leq 1000}\neg snk_{i-15}) \rightarrow \bigcirc error]$$

P_4 : The final property states that if play is selected then it happens exactly $5ms$ after a frame is received.

$$\Box\,[snk_i \wedge (\Diamondblack_{\leq 1000} snk_{i-15} \wedge \Diamondblack_{\leq 1000} snk_{i-20}\ \Diamondblack_{\leq 1000}\neg snk_{i-21}) \rightarrow \Diamond_{=5} play)]$$

Figure 2 shows the generated event schedulers for the SQTL assertions (initial states correspond to state 0). These event schedulers composed with the LOTOS-associated LTS are used to construct a real-time model corresponding to the stream system.

Figure 3 illustrates the complete real-time model that corresponds to the composition of LOTOS-associated labelled transition system (generated by the tool SMILE [9]), and the event schedulers derived from the SQTL specification.

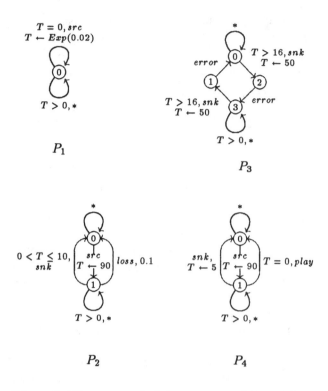

Figure 2: The event schedulers generated from SQTL formulae

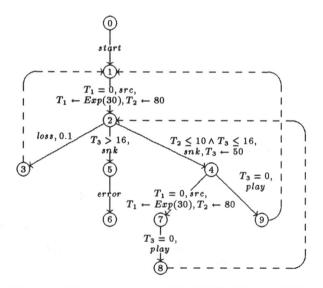

Figure 3: The composition of LOTOS LTS and SQTL schedulers

7 Verification

The verification problem addressed here concerns how to check if all infinite computations of a timed automaton A satisfy a real-time linear temporal logic formula ψ. This problem is known as the *model-checking* problem [8] and can be solved either by a *tableau based technique* or an *automata-theoretic technique*. In [21, 20], is presented a tableau-based technique to check the satisfiability of formula from untimed temporal logic. A real-time version of this method can be found in [10] and [6]. Checking the validity of a linear time formula ψ is then reduced to the problem of checking if $\neg \psi$ is satisfied. The foundations of automata-theoretic approach is first introduced in [20] and [19] in the context of untimed temporal logic and finite state automata. Specifically, it is stated in [20] that it is possible to build a *Büchi automaton A_ψ* that accepts exactly the infinite words satisfying a propositional linear temporal formula ψ. In addition, [2] presents the theory of timed version Büchi automata. A timed Büchi automaton is defined by the structure $A = \langle S, \Sigma, C, E, s_0, F \rangle$ where:

- S is finite set of control states and $s_0 \in S$ is the initial state

- Σ is finite set of actions

- C is a finite set of clocks where $\Phi(C)$ represents the set of time constraints on C

- $E \subseteq S \times \Sigma \times \Phi(C) \times 2^C \times S$ is a timed transition relation where transitions $s \xrightarrow{\mu, a, \nu} s'$ are guarded with constraints μ from $\Phi(C)$ and once executed, reset $\nu \subseteq C$ to zero

- $F \subset S$ is the set of final states.

In order to take advantage of this work, we adapt timed automata to event schedulers. Indeed, we translate clocks to timers where the 0-resetting function is replaced by a positive number resetting function. The set of final state will correspond to the states where the interpretation process terminates, i.e the *True*-state. The following is a predicate function deciding the final states associated with a formula interpretation process.

$$
\begin{array}{lcl}
Ter(True) & = & True \\
Ter(a) & = & False \\
Ter(\neg \psi) & = & \neg\, Ter(\psi) \\
Ter(\psi_1 \vee \psi_2) & = & Ter(\psi_1) \vee Ter(\psi_2) \\
Ter(\bigcirc_X \psi) & = & False \\
Ter(\psi_1 \, \mathcal{U}_X \, \psi_2) & = & Ter(\psi_2)
\end{array}
$$

The verification procedure is as follows. We first build a finite-automaton on infinite words for the negation of the formula ψ. The resulting automaton $A_{\neg\psi}$ accepts all sequences of states that violate ψ. Then we compute the product automaton $A_G = A_{Sch} \times A_{\neg\psi}$. Unfortunately, timed Büchi automata turn out not to be closed under complementation or under intersection [2]; i.e, it is a formally hard problem to build $A_{\neg\psi}$ from A_ψ. However, it is stated in [2] that complementation of a deterministic[2] timed automata with the *Muller condition* is decidable. A timed automaton possesses the Muller condition if its final states $F \subseteq 2^S$ and every accepted state sequence $(s_0, v_0)(s_0, v_0)...(s^w, v^w)$ contains a state from F which is appearing infinitely.

This product automaton accepts all infinite computations of Sch that are accepted by the automaton $A_{\neg\psi}$, i.e, all computations that violate the formula ψ. Finally we check if the automaton A_G is empty, i.e if it accepts any sequences. If A_G is empty, we have proven that all infinite computation of Sch satisfy the formula ψ. The emptiness of the language $\mathcal{L}(A)$ accepted by a timed automaton A can be checked in $O((|S| + |E|).2^{|\delta(A)|})$ [2] where S is the set of states of A, E the set of its edges and $\delta(A)$ represents the length of its time constraints.

8 Conclusion

In this paper we have introduced a new approach that uses the standardized LOTOS specification language together with a stochastic real-time temporal logic, SQTL. Timing modalities have been defined to extend LOTOS specifications with time critical and stochastic constraints. Two styles of constraints are identified. Firstly, real-time assumptions impose constraints on the underlying LOTOS specification reducing non-determinism, denoting time distances between action occurrences and fixing the delay of process synchronization. Secondly, real-time requirements state the desired properties of the resulting timed model.

The main contribution of this paper is the description of a verification technique for the dual language approach. Firstly, the creation of event schedulers from SQTL formulae is described. Event schedulers from real-time assumptions are combined with the labelled transition system produced from LOTOS to provide a timed model of the system behaviour. An example of this process is given (the multimedia stream example). Our approach to verifying real-time requirements against the timed model is then described.

---

[2] a timed automaton is said to be deterministic if $\forall s \in S, \forall a \in \Sigma$ if $s \xrightarrow{\mu_1, a, \nu_1} s_1$ and $s \xrightarrow{\mu_2, a, \nu_2} s_2$ then $\mu_1 \wedge \mu_2$ is unsatisfiable

Ongoing research is developing a toolkit for this approach. This toolkit will feature both formal verification and non-exhaustive simulation techniques.

References

[1] R. Alur, C. Courcoubetis, and D.L. Dill. Model-checking for probabilistic real-time systems. In *Automata, Languages and Programming: Proceedings of the 18th ICALP*, Lecture Notes in Computer Science 510, pages 115–136, 1991.

[2] R. Alur and D. Dill. A theory of timed automata. *Theoretical Computer Science*, 126, 1994.

[3] R. Alur and T.A. Henzinger. Real-time logics: complexity and expressiveness. *Information and Computation*, 104(1):35–77, 1993. Preliminary version appears in the Proc. of 5th LICS, 1990.

[4] G. Blair, L. Blair, H. Bowman, and A. Chetwynd. Time versus abstraction in formal description. In *6th International Conference on Formal Description Techniques, Boston, USA*, 1993.

[5] G. Blair, L. Blair, H. Bowman, and A. Chetwynd. A framework for the formal specification and verification of distributed multimedia systems. In *Workshop on Quality of Service and Performnce, Aachen, Germany*, 1994.

[6] L. Blair. *The Formal Specification and Verification of Distributed Multimedia Systems*. PhD thesis, Lancaster University, 1994.

[7] T. Bolognesi and E. Brinksma. Introduction to the iso specification language lotos. *Computer Networks and ISDN Systems, North-Holland*, vol. 14, No. 1, 1988.

[8] E. M. Clarke, E. A. Emerson, and A. P. Sistla. Automatic verification of finite state concurrent systems using temporal logic specifications. In *ACM TOPLAS*, volume 8(2), pages 244–263, 1986.

[9] H. Eertink and D. Wolz. Symbolic execution of LOTOS specifications. In Michel Diaz and Roland Groz, editors, *5th International Conference on Formal Description Techniques*, Lannion, France, October 13-16 1992.

[10] E. Harel, O. Lichtenstein, and A. Pnueli. Explicit clock temporal logic. In *IEEE 5th Annual Symposium on Logic in Computer Science*, pages 402–413, Philadelphia, June 1990.

[11] R. Koymans. Specifying real time properties with metric temporal logic. *Journal of Real Time Systems*, 2, 1992.

[12] A. Lakas, G. S. Blair, and A. Chetwynd. Specification of stochastic properties in real-time systems. In *11th UK Computer and Telecommunications Performance Engineering Workshop*, Liverpool, UK, September 1995.

[13] E. Madelaine and D. Vergamini. AUTO: A verification tool for distributed systems using reduction of finite state automata networks. In *2nd International Conference on Formal Description Techniques*, Vancouver, Canada, May 1989.

[14] E. Madelaine and D. Vergamini. Finiteness conditions and structural construction of automata for all process algebras. In R. Kurshan, editor, *Proceedings of Workshop on Computer Aided Verification*, New-Brunswick, Jun 1990.

[15] C. Miguel. Extended LOTOS definition. Technical Report OSI95/DIT/B5/8/TR/R/V0, OSI'95, Depto. Ingenieria de Sistemas Telemáticos, Univbersidad Politécnica de Madrid, Spain, November 1991.

[16] R. Milner. *A Calculus of Communicating Systems*, volume 92 of *Lecture Notes in Computer Science*. Sringer-Verlag, 1980.

[17] J. S. Ostroff. *Temporal Logic for Real Time Systems*. Research Studies Press, 1989.

[18] R. Segala and N. A. Lynch. A compositional trace-based semantics for probabilistic automata. In *Proceedings of CONCUR'95*, Philadelphia, PA, USA, August 1995.

[19] A. P. Sistla, P. Wolper, and M. Y. Vardi. The complementation problem for buchi automata with applications to temporal logic. In *Proc. 12th Int. Colloque on Automata, Languages and programming, Nafplion*, volume 194, pages 465–474, 1985.

[20] M.Y. Vardi and P. Wolper. An automata-theoretic approach to automatic program verification. In *Proc. IEEE Symp. on Logic in Computer Science*, pages 332–344, Boston, Jul 1986.

[21] P. Wolper, M. Y. Vardi, and A. P. Sistla. Reasoning about infinite computation paths. In *Proc. 24th IEEE Symposium on Foundations of Computer Science, Tuscon*, pages 185–194, 1983.

Requirements Elicitation Driven by Interviews:
The Use of Viewpoints

Julio Cesar Sampaio do Prado Leite[*]
Departamento de Informática PUC- Rio
R. Marquês de São Vincente 225
22453-900 - Rio de Janeiro, Brasil
e-mail: julio@inf.puc-rio.br

Ana Paula Pinho Gilvaz
Johnson Wax
Av. Comandante Guaranys 599
22275-610 - Rio de Janeiro, Brasil

Abstract

Requirements elicitation in the context of organizational information systems is well know to be a very hard task, much dependent on the experience and cleverness of the team performing the elicitation. In such a context the use of interviews is frequent and pointed out as the major technique for getting the requirements from the actors in the organization. We have been working with the idea of a general interview assistant and our first results are promising. In this article we elaborate on our original proposal in order to augment its assistant capability, without loosing its simplicity. We show how the use of viewpoint analysis improves the inference capability of our assistant.
Key-words: Interview, requirements elicitation, conceptual model, intelligent assistance.

1. Introduction

Our work is aimed at supporting the software engineer (systems analyst) in eliciting information for corporate information systems. We used well established IS techniques to build a prototype CASE tool called FAES [4]. FAES was designed to support an interview process based on a general framework of questions. Using a conceptual model and some analysis heuristics we managed to provide to the software engineer an automated support for his work of finding out important information in a given information system. As such, the work we will describe here is focused on a particular instance of computer automated support, namely the elicitation of information by interviews. FAES was built with the

purpose of supporting and evaluating our strategy. Preliminary data supports our hypothesis that in using FAES there is an increase in productivity during interviews [4].

During FAES's presentation at Case'95 [4], several questions from the audience encouraged us to rework some of its original architecture, making it more flexible and more powerful, but still maintaining its simplicity. FAES uses a simple conceptual model. Its shallowness is a positive factor in the tool performance, not only because it requires less computing power, but also because its structure is well understand by its users.

The literature [10] [8] has been pointing out the need of intelligent assistance to support upstream activities. The gap from informal to formal is not well addressed by the existing CASE technology. Although some, like [10] [9], believe that it is necessary to use deep representation strategies to bridge this gap, thus relying heavily on previous encoded domain knowledge, we firmly believe that it is possible to provide assistance, and thus decreasing the gap, by using simpler models at least at the stage of "reconnoitering the requirements" [2]. A previous work on viewpoints [7] does also use this approach, that is exploring the very first step in understanding a future software system.

In this article we will address two "problems" observed in FAES. The first one is related to the lack of flexibility in questioning. The second one is related to the lack of more powerful heuristics. Regarding the

---

[*] This work was supported by CNPq

flexibility aspect we re-designed the flow of questions, making it possible to interleave the fixed questions of the original FAES with questions on demand. With respect to more powerful heuristics we decided to fully explore the FAES capability of looking into previous interviews, by reusing our experience and heuristics described in Leite and Freeman's viewpoint work [7].

Section 2 provides a general description of the interview process and of the original FAES. Section 3 describes the new questioning schema. Section 4 details the viewpoint approach proposed for the new FAES. We conclude by pointing out how the improvements will impact on the automation support for interviews and how our work relates to other work in the area.

2. FAES

This section summarizes the original FAES work [4] and uses parts of that paper to explain the general context. FAES is the central part of an interview process that covers three basic interview questions: What to ask? How to ask? Whom to ask? The process has automation support for the first two questions and relies on general guidelines to the third question. Following the process, we build a knowledge base organized according to a conceptual model and analyzed according to special heuristics. The conceptual model was built upon three well-know information system techniques: BSP (Business System Planning) [6], CSF (Critical Success Factors) [11] and E/M (End Means Analysis) [12] and follows the integration model proposed by [13]. FAES knowledge base is an important factor for providing an organized model of corporate information, and its automation strategy supports the boring clerical tasks associated with interviews.

2. 1 The Process

The interviews are conducted individually with each person found to be important to interview [4]. The software engineer asks the questions suggested by FAES and annotates the answers trying to be as factual as possible given the respondents answer and trying to be as clear as possible. The software engineer can also comment on the answers he is annotating. It is important to note that the tool offers two feedback mechanisms: one at the time the question is being annotated and the other as the interview ends. At the end of the interview a report is generated which mirrors the knowledge base and provides some diagnoses of the captured information.

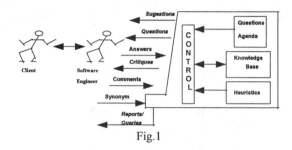

Fig.1

The interview assistant (Figure 1) applies a basic set of questions that would fill in the conceptual model. The interview assistant has a set of heuristics based on the conceptual model and on general common sense. These heuristics have been written to validate the answers, verify the existence of relationships between the answers and discover the need for more answers. FAES has four basic components: control, questions, knowledge base and heuristics. Control deals with the interface, the order of questions and heuristic's application. Heuristics are activated by a particular question or by the end of the interview. The questions are based on the conceptual model and contain the information necessary to instantiate the model. The knowledge base stores the answers, the diagnoses and the entries made by the software engineer (observations and synonyms).

2. 2 The Conceptual Model

The conceptual model is based on Wetherbe's work on executive information requirements [13]. According to Wetherbe, a common mistake made in determining information requirements is to ask the wrong question: "What information do you need from the new system ? " . Although this is the obvious question, it is not all helpful to clients attempting to determine what information they need. In order to minimize this problem, Wetherbe proposes an approach to interviewing that uses indirect questions. The interview scheme is composed of types of questions from three methods/techniques defined mentioned before: BSP, CSF and E/M analysis. Figure 2 shows the conceptual model we developed based on Wetherbe's approach. The conceptual model links the different types of questions and includes a lot of new information found necessary to support the interview. The model nodes represent the information to be

defined and the arcs the relationships among the information. The nodes serve as basis for the questions posed by the assistant. The arcs provide relationships that will help the analysis of the answers. The model has passed through several versions, as we tested its instantiation with a couple
of case studies.

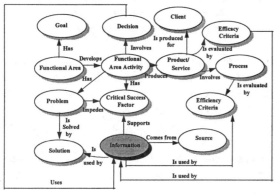

Fig. 2

2.3 Automation Strategy

In order to fill in the model with information, FAES uses 22 instantiation's questions. These questions have a fixed and a variable part. The fixed part is determined by the model and the variable part is used to establish the chain of questions. Below we list some of the instantiations questions.

4. What are the best solutions for < problem > ?
5. What information does support < solution > ?
6. Who does provide < information > ?
7. What are the decisions related to < activity > ?
8. What information does support < decision > ?

The questions that are used to fill in the model use the concept of information chaining, that is each question is composed of a fixed part and a variable part (< >). The variable part is an answer given to another question already answered, thus making a chaining process, since each of the answers of a given question will produce a different question for one of the fixed patterns. Besides the basic 22 questions, there are some heuristics that trigger other kind of questions in order to elaborate or to criticize the answers provided by users. Below we exemplify how the heuristics may trigger questions.

Completeness Heuristics - happen whenever a relation heuristic is confirmed and has an objective of relating

model entities with information already available for other entity.

Example:

Given a critical factor and a decision and also considering that a previous heuristic found a relation between them, then the information that supports the critical factor may also be relevant to the decision.

Question:
Does < Information > support < Decision > ?

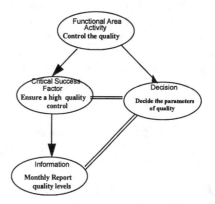

Does *<Monthly report of quality levels >* support *<decide quality parameters>*?

In this case the critical factor <ensure a high quality control> and the decision <Decide the quality parameters> were related by the confirmation of a relation heuristic that happened during the interview. As a consequence, the completeness heuristic was activated, thus creating a link between information and decision, which does not exist in the original model (Fig. 2).

FAES uses a standard production system scheme for dealing with the heuristics. Once a given node in the conceptual model is filled in by one of the questions from the automation strategy, the control mechanism activates the production memory to check if a rule will fire given the state of the knowledge base. These types of rules fire during the interview process. Other types will only be fired once the interview has ended.

2. 4 The Assistant

FAES was developed using an object oriented language, ENFIN, and a database tool, SQLBase. ENFIN is a Windows compatible software and as a result has the advantage of easily interfacing with other software. It implements the functionality described above, but has problems regarding performance, mainly due to the use of SQLBase.

Figure 4 shows the main window. On its top it poses a question to be asked to the client. The software engineer will use the <Answer> frame to type the answer. A frame labeled <Preview Answers> shows answers previously given by other respondents for this same question and this same functional area. The <Questions triggered by heuristics> frame shows all the questions generated by the heuristics. In order to answer a question posed by a heuristic, a special window is activate. The OBS bottom makes it possible to add comments to the answer. The Synonym bottom makes it possible to associate chosen terms in the <Answer> with other terms.

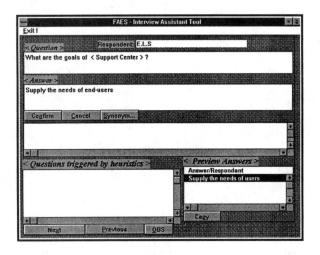

Fig. 4

3. The New Questioning Schema

One of the aspects in the original proposal was it's fixed set of questions. It was a feature in the sense that by following the script the elicitor would have filled the necessary information according to the meta-model, on the other hand it was also a barrier to the elicitor in terms of adding new information or following a different pattern of questioning. Considering that, we have analyzed our original approach and modified it in order to create an alternated form of questioning. The basic idea was to create an escape mechanism to allow the software engineer to follow, or investigate a different pattern of questioning, without loosing the original fixed set of questions.

As we can observe from Figure 5, there are four main paths we can follow in questioning. Each path of these paths instantiates their questions with respect to the list of activities answered at question 2 (the principle of chaining). The control structure in the original architecture was a fixed one. We now allow the interviewer to navigate on the control structure as well as to ask questions not in the agenda.

In order to make the navigation possible we used a stack to store the last state of the questioning. As such, we may advance to new questions or revisit questions previously answered. We anticipated that such a facility would only be effective for those familiar with the questioning structure of FAES. As we can see in Figure 5, the new control strategy gives more freedom to the interviewer.

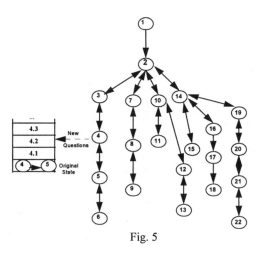

Fig. 5

Another feature that we added to FAES is the possibility that at any point in the interview process the interviewer makes a non planned question. This new feature also uses the stack mechanism showed above. In that case, we create a sub-tree, where the root is the last question of the prefixed agenda. Each question asked has to be annotated by the interviewer and will be stored together with the answer as a sub-node of the node that would hold the answer for the last questionnaire question asked. So in terms of the conceptual model, see Figure 2, we are creating a network of sub-nodes in a freely manner, but with the constraint that each node does have a link to the original node in the conceptual model. Figure 6 gives an example of such sub-network.

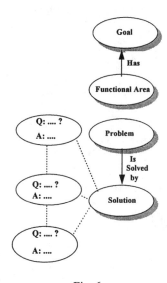

Fig. 6

It is important to note that when creating the sub-network, we still use the chaining technique, that is the next question may use the answer of the previous question.

4. Viewpoints

The heuristics used in the original version of FAES were simple and were basically driven to find out possible links in the conceptual model. It is important to note that the simplicity of the heuristics was due to the non usage of domain knowledge. One possibility of increasing the quality of the critique provided by the assistant, without relying on domain knowledge, is to follow the idea of previous answers as pointed out in [4] (see the original screen of FAES, Figure 5). We have developed this idea and used the ideas of viewpoints [7] to enhance the possibility of an on-line critique based on previous interviews.

In [7] we devised a process and a technique to compare very early requirements expressions. The technique proposed encompassed an automatic comparison of pairs of viewpoints that were expressed in a language, VWPl. The language was built on top of the production system paradigm, and basically was a typed manner of expressing rules about the problem being addressed. The language was designed to make it easier its use. Facts about the problem were described by production rules and the behavior was modeled by adding and deleting facts from the working memory.

Automatic comparison of viewpoints was performed by an AI based program that used both pattern matching and semantic information to analyze a pair of views expressed in VWPl. The comparison was driven by several heuristics which were classified according to an analogy framework described by Hall [5]. This framework is composed of the following phases: recognition, elaboration, evaluation and consolidation.

Leite's original analyzer was able to point out three types of discrepancies between views: **a)** wrong information, contradiction between the facts of the different rule sets, **b)** missing information, incomplete hierarchies with respect to rule facts, missing rules and missing facts, and **c)** inconsistency, contradiction between a fact and the hierarchy and redundancy in the same rule set. The analyzer was implemented as a Scheme program that analyzes the given VWPl descriptions.

FAES was not developed with the idea of viewpoints, although Gilvaz and Leite had discussed the possible links with Leite's previous work. As mentioned before, the comments at Case'95 were a motivation for coming back to FAES and looking at how it could be enhanced with the viewpoint ideas. In studying in more detail the relationship between the two works we found out that: **a)** the viewpoint analyzer was very dependent on VWPl, **b)** it was not reasonable to ask the interviewer to express the answers of the interviewee on VWPl, **c)** the analogy framework used by the viewpoint analyzer could be applied and d) some of the heuristics geared to VWPl could be restated, if we would consider FAES conceptual model as the base representation.

With these first observations, we decided to adopt the following general strategy:

The comparison strategy would take in consideration all the models available in the FAES knowledge base, and would use three possible perspectives: goals, functional areas and clients.

In order to make the statement above more clear we have to define what do we mean by models available and the notion of perspective. First, a model is an instantiated conceptual model, that is, the result of an interview. As such, a model has always attached to it the identification of the respondent. Second, we call a perspective the following nodes of the conceptual model: <u>goals</u>, <u>functional areas</u> and <u>clients</u>, since we believe each of them to be representative of a different perspective of the model. These perspectives will be used to find out similarities between models.

Using this as the basis, we have devised two group of heuristics to help the detection of wrong information and one group to detect incompleteness. First of all, we show the fine matching algorithm used in all groups. The purpose of this algorithm is to find similar text strings in two different sets. At the end of the section we present an example of the use of those heuristics.

4.1 The Matching Strategy

The matching strategy is based on the fine-matching algorithm used in [7] augmented by the use of FAES dictionary.

Fine-matching-with-dictionary
    Filter the answers by getting rid of articles and prepositions
    Find the shortest answer (measured by the number of words)
    member-count <-- 0
    For each word in the shortest answer
        If a word is a member of the longest answer
        then
            add 1 to member-count.
        else
            If word is in dictionary and its synonym is a member of longest answer
            then
                add 1 to member-count
    End_For
    Score <-- member-count / number words in the shortest answer
    /* OBS:. the member function is sensitive to
    /* regular verb tenses,
    /* so talk is a member in the sentence "She talked
    /* all night"
End_Fine-matching-with-dictionary

4.2 Group I, Finding Wrong Information

The group of heuristics presented below have the objective of finding out, at the time a question is answered and annotated by the system analyst, if there are relevant previous questions that are worth to be presented to the system analyst. The main rationale for this group is that by showing possible discrepancies between "related questions" we may alert the interviewer of a problem with that question, in the sense that there is a possible conflict of answers between two similar models. It is up to the interviewer to use the information which will be presented to him/her. The justification is that a 60% of complete different terms is a reasonable indication of a possible different answer (less than .4 fine matching score, scores are computed by matching the actual perspective with the models built by previous interviews).

1. Order the previous models by the highest score (maximum score is 3, that is 1 for each of the three perspectives).
2. Select the top two models
3. For each question do:
    3.1. Compute the fine-matching between the models' answers and the answer for the question at hand.
    3.2. If the best score is below .4 then
        3.2.1. Show the previous answers not matched to the interviewer
    3.3. If the questions matched have links to a sub-network, then
        3.3.1 Show these auxiliaries questions and answers to the interviewer.

4.3 Group II, Finding Wrong Information

The group of heuristics presented below have the objective of finding out, in three types of questions, if there is a possibility of wrong information at the time a question is answered by the respondent and annotated by the system analyst. The main rationale for this group is that answers to the "almost the same question" (the fixed part is the same and the variable part has a 70% fine matching) on problems, clients and sources for the same functional area must be "similar". In our case, we use the 70% fine matching as a measure for "almost the same question", and consider a "not at all similar" answers if there is less than 40% fine matching. Note that this group of heuristics issues a message about the possibility of wrong information, so the elaboration aspect of the analogy is more relevant in this group.

1. Given a matching functional area
   1.1 If there is a match, fine-matching with
   score > .7, on problem then
      1.1.1 compare fine-matching, solutions
      of the matched problem
         1.1.1.1 if score < .4 then
            1.1.1.1.1 give a msg
            reflecting a possible
            wrong information
   1.2 If there is a match, fine-matching with
   score > .7, on product/service then
      1.2.1 compare, fine-matching,
      clients
         1.2.1.1 if score < .4 then
            1.2.1.1.1 give a msg
            reflecting a possible
            wrong information
   1.3 If there is a match, fine-matching
   with score > .7, on information then
      1.3.1 compare, fine-matching,
      sources
         1.3.1.1 if score < .4 then
            1.3.1.1.1 give a msg reflecting
            a possible wrong information

4.4 Group III, Finding Incompleteness

The group of heuristics presented below have the objective of finding out if a given model is incomplete with respect to others. These heuristics are only applied to goals and clients. The rationale behind the heuristics is: given a similar model (main strategy), if the number of goals and clients are reasonable lower between the present model and the previous ones, then there is a great possibility of incompleteness in the present model. The heuristic for comparing the numbers uses a weight average (max, med, min) for the top two models.

1. Order the models by the highest score (maximum score is 3, that is 1 for each of the three perspectives).
2. Select the top two models
3. Compute the max, med, and min numbers of goals
5. Compare number of goals with the numbers computed at 3. Give a proper msg, in case of incompleteness
6. Compute the max, med, and min numbers of clients

7. Compare number of clients with the numbers computed at 6. Give a msg in case of Incompleteness

4.5 The Analogy Process

Our use of viewpoints in FAES is less powerful than the one used in [7], since there are several aspects that the conceptual model given by FAES is not able to capture, and does not provide the opportunity for analysis. We basically detected possibilities of wrong information and missing information, but not of inconsistency. Contrary to the schema used in [7] we use the results of the analogy analysis to take actions (first group). In our case the action is showing to the interviewer answers and questions of a previous interview.

4.5 An Example

At [4] we reported on the case study we conducted with the FAES tool in July of 1994 at Johnson's Wax information support center. At that time one member of the information center was interviewed with the assistance of the tool and the results were very positive with respect to our proposal, we managed to acquire more reliable information in a structured way. In order to exemplify our extension to FAES, one of us interviewed in December of 1995 another member of the Johnson's Wax information support center. Although this interview was performed partially, that is not all the branches of the questioning scheme were instantiated, due to time constraints, we managed to get enough data to run our example.

Once we had the interview data, we applied, by hand, the proposed heuristics using the new data and the original data collected in 1994. We will list below parts of the hand simulation we had performed for each group of proposed heuristics. The first and second group of heuristics are to be applied on the fly, that is at the moment when the interviewer enters the response to a given question. The third group are heuristics activated at the end of the interview, which may direct the interviewer to come back to a problematic question.

4.5.1 Finding Wrong Information, I

94 Interview: Question 2. *What are the activities of <information support center>?*
Answers: 1) Support PC users.
2) Manage the installed equipment.

95 Interview: Question 2. *What are the activities of <information support center>?*
Answers: 1) Give support to PC users.
2) Give support to the PC environment.

In this case, we will find that for the first answer of the actual interview (95) nothing should be shown (the score is 1 if we match answer 1 with 94 answer 1), for answer 2 there is also no reason to show the previous answers (the score .66 with 94 answer 1).

94 Interview: Question 3. *What are the problems of <Support PC users>?*
Answers: 1) Lack of user training.
2) Lack of human resources in certain areas of the support center.
3) Need to provide support to activities not belonging to the area.

95 Interview: Question 3. *What are the problems of <Give support to PC users>?*
Answers: 1) Lack of resources in the support center.
2) Little knowledge of the users.

In this case, for the first answer nothing should be shown (there is a .66 score with 94 answer 2), for answer 2, 94 answers 1 and 3 will be shown (since the best score with 94 answer 1 is below .4)

94 Interview: Question 10. *What are the critical success factors of <Support PC users>?*
Answers: 1) Good knowledge of the tools used by users.
2) Availability of human resources.

95 Interview: Question 10 *What are the critical success factors of <Give support to PC users>?*
Answers: 1) Availability of the support center employee.

In this case, for the first answer the two 94 answers will be shown (the score with 94 answer 2 is .33, that is one hit (*availability*) divided by the total number of words, less articles or prepositions, of the shorter sentence - 94 answer 2 with 3 words).

4.5.2 Finding Wrong Information, II

94 Interview: Partial list of "Information". 1) Experience. 2) Time of the task. 3) Understanding of the problem. 4) Locale of equipment.   5) Software description. 6) Know how of the training company. 7) Technical knowledge of the specialist. 8) Employee work load.

95 Interview: Question 17. *Who provides <execution time of a task>?*
Answer: Support center employee.

95 Interview: Question 5. *Who provides <employee experience>?*
Answer: Data processing manager.

Question 17 is of the type *Who provides <information>?* (see 1.3 of 4.3), as such we have to find a matching information on the previous models and compare the answers (sources). For instance, comparing the answer (source of information) of question 17 with the answer of the corresponding 94 question (*Who provides <time of a task>? --* **Answer:** Analyst), we get a non match, thus issuing a message of a possible wrong information. If we compare the sources for question 5 (Data processing manager) and the 94 corresponding answer (Analyst) we also get a non match and the proper message.

4.5.3 Finding Incompleteness

The 94 interview had one goal and the 95 interview also had detected just one goal., so no message is issued here. In the 94 interview two clients were identified and in the 95 interview just one, in this case a message indicating a possible incompleteness will be issued.

4.5.4 Comments on the Example

Our intention with the example was to induce the reader to follow the heuristics and to come to their own conclusions. Nonetheless, we would like to point out some of the facts observed. First of all, we believe that the example reinforced our hypothesis that the viewpoint matching approach is a sensible way of providing automated support validation. If we examine group I we will observe that not all the questions in an interview will be candidates for comparison, since only questions derived of a previous match will be analyzed, in that sense this is positive because these heuristics will be only applied when appropriated.

If we examine question 3 of group I above, we will note that for 95 answer 2 the 94 answers 1 and 3 will be shown to the interviewer. Showing 94 answer 3 to the interviewer detects that the respondent may have failed to observe a problem pointed out by a previous respondent, on the other hand, the fact that 94 answer 1 is shown points out the limitation of syntax matching, but the interviewer may filter the information and use it as a confirmation of the answer given. With respect to question 10 the interviewer may brought to light the question of user training.

If we examine the results got from group II we believe is more evident the kind of support that this approach can provide to the interviewer. For the question of type 5 is clear the difference in viewpoints between the respondents, probably the 95 respondent did a better job in identifying the source of the information. For question type 17 the answer is a generalization of the answer previously given, the approach does not detect this (VWPl hierarchies [7] would detect this type of match) so it complains of a possible wrong information.

Group III provides a critique at the end of the interview, and the result may lead the interviewer to came back to a previously answered question of type 15 *(Who are the clients of < products/services>)*. In the example we have found out that the 95 interview may have failed to identify a client.

5. Conclusion

This article elaborates on the result of previous research. We [4] showed an architecture for an interview assistant and gave data of its use in a case study. Considering that work and encouraged by the discussions of FAES at Case'95 we have proposed in this article an improvement on the assistant heuristics based on Leite and Freeman's work on viewpoints. Here as in [4] the main focus is on very early elicitation. In this article we have shown how we can easily include flexibility in our questioning scheme as well how viewpoint analysis can improve the feedback provided by the assistant.

Your contribution is well focused. We managed to show how a simple and non domain oriented elicitation strategy could be improved by established results in the field of viewpoint software engineering.

Although we did not conducted a complete case study with the new FAES architecture, the example showed that we have solid grounds to hypothesize the improvement in performance by adding viewpoint analysis as well as free questioning.

With respect to viewpoint analysis our previous experience shows that the kind of heuristics we have included in FAES are very effective. On the other hand our experience with the original FAES has shown, by the use of the OBS bottom (see Figure 5), that allowing free questions and answers would help the software engineer.

Reubenstein [9] and Drake [3] also dealt with interview automation. Reubenstein has developed a general assistant to gather information in the process of knowledge acquisition, but his strategy is based on a previous encoded knowledge base, which will serve as an oracle for the acquisition of requirements. Drake proposed an assistant to guide the client in answering questions anchored on a general model geared towards input/output. As we stressed before, our approach is not dependent on previous encoded knowledge, but the viewpoint analysis strategy will work better if our knowledge base is populated with interviews models (previous interviews). Contrary to the original proposal in [7], which used a special language for expressing viewpoints, we have developed analysis heuristics for an existing representation scheme. For that matter, this approach is similar to Finkelstein et al [1], since they have written heuristics to compare different instances of well-known software engineering representation schemes.

Future work should be geared towards an efficient implementation of the new FAES and its use in other case studies. The major problem regarding implementation will be how to integrate the original heuristic application with the necessity of dealing with more than one instantiated conceptual model at once.

Acknowledgments

We would like to acknowledge the contributions at those at the Case'95 session, whom by asking questions prompted us to extend FAES capabilities. In special we thank Jeff Kramer, since his question on viewpoints was the main reason for this article. The review process improved our paper, we are grateful to the referees for their comments.

References

[1] Finkelstein, A., Gabbay, D., Hunter, A., Kramer, J., Nuseibeh, B.;., Nuseibeh, B.; Inconsistency Handling in Multi-Perspective Specifications; *IEEE Trans. on Software Eng.*, Vol. 20, n. 8, Aug. 1994, pp. 569--578.

[2] Feather, M.S., Requirements Reconnoitering at the Juncture of Domain and Instance, *RE93, Proceedings of the Intl. Symposium on Requirements Engineering, IEEE Computer Society Press;* Jan. 1994, pp. 73--76.

[3] Drake J. M., Xie W. W., Tsai W. T. A Case Study of Requirement Analysis where End Users take an Active Role *Proceedings of the 15th International Conference on Software Engineering, IEEE Computer Society Press*, 1993, pp. 177-186.

[4] Gilvaz, Ana Paula, Leite Julio Cesar S. P. FAES: A Case Tool for Information Acquisition; *Case'95, Proceedings of the Seventh Intl Work. on Computer-Aided Soft. Eng. IEEE Computer Society Press;* Jul. 1995, pp. 260--269.

[5] Hall, R.; Computational approaches to analogical reasoning: a comparative analysis; *Artificial Intell.;* vol. 21, no. 1, Jan. 1988, pp. 241--250.

[6] *Information Systems Planning Guide, Application Manual*, GE20-0527-3, Third Edition, IBM Corporation (July 1981)

[7] Leite, Julio Cesar S P. and Freeman, P.A. Requirements Validation Through Viewpoint Resolution, *IEEE Trans. on Soft. Eng.*, Vol. 17, No. 12, Dec. 1991, pp-1253--1269.

[8] Loucopoulos, Pericles and Karakostas, Vassilios *System Requirements Engineering*, McGraw Hill International Series in Software Engineering, 1995.

[9] Reubenstein Howard B., Waters Richard C. The Requirements Apprentice: Automated Assistance for Requirements Acquisition
IEEE Transactions on Software Engineering,, vol 17, (3) 1991, pp. 226-240.

[10] Rich, Charles, Waters Richard C. Knowledge Intensive Software Engineering Tools, *IEEE Transactions on Knowledge and Data Engineering, 1992, vol 4, (5),* , pp. 424 -- 430.

[11] Rockart, J. F. Critical Success Factors *Harvard Business Review, 1979, (March-April), vol 57, (2)* pp. 81 -- 91.

[12] Wetherbe James C. *Systems Analysis and Design,* West Publishing Company, St.Paul, MN, 1988.

[13] Wetherbe James C. Executive Information Requirements: Getting It Right *MIS Quarterly, March* 1991 pp. 50 --65.

Formalising System Structure

Matthias Radestock and Susan Eisenbach
Department of Computing
Imperial College of Science, Technology and Medicine
180 Queen's Gate, London SW7 2BZ, United Kingdom
E-mail: {M.Radestock,S.Eisenbach}@ic.ac.uk

Abstract

Darwin is a language designed for configuring distributed systems. A system is modelled as a decompositional hierarchy of components with interfaces. Connections are represented as bindings between interfaces. Darwin programs define component types. Configurations of a system are obtained by instantiating these types. Configurations have to comply with a number of constraints on the system structure. It is therefore intuitive to express these constraints in the domain of configurations rather than on the language level. To succeed in this endeavour we need to precisely express the relation between Darwin programs and configurations. We do this in terms of a first-order logic theory of Darwin programs and configurations. Models of the theory provide a straightforward mapping from Darwin programs to configurations and vice versa. Most of the constraints on configurations as well as structural transformations can be specified by adding just a few axioms to the theory. Also the theory enables us to generate Darwin programs from configurations thus allowing for the inclusion of existing systems into new programs.

1 Introduction

It has been observed in the Software Engineering community that systems which are constructed from a large number of components have organisational difficulties [7, 14, 6]. There is a real need for clear design specifications of component based systems at this level. This is the level of the design which deals with the high-level organisation of computational elements and the interactions between those elements.

We are concerned with the demonstration of soundness of the tools for the design and construction of distributed systems. We use structural configuration languages [12, 9, 11] as a means of specifying and managing system structure. Systems are constructed from components. The overall architecture of a system is described as a hierarchical composition of primitive components which at execution time may be located on distributed computers. There are a variety of different configuration languages designed for a similar purpose such as Polylith [15], Durra [2] and LEAP [8].

This paper discusses the Darwin notation for specifying this high-level organisation. Darwin is a declarative binding language which can be used to define hierarchic compositions of interconnected components. The language supports the specification of both static structures and dynamic structures which may evolve during execution. The central abstractions managed by Darwin are component types and interfaces. The structure of a system is obtained by hierarchically instantiating component types at run-time. Interfaces are the means by which components interact. It is important to specify any programming language; without a formal specification a language is defined by its compiler. Even with the best intentions several compilers for a language will lead to several variants. The aim of this paper is to help formalise the definition of the Darwin programming language.

The paper introduces the Darwin programming language and its representation in first order logic. The definitions and axioms of the logic representation form a theory. From this theory we derive notations of validity for both programs and configurations as well as an important property of Darwin programs – a running configuration can be extended without requiring reconfiguration. The theory is extended to cover current in Darwin such as prevention of multicasting, unbound interfaces, circular binding and unbounded decomposition. We look at distinction between composite and primitive components and the flattening process which removes much of the structure of Darwin programs in the corresponding configurations. We conclude with a discussion of how this work relates to previous work on a π-calculus model [16, 10, 4, 13].

There has been some related work on a formal model for module interconnection languages presented in [18] by Rice and Seidman, but the focus of our paper

Proceedings of IWSSD-8

is different. Whereas there the authors are concerned with the construction process of a system structure specification we investigate the relation between programs and configurations. Allan and Garlan's work [1] makes assumptions about the primitive component's interaction mechanisms which is in contrast to our work where only the structuring of the composite components is examined.

2 Darwin

The Darwin language[3, 11, 9] is intended for the description of hierarchical configurations of components. Composite components are written in the configuration language itself and primitive components are written in an implementation language like C++. The Darwin system grew out of Conic which has been used in large scale industrial problems[12]. An important characteristic of the Darwin system is that it enables systems to be conFig. d dynamically.

The basic unit of the configuration language is a component. A Darwin component type definition consists of a list of declarations. Instances of components are declared using the **inst** keyword, which causes a component to be created. The interface of a component with its environment is a vector of names identifying services that are **provide**d by the component, and another vector of names identifying services that are **require**d by the component. Interfaces are typed. The Darwin configuration language does not place restrictions on the types (but it ensures that program construction is type safe).

A **bind** declaration is used in order to bind the provisions and requirements of two components together to enable the transfer of data . It is the core statement of the configuration language. The statement may refer to interfaces of sub-components or to interfaces of the component being defined.

Darwin enables a limited amount of control structuring of its declarations. **When** declarations are guards that enable one or more declarations to be optionally declared. Since it is not uncommon to want to perform the same declaration repetitively there are **forall** declarations.

The following is an example of a Darwin program:

```
component B {
provide a;
require b,c;
        }

component A(int n) {
provide a, c, e;
require b, d;
```

```
array   B[n]:B;
forall i:0..n
        inst B[n];
forall i:0..n-1 {
        bind    B[i].b--B[i+1].a;
                B[i].c--B[i+1].a;
                }
bind    a--B[0].a; e--B[0].a;
        B[n].b--b; B[n].c--b;
        c--d;
        }
```

The abstract component B has three interfaces – one provided (a) and two required (b,c). The component A has three provided interfaces (a,c,e) and two required interfaces (b,d). Inside A $n+1$ instances of the abstract component B are chained together by connecting their required interfaces b,c to the provided interface a of the next component in the chain. The provided interface a of the first component is connected to the provided interfaces a and e of the composite component. Similarly the required interfaces b and c of the last component in the chain are connected to the required interface b of the composite component. Finally there exists a direct link between the provided interface c and the required interface d.

3 First Order Logic Representation

Darwin is a language for defining *types* of system components. When a program is executed a parameter (from the command line) determines the type of the top-level component. Starting with this component a hierarchical instantiation of component types unfolds and bindings are established between interfaces of these instances. Some types may get instantiated multiple times and in different contexts, whereas other types may not get instantiated at all. The result of the instantiation is a *configuration*. It can be viewed as a collections of components (ie. instances of component types) with interfaces and bindings between those interfaces. A Darwin program defines a class of configurations consisting of all configurations that can be obtained by instantiating component types defined in the program.

The logic specification is given in form of a theory δ. The purpose of it is twofold. It serves as a framework for representing both Darwin programs and actual system configurations.

3.1 Definitions

The specification requires six sorts

C_NAME, C_TYPE, I_NAME, I_TYPE, CID, IID

The first four (C_NAME, C_TYPE, I_NAME, I_TYPE) represent the names and types of components and interfaces and are thus directly derived from Darwin programs. The remaining two sorts (CID, IID) are needed for the specification of system configurations. Each component in a configuration is assigned a unique component identifier (i.e. an element of the sort CID) and each interface gets a unique interface identifier (i.e. an element of the sort IID). Hence, although in Darwin several components and interfaces can have the same name as long as they are defined at different points in the decompositional hierarchy, the component identifiers and interface identifiers provide a means of globally (i.e. without regard of the decomposition hierarchy) referring to components and interfaces in a configuration.

Only two constants are used in the specification:

Universe : CID
Top : C_TYPE

Universe refers to the top-level component in the decompositional hierarchy. Top is its type. It corresponds to the execution parameter of a Darwin program and thus needs to be defined explicitly.

We define the following functions:

c_name(CID) : C_NAME
i_name(IID) : I_NAME
c_type(CID) : C_TYPE
i_type(IID) : I_TYPE
c_cont(CID) : CID
i_comp(IID) : CID

The functions c_name and i_name establish the mapping of identifiers to names. Components and interfaces in Darwin are typed and the functions c_type and i_type are used for specifying these. Components in a configuration are part of a decomposition hierarchy whose root node represents the entire system. Thus, with exception of Universe, all components are part of other components. The function c_cont takes a component identifier and returns the component identifier of the containing component. Interfaces are always attached to components – they cannot exist independently. The component of an interface is returned by the function i_comp.

There are a number of predicates:

inst(C_TYPE, C_NAME, C_TYPE)
provide(C_TYPE, I_NAME, I_TYPE)
require(C_TYPE, I_NAME, I_TYPE)

binding_{SS}(C_TYPE, C_NAME, I_NAME, C_NAME, I_NAME)

binding_{SC}(C_TYPE, C_NAME, I_NAME, I_NAME)

binding_{CS}(C_TYPE, I_NAME, C_NAME, I_NAME)

binding_{CC}(C_TYPE, I_NAME, I_NAME)

prov(IID)
req(IID)
bind(IID, IID)

A Darwin program can be translated into logic using just four predicates – inst, provide, require and binding. These predicates can be obtained by a straightforward translation of the respective Darwin program statements. A Darwin program can be viewed as a set of component type definitions. Program statements are context dependent upon the component type definition they occur in. The first parameter of the predicates establishes that dependency. The remaining parameters are obtained from the parameters of the corresponding Darwin statement. The binding predicate occurs in four different forms to cater for the four different notations of the corresponding Darwin statement:

bind *component.interface -- component.interface*
bind *component.interface -- interface*
bind *interface -- component.interface*
bind *interface -- interface*

The indices of the predicate indicate whether it's in internal binding between the interfaces of two sub-components (SS), a binding between an interface of a sub-component and an interface of the container component (SC), a binding between an interface of the container component and an interface of a sub-component (CS) or a binding between two interfaces of the container component (CC).

Of the remaining three predicates prov and req are employed for specifying that an interface is a provision or requirement respectively, whereas the bind predicate denotes a binding between two interfaces.

3.2 Axioms

The theory contains a number of axioms. The following are the *base case axioms*:

$$\text{c\_cont}(c) = c \iff c = \text{Universe}$$
$$\text{c\_type}(c) = \text{Top} \iff c = \text{Universe}$$

The first axiom defines the container component of the top-level component in the decomposition hierarchy. Making the Universe object a sub-object of itself is done for convenience only, as it makes c_cont a total function and allows us to specify further axioms without having to cater for special cases. The second axiom defines the type of the top-level component. Note that both axioms also ensure that the top-level component is unique.

The set of axioms in Fig. 1 defines how a Darwin program can be translated into an actual configuration and visa versa (note the double arrow). On the left hand side we find only predicates which can be derived directly from a Darwin program while all the predicates and functions on the right hand side can be derived from an actual configuration. There is currently no direct support for some Darwin constructs, such as control structures, in the translation axioms. Note, however, that these constructs can be *unfolded* prior to application of the axioms. The first axiom in the list is of special significance. It is the only axiom that has the c_type function on both sides. It introduces a new component to the configuration by instantiating a component type. All the other axioms can then be applied to deduce further properties of that component in the system. A re-application of the axiom itself introduces the sub-components of that particular component to the system.

Darwin programs don't specify the top-level component of the decompositional hierarchy. It gets defined as an execution parameter. In order for the first axiom to be applicable an additional formulae has to be added to the logical representation of a Darwin program. That formulae must define which component type is to be identified with Top. Thus the first time the axiom is applied it can only be applied to the Universe component (cf. the second base case axiom). Intuitively, no component will exist in an actual system unless the Universe component exists.

The set of axioms in Fig. 2 deals with naming constraints in Darwin programs. The first axiom ensures that an interface cannot be both a provision and a requirement. The remaining two axioms imposes certain constraints on the naming of components and interfaces. In Darwin the names of interfaces of a component must be distinct. The same holds for the names of sub-components.

Darwin imposes a number of constraints on the binding of interfaces. Bindings can only occur between interfaces of the same component, interfaces of sub-components of the same component, an interface of a component and an interface of its sub-component. The first axiom in Fig. 3 ensures that these constraints are satisfied and that only interfaces of the same type are linked. Provisions and requirements cannot be bound in an arbitrary fashion. The remaining axioms impose constraints depending on which of the cases of hierarchical binding occurs.

The above definitions and axioms form a theory which we shall give the name δ.

3.3 Theory, Programs and Configurations

Darwin programs contain a finite number of component type definitions and configurations consist of a finite number of components and interfaces. Hence the sorts, functions and predicates in our theory can all be interpreted as finite sets. Further adding the interpretation of the constants we can obtain a so-called *signature* of δ, denoted by $\mathcal{S}^\delta$. The signature ([5]) can be viewed as a set of all possible *realizations* of δ. A realization provides one particular interpretation for each element in the signature. Darwin programs and configurations are related to δ via its models. *Models* are realizations that obey all the axioms of the theory:

Lemma 1 $M \models \delta \Longrightarrow M \in \mathcal{S}^\delta$

Definition 1 *The set of all models is denoted by $\mathcal{M}^\delta$:*
$M \models \delta \Longleftrightarrow M \in \mathcal{M}^\delta$

From the preceding lemma and definition we can derive the following lemma:

Lemma 2 *Models are realizations:* $\mathcal{M}^\delta \subseteq \mathcal{S}^\delta$

We can define a $\subseteq$ and $\preceq$ relation between realizations. These relations will be used later on for the definition of properties of the translation from Darwin programs and configurations into realisations.

Definition 2 $\forall M, N \in \mathcal{S}^\delta. M \subseteq N \Longleftrightarrow \forall I \in \mathcal{I}^\delta. M_I \subseteq N_I$

Definition 3 $\forall M, N \in \mathcal{S}^\delta. M \preceq N \Longleftrightarrow \forall I \in \mathcal{I}^\delta. M_I \neq \bot \Longrightarrow M_I = N_I$

The above definitions utilise indices for element extraction. In case of the signature these elements are sets corresponding to possible interpretations for a particular sort, constant, function or predicate. The set of the indices is denoted by $\mathcal{I}^\delta$. To extract all possible interpretations of the c_NAME sort from the signature, we would write $\mathcal{S}^\delta_{\text{C\_NAME}}$. We can also extract the elements of a particular realization by using indices, eg. $s_{\text{C\_NAME}}$ where $s \in \mathcal{S}^\delta$.

3.3.1 Translating Darwin Programs into Realizations of δ

Definition 4 *A Darwin program P can be translated into a realization $\mathcal{M}_P$ of δ by an application of the translation function $\mathcal{M}_P = [[P]]^{\mathcal{P}}$ where $\mathcal{M}_P \in \mathcal{S}^\delta$.*

$$\begin{array}{lcl}
\exists t' \in \text{C\_TYPE}.\text{c\_type}(c') = t' & \Longleftrightarrow & \exists c \in \text{CID}.\text{c\_name}(c) = n \wedge \text{c\_type}(c) = t \\
\wedge\text{inst}(t', n, t) & & \wedge\text{c\_cont}(c) = c' \\[4pt]
\exists t' \in \text{C\_TYPE}.\text{c\_type}(c') = t' & \Longleftarrow & \exists i \in \text{IID}.\text{i\_name}(i) = n \wedge \text{i\_type}(i) = t \\
\wedge\text{provide}(t', n', t) & & \wedge\text{prov}(i) \wedge \text{i\_comp}(i) = c' \\[4pt]
\exists t' \in \text{C\_TYPE}.\text{c\_type}(c') = t' & \Longleftarrow & \exists i \in \text{IID}.\text{i\_name}(i) = n \wedge \text{i\_type}(i) = t \\
\wedge\text{require}(t', n', t) & & \wedge\text{req}(i) \wedge \text{i\_comp}(i) = c' \\[4pt]
\exists t' \in \text{C\_TYPE}.\text{c\_type}(c') = t' & \Longleftrightarrow & \exists i_1, i_2 \in \text{IID}, c_1, c_2 \in \text{CID}.\text{bind}(i_1, i_2)\wedge \\
\wedge\text{binding}_{SS}(t', cn_1, in_1, cn_2, in_2) & & \wedge\text{i\_name}(i_1) = in_1 \wedge \text{i\_comp}(i_1) = c_1 \\
& & \wedge\text{i\_name}(i_2) = in_2 \wedge \text{i\_comp}(i_2) = c_2 \\
& & \wedge\text{c\_name}(c_1) = cn_1 \wedge \text{c\_cont}(c_1) = c' \\
& & \wedge\text{c\_name}(c_2) = cn_2 \wedge \text{c\_cont}(c_2) = c' \\[4pt]
\exists t' \in \text{C\_TYPE}.\text{c\_type}(c') = t' & \Longleftrightarrow & \exists i_1, i_2 \in \text{IID}, c_1 \in \text{CID}.\text{bind}(i_1, i_2)\wedge \\
\wedge\text{binding}_{SC}(t', cn_1, in_1, in_2) & & \wedge\text{i\_name}(i_1) = in_1 \wedge \text{i\_comp}(i_1) = c_1 \\
& & \wedge\text{i\_name}(i_2) = in_2 \wedge \text{i\_comp}(i_2) = c' \\
& & \wedge\text{c\_name}(c_1) = cn_1 \wedge \text{c\_cont}(c_1) = c' \\[4pt]
\exists t' \in \text{C\_TYPE}.\text{c\_type}(c') = t' & \Longleftrightarrow & \exists i_1, i_2 \in \text{IID}, c_2 \in \text{CID}.\text{bind}(i_1, i_2)\wedge \\
\wedge\text{binding}_{CS}(t', in_1, cn_2, in_2) & & \wedge\text{i\_name}(i_1) = in_1 \wedge \text{i\_comp}(i_1) = c' \\
& & \wedge\text{i\_name}(i_2) = in_2 \wedge \text{i\_comp}(i_2) = c_2 \\
& & \wedge\text{c\_name}(c_2) = cn_2 \wedge \text{c\_cont}(c_2) = c' \\[4pt]
\exists t' \in \text{C\_TYPE}.\text{c\_type}(c') = t' & \Longleftrightarrow & \exists i_1, i_2 \in \text{IID}.\text{bind}(i_1, i_2)\wedge \\
\wedge\text{binding}_{CC}(t', in_1, in_2) & & \wedge\text{i\_name}(i_1) = in_1 \wedge \text{i\_comp}(i_1) = c' \\
& & \wedge\text{i\_name}(i_2) = in_2 \wedge \text{i\_comp}(i_2) = c'
\end{array}$$

Figure 1: Translation axioms

$$\begin{array}{rcl}
\text{prov}(i_1) \wedge \text{req}(i_2) & \longrightarrow & i_1 \neq i_2 \\
\text{i\_comp}(i_1) = \text{i\_comp}(i_2) \wedge i_1 \neq i_2 & \Longrightarrow & \text{i\_name}(i_1) \neq \text{i\_name}(i_2) \\
\text{c\_cont}(c_1) = \text{c\_cont}(c_2) \wedge c_1 \neq c_2 & \Longrightarrow & \text{c\_name}(c_1) \neq \text{c\_name}(c_2)
\end{array}$$

Figure 2: Naming constraints

$$\begin{array}{lcl}
\text{bind}(i_1, i_2) \wedge \text{i\_comp}(i_1) = c_1 \wedge \text{i\_comp}(i_2) = c_2 & \Longrightarrow & (c_1 = c_2 \vee cc_1 = cc_2 \\
\wedge\text{c\_cont}(c_1) = cc_1 \wedge \text{c\_cont}(c_2) = cc_2 & & \vee c_1 = cc_2 \vee c_2 = cc_1) \\
& & \wedge\text{i\_type}(i_1) = \text{i\_type}(i_2) \\[4pt]
\text{bind}(i_1, i_2) \wedge \text{i\_comp}(i_1) = c_1 \wedge \text{i\_comp}(i_2) = c_2 & \Longrightarrow & \text{prov}(i_1) \wedge \text{req}(i_2) \\
\wedge c_1 = c_2 & & \\[4pt]
\text{bind}(i_1, i_2) \wedge \text{i\_comp}(i_1) = c_1 \wedge \text{i\_comp}(i_2) = c_2 & \Longrightarrow & \text{req}(i_1) \wedge \text{prov}(i_2) \\
\wedge\text{c\_cont}(c_1) = \text{c\_cont}(c_2) & & \\[4pt]
\text{bind}(i_1, i_2) \wedge \text{i\_comp}(i_1) = c_1 \wedge \text{i\_comp}(i_2) = c_2 & \Longrightarrow & (\text{prov}(i_1) \wedge \text{prov}(i_2)) \\
\wedge(\text{c\_cont}(c_1) = c_2 \vee \text{c\_cont}(c_2) = c_1) & & \vee(\text{req}(i_1) \wedge \text{req}(i_2))
\end{array}$$

Figure 3: Hierarchical binding constraints

As most Darwin constructs have corresponding predicates, the translation function is straightforward. The following is an example of a translation.

```
component B {
provide a;
require b, c;
        }

component A {
provide a, e;
        c<port>;
require b;
        d<port>;
inst    B0:B;
        B1:B;
bind    a--B0.a; e--B0.a;
        B0.b--B1.a; B0.c--B1.a;
        B1.b--b; B1.c--b;
        c--d;
        }
```

This program can be translated into the following realization of δ:

$$
\begin{aligned}
\text{C\_NAME} &= \{\text{A}, \text{B0}, \text{B1}\} \\
\text{C\_TYPE} &= \{\text{A}, \text{B}\} \\
\text{I\_NAME} &= \{\text{a}, \text{b}, \text{c}, \text{d}, \text{e}\} \\
\text{I\_TYPE} &= \{\text{port}, \text{void}\} \\
\text{inst} &= \{(\text{A}, \text{B0}, \text{B}), (\text{A}, \text{B1}, \text{B})\} \\
\text{provide} &= \{(\text{B}, \text{a}, \text{void}), (\text{A}, \text{a}, \text{void}), \\
&\quad (\text{A}, \text{e}, \text{void}), (\text{A}, \text{c}, \text{port})\} \\
\text{require} &= \{(\text{B}, \text{b}, \text{void}), (\text{B}, \text{c}, \text{void}), \\
&\quad (\text{A}, \text{b}, \text{void}), (\text{A}, \text{d}, \text{port})\} \\
\text{binding}_{SS} &= \{(\text{A}, \text{B0}, \text{b}, \text{B1}, \text{a}), (\text{A}, \text{B0}, \text{c}, \text{B1}, \text{a})\} \\
\text{binding}_{SC} &= \{(\text{A}, \text{B1}, \text{b}, \text{b}), (\text{A}, \text{B1}, \text{c}, \text{b})\} \\
\text{binding}_{CS} &= \{(\text{A}, \text{a}, \text{B0}, \text{a}), (\text{A}, \text{e}, \text{B0}, \text{a})\} \\
\text{binding}_{CC} &= \{(\text{A}, \text{c}, \text{d})\}
\end{aligned}
$$

The above model structure only gives interpretations of some of the sorts, functions and predicates in δ. The remaining (unmentioned) elements are interpreted as $\perp$. Such a model structure can therefore never be a model of δ. We have the following important definitions:

Definition 5 *Let P be a Darwin program. P is a* **valid** *Darwin program iff $\exists A \in \mathcal{M}^{\delta} . [[P]]^{\mathcal{T}} \preceq A$*

What the definition says is the following: If and only if we can find a model which looks exactly like the realization obtained from the program translation but has all the $\perp$ elements filled in then the program is valid. This makes sense because all the $\perp$ elements in a realization obtained from the translation of a program are related to configurations. A program is only valid if there is a matching configuration and together they obey all the axioms of the theory δ. We can thus check the validity of Darwin programs using our theory and catch errors in the specification of systems. From the axioms that 'fail' it is possible to deduce where and why a specification is erroneous.

We can define a $\subseteq$ relation between Darwin programs:

Definition 6 *Let P and Q be two Darwin programs. If $P \subseteq Q$ then Q can be obtained from P by adding*

- *component type definitions,*
- *interface or instance definitions to component type definitions,*
- *bindings to component type definitions.*

Q is called an extension *of P.*

As we have included identity Q need not be a *proper* extension. Neither need it be a *valid* extension as we could for instance add a binding without defining the interfaces involved. All the above operations, if executed on the realization rather than the Darwin program, are just set extensions of the elements of the realization. Hence $[[\_]]^{\mathcal{P}}$ is a monotonic function, ie. the following lemma holds:

Lemma 3 *Let P and Q be two Darwin programs, then $P \subseteq Q \Longrightarrow [[P]]^{\mathcal{P}} \subseteq [[Q]]^{\mathcal{P}}$.*

3.3.2 Translating Configurations into Realizations of δ

Definition 7 *A configuration C can be translated into a realization $\mathcal{M}_C$ of δ by an application of the translation function $\mathcal{M}_C = [[C]]^{\mathcal{C}}$ where $\mathcal{M}_C \in \mathcal{S}^{\delta}$.*

There is currently no language for describing actual configurations. We could either use a simplified version of Darwin or the logical representation itself. In the first case the translation function would be very similar to the function $[[\_]]^{\mathcal{P}}$ as we could establish a similar straightforward mapping from program constructs to the predicates describing configurations. In the latter case the translation function is the identity function. The following is an example of the result of a translation of a configuration into a realization of δ:

$$
\text{I\_TYPE} = \{\text{port}, \text{void}\}
$$

$$\text{CID} = \{\text{C}, \text{C0}, \text{C1}\}$$
$$\text{IID} = \{\text{IA}, \text{IB}, \text{IC}, \text{ID}, \text{IE},$$
$$\text{IA0}, \text{IB0}, \text{IC0}, \text{IA1}, \text{IB1}, \text{IC1}\}$$
$$\text{Universe} = \text{C}$$
$$\text{c\_cont} = \{(\text{C0}, \text{C}), (\text{C1}, \text{C}), (\text{C}, \text{C})\}$$
$$\text{i\_type} = \{(\text{IA}, \text{void}), (\text{IB}, \text{void}),$$
$$(\text{IC}, \text{port}), (\text{ID}, \text{port}),$$
$$(\text{IE}, \text{void}),$$
$$(\text{IA0}, \text{void}), (\text{IB0}, \text{void}),$$
$$(\text{IC0}, \text{void}), (\text{IA1}, \text{void}),$$
$$(\text{IB1}, \text{void}), (\text{IC1}, \text{void})\}$$
$$\text{i\_comp} = \{(\text{IA}, \text{C}), (\text{IB}, \text{C}), (\text{IC}, \text{C}),$$
$$(\text{ID}, \text{C}), (\text{IE}, \text{C}),$$
$$(\text{IA0}, \text{C0}), (\text{IB0}, \text{C0}), (\text{IC0}, \text{C0}),$$
$$(\text{IA0}, \text{C1}), (\text{IB0}, \text{C1}), (\text{IC0}, \text{C1})\}$$
$$\text{prov} = \{\text{IA}, \text{IC}, \text{IE}, \text{IA0}, \text{IA1}\}$$
$$\text{req} = \{\text{IB}, \text{ID}, \text{IB0}, \text{IC0}, \text{IB1}, \text{IC1}\}$$
$$\text{bind} = \{(\text{IB0}, \text{IA1}), (\text{IC0}, \text{IA1}),$$
$$(\text{IB1}, \text{IB}), (\text{IC1}, \text{IB}),$$
$$(\text{IA}, \text{IA0}), (\text{IE}, \text{IA0}), (\text{IC}, \text{ID})\}$$

As in the case of the representation of a Darwin program we observe that such a realization cannot be a model of δ because $\bot$ is assigned to the undefined (and unmentioned) elements. However, the validity of a configuration can be established by the following definition (cf. Definition 5):

Definition 8 *Let C be a configuration. C is a* **valid** *configuration iff $\exists A \in \mathcal{M}^\delta.[[C]]^C \preceq A$*

This definition makes sense for reasons similar to those given for Definition 5.

$[[\_]]^C$ must be a monotonic function, ie. the following lemma must holds:

Lemma 4 *Let P and Q be two configurations, then $P \subseteq Q \Longrightarrow [[P]]^P \subseteq [[Q]]^P$.*

For the first of the two translation functions mentioned above this is true because of its resemblance to $[[\_]]^P$ and Lemma 3. For the second of our translation functions, identity, the lemma obviously holds.

3.3.3 Relation between Darwin Programs and Configurations

So far we have only investigated Darwin programs and configurations separate from each other. The execution of a program yields a configuration. We would like to express this relation in our logic. The obvious candidate for such a relation is *implements*:

Definition 9 *Let P be a Darwin program and C be a configuration. C implements P, written $C \models P$, iff $\exists A \in \mathcal{M}^\delta.[[P]]^P \preceq A \wedge [[C]]^C \preceq A$*

Note that we implicitly enforce the validity of both program and configuration (cf. Definitions 5, 8). With the following two definitions we can ensure that a compiler will be able to find a corresponding configuration for every valid Darwin program. We can also imagine a program that creates Darwin programs from existing configurations. Essentially these definitions ensure that the expressiveness of the Darwin language and the language for configurations is the same:

Definition 10 *Let P be a valid Darwin program, then $\exists C.C \models P$.*

Definition 11 *Let C be a valid configuration, then $\exists P.C \models P$.*

The following lemma is very important for the design process. It follows from the investigation into the monotonicity of the translation functions $[[\_]]^P$ and $[[\_]]^C$. If we construct our Darwin program by extending an existing program then we can do the same with the corresponding configuration. Thus we can extend a system dynamically without having to completely reconFig. it:

Lemma 5 *Let P and Q be Darwin programs and C and D be configurations. $P \subseteq Q \wedge C \models P \iff \exists D.D \models Q \wedge C \subseteq D$*

4 Extensions of the Theory

In order to enforce constraints on Darwin programs and to deduce properties the core theory δ can be extended by adding axioms.

4.1 Constraints on Darwin Programs

There are a number of constraints that apply to Darwin programs. Fig. 4 serves as a illustration for the following description of the constraints by means of a graphical representation of a Darwin program.

4.1.1 Multicast

Viewing provisions as data sinks and requirements as data sources Darwin allows the binding of many sources to one sink. However, it doesn't allow the binding of a source to multiple sinks. The following axioms ensure this:

$$\begin{aligned}
\text{bind}(i_1, i) &\Longrightarrow (\text{prov}(i_1) \wedge \text{prov}(i_2) \wedge \text{prov}(i)) \\
\wedge \text{bind}(i_2, i) & \vee (\text{req}(i_1) \wedge \text{req}(i_2) \wedge \text{req}(i)) \\
\wedge i_1 \neq i_2 & \vee (\text{req}(i_1) \wedge \text{req}(i_2) \wedge \text{prov}(i))
\end{aligned}$$

$$\begin{aligned}
\text{bind}(i, i_1) &\Longrightarrow \text{prov}(i) \wedge \text{req}(i_1) \wedge \text{req}(i_2) \\
\wedge \text{bind}(i, i_2) & \\
\wedge i_1 \neq i_2 &
\end{aligned}$$

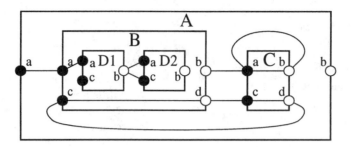

Figure 4: Example of an Incorrect Configuration

The binding of the interface D1.b to D2.a and D2.c in Fig. 4 is an example of multicast.

4.1.2 Unbound Interfaces

Unbound interfaces are an indication of a possible mal-configuration and are prevented with the axioms

$$\text{prov}(i) \implies \exists j \in \text{IID.bind}(i,j) \vee \text{bind}(j,i)$$
$$\vee \text{req}(i)$$

The current compiler does not detect these. In Fig. 4 the interfaces D1.c, D2.b and A.b are unbound.

4.1.3 Circular Bindings

A circular binding binds an interface to itself. While their direct occurrence is easy to detect in a Darwin program the indirect circular bindings across several levels of the decompositional hierarchy poses a more difficult task. However, in the logic specification three simple axioms are sufficient to achieve this goal. Using the fact that the bind predicate also expresses a directionality for an imaginary data flow from data sources to sinks, we can compute the transitive closure bind_T of that relation. Circular (and *only* circular) bindings will thus result in reflexive elements:

$$\text{bind}(i_1, i_2) \implies \text{bind}_T(i_1, i_2)$$
$$\text{bind}_T(i_1, i) \wedge \text{bind}_T(i, i_2) \implies \text{bind}_T(i_1, i_2)$$
$$\neg\text{bind}_T(i, i)$$

The binding between C.b and C.a in Fig. 4 is a direct circular binding whereas the circularity established by the binding between C.d and B.c is indirect.

4.1.4 Unbounded Decomposition

An unbounded decomposition occurs when a component has the same type as its container component

or any other component above that in the decompositional hierarchy. The Darwin compiler doesn't detect this and the resulting program creates an infinitely growing system structure. In our logical representation we would encounter infinitely many possible applications of the translation axioms. To prevent this we compute the transitive closure contains_T of the relation established by the c_cont function and ensure that the two elements of the relation never have the same type:

$$\text{c\_cont}(c) = c' \implies \text{contains}_T(c', c)$$
$$\text{contains}_T(c_1, c) \implies \text{contains}_T(c_1, c_2)$$
$$\wedge \text{contains}_T(c, c_2)$$
$$\text{contains}_T(c_1, c_2) \implies \text{c\_type}(c_1) \neq \text{c\_type}(c_2)$$

4.2 Primitive and Composite Components

The Darwin compiler distinguishes two classes of components – primitive and composite components.

Definition 12 *A primitive component is a component that contains no sub-components. A composite component is a component that contains at least one sub-component.*

Two predicates, composite and primitive, can be defined:

$$\exists c' \in \text{CID}.c' \neq \text{Universe} \implies \text{composite}(c)$$
$$\wedge \text{c\_cont}(c') = c$$
$$\neg\text{composite}(c) \implies \text{primitive}(c)$$

The fact that the Universe component is considered to be part of itself makes the first axiom slightly more complicated as we have to make sure that Universe is only regarded as a composite component if it *really* contains other components.

The distinction between the two classes of components is made to enable the Darwin compiler to impose further constraints on the structure of systems.

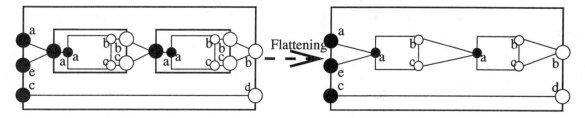

Figure 5: Example of Flattening

Processes must only be attached to primitive components. This way primitive components are the only *active components* in the system while the sole purpose of composite components is the structuring of the system. As a result we can strengthen the constraint dealing with unbound interfaces and carry out a structural transformation known as *flattening*.

4.2.1 Unbound Interfaces of Composite Components

Viewing the interfaces as data sources and sinks the axiom

$$(\mathsf{prov}(i) \vee \mathsf{req}(i)) \implies \exists j, k \in \textsc{iid}.\mathsf{bind}(j,i)$$
$$\wedge \mathsf{composite}(c) \qquad \wedge \mathsf{bind}(i,k)$$

ensure that the data flow originates and terminates at primitive components. Given these additional constraints the interface B.b of the configuration in Fig. 4 can be identified as being unbound. The axiom also prevents the Universe component from having any interfaces at all.

4.2.2 Flattening

As the active components are primitive components the system structure can be simplified by eliminating all composite components and replacing them by direct bindings between interfaces of the primitive components in the system. The new configuration consists of primitive components and bindings between their interfaces. It is behaviourally equivalent to the original configuration. The bindings between the primitive components can be obtained using the transitive closure bind_T (cf. Sect. 4.1.3) of the bind predicate:

$$\mathsf{bind}_T(i_1, i_2) \implies \mathsf{bind}_F(i_1, i_2)$$
$$\wedge \mathsf{primitive}(\mathsf{i\_comp}(i_1))$$
$$\wedge \mathsf{primitive}(\mathsf{i\_comp}(i_2))$$

As the directionality of bindings is preserved in the transitive closure the new predicate bind_F can be derived easily from bind_T. A flattened system can be described by a set of *configuration formulae* with the modifications that component identifiers make the primitive predicate true and that the bind predicate is replaced by bind_F. Fig. 5 shows an example of Flattening. As the component has interfaces it must be contained in another component in an actual configuration. The Flattening would eliminate those interfaces and the component boundary as well.

5 Summary and Future Work

Configuration languages like Darwin that incorporate the notions of types and decomposition are a means for describing system configurations in a way that facilitates reuse and flexibility. However, because of their abstract nature, it is difficult to reason about programs in these languages. For this we need direct representations of configurations. Such representations wouldn't be of much use though, unless their relation to the representation language is defined precisely. By using logic to specify a theory δ of Darwin programs and configurations we are able to provide a framework in which constraints and properties of configurations can be expressed easily by adding axioms to the theory. The theory also establishes the relationship between Darwin programs and configurations and links the validity of the former to the validity of the latter. Hence it can serve as a specification for the instantiation process. The operational semantics of instantiation can be described in terms of the π-calculus (cf. [10, 17]). In our future research we intend to show that it indeed satisfies the specification.

The results that have been presented in this paper combine well with our research on the semantics of Darwin (cf. [16]). The π-calculus semantics can be used to specify and analyse dynamic behaviour but is too complicated for expressing structural constraints, properties and program transformations such as Flattening. The converse is true of the theory presented here. As distributed programs combine both static (structural) and dynamic aspects the combination of the first order logic theory with the π-calculus semantics will enable us to reason about such programs. We've shown how the theory helps us in the design process by relating the extension of programs to the extension of configurations. The validity and extension lemmas from the theory, together with the notions of behavioural equivalence from the π-calculus, can be the basis of powerful tools for the system designer. They will enable the redesign of systems while preserving desirable properties, such as being able to extend a system dynamically without requiring complete reconfiguration. Our future research will therefore attempt to formalise the combination of the logic theory with the π-calculus semantics.

6 Acknowledgements

We gratefully acknowledge the advice and help provided by the Distributed Software Engineering Research Section at the Imperial College Department of Computing, and the financial support provided by the DTI under grant ref: IED4/410/36/002.

References

[1] R. Allan and D. Garlan. Formalizing architectural connection. In *Proc. of the 16th Int. Conf. on Software Engineering*, May 1994.

[2] M. Barbacci, C. Weinstock, D. Doubleday, M. Gardner, and R. Lichota. Durra: A structure description language for developing distributed applications. *IEE Software Engineering Journal*, 8(2):83–94, March 1993.

[3] N. Dulay. The Darwin configuration language. Imperial College Department of Computing Internal Report, March 1992.

[4] S. Eisenbach and R. Paterson. π-calculus semantics for the concurrent configuration language darwin. In *Proc. of the 26th Annual Hawaii Int. Conf. on System Sciences*, volume 2. IEEE Computer Society Press, 1993.

[5] N. Fenton and G. Hill. *Systems Construction and Analysis: A Mathematical and Logical Framework*. McGraw-Hill International Series in Software Engineering, 1993.

[6] D. Garlan and D. Perry. Software architecture: Practice, potential and pitfalls. In *Proc. of the 16th Int. Conf. on Software Engineering*, May 1994.

[7] D. Garlan and M Shaw. An introduction to software architecture. In *Advances in Software Engineering and Knowledge Engineering*, volume 1. World Scientific Publishing Co., 1993.

[8] H. Graves. Lockheed environment for automatic programming. In *Proc. of KBSE'91, 6th IEEE Knowledge Based Software Engineering Conf.*, pages 68–76, 1991.

[9] J. Kramer, J. Magee, M. Sloman, and N. Dulay. Configuring object-based distributed programs in REX. *IEE Software Engineering Journal*, 7(2):139–149, March 1992.

[10] J. Magee, N. Dulay, S. Eisenbach, and J. Kramer. Specifying distributed software architectures. In *Fifth European Software Engineering Conf.*, Barcelona, 1995.

[11] J. Magee, N. Dulay, and J. Kramer. Structuring parallel and distributed programs. *Software Engineering Journal*, 8(2):73–82, March 1993.

[12] J. Magee, J. Kramer, and M. Sloman. Constructing distributed programs in conic. *IEEE Transactions on Software Engineering*, 15(6), 1989.

[13] R. Milner. The polyadic π-calculus: a tutorial. Technical Report ECS-LFCS 91-180, University of Edinburgh, October 1991.

[14] D.E. Perry and A.L. Wolf. Foundations for the study of software architectures. *ACM SIGSOFT Software Engineering Notes*, 17(4):40–52, 1992.

[15] J.M. Purtilo. The polylith software bus. *ACM Transactions on Programming Languages*, 16(1):151–174, January 1994.

[16] M. Radestock and S. Eisenbach. What do you get from a π-calculus semantics? In *Proc. of PARLE'94 Parallel Architectures and Languages Europe*, number 817 in Lecture Notes in Computer Science, pages 635–647. Springer-Verlag, 1994.

[17] M. Radestock and S. Eisenbach. Semantics of a higer-order coordination language. In *COORDINATION'96 Proceedings*, Lecture Notes in Computer Science. Springer-Verlag, 1996. to appear.

[18] M.D. Rice and S.B. Seidman. A formal model for module interconnection languages. *IEEE Transactions on Software Engineering*, 20(1):88–101, January 1994.

A Framework for Heterogeneous Concurrency Control Policies in Distributed Applications

António Rito Silva, João Pereira and José Alves Marques

INESC/IST Technical University of Lisbon

Lisboa, Portugal

email: Rito.Silva@inesc.pt, joao@sabrina.inesc.pt, jam@inesc.pt

Abstract

Several concurrency control policies for distributed systems have been proposed both by theorists and practitioners. In this paper we present an abstract framework for concurrency control policies for the serial model. This framework supports a wide range of policies and permits the integration of different policies within the same application. It is shown how the framework is instantiated for several policies: strict two-phase locking, strict timestamping, optimistic and local timestamping. The framework defines a uniform interface for distributed concurrency control policies, such that a smooth replacement of policies during development is possible.

1 Introduction

Usually concurrency control deals with the isolation property of transactions. Isolation ensures serial execution of transactions in face of concurrency. Recently, it has been raised that some applications need to relax isolation to allow interference, e.g. cooperative work applications [1]. So, in a wider sense, concurrency control should allow a particular model of transaction interference. We call these models concurrency control models.

Each concurrency control model can be supported by different concurrency control policies. For instance, the serial model, where each transaction sees only the effects of committed transactions, is supported by two kind of policies: pessimistic and optimistic [2]. Both kinds can use different synchronization primitives, such as locking [3] or timestamping [4].

Concurrency control policies are built on top of lower level components which implement concurrency control mechanisms, including synchronization and communication components such as conditions or atomic broadcast.

We present an abstract framework that establishes a uniform interface to distributed concurrency control policies for the serial model (serializability policies). Particular policies are built by derivation of the framework.

The framework also permits the coexistence of heterogeneous concurrency control policies within the same application. Policies are constructed by instantiating three characteristics: transaction execution order definition time; object accesses consistency check time; and used synchronization primitives.

The framework specifies an architecture for a logically distributed application which integrates the design of several heterogeneous concurrency control policies.

2 Related Work

Domain specific architectures result from a domain analysis [5] activity which abstracts the domain and defines the structure and behavior holding its reusable part. Several authors have addressed the issue of distributed concurrency control in depth:

- Concurrency control policies can be implemented following two different perspectives [6]: pessimistic, when the application is expected to have high contention, and optimistic, when the level of contention is supposed to be low. Policies are further distinguished by their synchronization primitives: locking or timestamping.

- Weihl defines concurrency control in the context of atomic objects [7]. An atomic object encapsulates concurrency control and recovery control. Global serializability is achieved using local object properties [8]. Three local properties are explored: dynamic protocols, in which the serialization order of transactions is determined from the order in which they access the objects; static protocols, in which the serialization order of transactions is defined at transaction creation time; and hybrid protocols, which define the serialization order when a transaction finishes. All atomic objects accessed by a transaction must use the same local atomicity properties, otherwise global serializability cannot be achieved [8].

- Concurrency control is supported by several systems which implement atomic objects and local atomicity,

Proceedings of IWSSD-8

for instance Argus [9], Avalon [10], Arjuna [11] and Hermes/ST [12]. These systems use nested transactions and two-phase locking as their default concurrency control policies. It is possible to use other policies but they must be implemented by the programmer without explicit support.

Guerraoui describes an object-oriented system that abstracts some of the aspects of distributed concurrency control policies [13]. Starting from Weihl's work, he proposes an object-oriented system where objects can possess different local atomicity properties if some global serialization protocol exists. The global serialization protocol defines a global serial order of execution which is defined outside objects. Global serialization protocols are grouped in three classes: static, dynamic and hybrid, as in [8].

The object-oriented approach is claimed to be suitable for the development of distributed applications [14]. Object-oriented analysis and design methods, e.g. [15, 16], are becoming widely used in the development of applications. Nevertheless, developing applications for distributed object-oriented systems involves issues that suggest deep changes in current methods [16]. Object-oriented frameworks [17] can support the structure and behavior resulting from a domain analysis. In particular, Schmidt proposes a framework [18] which simplifies the development, configuration and reconfiguration of applications.

We propose an approach to the development of applications with distributed concurrency control based on an object-oriented framework. This is a novel work since it is independent of a specific platform and integrates a wide range of concurrency control policies.

3 Abstract Framework

The design of concurrency control policies for the serial model is guided by an abstract framework. An object oriented framework is an aggregation of collaborating classes with a common purpose. It constitutes a skeleton which should be fleshed out to build complete applications [17]. The framework permits the design of concrete systems where heterogeneous policies can coexist.

To support transactions the usual basic architecture of transactional systems (transactions, transaction managers and object managers) is adopted as the main structure. A structure to represent logic distribution is also supported by the framework.

We divide concurrency control policies into three parts: order definition, order control and recovery control. Specialization of these parts results in concrete systems.

Order definition and order control together constitute what is usually referred to as serial control. Serial control guarantees that transactions execution is serializable and separates execution order definition from object access control. This allows for objects to have their own local concurrency control policies independently of the global serial order as in [13]. Recovery control guarantees preservation of a consistent state in spite of transaction failures.

Emphasis is put on order definition and order control. Recovery control functionality is isolated in the architecture but particular solutions are not discussed.

The notation in this paper follows [15].

3.1 Structure

The framework's structure is centered on the support of logic distribution, transactions and atomic objects.

3.1.1 Logic distribution

The framework supports introduction of concurrency control into the specification of a distributed application. A specification is divided into worlds. Application objects must belong to one and only one world and objects belonging to different worlds should communicate by explicit message passing. This approach is based on the definition of logically distributed software [19]. Logically distributed worlds abstract a wide range of distributed applications since they only establish the concept of world, postponing decisions about other characteristics of a distributed system.

Worlds are represented by classes (figure 1) and are responsible for objects registration and system configuration. Worlds are autonomous entities with a predefined interface to other worlds.

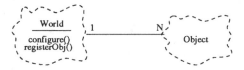

Figure 1: Logic Distribution

Objects registration within worlds permits to logically distinguish between inter-world communication, when the objects involved in the communication belong to different worlds, and intra-world communication, when the objects belong to the same world. Inter-world communications are also called remote communications and will be relevant in the creation of distributed sub-transactions.

Configuration may be dynamic, if worlds can be created or destroyed during the system's lifetime, or static, otherwise.

In order to introduce distributed concurrency control policies in a specification the designer should first use the framework to specify logic distribution.

3.1.2 Transactions

Worlds can have different concurrency control policies, i.e., the design of concurrency control is done on a per world.

We use transactions to support concurrency control. A transaction is a transient entity representing atomic execution of several operations. Transactions ensure isolated execution of their operations.

The framework uses nested and distributed transactions to handle distribution. Nested transactions [20] define a tree of transactions allowing concurrency among sub-transactions and partial recovery of sub-transactions.

The tree of transactions may span several worlds. The set of transactions of a tree of transactions belonging to a world is part of the distributed structure of that tree. Each of these sets is called the top transaction's distributed set in that world. The distributed set of a transaction in a world is useful for the definition of the distributed commit protocol.

For example, the tree of transactions in figure 2 has three distributed sets: {t1,t5,t6}, {t2,t3} and {t4} in worlds W1, W2 and W3 respectively.

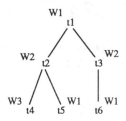

Figure 2: Tree of transactions

Each world (figure 3) has a transaction manager object responsible for the definition of the transactions' execution order. Transaction managers are also responsible for the creation, commit, abort and destruction of transactions. The framework defines transaction managers and transaction classes in the context of worlds. Note that the distributed set of a transaction in a world can be derived from existing relationships.

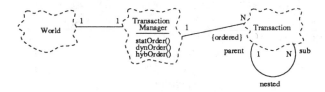

Figure 3: Transactions and Transaction Managers.

Concurrency control policies establish different ways of defining transactions execution order [8]. Worlds must be capable, via transaction manager, of autonomously define their local transactions' execution order. The transaction manager can use a static policy (operation statOrder), a dynamic policy (operation dynOrder) or an hybrid policy (operation hybOrder). A problem appears if the several local orders of execution defined in each world are incompatible. Our solution for this problem follows [21]: a local transactions' execution order is defined in each world and a global execution order is constructed using local orders. If the global order is acyclic the transaction commits, otherwise it must abort.

3.1.3 Atomic objects

Atomic objects control the transactions' execution order and are responsible for recovery from operations of aborted transactions. They encapsulate recovery control policies and cooperate with the transaction manager to support a particular concurrency control policy. In order to achieve atomicity, transactions should act upon atomic objects.

As in [8], we support both atomic and non-atomic objects. Incomplete transactions have no effects on atomic objects and accesses are serializable. Atomic objects can only be accessed within a transaction. Transactions may access both kinds, atomic and non-atomic objects. Accesses to non-atomic objects are neither serializable nor recoverable. We support non-atomic objects for efficient implementation of temporary and non-shared objects. In this paper we only consider atomic objects.

To allow a higher degree of concurrency, besides the ordinary distinction between read and write operations, atomic objects can use knowledge of operation semantics [22]. A matrix of operation compatibility must be defined for each class. Two operations are compatible when they can execute concurrently within the same object and their effects are serializable.

Atomic objects are implemented from the original Object and Atomic Interface, Recover, Controller and Access objects (figure 4). Class Object defines part of the application semantics ignoring synchronization. Atomic objects are encapsulated by Atomic Interface objects that intercept all accesses to them. The only accesses we considered to objects are invocations. Controller objects are responsible for managing concurrent accesses and Recover objects for recovery. Operations are associated with Access classes denoting the mode of access, e.g. read. In each instant, Controller objects hold the set of current accesses of unfinished transactions, i.e., neither committed nor aborted. Recover objects encapsulate recovery control policies.

The matrix of operation compatibility is split into definitions of Access subclasses. Each Access object knows its compatibility with a set of known Access subclasses and delegates to other Access objects if its class is not a member of this set. Therefore it is possible to increment

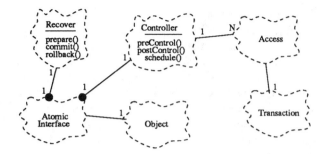

Figure 4: Atomic Object Structure.

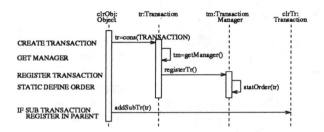

Figure 5: Transaction creation.

the matrix without updating previously defined `Access` classes.

3.2 Behavior

The framework's behavior is centered on the cooperation of objects to support concurrency control policies. We describe some relevant cooperations: transaction creation, atomic object access, two-phase commit protocol, object commit and object abort.

3.2.1 Transaction creation

For good design we consider transaction creation and transaction start as different events. Transaction creation corresponds to the creation of a new transaction object and its connection to a tree of transactions. Afterwards, transactions can be started synchronously or asynchronously, allowing concurrency between transactions belonging to the same tree.

Transactions are created either explicitly or implicitly. Transactions can be explicitly created by programmers either to start a top transaction or to create a local non-distributed sub-transaction. Transactions are created implicitly during inter-world communications to define distribution boundaries in the transaction tree and to allow distributed commit and recovery. A sub-transaction is created in the invoked world.

Static policies require execution order to be defined when transactions are created. The transaction manager responsible for the new transaction must implement the `statOrder` operation to set a transaction execution order before the transaction starts.

Transaction creation design is presented in the interaction diagram shown in figure 5. A transaction object must know the object and operation where the transaction starts. This are given as arguments of the constructor of `Transaction` class[1]. The new transaction, `tr`, registers itself in the transaction manager of the invoked object, and in the parent transaction if the new transaction is a sub-transaction.

---

[1]This is not shown in the figure for the sake of simplicity.

This design is intended to uniformly cover all possible situations of transaction creation: creation of a transaction in the same world (invoker and invoked objects belong to the same world) and distributed creation (invoker and invoked objects belong to different worlds). The creation of a transaction in the same world covers both top transaction creation and sub-transaction creation. The only difference is whether operation `addSubTr` is invoked or not.

3.2.2 Atomic object access

Once created, a transaction can be started and access the first object. Further invocations from this object to other atomic objects are in the context of this transaction.

Each access to an atomic object is controlled using an access protocol after which the operation is invoked on the original object. This protocol is divided in order control and recovery control.

Order control for pessimistic policies enforces that access to atomic objects be checked, i.e., only compatible operations can execute concurrently. Order control determines whether an access should proceed, wait or abort. For optimistic policies accesses to atomic objects are not controlled.

An `Access` object is created when a transactional operation is invoked. It denotes operation semantics and will be used in the access protocol to check compatibility among concurrent accesses to objects. Furthermore, `Access` objects allow programmers to insert non-trivial semantic knowledge to achieve a greater concurrency degree.

The access protocol is represented in figure 6. The operations encapsulated by `preControl` and `prepare` support order control and recovery control, respectively. Operations `compatible` and `cmpOrder` verify if the transaction can access the object and return: eERROR, when an internal abort is triggered within the transaction; eDELAY, when the execution should be delayed; eCONTINUE, when the transaction can access the atomic object. Dynamic policies order transactions during object accesses (operation `dynOrder`).

The access protocol must be executed in mutual exclusion to prevent interference among transactions trying to

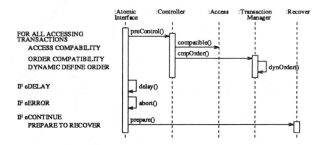

Figure 6: Access protocol.

access the same atomic object simultaneously. For the sake of simplicity, this is not shown in the interaction diagram.

3.2.3 Two-phase commit protocol

Due to distribution and policy heterogeneity we distinguish transaction termination from transaction commit and abort. A transaction terminates when the initial invocation of a top transaction returns. A transaction commits or aborts only after completion of a protocol that ensures the transaction leaves the system consistent. Since policy heterogeneity can generate different execution orders, the protocol needs to determine if the local orders are compatible, i.e., whether they can generate a serial global order. This protocol is started when a top transaction terminates.

The framework supports a two-phase commit protocol. The two-phase commit protocol is used to ensure atomic commitment of distributed transactions [23]. The framework includes the behavior necessary to generate the serial global order in the two-phase commit protocol to reduce the number of messages exchanged.

Transaction managers play the roles of both coordinators and participants in the two-phase commit protocol. Briefly, when asked by the coordinator (transaction manager of the top transaction), participant transaction managers reply with their local execution orders (first-phase) if the transaction can commit locally, or with an abort result otherwise. After the coordinator has received all the replies, if all participants can commit locally and the local orders generate a serializable global order, the coordinator sends a commit message to the participants, otherwise it sends an abort message (second-phase).

The protocol acts upon the worlds where distributed sets of the top transaction exist. Each transaction manager of these worlds is a participant. Control flow does not follow the structure of the tree of transactions.

Optimistic policies require that, during the first phase of the two-phase protocol, object accesses done by the preparing transaction must be controlled to verify if only compatible operations have been executed concurrently. For pessimistic policies this is not necessary because atomic objects are already in a consistent state.

During the first phase the local execution orders can be constructed to implement hybrid policies.

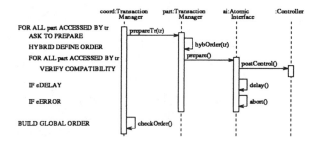

Figure 7: Two-phase commit protocol: first phase.

During the first phase (figure 7), message `prepareTr` is sent by the coordinator to each participant asking for the transactions' execution local order. Participant `Transaction Manager` objects define an execution order, used by hybrid policies, invoking `hybOrder`. Objects accessed by the transaction execute a post order control. If operation `postControl` returns eERROR, object `part` is notified that the transaction should abort; if it returns eCONTINUE object `part` is informed that the atomic object complies with the local serial order; if it returns eDELAY, operation `delay` is executed and the transaction is delayed. This operation, `postControl`, is implemented only for optimistic policies.

When the participant transaction manager has received all the answers from accessed atomic objects it returns to the coordinator if the transaction can commit locally and, in the affirmative case, which is the serial local order of execution.

3.2.4 Object commit and abort

The second phase of the two-phase protocol consists of a commit or abort. The transaction's commit/abort requires that all objects accessed by it execute operation `commitTr`/`abortTr` to confirm/rollback the object's current state. During commit/abort, recovery policies must restore the state or discard recovery objects.

Upon commit/abort delayed transactions may be rescheduled for execution.

Commit or abort of an atomic object (figure 8) invokes operation `commit` on the `Recover` object, destroys all `Access` objects created by the transaction (behavior associated to operation `housekeep`) and verifies whether other delayed transactions can now access the object by invoking operation `Schedule`.

4 Concrete Systems

In the previous sections we have defined an abstract framework for the construction of concurrency control poli-

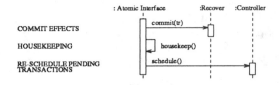

Figure 8: Atomic object commit.

cies. The concrete policies are built by derivation of this abstract framework, redefining some operations of some abstract classes and possibly defining some new operations. For each concrete policy we will have to create subclasses of classes defined in the framework to implement the needed redefinitions and the new operations.

In table 9 we show which operations should be redefined for each policy.

	pessimistic	optimistic	static	dynamic	hybrid
preControl()	yes				
postControl()		yes			
schedule()	yes	yes			
statOrder()			yes		
dynOrder()				yes	
hybOrder()					yes

Figure 9: Operations Redefinition and Policies.

For pessimistic policies we need to ensure that transactions accesses to atomic objects happens in a serial way. In this case, operation preControl must be redefined (figure 6). In optimistic policies verification of serial accesses to atomic objects is done only when a transaction tries to commit. For this policy type, operation postControl must be redefined (figure 7).

In our system, serialization order for hybrid policies is defined only when a transaction tries to commit, so we need to redefine operation hybOrder (figure 7). For static policies, as the serialization order is defined when a transaction is created, we need to redefine operation statOrder (figure 5). Dynamic policies define the serialization order using operation dynOrder during object access in pessimistic policies (figure 6) or during object prepare (included in operation postControl) in optimistic policies. The latter case occurs when the Controller object is verifying order compatibility (not explicitly shown in figure 7).

Any policy using operation delay should also redefine operation Schedule so that suspended transactions can be resumed.

We allow simultaneous existence of heterogeneous policies within same application. Furthermore, worlds can independently define their own concurrency control policies. Weihl proved that global serializability is achieved if all atomic objects use the same policy[8]. Since each world

has a single policy we achieve a local order of serialization within each world. As already referred, to obtain a global serial order, the coordinator's transaction manager constructs a serialization order using the participant's local orders. The transaction can commit if the generated global order is serializable, otherwise it aborts.

4.1 Traditional Policies

We now present concrete systems for some traditional policies. The name of each subclass identifies the concurrency control policy.

4.1.1 Strict two-phase locking policy

Strict two-phase locking is a pessimistic dynamic locking policy. This policy was proposed in [3].

To support this policy, we defined specialized subclasses of Transaction Manager and Controller.

When using this policy, locks are represented by Access objects, and transactions need to obtain a lock on an object to access it.

During object accesses operation preControl (figure 6) verifies if the required access is compatible with accesses currently granted by the object to transactions accessing it. If the required access is compatible the transaction is allowed to access the object, otherwise it is suspended by invoking operation delay.

An atomic object can resume execution of delayed transactions when a transaction that has accessed it commits or aborts. Transactions can be resumed according to the order they were suspended by (FIFO) or not, depending on whether the abstract mechanisms being used offer strong fairness or not. This behavior is defined by operation schedule (figure 8). Afterwards, each resumed transaction checks whether it can access the object. If this is not the case, it will be suspended again.

The framework allows two different versions of the two-phase locking policy, depending on whether there is an explicit local order definition or not. The first orders conflicting transactions using operation dynOrder while in the second case transactions are implicitly ordered only when they commit. By using explicit local order the Controller object is able to detect situations of local deadlock[2] in which case a eERROR value should be returned.

To avoid deadlocks a transaction only waits a certain amount of time to obtain the lock and, if there is a timeout, aborts.

4.1.2 Strict timestamping policy

Strict timestamping is a pessimistic static timestamping policy. Transactions are serialized according to a unique

---
[2]Deadlocks can always occur without being detected due to distribution - global deadlock.

global order usually relating to the top transaction's creation time. A transaction aborts when it accesses an object that has already been accessed by a transaction with a higher timestamp. This policy was proposed in [4].

To support this policy, we defined subclasses of `Transaction Manager` and `Controller`. A new class is defined (`Generator`) which generates unique timestamps.

When a transaction is created, operation `statOrder` (figure 5) is invoked to generate its execution order which is identified by a global timestamp. The operation communicates with a central independent entity, a `Generator` object, that knows the global timestamp associated with each transaction family. If the transaction is a top one, this central entity generates a unique global timestamp for it, otherwise it gets the global timestamp associated with the top transaction.

In this policy object accesses are checked by operation `preControl`. This operation checks the local order and the access mode to decide if an access should be permitted. The transaction is aborted if the object has already been accessed by a transaction with a higher serial order and the corresponding accesses are incompatible. The transaction is delayed when transactions concurrently accessing the object have incompatible accesses, otherwise it proceeds.

As with the previous policy we also need to redefine operation `schedule` and it has a similar behavior. A difference is that transactions should be resumed by the order defined by their timestamps, which implies that abstract mechanisms should support a priority scheduling.

4.1.3 An optimistic policy

There are several policies usually classified as optimistic. We describe an optimistic hybrid timestamping policy where a local order is assigned to each transaction by timestamping. This policy uses the parallel validation algorithm proposed in [2].

During the first phase of the two-phase commit protocol operation `hybOrder` generates a local serial order (figure 7). Operation `postControl` has to verify if the transaction can commit locally. It returns `eCONTINUE` if the transaction's access is compatible with those of other transactions that have already committed[3], taking into consideration local order and access semantics, otherwise it returns `eERROR`.

Since in this policy transactions are not delayed it is not necessary to redefine operation `schedule`.

Due to asynchronous inter-world communication this policy can generate unnecessary conflicting local orders because timestamps are locally generated.

---

[3]In reality, to be more precise, these are not transactions that have committed but all transactions that have done the first-phase of the commit protocol and have not yet aborted.

4.1.4 Local Timestamping Policy

This policy differs from the timestamping policy presented in section 4.1.2 because timestamps are created by a local entity, not by a central entity. A different `Generator` object is associated with each `Transaction Manager` object, i.e., a `Generator` object is not a central entity known by every `Transaction Manager` object. This local entity knows the local timestamp associated with each transaction family presented in the world. When a transaction family first appears in a world, the local `Generator` object creates a local timestamp and associates it to the transaction family. Relatively to strict timestamping policy, it is only necessary to modify operation `statOrder` (see figure 5).

This policy has the advantage of not depending on a central entity for the management of timestamps. Nevertheless, since local orders do not follow the global order we can have unnecessary aborts due to transactions that do not conflict with others but have associated incompatible local orders.

4.2 Cooperation and Autonomy

In this section we discuss how worlds can cooperate and what is meant by autonomous policies. There is a tradeoff between autonomy and cooperation, autonomy improves application extensibility and cooperation improves application performance.

4.2.1 Cooperative Worlds

There are several ways in which worlds can cooperate. One way is the creation of a global order from local serialization orders, but this is not the only way. Greater degrees of cooperation imply more communication between entities in the system, especially between `Transaction Manager` objects.

There are several reasons for the cooperation between worlds. They can cooperate to improve the performance of the global system or to avoid unnecessary aborts[4], for example.

An example of cooperation is the definition of the local order in the invoked `Transaction Manager` object taking into account the local order already defined in the invoker `Transaction Manager` object.

In figure 10, the local timestamping policy, presented in section 4.1.4, is adapted to cooperate with the caller (remote transaction manager).

The local order is enriched with the caller's local order. Thus, it is possible to immediately abort the transaction if they are not compatible and not later when the transaction will try to commit.

---

[4]In our system we can have transactions that in reality are unrelated, but apparently conflict due to their serialization order.

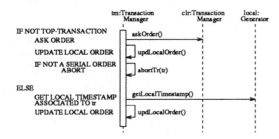

Figure 10: Operation `statOrder` redefinition.

4.2.2 Autonomous Policies

A policy is autonomous if its integration with other policies does not imply their modification. A policy is autonomous if it does not need to be aware of other worlds' policies.

The design of the strict timestamping policy can be non-autonomous. In operation `statOrder` (figure 11), object `Transaction Manager` gets the global timestamp from the top transaction manager. Because transaction managers can have different policies, operation `getGlobalTimestamp` must be present in the interface of all `Transaction Manager` classes, even if they provide different policies.

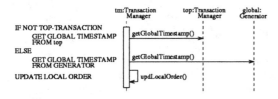

Figure 11: Operation `statOrder` redefinition.

The framework we propose supports the definition of both autonomous and non-autonomous policies. The difference is that an autonomous policy uses the framework's abstract interface while a non-autonomous one needs to use interfaces of particular policies, which becomes a penalty for application maintenance.

5 Conclusions

This work is part of the definition of a global development process of distribution applications centered on separation of concerns [24]. Concerns, relevant for the development of distributed applications, are divided into three levels of abstraction: model, policy and mechanism. Models describe users expectations about the application or system behavior, e.g. serial execution of transactions. Policies define algorithms which support application models, e.g. strict two-phase locking. Mechanisms offer components which are used by policies to implement their algorithms, e.g. threads.

This approach guarantees two levels of independence: policy independence and mechanism independence. Policy independence permits modular replacement of policies for the same model without interfering with application semantics. Mechanism independence keeps policies independent from specific mechanisms, such as threads packages or synchronization primitives.

We present a generic abstract framework for the serial model of transactions concurrency control. This framework allows definition of concrete specializations supporting a wide set of concurrency control policies. Moreover, the framework permits several per-world policies running within the same application, being possible to replace a policy without needing to change other worlds' specifications. Semantic knowledge of objects can be used to allow a greater level of concurrency. Our framework is platform-independent since we use abstract mechanisms as in [25].

New policies can be defined using knowledge about other worlds' policies. This violates policy autonomy but can become a powerful optimization technique. In this case, policy independence is not achieved.

We allow dynamic order definition, e.g. strict two-phase locking policy, static order definition, e.g. strict timestamping policy, or hybrid order definition, e.g. optimistic policies. Furthermore, we allow different worlds to have different local serial orders because transaction managers can make decisions about their own order policies: dynamic, static or hybrid. Our framework can emulate Guerraoui's system [13] if we consider our worlds as his objects, which is natural since both solve the same problems. The same policy is implemented for all of a world's objects for performance reasons.

The framework achieves a structural separation between control and recovery control. Nevertheless, as pointed out in [26], serial policies are not independent from recovery policies. This means that a given framework instantiation using a particular serializability policy restricts the set of possible recovery policies. This paper does not present any particular recovery control policy but they can be found in [27].

Several object-oriented design patterns [28] have been identified in the framework [27, 29, 30].

An implementation [31] was done in C++ on UNIX using the DCE threads package. The implementation allows the construction of centralized prototypes with logic distribution which can be debugged without interference of communication faults, errors or delays. Currently another implementation is going on on top of the ACE environment [32].

In the near future we intend to integrate within this

framework concurrency control with replication. Extending the framework to support non-strict models of concurrency control is the next evolutionary step.

Acknowledgments

We would like to thank Pedro Sousa for the fruitful discussions. We also thank David Matos for his careful proofreading.

References

[1] Naser S. Barghouti and Gail E. Kaiser. Concurrency Control in Advanced Database Applications. *ACM Computing Surveys*, 23(3):269–317, September 1991.

[2] H. Kung and J. Robinson. On optimistic methods for concurrency control. *ACM Transactions Database Systems*, 6(2):213–226, June 1981.

[3] K.P. Eswaran, J.N. Gray, R.A. Lorie, and I.L. Traiger. The Notions of Consistency and Predicate Locks in a Database System. *Comunications of the ACM*, 19(11):624–633, November 1976.

[4] Robert H. Thomas. A Majority Concensus Approach to Concurrency Control for Multiple Copy Databases. *ACM Transactions on Database Systems*, 4(24):180–209, June 1979.

[5] Guillermo Arango and Ruben Prieto-Diaz, editors. *Domain Analysis and Software Systems Modeling*. IEEE Computer Society Press, 1991.

[6] M. Tamer Ozsu. *Principles of Distributed Database Systems*. Prentice Hall, 1991.

[7] William Weihl. *Specification and Implementation of Atomic Data Types*. PhD thesis, MIT, 1984.

[8] William Weihl. Local Atomicity Properties: Modular Concurrency Control for Abstract Data Types. *ACM Transactions on Programming Languages and Systems*, 11(2):249–282, April 1989.

[9] Barbara Liskov. Distributed Programming in Argus. *Communications of the ACM*, 31(3):300–312, March 1988.

[10] Jeffrey L. Eppinger, Lily B. Mummert, and Alfred Z. Spector. *Camelot and Avalon: A Distributed Transaction Facility*. Morgan Kaufmann, 1991.

[11] Santosh K. Shrivastava, Graeme N. Dixon, and Graham D. Parrington. An overview of the arjuna distributed programming system. *IEEE Software*, January 1991.

[12] Michael Fazzolare, Bernhard G. Humm, and R. David Ranson. Concurrency control for distributed nested transactions in hermes. *International Conference for Concurrent and Distributed Systems*, 1993.

[13] Rachid Guerraoui. Atomic Object Composition. In *ECOOP'94*, pages 118–138, Bologna, Italy, July 1994.

[14] Gordon S. Blair, Javad Malik, John R. Nicol, and Jonathan Walpole. A synthesis of object-oriented and functional ideas in the design of a distributed software engineering environment. *Software Engineering Journal*, 5(3):193–204, May 1990.

[15] Grady Booch. *Object-Oriented Analyis and Design with Applications*. The Benjamin/Cummings Publishing Company, Inc., 1994.

[16] Derek Coleman, Patrick Arnold, Stephanie Bodoff, Chris Dollin, Helena Gilchrist, Fiona Hayes, and Paul Jeremes. *Object-Oriented Development: The Fusion Method*. Prentice-Hall, 1994.

[17] Rebecca Wirfs-Brock, Brian Wilkerson, and Lauren Wiener. *Designing Object-Oriented Software*. Prentice-Hall, 1990.

[18] Douglas C. Schmidt and Tatsuya Suda. An Object-Oriented Framework for Dynamically Configuring Extensible Distributed Systems. *BCS/IEE Distributed Systems Engineering Journal*, 1995.

[19] Henri E. Bal, Jennifer G. Steiner, and Andrew S. Tanenbaum. Programming Languages for Distributed Computing Systems. *ACM Computing Surveys*, 21(3):261–322, September 1989.

[20] David P. Reed. Naming and synchronization in a decentralized computer system. Technical Report 205, Ph.D. Thesis, M.I.T. Dept. of Elec. Eng. and Comp. Sci, available as M.I.T. Lab. for Comp. Sci. Technical Report 260, Sept 1978.

[21] Calton Pu. Superdatabases for Composition of Heterogeneous Databases. In *Proceedings of the 4th Data Engineering Conference*, pages 548–555, Los Angeles, USA, February 1988. IEEE.

[22] Hector Garcia-Molina. Using Semantic Knowledge for Transaction Processing in a Distributed Database. *ACM Transactions on Database Systems*, 8(2):186–213, June 1983.

[23] Jim Gray. Notes on Data Base Operating Systems. In R. Bayer, R. M. Graham, and G. Seegmuller, editors, *Operating Systems: An Advanced Course*, pages 393–481. Springer-Verlag, New-York, 1979.

[24] António Rito Silva, Pedro Sousa, and José Alves Marques. Development of Distributed Applications with Separation of Concerns. In *Proceedings of the 1995 Asia-Pacific Software Engineering Conference APSEC'95*, pages 168–177, Brisbane, Australia, December 1995. IEEE Computer Society Press.

[25] Douglas C. Schmidt. An OO Encapsulation of Lightweight OS Concurrency Mechanisms in the ACE Toolkit. Technical Report WUCS-95-31, Washington University, St. Louis, 1995.

[26] William Weihl. The Impact of Recovery in Concurrency Control. *Journal of Computer and System Sciences*, 47(1):157–184, August 1993.

[27] António Rito Silva, João Pereira, and Pedro Sousa. The Recovery Pattern, August 1995. INESC Technical Report.

[28] Erich Gamma, Richard Helm, Ralph Johnson, and John Vlissides. *Design Patterns: Elements of Reusable Object-Oriented Software*. Addison Wesley, 1995.

[29] António Rito Silva, João Pereira, and Pedro Sousa. Local Serialization Pattern, October 1995. Presented at OOPSLA'95 Workshop on Design Patterns for Concurrent, Parallel, and Distributed Object-Oriented Systems.

[30] António Rito Silva, João Pereira, and Pedro Sousa. The Global Serialization Pattern, September 1995. INESC Technical Report.

[31] João Pereira. Enriquecimento com Controlo de Concorrência de Especificações Orientadas por Objectos. Tese de mestrado/Master thesis, Instituto Superior Técnico, Universidade Técnica de Lisboa, Lisboa, Portugal, Setembro 1994.

[32] Douglas C. Schmidt. The ADAPTIVE Communication Environment: An Object-Oriented Network Programming Toolkit for Developing Communication Software. In *11th and 12th Sun User Group Conferences*, San Jose, California and San Francisco, California, December 1993 and June 1994.

Visual Presentation of Software Specifications and Designs

Gruia-Catalin Roman, Delbert Hart, Charles Calkins
Department of Computer Science
Washington University, St. Louis, MO 63130

Abstract

Formal methods hold the promise for high dependability in the design of critical software. However, software engineers who employ formal methods need to communicate their design decisions to users, customers, managers, and colleagues who may not be in a position to acquire a full understanding of the formal notation being used. Visualizations derived from formal specifications and designs must be able convey the required information precisely and reliably without the use of formal notation. This paper discusses an attempt to integrate a design methodology based upon specification and program refinement with a state-of-the-art approach to rapid visualization of program executions. The emphasis is placed on how to convey graphically various kinds of formally-stated program properties. The illustrations are extracted from a case study involving the formal derivation of a message router. The ultimate goal is to identify issues fundamental to the use of visualization in conjunction with formal methods and to catalog methods which achieve effective visual communication without compromising formal reasoning.

1. Introduction

As amply demonstrated by two recently published surveys [6, 12], program visualization is an area of significant research growth. Although to date its impact on software development methods has been relatively small, our own experiments identify requirements validation, rapid prototyping, training, monitoring, and testing as areas of immediate, high-payoff potential. It is less clear, however, what role program visualization ought to play during design. Since program visualization does not come for free, one must ensure that the benefits outweigh the potential costs associated with constructing visualizations. Predefined visualizations practically eliminate the construction costs, but may not be responsive to the needs of a specific design effort. Rapid visualization techniques which allow one to develop custom visualizations with minimal effort offer an attractive alternative. This idea was the key motivating factor behind the development of Pavane [7] and the use of declarative visualization as its foundation. Experiments with Pavane showed that programmers with no prior visualization experience can construct relatively sophisticated program visualizations within half a day. Despite this, we believe that much more drastic reductions in the visualization development effort must be achieved before custom visualizations are likely to impact to a significant degree the typical design process.

There is, however, one design area where visualization may prove to be not only a cost-saving technique but a basic necessity. What we have in mind is the use of formal methods in the development of high-dependability software involved in critical applications. Formal methods involve specialized expertise not widely available. Yet, the designs must still be scrutinized by customers, users, managers, and colleagues who may not be in a position to become versed in the use of formal notation. Concrete visual representations of the evolving design could become a practical communication medium between designers and the rest of the community. This is not actually a new idea. Architects make use of scale models and elevation views to explain projects, gain approval, and to explore options. In this paper we investigate ways of incorporating a similar visual presentation strategy into a formal design process.

A particularly attractive formal technique is program derivation. It entails the application of a series of correctness-preserving transformations to some formal description of the problem to be solved. In sequential programming, where the approach enjoys a long standing and prestigious tradition, the starting point for the derivation is a pair of assertions. In concurrent programming the starting point may be either a program or a set of assertions about some computation. In one case, the program is gradually transformed into another program having certain more desirable properties, e.g., it can be implemented efficiently on a particular architecture; in the other case, the initial abstract specification is gradually refined up to a point when it is sufficiently concrete as to have a trivial encoding into some target programming language.

All the visualizations presented in this paper have been produced using Pavane. They involve one or more worlds (windows) of three-dimensional geometric objects, full-color, and smooth animation. Each visualization is constructed by writing a set of rules that map program states to graphical representations. Pavane supports rapid visualization of C and Swarm [8] programs. Swarm employs tuple-based communication à la Linda [2] and has a UNITY-style proof logic [3] which may be used to carry out specification refinements or prove Swarm programs correct. In addition, state changes in a Swarm program are automati-

1063-6765/96 $5.00 © 1996 IEEE

Proceedings of IWSSD-8

115

cally supplied to Pavane thus obviating any need to modify the program being visualized. These considerations make Swarm the language of choice for our work on formal design methods. The Swarm logic is used to build the specifications and carry out the refinements, the Swarm programming notation is used to write abstract programs that satisfy the specifications, and Pavane is used to construct the visualizations that convey the design decisions associated with each refinement step.

The specific case study presented in this paper involves a message router. In the simplest terms, the message router is a device which accepts messages on a number of input lines and delivers them to its output lines. Each message consists of a header, one or more body packets, and a tail. The header contains the packet destination. Packet ordering within a message is preserved, packets belonging to different messages are not interleaved, and messages from the same input line going to the same output line are not reordered. A full formal derivation of a message router design employing wormhole routing in a cross-bar switch [4] already existed prior to the start of this work. The general question we try to address in this paper is how can the various stages of the design be presented visually. We used the case study to identify challenging issues and helpful techniques.

The remainder of the paper is organized as follows. Section 2 provides an informal overview of our design methodology and the application domains where it was used. Section 3 reviews very briefly: the UNITY-logic to help the reader understand the basic nature of the formal specifications we employ; the Swarm notation used to construct abstract programs; and Pavane's rule-based notation which facilitates the declarative specification of three-dimensional, full-color, smoothly animated graphical representations of executing programs. Section 4 outlines the router design (stage by stage) and uses it as a backdrop against which to discuss a variety of useful visualization techniques. Brief concluding remarks follow in Section 5.

2. Design Methodology Overview

Central to our research is the idea that the lessons we have learned from exercises in program derivation can reshape the process by which we design concurrent systems. Critics of formal derivation make the claim that such techniques are tedious and costly and require highly-specialized skills and training. We contend that the tedium is not intrinsic to program derivation and that costs relate to the degree of reliability one attempts to achieve. We do not dispute, however, the fact that the application of formal techniques demands special skills. For this reason we are exploring a scenario involving designers comfortable with formal specifications who navigate expeditiously through the refinement process, providing some formal justification for each step along the way but not necessarily slowing down to carry out all the proofs. One important practical objective of our work is to understand better what combination of skills is essential to the successful application of

program derivation on industrial-grade problems by a group of highly-trained specialists. To accomplish this we focused our attention on refinement methods and visual communication techniques. The former are the intellectual blueprint for the way in which design is approached and managed; the latter provide the means by which design decisions expressed in rigorous formal notation may be communicated to a broad audience and project progress may be monitored. These two issues and their interplay may not capture all that is needed to make industrial application of formal derivation possible but they are central to such an undertaking.

Formal derivation. Program derivation is a technique for generating correct programs from some initial formal specification by means of stepwise refinement. The initial specification is usually highly abstract. Each refinement produces an increasingly more concrete and detailed specification with the final result being a compilable program. Successive specifications along the refinement path relate to each other in terms of some *implements* relation. Generally, specifications are expressed in a logic-based notation while programs are given in terms of a programming language. As many authors have noted, the distinction between the two is merely pragmatic. A program is also a specification, one which has an efficient implementation and exhibits a low level of abstraction. Because many of the "desired program characteristics" can not be expressed formally, program derivation is aided by criteria which are entirely outside the logic and are supplied by the designer as "informal motivation" for the individual refinement steps.

Previous approaches to formal derivation of concurrent programs can be classified into two broad categories. The first category includes methods which emphasize specification refinement with the program being generated at the very last step as a trivial coding exercise, e.g., [3]. The second category includes methods that start with an initial program which is subjected to a series of transformations which are guaranteed to preserve program correctness until a program having all the desired (informally stated) characteristics is obtained, e.g., [1]. In our experience, mixed specification and program refinement offers some important practical advantages. Working on formal derivation of concurrent rule-based systems [10], we found it helpful to combine specification refinement and program refinement. Specification refinement was used to generate an initial program correct in all respects except that it was non-terminating. During program refinement we applied a series of optimizations which led to proper termination, to the elimination of operations too expensive for the target implementation, and to the elimination of busy-wait cycles. Similarly, during our investigation into architecture-driven refinement [11] we found it beneficial to generate initially a program which satisfies all functional requirements but fails to meet many of the architectural constraints. Subsequent program transformations lead to a program that satisfies both. In both areas we employed a UNITY-like specification refinement and generated Swarm programs which (when needed) were transformed mechanically to the target language.

Visualization. Program visualization is defined as the graphical presentation, monitoring, and exploration of programs. While, in general, program visualization includes the graphical presentation of code, our interest in visualization is centered around abstract formal properties of programs. In large concurrent systems, code visualization is of limited value when trying to explain or explore the system's behavior. The complexity of the visualization overwhelms both the screen real estate and the cognitive capacity of the viewer. Furthermore, operational views of the system behavior convey the mechanics of the computation and not its rationale. The viewer may be able to observe every aspect of a program but still fail to understand its behavior. Consequently, our methodology relies on custom-built visualizations which capture formally stated assertions about the program being derived. To accomplish this, one needs access to rapid visualization capabilities and an innovative approach to visual representation of concurrent computations. The former is provided by Pavane [7, 12] while the latter is the research subject of this paper.

Pavane visualizations span multiple windows each containing a three-dimensional, full-color world of geometric objects. The scene being displayed is controlled directly by the state of the program being visualized. Each state change triggers a change of scene. The transitions from one scene to the next may involve highly synchronized and complex animations. The scenes capture abstract program properties. The animations are meant to enhance the aesthetic value of the presentation and to provide a visual commentary on the behavior of the program by focusing attention on specific objects, events, or relations among them. In Pavane, the scenes and the animations are constructed by defining mappings from program states to sets of three dimensional objects from a predefined visual vocabulary, objects whose attributes can be a function of time (actually frame number). Each state transition is followed by the application of the mapping which, in turn, is followed by the display of the multiple frames required to accomplish a smooth transition from the previous to the new scene, i.e., an animation. The overall mapping is generally a composition of several simpler mappings. Each mapping is specified using a rule-based notation which is sufficiently powerful to allow for the computation of arbitrary history variables and fixpoints.

The typical program visualization process entails three steps. First, a program is constructed without any consideration being given to visualization. Since Pavane can visualize only programs, specifications are approached indirectly—by constructing a highly abstract program that satisfies the specification and visualizing the properties the program is supposed to satisfy. Next, some property of interest is selected for visualization. The property may emerge during attempts to formally verify the program or may be present in its specification. Other times, the designer may simply want to explore visually the validity of some

hypothesis or understand some processing (even performance) pattern that might suggest a simpler formulation of some complex property. A tentative graphical representation is selected next and a Pavane mapping is constructed. After some experimentation and a preliminary evaluation of the suitability of the selected graphical representation, full animation is added.

Pavane's effectiveness as a rapid visualization tool has been evaluated in a variety of settings including scientific visualization, algorithm animation, rapid prototyping, requirements validation, program testing, debugging, and instruction. However, the question of how to integrate visualization into the design process is the most challenging task we have attempted to date.

3. Specification Methods and Notation

A distinctive feature of our strategy for integrating formal methods and visualization is the synergy among the program specification, programming notation, and visualization method. They all deal with global abstract views of concurrent programs and employ a tuple-based notation. Moreover, both the specification and the visualization methods are state-based and non-operational. The UNITY-logic involves assertions over the global state of the computation and the lowest level predicates look like tuples, i.e., predicate name and arguments. In Swarm, data and actions (called transactions) assume a tuple format and coexist in a global tuple-space called a dataspace. Declarative visualization maps program states, sets of Swarm tuples, to graphical objects which also assume a tuple format. In this section we provide a very brief overview of the three models and associated notations.

Program Properties. The basic program specification method we employ is due to Chandy and Misra [3]. It is a specialization of the temporal logic used to derive and verify UNITY programs—henceforth called UNITY logic or simply UNITY. As is the case with other logic-based models, the program behavior is given in terms of two classes of properties: safety and progress. Safety properties specify that certain actions (i.e., state transitions) are not possible, while progress properties specify that certain actions will eventually take place. In UNITY, the basic safety property is the **unless** relation. The formula p **unless** q states that if the program enters a state in which the predicate p is true and q is false, every program action will either preserve p or establish the predicate q. All other safety properties, such as **invariant**, **constant**, and **stable** are defined in terms of **unless**. The basic progress properties are **ensures** and **leads-to** (written $\mapsto$). The formula p **ensures** q states that p **unless** q holds and, in addition, there is some action which establishes q, an action the program is guaranteed to take in a bounded number of steps. Similarly, the formula $p \mapsto q$ states that if the program enters a state in which p is true, the program will eventually enter a state in which q holds, although p need not remain true until q becomes true.

For illustration purposes, let us consider a program in

117

which data is moving from one register (say i) to the next (say $i+1$) in a finite length queue. Using UNITY, two aspects of the basic queue behavior can be stated simply as

$$\text{reg(i,x)} \ \textbf{unless} \ \text{reg(i,nil)} \wedge \text{reg(i+1,x)}$$
$$\text{reg(i,x)} \mapsto \text{reg(i+1,x)}$$

where i and x are universally quantified by convention; the first formula prevents the register i from receiving a new value before x is passed on to the next register in the queue and imposes an asynchronous movement of values by requiring a register to become empty (*nil* value) at the time its value is transferred to its successor; the second formula introduces a requirement that values must actually move along the queue.

UNITY specifications are simple and intuitive. There are few modeling artifacts introduced by the method, the state representation is direct, and the careful and creative use of auxiliary variables allows very sophisticated problems to have simple behavior specifications. Reasoning about global program states is more intuitive than reasoning about execution sequences. The UNITY logic may be used both as a specification language (during derivation) and as a proof logic (during verification). Although this paper avoids showing the formal specifications, familiarity with these concepts is necessary to appreciate the issues facing the designer who is attempting to confer graphical representations to such properties.

Programs. The only distinction between the UNITY and Swarm logics is in the way **unless** and **ensures** properties are proved using the program text. Since specification refinement involves neither writing nor proving programs, the target of the derivation may be either a UNITY or a Swarm program—UNITY is a proper subset of Swarm, subject to minor mechanical translation. Distinctions become important only when program refinements are involved. UNITY assumes that a program consists of a fixed finite set of variables and statements and that each statement is a conditional multiple assignment—thus the state is captured by the current values of the variables and an action corresponds to the execution of one of the statements. Swarm [8] and its logic [5, 9] has shown that applicability of the UNITY logic can be extended to models which exhibit a very different set of characteristics: content-based access to data as in rule-based programming and Linda, dynamic creation of statements and data, and dynamic changes in the mode of execution (synchronous, asynchronous, and mixed).

Since the syntax of Swarm is very close to logical notation, many specifications have obvious representations as abstract Swarm programs, a fact which enables us to execute specifications with minimal effort. To illustrate this, we present the definition of a simple Swarm transaction *Move(i)* which forwards data along the queue discussed earlier. In Swarm, this requires one to create a parameterized transaction class called *Move* (shown below) and to place all the needed transaction instances in the dataspace (at initialization or dynamically):

$$\textbf{Move(i)} \equiv$$
$$\text{x : reg(i,x)} \wedge \text{reg(i+1,nil)}$$
$$\rightarrow \text{reg(i,x)}\dagger, \text{reg(i+1,nil)}\dagger,$$
$$\text{reg(i,nil)}, \text{reg(i+1,x)}$$
$$\parallel \ \textbf{true}$$
$$\rightarrow \text{Move(i)}$$

According to the definition above, a transaction *Move(i)* consists of two subtransactions that are executed in parallel. The first one, involves a query which extracts the current value x for register i and checks if the register $i+1$ is empty. If the query is successful the associated action part (following "$\rightarrow$") is executed by first deleting from the dataspace the tuples holding the old register values (marked by a dagger "$\dagger$") and inserting tuples representing the new register states. If the query fails the first subtransaction has no effect. The query of the second subtransaction (following "$\parallel$") always succeeds and recreates the transaction instance which otherwise would be implicitly deleted from the dataspace as soon as it is executed. Transactions are selected fairly and parallel execution (which extends to groups of transactions) follows a basic three-phase pattern: query evaluations precede data-tuple deletions which, in turn, precede data-tuple and transaction insertions into the dataspace.

Visualizations. In Pavane, visualizations are implemented as mappings from the state of the program to a collection of graphical objects in a four-dimensional space—the three spatial dimensions plus time. For notational convenience, we express both the state of the underlying computation and the final set of four-dimensional graphical objects as collections of tuples, called respectively the *state space* and *animation space* of the visualization. The overall mapping from state space to animation space can be decomposed into a pipeline of any number of sub-mappings, with each intermediate mapping transforming one space into the next in the pipeline; each of these intermediate spaces is also a collection of tuples. Although the Pavane rules look very similar to Swarm transactions, the visualization semantics is radically different from the transaction execution semantics. Pavane assumes that the underlying computation progresses by means of a series of atomic transitions which modify the state. After each transition, the visualization rules are re-applied to the new state and the resulting animation space is rendered.

To construct a very simple visualization of a program implementing the queue, we may want to represent an empty register as an unfilled square, a register holding some value as a filled square, and a *Move* transaction as a line. The picture below shows three empty registers and reveals an initialization error—a missing transaction.

Only two trivial Pavane rules are required to construct this kind of picture

DrawRegister ≡
  i, x : reg(i,x)
  ⇒ _box(_center:=[3*i,0,0], _size:=1, _fill:=(x≠nil))

DrawPotentialFlow ≡
  i : Move(i)
  ⇒ _line(_from:=[3*i,0,0], _to:=[3*(i+1),0,0],
          _chop:=0.5)

The result of a rule application is the union of the results of every successful instantiation of each rule.

Adding animation is less trivial. The increase in the complexity of the rules is determined by the sophistication of the animation being constructed. For this example, a simple animation may involve reemphasizing the flow of data by showing a little ball that retraces the data movement to attract attention to a value which just changed registers instantaneously.

Only one rule would be required in this case

DrawActualFlow ≡
  i, x : old.reg(i,x) ∧ x≠nil ∧ reg(i,nil) ∧ old.reg(i+1,nil)
        ∧ reg(i+1,x)
  ⇒ _sphere (_center:=
              ramp(0,[3*i,0,0],10,[3*(i+1),0,0]),
              _radius:=0.2,
              _color:=[200,0,0])

This rule is triggered whenever the register i is empty but was observed to be non-empty in the preceding state. A sphere whose center moves from one register to the next over ten video frames is generated. Note that for a correct program the query part of the Pavane rule is overspecified. It was designed, however, to ensure the detection of possible program errors—if a register is emptied under the wrong conditions no sphere is displayed!

As the rules above already suggest, the overall process of visualization is data-driven; the rendering computation must wait for data from the visualization computation, which in turn waits for data from the underlying computation. It is not, however, synchronous. The underlying computation is permitted to send state changes more rapidly than the visualization computation is able to process them, and similarly the visualization can send animation spaces faster than the renderer can translate them into images. The latter often happens, simply because the process of generating an image (and, more importantly, the comprehension of that image by the viewer) is much slower than the other two computations. If synchronous execution is desired, it can be requested when the computation is started; the underlying computation is then forced to wait for the rendering computation to complete the display of an

animation space. This is particularly useful when contrasting two or more different visualizations by displaying them in separate windows, since synchronization guarantees that all the images represent the same state of the underlying computation.

Pavane's graphical model provides one or more three-dimensional "worlds", each containing a collection of graphical objects. The animator defines one "window" for each world; the window definition includes the world's properties (center, scaling, background color, and so forth), the properties of the screen window which will be opened (dimensions, position, etc.), and the types of transformations that the viewer is permitted to make. Subject to any such limitations that the animator requires, the viewer can examine each world "through" its window from any point in the world's coordinate system. The ability to use multiple windows is especially convenient when the effectiveness of two or more visualizations is being compared or when multiple properties of the same program need to be examined together.

Pavane has undergone many repeated developments and redesigns. It consists of a compiler for visualization rules, a display subsystem, and a number of run-time libraries for monitoring C++ and Swarm programs, for executing visualization rules, and for supporting the display process. The most recent version is written in C++ under UNIX and requires X Window System® support. The display subsystem makes use of Open Graphics Library™ (OpenGL) and OpenInventor™ Libraries.

4. Visualization Techniques

The discussion in this section is informal by intent as it is meant to be equally accessible to formalists and practitioners. No UNITY assertions, Swarm programs, or Pavane rules are shown. The initial specification of the router and the key refinements leading to the final design are presented in a summary form and used primarily as a backdrop against which we organize a discussion of techniques which we found helpful in the visualization of the router and of other programs as well. Special emphasis is placed on identifying general graphical representation principles and strategies that transcend the specifics of this particular case study. We also identify several problems for which we did not find a satisfactory solution yet. Furthermore, even though the full derivation of the router predates this case study, we went to a great effort to make sure that in visualizing each refinement we used only information available at that specific point in the design process.

4.1. Initial Specification: A message router

We consider a communication network that connects N senders of messages to M receivers via a message router. Each sender is connected to one of the input ports of the router, and each receiver to one of the output ports. Each message is composed of a finite number of packets that can be of three different types: *header*, *body*, and *tail*. The

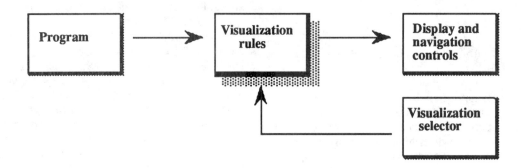

Figure 1. Basic visualization structure and controls.

header, which is the first packet of the message, contains the port address of the message destination. Each header is followed by one or more body packets which contain the actual data. Finally, the tail packet marks the end of the message. The externally observable behavior of the router is defined by the following requirements:

(R1) The value of the body packets must not be modified, but, for control purposes, the router may modify the value of the header and tail packets.

(R2) Packet ordering within a message must be preserved (at the receiver).

(R3) Messages from the same source going to the same destination must not be reordered (at the receiver).

(R4) Messages from different sources going to the same destination must not be interleaved (at the receiver).

(R5) Each packet that is sent must eventually be delivered to the intended receiver.

These five properties are ultimately captured by eleven formal assertions and a number of assorted definitions. Since Pavane can only visualize programs, the first step towards building a visualization is to generate a program P which embodies the initial specification S. This needed intermediary step raises issues regarding the effort and accuracy associated with the approach. The cost of developing the program is minimal because Swarm is a very high level language allowing arbitrary queries over the state space expressed in a notation similar to that used to write logical assertions. Accuracy is a more complicated issue. It is easy to guarantee that the program is correct but it is more difficult to make sure that all behaviors permitted by the specification are actually captured by the program. This can be a serious drawback if the program is used to explore the specifications but it is less of a problem when used to communicate ideas the designer explicitly decided to present. (Possible mechanical solutions for the former case are: to

make the specifications executable or to work with program refinement.)

Once the program is written one needs to decide on the desired visual representation and write Pavane rules that map the program state to the graphical objects on the screen (Figure 1). Smooth animation and other special effects are added to the rules once the basic representation is considered satisfactory. Although not a necessity, we find it convenient to allow the viewer to select from among a set of available visualizations during program execution—a rule selector window is constructed providing a list of visualizations, annotations explaining how they relate to the formal specifications, and buttons to turn them on and off. One visualization selector and set of rules was constructed for each specification generated during the router design. The visualization selectors listed all the relevant formal properties and provided buttons that enabled the visualization of one desired property at a time. In addition, Pavane provides a standard set of 3D navigation controls.

This section, however, is not about the mechanics of visualization but about representation. We turn our attention next to the concepts we need to visualize and the methods that help us convey them graphically. To help the reader recall and refer to specific techniques we gave them names. Very few of these names enjoy general acceptance in the field now but, as the area matures, a standard terminology must eventually emerge and we hope that some of our terms will be part of it.

Steel gray. From the very start we realized that a single visualization able to capture all the important formal properties of the router is neither feasible nor desirable. Nevertheless, all the visualizations must contribute to a single unified mental picture and must relate easily to each other, especially when the visualization changes midstream. The solution was to create one single common reference point shared by all the visualizations, a mostly neutral image that provides a contextual framework on which to highlight other properties. In the case of the router the input and output queues readily suggest a simple rectangular structure for the router with the input queues on the left to imply a starting origin and the output queues at the top to hint at a sense of progress. We use shades of gray to allow the image to recede in the background and to lower the viewer's expectation in terms of the amount of information being communicated.

Thin air. In the steel gray image the messages look like nuts on a rod. What should happen when a message travels from input to output? One subtle point about the initial specification is that it defines only the behavior observable in the environment of the router and says nothing about how the router should be realized. Showing the router as a black box is not reasonable because the specification states that each packet is present some place at all times. Our approach is to show the presence of packets in the router while making clear that their behavior and existence there does not have the same reality as on the inputs and outputs. The router exhibits no internal structure while packets float in thin air and bounce off the walls like elastic balls. The result is not suggestive of any design while the continued existence of packets is evident.

Spot color. Some of the formal properties are concerned with the structure of the messages and others with the ordering of packets. Because these properties apply to all the messages, there is a tendency to try to color code each message. This may create a pleasing image but it fails to focus the viewer's attention on anything in particular and provides more information than necessary. Such images require additional (unnecessary) oral explanations whose sole purpose is to force the viewer to concentrate on one particular aspect of the image, i.e., to ignore the rest. Take, for instance, the property that packets belonging to different messages are not interleaved (on output). One can think of this property as a relation among all the messages but it is much more profitable to view it as a relation between one particular message and all the rest. This can be easily captured by assigning a color to one of the messages and leaving all the others gray. For reasons having to do with keeping the number of visualizations small, we opted to use spot colors also for the source and destination queues associated with the colorized message and to differentiate the header and the tail packets. Only when we want to show that ordering is preserved among messages that have the same source and destination we spot color a pair of messages.

Event compression. Most models of concurrency assume that atomic actions associated with a concurrent computation are executed serially although an actual system may schedule them in parallel if the resources are available and the observable effect is the same as some serial execution. The abstract program associated with the initial router specification, for instance, treats the movement of individual packets as separate atomic actions. The specification, however, does allow for several packets to move simultaneously. To actually capture this behavior in the program entails additional coding and performance costs. We found that one simple way to get around this added burden is to allow the program to take multiple steps which are visually captured as a single combined synchronous transition. One must exercise care not to create visual transitions that are not permitted by the specification. If individual atomic steps affect distinct graphical objects appearing in the visualization, it is relatively easy to combine them into a single visual transition thus offering the viewer the illusion of parallel or synchronous execution. It is possible, for instance, to advance by one position synchronously a whole set of adjacent packets located on the same input queue. The approach would not work, however, if the packet closest to the router advances two positions while the rest advance only one. In our case study the rule selector allows the viewer to choose between a serial execution and one involving combined presentation of multiple atomic actions.

Free walk. The last issue we faced in visualizing the initial specification was how to handle the nondeterministic behavior implicit in the specification. One option is to introduce randomness in the selection of the program statements. A second option is to involve the viewer in the choice of action to be executed next. We opted for the latter because it promotes active exploration of the program's behavior and also because Pavane already supports this kind of viewer control over the execution of Swarm programs (but not for C++ programs which are sequential).

These techniques were used extensively throughout the remainder of the case study and, as we continue looking at successive design refinements, we will try to showcase only those presentation methods that have not be discussed already in a previous section.

4.2. Refinement 1: Router topology

The first refinement defines the general topology of the router as a grid of $N{\times}M$ switches. The N input lines and M output lines are thus extended inside the router. Each switch can receive packets from its left neighbor on the row or its bottom neighbor on the column, and can route them either to its right neighbor on the row or to its upper neighbor on the column, depending on the destination of the packets. So, to move from its source row to its destination column, each packet first travels along the row (one switch at a time) until it reaches the destination column, and then just moves up the column (also one switch at a time). Each row-column intersection has a switch that holds two registers and some yet to be specified control logic.

Continuity of structure. Visually, the steel gray representation is extended into the router. The thin air behavior is replaced by packet movement from one register to the next. A packet travels along the row up to the point when the destination column is reached. Then it moves from the current row register to column register on the row above and continues to travel along the column registers. It is important to exploit the viewer's familiarity with the earlier view of the router and its environment and extend the representation to include the new structural elements. This strategy can speed up understanding and reduce the amount of verbal explanations required to interpret the imagery.

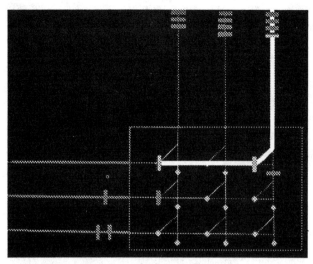

Figure 2. One message path through the router (tracing)

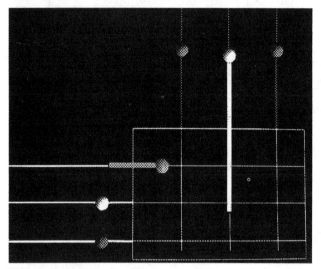

Figure 3. Message paths through the router (emaciation)

Scenario recycling. The essence of the first refinement is the extension of properties true outside the router to the router itself. Most formal assertions associated with Refinement 1 actually have forms identical to those of their counterparts in the initial specification. Consequently, it is not surprising that the presentation scenarios introduced earlier can be used again with the refined structure. This simplifies understanding and saves some of the effort involved in the development of visualization rules. While the program being visualized changed, many of the visualization rules can be reused.

4.3. Refinement 2: Arbitration logic

The second refinement provides additional details about the behavior of each single switch, by defining the mechanism that prevents messages from being interleaved along the columns. This can be done by associating two mutually exclusive signals—*turn* and *up*—with each switch. Signal *turn* prevents messages from moving through the switch along the column when a message is currently passing through the switch from the row to the column, and the other way around for the signal *up*.

Choreography. The value of the signals is determined by the movement of the header and tail packets through each switch. This coupling between packet movement and signal changes can acquire a visual counterpart by carefully choreographing the timing of the corresponding changes in the image. A header reaching the destination column is involved in three transitions: arrival in the row register, the setting of the *turn* signal to true, and the transfer to the column register on the row above. These transitions are sequenced in this manner by the program and naturally appear as such in the animation. The tail packet, however, is required to reset the corresponding signal (*turn* or *up*) upon exiting the switch. Let's assume that the switch state is shown in terms of the paths currently open through it. Changing the switch configuration while the packet is moving or immediately after it stopped moving can be misleading by making the packet travel on an apparently nonexistent line or by suggesting an ordering that does not exist. Our solution takes advantage of Pavane's fine grained synchronization capabilities by scheduling the change in the switch configuration to start at the time the tail packet is almost entering the next switch and to end at the same time as the packet movement.

Tracing. Many of the formal assertions associated with this refinement are invariants that relate the state of the switches to the distribution of packets across the router—along the path laying between the header and the tail all the switches must be properly set. We show this by simply coloring the path taken by the header of one particular message and by having the tail erase the color (Figure 2). This one single visualization covers a number of assertions each dealing with a distinct header/tail location pattern. The location patterns map visually to shapes of the color trace.

Emaciation. Throughout the case study we tried to keep visual representations simple through the frugal use of color. One other approach to simplification is to create more abstract representations. This is highly recommended when the viewer wants to see global patterns or relationships involving multiple objects. Such properties tend to correspond to formal assertions that are not part of the specification but can be derived from it. As an example, one may want to see the message traffic through the router. To do this we can reduce the router to a simple grid, represent messages by their headers (balls whose color indicates the destination column), and turn on the tracing mechanism for all messages in the router (Figure 3). The result is a trade-off between level of detail and volume of information.

4.4. Refinement 3: Fairness constraint

In the third refinement, we specify further the behavior of the switches by introducing a strong fairness constraint,

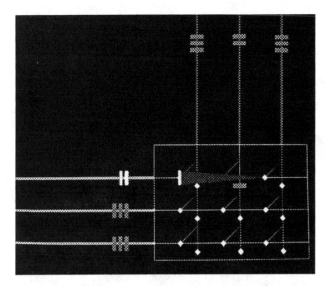

Figure 4. Header value decrement (foretelling)

i.e., the existence of a constant upper bound on the number of messages that can block a particular message from passing through each switch. We choose a design in which a message waits for at most one other message to pass through the switch before it can proceed.

Uncloaking. To render the fair behavior we need to highlight to the user the conditions under which a message may be blocked and than show that this does not happen. Colorizing an arbitrary message is not useful here. The particular message may not enter in a situation where indefinite blocking occurs while other messages may be blocked without the viewer realizing it. The solution we adopted is to colorize all packets of a message whose header is blocked at a switch and remove the colorization as soon as packet moves on towards its destination. We also highlight the blocking message to show that the blocking message is making progress.

4.5. Refinement 4: Destination address

At this point in the design, each switch on the rows makes the decision to route messages either to the next switch on the row, or to the next switch on the column, by comparing the message destination to the number of the column it is located at. This implies that each switch has to know its location. The purpose of the fourth refinement is to eliminate this knowledge by using the value of the header packets. We make the value of each header packet decrease by one each time the packet passes through a switch along the row. Since the value is initially equal to the destination column, this implies that a message will have to take a turn when the value is equal to 1.

Foretelling. Formally, the changes in the header value are tied to its current position on the row by an invariant relation. Given the current position and the header value we can foretell where the header will eventually move to the destination column. This allows us to materialize the header value as a beam of light originating in the header packet and focused on the switch where the turning on the column will occur (Figure 4). As the packet gets closer to the destination column, the focal distance of the beam is reduced until it goes down to zero. This kind of visual representation plays a key role in the visualization of two important classes of assertions. First, many progress properties (e.g., *"eventually the header reaches the destination column"*) are proved using a variant function over a well-founded set (e.g., the remaining distance to the destination column). By showing a graphical representation of the metric one can actually see how progress is being measured. Second, **unless** properties (by their very nature) constrain the set of possible state transitions. In complex situations, it becomes helpful to depict the set of possible transitions by showing both some aspect of the current state such as the current packet position and the positions the packet can occupy next. Of course, when there are not many choices, as is the case in a cross-bar router, this use of foretelling is not necessary.

4.6. Refinement 5: Asynchronous movement

The last refinement deals with the execution control we impose on the switches. A possible choice is to have the switches running asynchronously, another choice is to have them working in a synchronous way. We chose the more realistic asynchronous behavior. Since each location can contain at most one packet, this implies that a packet is not able to move to the next location, unless it is empty. This refinement is constructed simply by adding a single unless property that requires a packet to leave an empty register behind when it departs the switch. Trying to visualize that certain behaviors are no longer permitted is a little tricky. A simple solution is to foretell the situations in which packet movement is feasible by highlighting registers which could receive a packet in the next transition.

Magnification. Because at this point it is possible to write the final program, it is conceivable that one might want to present a visualization that includes details such as dataflows or even wires connecting the registers. We opted to combine one of the previous visualizations with a detailed visualization of the processing logic for a switch and its connections to its four neighbors. The absence of animation makes understanding the image more difficult. We present an annotated description of the switch representation (Figure 5) to clarify the image. The former visualization provides the global context while the latter shows the internal workings of a small portion of the switch. The two visualizations appear in separate windows exhibiting fully synchronized behaviors. The choice of switch to be shown in a close-up is at the viewer's discretion.

5. Conclusions

In some earlier work [7] we proposed a *proof-based* methodology for the visualization of concurrent computa-

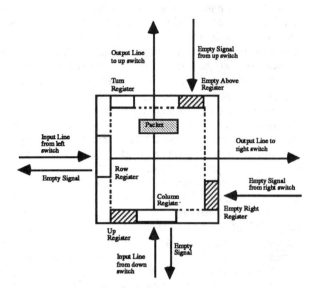

Figure 5. Annotated description of the switch level visualization.

tions. We sought to find correspondences between formal properties of concurrent programs and appropriate visual counterparts. The case study described in this paper builds upon those early ideas but shifts the emphasis from after-the-fact program presentation to the integration of visualization into the design process. The paper showed the kinds of representations that emerge during a rigorous program design process and considered their interactions along a sequence of refinements. This type of investigation represents an important first step towards understanding how visualization can support the application of formal design methods. The case study revealed many useful elements of a systematic visualization methodology. They, in turn, contribute to defining the kinds of features that ought to be included in the next generation of program visualization systems.

Acknowledgements

This material is based upon work supported by the National Science Foundation under Grant No. CCR-9217751. Any opinions, findings, and conclusions or recommendations expressed in this material are those of the authors and do not necessarily reflect the views of the National Science Foundation.

6. References

[1]   Back, R. J. R., and Sere, K., "Stepwise Refinement of Parallel Algorithms," *Science of Computer Programming*, vol. 13, no. 2-3, pp. 133-180, 1990.

[2]   Carriero, N., and Gelernter, D., "Linda in Context," *Communications of the ACM*, vol. 32, no. 4, pp. 444-458, 1989.

[3]   Chandy, K. M., and Misra, J., *Parallel Program Design: A Foundation*, Addison-Wesley, New York, NY, 1988.

[4]   Creveuil, C., and Roman, G.-C., "Formal Specification and Design of a Message Router," *ACM Transactions on Software Engineering and Methodology*, vol. 3, no. 4, pp. 271-307, 1994.

[5]   Cunningham, H. C., and Roman, G.-C., "A UNITY-Style Programming Logic for a Shared Dataspace Language," *IEEE Transactions on Parallel and Distributed Systems*, vol. 1, no. 3, pp. 365-376, 1990.

[6]   Price, B. A., Baecker, R. M., and Small, I. S., "A Principled Taxonomy of Software Visualization," *Journal of Visual Languages and Computing*, vol. 4, pp. 211-266, 1993.

[7]   Roman, G.-C., Cox, K. C., Wilcox, C. D., and Plun, J. Y., "Pavane: A System for Declarative Visualization of Concurrent Computations," *Journal of Visual Languages and Computing*, vol. 3, no. 1, pp. 161-193, 1992.

[8]   Roman, G.-C., and Cunningham, H. C., "Mixed Programming Metaphors in a Shared Dataspace Model of Concurrency," *IEEE Transactions on Software Engineering*, vol. 16, no. 12, pp. 1361-1373, 1990.

[9]   Roman, G.-C., and Cunningham, H. C., "Reasoning about Synchronic Groups," in *Research Directions in High-Level Parallel Programming Languages*, J. P. Banâtre, D. L. Métayer, Eds., Springer-Verlag, New York, NY, vol. 574, pp. 21-38, 1992.

[10]   Roman, G.-C., Gamble, R. F., and Ball, W. E., "Formal Derivation of Rule-Based Programs," *IEEE Transactions on Software Engineering*, vol. 19, no. 3, pp. 227-296, 1993.

[11]   Roman, G.-C., and Wilcox, C. D., "Architecture-Directed Refinement," *IEEE Transactions on Software Engineering*, vol. 20, no. 4, pp. 239-258, 1994.

[12]   Roman, G. C., and Cox, K., "A Taxonomy of Program Visualization Systems," *IEEE Computer*, vol. 26, no. 12, pp. 11-24, 1993.

How Modeling Methods Affect the Process of Architectural Design Decisions: A Comparative Study

Tetsuo Tamai

Graduate School of Arts and Sciences

University of Tokyo

Tokyo, Japan 153

tamai@komaba.ecc.u-tokyo.ac.jp

Abstract

A number of modeling methods have been proposed and practiced for the analysis process of software development. As many modeling methods cover the design process as well, it would be natural to ask how those methods affect the critical decisions made during the transition phase from the analysis to the architectural design, but little research activities seem to be visible tackling this problem. The reasons might be the difficulties of finding an appropriate approach and an appropriate comparison framework.

We take an approach of analyzing a set of case studies that treat a common example problem and use a formal method to clarify critical design issues. This paper reports some significant results obtained by the analysis of example problem solutions, based on a formally described comparison framework.

1 Introduction

The importance of domain analysis is well recognized in the software engineering community and a number of modeling methods have been proposed and practiced for the analysis process. Some have acquired a large number of followers, e.g. the structured analysis and the object-oriented analysis, and some have been practiced in relatively small communities. Most of them share some basic concepts such as processes, states and data structures but the way they view and relate these concepts is different, which characterizes the uniqueness of each method.

From the engineering point of view, one of the crucial issues is how to make the architectural design decision based on the domain model obtained by the analysis. As many methods, or methodologies to use a term preferred by some advocates, cover the design phase as well, it would be natural to pose a question whether the modeling method used in the analysis phase affects the architectural design decisions. Each method may have a specific tendency of preferring certain types of architectures, and therefore, the eventual architectural design might turn out different depending on the analysis methods chosen. Our goal of research is to clarify the relationship between modeling methods and derived final designs.

It is hard to find similar research objectives and activities in the literature. The main reasons might be the difficulties in finding an appropriate approach to conduct this kind of research. We take the following steps.

1. Take a sample problem, *Sake Warehouse Problem*, which had been treated in more than a dozen papers for illustrating various analysis and/or design methodologies.

2. Identify crucial design issues of the problem and write precise descriptions of those issues using a formal specification language Z.

3. Compare the various design architectures given in the published papers, focusing on the issues described above. The specification in Z will be used as a basis to proceed the comparison study of analyzing the relationship between analysis methods and derived architectures.

An alternative approach might be an experiment; several teams are organized, each assigned with a specific modeling method and given the same problem. However, it is almost impossible to plan and execute a well-controlled experiment. The results will certainly be affected not only by the assigned methods but also by other factors, such as the diversity of human skills and preferences. Moreover, it will take much time and budget.

If it is difficult to eliminate irrelevant factors anyhow, it would be wise to use published design solutions for a common example problem. There are several reasons for selecting the sake warehouse problem for this purpose.

1. As described in Section 2, the problem has appropriate complexity, i.e. not trivial but not too complex either.

2. Most of the solutions were published in special issues of a journal for a kind of modeling/design competition under the same condition.

3. All the authors, either software practitioners or researchers, are specialists of designated methods and the solutions are elaborately written by them.

125

Proceedings of IWSSD-8

As the original problem and the solutions are written in Japanese and published in Japan, the problem is hardly known outside of Japan, in contrast with the well known problems like the library problem and the elevator problem. It is often argued the software engineering community will benefit by many good sample problems [21]. We hope introducing this problem will contribute to the community as the by-product of this paper.

We use a formal specification language Z to rigorously write key design issues of the problem. In general, a formal method itself can be regarded as one of modeling methods, a candidate for our analysis target. Although Z is relatively independent from a specific method (thus named Z *notation*), as opposed to VDM (Vienna Development *Method*), the difference between Z and VDM is not so large. Z is usually used to specify state machines characterized by a set of input and output data and state transitions, for which useful constructs are provided by the language just like VDM.

At the same time, a formal specification language can be used just as a notation, neutral to any modeling method. We intentionally use Z at a higher abstraction level, taking advantage of higher order functions. By this way, the description obtained is abstract and neutral and thus can be used as a framework for comparing various modeling methods.

2   The Example Problem

The *Sake Warehouse Problem*, created by T. Yamasaki [27], is well known among the software engineering researchers in Japan. Various solutions of the problem have been published in journals and conference proceedings. The problem is relatively simple and succinctly described but it contains certain complexities that are typically found in many business application software designs.

The problem is as follows.

A warehouse of X Sake Retailing Company accepts several containers everyday. Each container contains sake bottles, possibly of multiple brands. The number of brands that can be mixed in one container is up to ten. The total number of brands to be treated is about 200.

A warehouse keeper stores each container carried into the warehouse without any rearrangement and sends a container contents notice to a clerk. He also ships out sake bottles by the shipment direction forwarded from the clerk. Stored bottles are never repacked into another container, nor kept in another place. An emptied container is immediately carried out of the warehouse.

container contents notice:
    container number (5 digits)
    carried-in time (hour/day, month/year)
    brand, quantity (repeat)

The clerk receives dozens of shipment orders per day and sends a shipment direction to the keeper for each order. An order comes by an order form or by telephone and each order must designate just one brand. If the brand is out of stock or in short for the ordered quantity, the clerk will tell it to the customer and adds the order to the waiting list. And when the designated brand is supplied to meet the order, the clerk will issue a shipment direction.

In a shipment direction, containers that will become empty are notified.

Develop a system that supports the work of the clerk (notifying out of stock status, issuing shipment direction forms and listing the outstanding orders).

shipment direction form:
        order number
        customer name
            container number ⎤
            brand, quantity   ⎥ (repeat)
            empty mark   ⎦

waiting list: customer name
                brand, quantity

- No loss of sake will occur either during the transportation or during the storage.

- As some part of the problem description may not be realistic, sophisticated functions such as exception handling can be minimal.

- Ambiguities may be resolved by appropriate interpretation.

Figure 1 shows the data flow diagram that gives the overall view of this problem. The diagram shows not only the flow of data but also the flow of things such as container in/out and sake shipment. Since this is not a part of the original problem description, the use of the data flow diagram here does not give advantage to the structured analysis method nor does it imply the problem fits well to the data flow approach. It is shown just to help the readers understand the problem intuitively.

3   Description in Z
3.1   Critical Design Issues

We surveyed 16 published solutions to this problem and found several key issues that affect architectural decisions. Among them, the following three are especially important.

1. Data corresponding to sake arrival are grouped by container, while data corresponding to sake shipment are sorted by brand. One set of sake shipment may be collected from multiple containers and thus some method of relating arrival information to shipment information is required, which

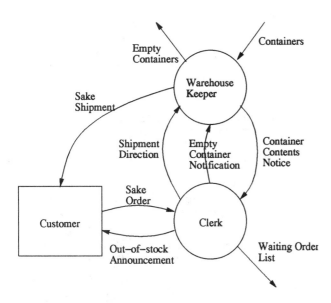

Figure 1: Data Flow Diagram of the Sake Warehouse Problem

is typically designed either as a search procedure among the data sorted by container or by data transformation applied to input so that they are sorted by brand.

2. A way of judging whether a shipment order can be met is required and how to implement it is one of the key design decisions.

3. Similarly, a way of judging whether a container gets emptied or not is required and how to implement it is another key design decision.

In the following, we precisely define the issues stated above using Z, without inflicting any design decision preference.

3.2 Basic Types and Schemas

Z is a formal specification language developed at Oxford University [23, 6]. A description in Z starts with the definition of basic types.

We assume $CONTAINER\_ID$ and $BRAND$ as basic types and also use a type $QUANTITY$ as the natural numbers greater than 0.

$$[CONTAINER\_ID, BRAND]$$
$$QUANTITY == \mathbb{N}_1$$

The warehouse stocks containers. We represent it as a schema $Warehouse$ as follows.

$\underline{\quad Warehouse \quad\quad\quad\quad\quad\quad\quad\quad}$
$container : CONTAINER\_ID \nrightarrow$
$\quad (BRAND \nrightarrow QUANTITY)$

The above schema does not have an axiom part but we may describe the condition that "one container can mix up to ten brands" as an axiom and get:

$\underline{\quad Warehouse \quad\quad\quad\quad\quad\quad\quad\quad}$
$container : CONTAINER\_ID \nrightarrow$
$\quad (BRAND \nrightarrow QUANTITY)$
$\overline{\forall c : \mathrm{dom}\, container \bullet \#(container\, c) \leq 10}$

The process of carrying a container into the warehouse is a typical data addition operation to a database and every textbook on Z starts with an example of specifying such a process, so we omit such description here.

3.3 Shipment Process

The first problem is how to process orders from customers. An order comes by brand, which requires searching containers by brand. Let us define a concept of $brand\_stock$ as follows.

$\underline{\quad\quad\quad\quad\quad\quad\quad\quad\quad\quad\quad\quad}$
$brand\_stock : BRAND \nrightarrow$
$\quad (CONTAINER\_ID \nrightarrow QUANTITY)$

We add this to the declaration part of $Warehouse$.

The crucial point of the problem is that these two data, $container$ and $brand\_stock$, are substantially the same. Let us think in a generalized framework. The type of $container$ and $brand\_stock$ has the form $(X \nrightarrow (Y \nrightarrow Z))$, which can be mapped to $((X \times Y) \nrightarrow Z)$ by one-to-one correspondence. This transformation is just the reverse of $currying$ operation, changing a multiple variable function to a sequence of single variable functions. This relation can be defined as follows.

$\underline{\quad [X, Y, Z] \quad\quad\quad\quad\quad\quad\quad\quad}$
$uncurry : (X \nrightarrow (Y \nrightarrow Z)) \rightarrowtail\!\!\!\rightarrow ((X \times Y) \nrightarrow Z)$
$\overline{\forall f : (X \nrightarrow (Y \nrightarrow Z)) \bullet}$
$\quad uncurry\, f =$
$\quad \{ x : X;\ y : Y;\ z : Z \mid$
$\quad\quad x \in \mathrm{dom}\, f \wedge y \in \mathrm{dom}\, (f\, x) \wedge$
$\quad\quad z = f\, x\, y \bullet (x, y) \mapsto z \}$

Next, we consider a transformation of exchanging the first argument and the second argument of a two-variable function.

$\underline{\quad [X, Y, Z] \quad\quad\quad\quad\quad\quad\quad\quad}$
$swap : ((X \times Y) \nrightarrow Z) \rightarrowtail\!\!\!\rightarrow ((Y \times X) \nrightarrow Z)$
$\overline{\forall f : (X \times Y) \nrightarrow Z \bullet}$
$\quad swap\, f = \{ x : X;\ y : Y;\ z : Z \mid$
$\quad\quad (x, y) \in \mathrm{dom}\, f \wedge z = f(x, y) \bullet$
$\quad\quad (y, x) \mapsto z \}$

Using the above higher order functions, $container$ can be transformed to $brand\_stock$ through $uncurry^{-1} \circ swap \circ uncurry$. The inverse of $uncurry$ had better be named $curry$, thus

$$curry == uncurry^{-1}$$

and

$$
\begin{array}{l}
\rule{0pt}{0pt}\underline{\quad Warehouse}\\
container : CONTAINER\_ID \nrightarrow \\
\qquad (BRAND \nrightarrow QUANTITY)\\
brand\_stock : BRAND \nrightarrow \\
\qquad (CONTAINER\_ID \nrightarrow QUANTITY)\\
\hline
brand\_stock = curry \circ swap \circ uncurry\ container
\end{array}
$$

3.4 Judgement on Quantity

In order to judge if a given order can be met, knowledge of the current total quantity of the specified brand should be necessary. In order to judge if a container is empty or not, the total amount of sake quantity of the container may be required. Functions that give these amounts should have the form:

$$
\begin{aligned}
brand\_stock\_quantity :\ & \\
& BRAND \nrightarrow QUANTITY\\
container\_quantity :\ & \\
& CONTAINER\_ID \nrightarrow QUANTITY
\end{aligned}
$$

To specify these functions, we need some preparation concerning bags. We define a bag version of *dom* (that returns the domain of the given function) and *ran* (that returns the range of the given function) as below.

$$
\begin{array}{l}
\rule{0pt}{0pt}\underline{\quad[X,Y]}\\
bdom : (X \leftrightarrow Y) \rightarrow \mathrm{bag}\ X\\
bran : (X \leftrightarrow Y) \rightarrow \mathrm{bag}\ Y\\
\hline
\forall R : X \leftrightarrow Y \bullet\\
\quad bdom\ R = \{\ x : \mathrm{dom}\ R \bullet\\
\qquad x \mapsto \#\{\ y : Y \mid x\ \underline{R}\ y\ \}\ \} \wedge\\
\quad bran\ R = \{\ y : \mathrm{ran}\ R \bullet\\
\qquad y \mapsto \#\{\ x : X \mid x\ \underline{R}\ y\ \}\ \}
\end{array}
$$

Next, we define a summation function over a bag on natural numbers, Σ, as follows.

$$
\begin{array}{l}
\rule{0pt}{0pt}\underline{\quad}\\
\Sigma : \mathrm{bag}\ \mathbb{Z} \rightarrow \mathbb{Z}\\
\hline
\Sigma[\![\,]\!] = 0\\
\forall x : \mathbb{Z} \bullet \Sigma[\![x]\!] = x\\
\forall B, C : \mathrm{bag}\ \mathbb{Z} \bullet \Sigma(B \uplus C) = \Sigma B + \Sigma C
\end{array}
$$

Here, $[\![\,]\!]$ stands for an empty bag, $[\![x]\!]$ for a bag with a single element x and $B \uplus C$ for a union of bags B and C.

Now, we can define a higher order function *subtotal* that can be applied to *container* and *brand_stock* to get *container_quantity* and *brand_stock_quantity*, respectively.

$$
\begin{array}{l}
\rule{0pt}{0pt}\underline{\quad[X,Y]}\\
subtotal : (X \nrightarrow (Y \nrightarrow \mathbb{Z})) \rightarrow (X \rightarrow \mathbb{Z})\\
\hline
\forall f : X \nrightarrow (Y \nrightarrow \mathbb{Z}) \bullet\\
\quad subtotal\ f = \{\ x : \mathrm{dom}\ f \bullet x \mapsto \Sigma \circ bran \circ f\ x\ \}
\end{array}
$$

Using this,

$$
\begin{aligned}
brand\_stock\_quantity &= subtotal\ brand\_stock\\
container\_quantity &= subtotal\ container
\end{aligned}
$$

Lastly, the overall schema of *Warehouse* can be rewritten as:

$$
\begin{array}{l}
\rule{0pt}{0pt}\underline{\quad Warehouse}\\
container : CONTAINER\_ID \nrightarrow \\
\qquad (BRAND \nrightarrow QUANTITY)\\
brand\_stock : BRAND \nrightarrow \\
\qquad (CONTAINER\_ID \nrightarrow QUANTITY)\\
brand\_stock\_quantity : BRAND \nrightarrow QUANTITY\\
container\_quantity : CONTAINER\_ID \nrightarrow \\
\qquad QUANTITY\\
\hline
brand\_stock = curry \circ swap \circ uncurry\ container\\
brand\_stock\_quantity == subtotal\ brand\_stock\\
container\_quantity == subtotal\ container
\end{array}
$$

We intended to write the key properties of the sake warehouse problem, method-independently. Taking advantage of higher order functions, we believe this intention is satisfied and the result can be used as a framework for comparing various modeling methods.

The above representation in Z can be extended to cover the whole specification of the problem, by adding the description of state change mechanisms for container arrival and sake shipment. We omit those parts in this paper for brevity but that work is already completed.

4 Comparative Study

4.1 Classification of Solution Models

We collected 16 published solutions for the sake warehouse problem. Most of the solutions appeared in three issues of the *Journal of Information Processing Society of Japan* (Vol. 25, Nos. 9, 11 and Vol. 26, No. 5). The problem was given as a design competition target, but each author started their study with the problem analysis.

The original papers were not sorted in any order, except that in the earlier two issues, relatively "conventional" approaches were included and in the last issue more "modern" approaches were collected.

We classify the modeling methods applied by these studies according to two dimensions: one is the modeling paradigm, i.e. structural, object-oriented and functional and the other is the basic property of model components, either data-oriented or process-oriented.

In the structural paradigm, a model is constructed by means of structure decomposition. A typical method of this category is the structured analysis/design. The methods in this class are relatively mature and practiced in the industry, especially for business applications.

In the object-oriented modeling methods, we include not only the typical O-O methodologies but also abstract data type approaches. As the time these solutions were written is prior to the publication of books on OMT, Booch's approach and Coad-Yourdon method, among others, no paper explicitly uses one of those methods, but all solutions categorized in this class follows the process of identifying objects, allocating behaviors or functions to each object and defining a structure made by these objects and thus they are justifiably qualified as object-oriented methods.

The third paradigm is functional. We find two subclasses of this category in the 16 solutions: the stream based model and the attribute grammar model.

The second dimension, data-oriented vs. process-oriented, can also be paraphrased as declarative vs. operational or static vs. dynamic. For each modeling paradigm, we find both the data-oriented subclass and the process-oriented subclass, as shown in Table 1, where the subclass (a) has the data-oriented property and the subclass (b) has the process-oriented property.

Table 1: Classification of Modeling Methods Used in 16 Solutions

1. Structural Paradigm

    (a) Data Decomposition Models

        - Warnier Method [24]
          Warnier Method was developed by J.-D. Warnier around 1970 in France. The key idea is to first define a hierarchical data structure and design the procedure structure based upon it.
        - Standard Structure Model [8]
          The standard structure model was developed by M. Kataoka et al. at Hitachi, Ltd. It is intended for practical use but incorporates abstract data types, data-oriented approach and description of hierarchical structures using regular expressions.
        - SP-FLOW [25]
          SP-FLOW was originated by Y. Usui, mainly for business application system development. It defines diagram notation to describe the data and program structures.
        - Mother System [15]
          Mother System is developed by T. Nishimura at Information-Technology Promotion Agency, Japan. It is a system to support developing COBOL programs, semi-automatically generating programs from declarative specifications of input/output data relations. It assumes the use of sequential files.

    (b) Function Decomposition Models

        - Composite Design [10]
          This is a design method developed by G. J. Myers. It is strongly related with the structured design by L. L. Constantine and E. Yourdon.
        - PAD/PAM [3]
          PAD (Problem Analysis Diagram) /PAM (Problem Analysis Method) was devised by Y. Futamura at Hitachi, Ltd. PAD is a kind of structured charts and PAM is a method of using PAD.

2. Object-Oriented Paradigm

    (a) Abstract Data Type Models

        - HISP [18]
          HISP, Hierarchical Specification Language, is one of algebraic specification languages, developed by K. Futatsugi and K. Okada at Electrotechnical Laboratory, Japan.
        - RSD [11]
          RSD (Reformed Structured Design) was developed by Y. Kuno. It intends to extend the structured design approach by introducing the abstract data type concept. Its target language is Clu.
        - IOTA [28]
          IOTA is a software development system based on a formal specification method. It was developed by R. Nakajima and his group at Kyoto University in 1970's and early 1980's.

    (b) Concurrent Object-Oriented Models

        - JSD [17]
          This is a well known method developed by M. Jackson.
        - ABCL [22]
          ABCL is a concurrent object-oriented language developed for research purpose by A. Yonezawa and his group.
        - Concurrent Prolog [16]
          Concurrent Prolog was developed by E. Shapiro. It is a programming language but can be used to describe concurrent models with its features of logic and concurrency expressions.

3. Functional Paradigm

    (a) Attribute Grammar Models

        - AG [9]
          AG stands for Attribute Grammar language. It can be regarded as a pure functional programming language with hierarchical constructs. It was developed by T. Katayama and its successor language, HFSP, is used for process programming.
        - DCG [14]
          Definite Clause Grammar is used here to specify the problem. It is automatically translated to Prolog.

    (b) Stream Based Models

        - Stella [12]
          Stella is a stream based language developed by K. Kuse at the University of Tsukuba.

- Valid [1]

  Valid is a functional programming language developed for a data-flow architecture machine by M. Amamiya et al. at NTT Electrical Communication Laboratory.

It may be controversial to classify JSD (Jackson System Development) to a concurrent object-oriented model. Although JSD was advocated long before the O-O analysis/design methods became in mode, we consider its characteristics of identifying *entities* as agents performing a set of *actions* well fit into the framework of concurrent object orientation.

4.2 Comparison Framework

How do we compare the architectural designs given by those modeling methods? In a way, each model provides its own "architecture" model, thus a trivial answer might be: the structural models give structural designs, the O-O models give O-O designs and the functional models give functional designs. We need an orthogonal criterion applicable across the paradigm difference.

In Section 3, we specified three key factors the design should make decisions upon. The most important among them is how to relate container based information to brand based information. We focus on this problem in the following discussions. We represented these two kinds of information as two functions in Z:

$$container : CONTAINER\_ID \nrightarrow$$
$$(BRAND \nrightarrow QUANTITY)$$
$$brand\_stock : BRAND \nrightarrow$$
$$(CONTAINER\_ID \nrightarrow QUANTITY)$$

Let us symbolically call the *container* type CBQ and the *brand_stock* type BCQ. Any design should reflect both types in some way but the strategy can be different. Three different strategies are conceivable:

1. make CBQ a first class citizen(1) and BCQ a secondary(2);

2. make BCQ a first class citizen(1) and CBQ a secondary(2);

3. make both CBQ and BCQ first class citizens.

We name these three strategies, 1-2, 2-1 and 1-1, respectively.

When we say CBQ or BCQ a first class citizen, it means the design intentionally and explicitly defines an object (or a module, a data structure, a file or whatever the method identifies as a unit component of the model) that mainly plays its role. The unit not only realizes the function of CBQ or BCQ but also updates its state according to the interaction of the system with the environment (i.e. arrival of containers and shipment of sake bottles). If CBQ or BCQ is a secondary class citizen, it realizes its function mainly using operations of other first-class citizens. Its role is not clearly bound to a single specific unit object but

is distributed over several objects or embedded in a composite type object.

A typical 1-2 type model of the conventional category is such that CBQ is directly realized as a data structure, e.g. a sequential file or a table, and BCQ is realized as a procedure that searches over the CBQ data. The intended design strategy classification, however, is not implementation dependent. Information hiding can certainly be employed to define CBQ or BCQ object. The point is whether an explicit player exists in the model that essentially corresponds to the role of CBQ or BCQ.

4.3 Analysis of the Solutions

Table 2 shows the result of determining the types of the models, either 1-2, 2-1 or 1-1. This result does not yield a simple interpretation as the following direct observation shows.

Table 2: Design Types of the Models

Category	Model	Type
Structural		
Data Decomp.	Warnier	1-2
	Standard Str.	1-1
	SP-FLOW	2-1
	Mother Sys.	1-2
Function Decomp.	Composite D.	1-2
	PAD/PAM	1-2
Object-Oriented		
ADT	HISP	1-1
	RSD	1-1
	IOTA	1-2
Concurrent O-O	JSD	1-1
	ABCL	1-2
	CP	1-1
Functional		
Attribute Grammar	AG	1-2
	DCG	1-1
Stream	Stella	1-2
	Valid	1-1

1. Only one model, SP-FLOW, has the type 2-1. The others are almost evenly divided between 1-2 and 1-1, 8 for 1-2 and 7 for 1-1.

2. 1-2 is preferred by the structural paradigm; 1-1 is favored by the object-oriented paradigm; and the break is even in the functional paradigm. However, this trend is not so definite. Among the models of the structural class, Warnier and PAD/PAM, assigned 1-2, are actually something in between 1-2 and 1-1. They do not have objects (or data structures in this case) corresponding to BCQ but both have a data structure of the type $B \nrightarrow \mathbb{P} C$, which, with $C \nrightarrow B \nrightarrow Q$, practically realizes $B \nrightarrow C \nrightarrow Q$. We assign them 1-2, because this structure $B \nrightarrow \mathbb{P} C$ appear to be tentative in nature, just for convenience of accessing

$C \twoheadrightarrow B \twoheadrightarrow Q$ from the sake brand key. But the difference may be subtle.

3. No clear correlations observed between the distribution of 1-2 and 1-1 and the data-oriented or process-oriented property of the models. The static model class has four 1-2 and four 1-1 types, whereas the dynamic model class has four 1-2 and three 1-1 types.

However, more careful analysis reveals some interesting findings. First, we see those models of type 1-2.

Some models almost automatically assume a specific kind of data structures for use. For example, Warnier method, Mother System, Composite Design and SP-FLOW, all in the structural paradigm, decide to use sequential files at the early stage of design without much discussions or almost by default. Whether to use a sequential file or not is a matter of detailed design but these methods decide it early, affecting the structure of the models. SP-FLOW is unique for deliberately choosing BCQ to maintain as a file, but the reason for this choice is not explained. Other three methods maintain CBQ as a file.

Once a sequential file is chosen to represent CBQ (or BCQ), it is almost inconceivable to represent BCQ (or CBQ) also as a file for the sake of performance (another implementation consideration). Thus, their models naturally fall into the type 1-2 or 2-1.

Similarly, ABCL and IOTA decide early to represent CBQ as a list. As lists share the same characteristics of sequence with sequential files, this decision leads them to the type 1-2. However, the process of reaching to this decision seems to be different here, because these O-O methods do not necessarily encourage the use of lists, whereas the structural models have traditionally been assuming the use of sequential files.

In our view, the major reason for this decision is probably related to the emphasis on the "naturalness" of models. For example, the solution by ABCL selects four objects to construct their model: clerk, warehouse, container and out-of-stock list. This model certainly reflects the real domain directly and then it would also be natural to see the warehouse as a collection of containers. The decision of using a list to represent a collection may be too specific and could have been postponed a while but it is probably a matter of taste or a habit. The function of BCQ is embedded in the clerk object. But as the clerk is human (or an agent), it is not "natural" to bind it with any static information structure; instead it performs the assigned responsibilities through dispatching functions to other objects. From the design point of view, the resulting model is not so clean, because the process of handling shipment orders are distributed among the three objects, clerk, warehouse and container and the interaction between them is fairly complicated.

It is interesting to note the two stream based models, Valid and Stella, produced different types of models. Although streams also have the property of sequential order, just as sequential files and lists, representing CBQ as a stream does not necessarily lead to the 1-2 type, because streams are almost the only objects the stream based models handle. Valid is purer than Stella in that sense and thus it is almost forced to represent BCQ also with a stream. On the other hand, Stella allows tables as supporting players and the decision is made to use a table for realizing BCQ.

Let us turn our attention to the 1-1 type models.

The Standard Structure model is the only one in the structural category that clearly belongs to the 1-1 type. This method follows the approach of decomposing data structures just like Warnier Method, but it explicitly distinguishes logical structures from physical structures. For the logical representation, such constructs as Cartesian products, disjoint unions and mapping are provided, which enables descriptions at an abstract level. Thus, BCQ can be represented without considering the constraints coming from physical data structures and the 1-1 type model is derived.

Typical examples of 1-1 type models are those of CP and DCG. In the case of CP, containers and brands are represented as objects, both of which have links to finer grained objects called stocks. Stocks are instances of $BRAND \times QUANTITY$ in each container. Thus, the roles of containers (CBQ) and brands (BCQ) are symmetric.

In the model of DCG, the triples ($CONTAINER\_ID$, $BRAND$, $QUANTITY$) are represented as Prolog clauses. Owing to the symmetric feature of Prolog clauses, the same data can be accessed by $CONTAINER\_ID$ and by $BRAND$, which means CBQ and BCQ are represented in dual at once.

The common factors of CP and DCG models are:

1. The granularity of considered objects is relatively small, probably because the pure top-down approach is not adopted for the analysis.

2. Each model depends on the specific features of underlying computational mechanisms; the CP model makes much use of the dynamic process creation and destruction mechanism of CP, which also enables natural linking between the creating and the created processes; the DCG model ingeniously exploits the symmetric access feature of Prolog data base.

The feature of finer granularity also explains the cases of HISP and RSD. In both models, CBQ and BCQ are treated almost equally, maybe because they started with not a very few number of objects. Their approach is more close to bottom-up rather than top-down.

The case of JSD is unique. Its model contains three objects (entities): containers, brands and customers. The choice of containers looks natural but brands and customers seem to be selected just by insight. Especially, the customer object looks ad hoc, because its function is just to judge whether the customer's order is satisfied by the current stock or not. The model itself is very well designed and it certainly belongs to the 1-1 type as the brand object corresponds to BCQ, but the process of obtaining this model looks much dependent on the engineers' insight.

4.4 Discussion

The above observation can be summarized as follows.

1. An early decision to adopt a sequential type of data leads to the design strategy of type 1-2 (or 2-1).

2. That decision is caused by the convention of the modeling methods (in most of the structural paradigm models) or by the intention of naturally mapping the real world to the domain model, basically following the top-down approach.

3. 1-1 type models are obtained either by 1) insights, 2) bottom-up approach, or 3) taking advantage of powerful features of underlining computational mechanisms.

So far, the evaluation was not explicitly made but it may have been obvious that we favor 1-1 type models over the 1-2 or 2-1 type models. The reason is that in most cases, 1-1 type models give articulate object separation and clean overall structures. The most impressive examples are the models of CP and DCG.

It is often advocated that object-oriented modeling has an advantage of mapping the real world to the model naturally. On the other hand, D. Parnas insists that designs that result from a careful application of information hiding are quite different from the "natural designs" [19, 20]. B. Meyer also insists that the criteria of naturalness should not be considered in building an object-oriented model [13]. How can we reconcile these two contradictory views?

One way might be to construct two models: an analysis model that is closer to the real domain and a system model that shows a fundamental architecture of system design. Since software models go through a series of transformation over the life-cycle of analysis, design, implementation and evolution, anyhow, it would be acceptable to have two separate models at the early stage of the life-cycle. The problem is if there is a significant difference between the structures of the two models, how can we bridge the gap?

Our suggestion is that we should occasionally abandon the appealing concept of the *seamless* development process of the object-oriented technology, if *natural* models potentially lead to unclear architectural designs, and consider a system model afresh, temporarily forgetting the analysis model. At the same time, as the models of CP and DCG show, there are the cases that good system models also pass as good domain models. Thus, there remains a possibility that excellent engineers with deep domain knowledge can build a single model which is good as a domain model and also as a system model.

5   Related Work

Comparison of 12 specifications for the library problem was done by J. M. Wing [26]. Her goal of comparison study was to clarify ambiguities and incompleteness in the original informal requirement description, how they were found and resolved by different specification approaches. Thus, her study approach is similar to ours but the objectives are different.

There are many case studies of writing specifications in Z and other formal specification languages [6, 2]. Most of introductory examples and practical case studies written in Z or VDM have been emphasizing the aspect of the state machine specification in the form of pre-conditions and post-conditions. Our study takes a different style and hopefully extends the possibility of using formal approaches.

The term software architecture is recently often used to denote the basic principle of software system structure, which should be determined at the early stage of design [4]. As our study is highlighting the relation between analysis models and basic design decisions, it should certainly be related to the works of software architecture. However, active researchers in this field seem to focus their research attention to the study of various styles or forms of architectures, e.g. pipe-filter, client-server, layered, blackboard, etc. [5], whereas we are more interested in domain specific and semantics oriented design decisions.

Our notion of describing the heart of the problem overlaps with the concept of *problem frame* by M. Jackson [7]. Related concepts and relations among them are uniquely and impressively explained in his book, which is stimulative to our current and future work.

6   Conclusion

We used a formal specification language, Z, in a unique way in terms of the objective and the approach:

- not to write the whole specification of the problem but to clarify crucial design decision issues;

- making much use of higher order functions to get highly abstract description, rather than specifying state machine transition processes.

Based on the description in Z, we set a framework for comparing 16 solution models for the sake warehouse problem. The framework is not so simple as just distinguishing modeling paradigms, e.g. structural, object-oriented and functional, but gives a criterion for comparing the models across those paradigms. Using that framework, we analyzed the models from various views and extended discussions over the relation between analysis models and design models.

In this paper, we only dealt with the design issue on relating the container information and the sake-brand information. The other two problems described in Z, i.e. how to design the judgement on out-of-stock status and the detection of empty containers, should be the next target of analysis, but they can be handled in a similar way.

Probably, a more interesting research topic is the process of handling waiting orders, which is deliberately omitted in this paper. The original description of the problem itself was a little ambiguous about this point. It said that those orders not met by the current stock should be added to the out-of-stock order list, but how they will be treated later when enough amount of a certain brand of sake arrives was not mentioned. The problem was revised later in the vol. 26, no. 6 issue of the *Journal of Information Processing Society* to state explicitly that outstanding orders should be processed when enough sake bottles arrive.

This seemingly little modification gives a new dimension to the problem. We did not treat this, because the given requirements are different between the solution models in the earlier issues and those in the last one, but we have already specified this requirement and start comparing solutions that are handling this requirement. Also, the process of revising the example problem itself gives an opportunity of exploring requirements change processes.

References

[1] Amamiya, M. and Murayama, M.: A Stock Management Program Written in Functional Programming Language Valid, *Journal of Information Processing Society of Japan*, Vol. 26, No. 5 (1985), pp. 506–520, in Japanese.

[2] Fields, B. and Elvang-Gøransson: A VDM Case Study in *mural*, *IEEE Transactions on Software Engineering*, Vol. 18, No. 4 (1992), pp. 279–295.

[3] Futamura, Y.: PAD/PAM: A Program Design Method, *Journal of Information Processing Society of Japan*, Vol. 25, No. 11 (1984), pp. 1237–1246, in Japanese.

[4] Garlan, D. and Shaw, M.: An introduction to software architecture, in Ambriola, V. and Tortora, G. eds.: *Advances in Software Engineering and Knowledge Engineering, Vol. 1*, World Scientific Publishing Company, 1993.

[5] Garlan, Allen, R. and Ockerbloom, J.: Exploiting Style in Architectural Design Environment, *Proc. 2nd ACM SIGSOFT Symposium on Foundation of Software Engineering*, December 1994, pp. 175–188.

[6] Hayes, I. ed.: *Specification Case Studies*, Prentice Hall, 2nd edition, 1993.

[7] M.A. Jackson, *Software Requirements & Specifications: a lexicon of practice, principles and prejudice*, Addison-Wesley, 1995.

[8] Kataoka, M., Miyamoto, F., Kondo, H. and Yamano, K.: Software Specification and Design Method Based on Integrated View of Structure Standardization, *Journal of Information Processing Society of Japan*, Vol. 25, No. 11 (1984), pp. 1220–1227, in Japanese.

[9] Katayama, T.: Description of an Inventory Control System by Attribute Grammar, *Journal of Information Processing Society of Japan*, Vol. 26, No. 5 (1985), pp. 478–485, in Japanese.

[10] Kubo, M.: Introduction to Composite Design, *Journal of Information Processing Society of Japan*, Vol. 25, No. 9 (1984), pp. 935–945, in Japanese.

[11] Kuno, Y.: A Structured Design Method Suitable for an Abstract Data Type Language, *IPSJ-SIG Software Engineering*, 39-3, November 1984, in Japanese.

[12] Kuse, K.: Programming an Inventory Control System using Stella – a Programming Language with Streams, *Journal of Information Processing Society of Japan*, Vol. 26, No. 5 (1985), pp. 497–505, in Japanese.

[13] Meyer, B.: Uses and Misuses of Inheritance, Invited Lecture at *Technology of Object-Oriented Language and Systems (TOOLS) 13*, Versailles, France, March 1994.

[14] Morisawa, Y.: A Step toward a Walkable Specification, *Journal of Information Processing Society of Japan*, Vol. 25, No. 11 (1984), pp. 1255–1260, in Japanese.

[15] Nishimura, T.: The Software Design and Production on the MOTHER SYSTEM, *Journal of Information Processing Society of Japan*, Vol. 25, No. 11 (1984), pp. 1247–1254, in Japanese.

[16] Ohki, M., Futamura, Y, Takeuchi, A. and Furukawa, K.: Description of Stock Management System by Concurrent Prolog, *Journal of Information Processing Society of Japan*, Vol. 26, No. 5 (1985), pp. 469–477, in Japanese.

[17] Ohno, T.: Jackson System Development, *Journal of Information Processing Society of Japan*, Vol. 25, No. 9 (1984), pp. 955–962, in Japanese.

[18] Okada, K.: Transformation Programming Based upon a Hierarchical Specification Language, *Journal of Information Processing Society of Japan*, Vol. 25, No. 11 (1984), pp. 1261–1267, in Japanese.

[19] Parnas, D. L.: On the Criteria To Be Used in Decomposing Systems into Modules, *Comm. ACM*, Vol. 15, No. 12 (1972), pp. 1053–1058.

[20] Parnas, D. L.: Software Aging, *Proc. 16th International Conference on Software Engineering*, May 1994, Sorrento, Italy, pp. 279–287.

[21] Shaw, M., Garlan, D., Allen, R., Klein, D., Ockerbloom, J., Scott, D. and Schumacher, M.: Candidate Model Problems in Software Architecture, Discussion draft 1.0 in circulation for development of community consensus, December 1993.

[22] Shibayama, E., Matsuda, H. and Yonezawa, A.: A Description of an Inventory Control System Based on an Object Oriented Concurrent Programming Methodology, *Journal of Information Processing Society of Japan*, Vol. 26, No. 5 (1985), pp. 460–468, in Japanese.

[23] Spivey, J. M.: *The Z Notation*, Prentice Hall, 2nd edition, 1992.

[24] Suzuki, K.: Structured Programming Warnier Method, *Journal of Information Processing Society of Japan*, Vol. 25, No. 9 (1984), pp. 946–954, in Japanese.

[25] Usui, Y.: System Design Procedure Based on Data Structures with "SP-FLOW", *Journal of Information Processing Society of Japan*, Vol. 25, No. 11 (1984), pp. 1228–1236, in Japanese.

[26] Wing, J. M.: A Study of 12 Specifications of the Library Problem, *IEEE Software*, July 1988, pp. 66–76.

[27] Yamasaki, T.: Surveys of Program Design Methods Using a Common Example Problem, *Journal of Information Processing Society of Japan*, Vol. 25, No. 9 (1984), p. 934, in Japanese.

[28] Yuasa, T.: Specification and Programming in the Modular Programming Language IOTA — A Practice on the Inventory Control Problem, *Journal of Information Processing Society of Japan*, Vol. 26, No. 5 (1985), pp. 486–496, in Japanese.

Proceedings of the 8th International

POSITION PAPERS

Workshop on Software Specification and Design

Learning from Inconsistency

Steve Easterbrook

NASA/WVU Software Research Lab
NASA IV&V Facility, 100 University Drive, Fairmont, WV 26554
steve@atlantis.ivv.nasa.gov

Abstract

This position paper argues that inconsistencies that occur during the development of a software specification offer an excellent way of learning more about the development process. We base this argument on our work on inconsistency management. Much attention has been devoted recently to the need to allow inconsistencies to occur during software development, to facilitate flexible development strategies, especially for collaborative work. Recent work has concentrated on reasoning in the presence of inconsistency, tracing inconsistencies with 'pollution markers', and supporting resolution. We argue here that one of the most important aspects of inconsistency is the learning opportunity it provides. We are therefore concerned with how to capture this learning outcome so that its significance is not lost. We present a small example of how apprentice software engineers learn from their mistakes, and outline how an inconsistency management tool could support this learning. We then argue that the approach can be used more generally as part of continuous process improvement.

1. Introduction

During the development of a specification, software developers are directed by methods (for technical guidance) and process models (for co-ordinating development activities). Although both are prescriptive, neither are perfect. We argue in this paper firstly that a flexible approach to the application of methods and process models is needed, and secondly that much can be learnt from studying instances of deviation, especially in terms of process improvement.

In the case of methods, any particular method is developed from experience on a set of cases in a particular domain or domains; it is rare that subsequent projects will map on to the original cases perfectly. In fact, most of the common methods available now have evolved considerably from their original design. Poor method fit has hampered the uptake of CASE tools: the tools often force developers to apply a method too rigidly for practical use. There is no reason to assume that because a method is mature enough to be used widely, it should not also continue to evolve.

In the case of process models, the long term rationale for process modelling is that it facilitates process improvement. This implies an acknowledgement that process models are never perfect, that there is always room for improvement. In general, there are two ways in which process improvements are identified: retrospectively or dynamically [7]. Retrospective improvement identifies areas of stress in the process enactment, and incorporates improvements based on hindsight. Dynamic process improvement allows developers to change the process model as problems are encountered. In both cases, adherence to the process model is maintained. In practice, a combination of the two approaches is desirable, incorporating the local contextual knowledge available in dynamic process improvement, with the benefit of hindsight offered by retrospective improvement. As Cugola *et. al.* [2] argue, this can be achieved by allowing deviations from the prescribed process, and providing support for dealing with the resulting inconsistencies.

In this paper, we are concerned primarily with (deviation from) specification methods. However, the arguments apply equally to the type of fine-grained process modelling described by Nuseibeh *et. al.* [9], and perhaps to process modelling in general.

2. Inconsistency Management

In Easterbrook *et. al.* [3] we introduced a broad definition of inconsistency, as any situation in which a relationship between two parts of a specification should hold but does not. This allows us to consider inconsistencies in any notation. Of course, this also makes inconsistency entirely method-dependent, as the method (or possibly the process model) defines which relationships should hold.

The need for a tolerant approach to inconsistency has been recognised by a number of authors [1; 5; 8; 10]. While these approaches offer ways of proceeding with development in the presence of inconsistency, and of analysing and resolving inconsistencies, none have yet addressed the question of what can be learnt from the occurrence of inconsistency. We regard the occurrence of inconsistency as a good indicator of problems in the prescribed development process. For example, in [4] we show how analysis of inconsistencies can reveal conceptual disagreements between developers.

Existing work on managing inconsistency concentrates on identifying the deviations, and reasoning about the correctness of the resulting process. For example, Cugola

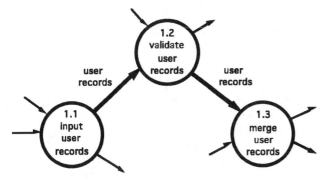

Figure 1: A portion of a dataflow diagram in which the author has deviated from the method, as process 1.2 passes its input to its output without transformation.

et. al. [2] introduce 'pollution markers', to track deviations from a process model, but do not offer any way of identifying lessons from such deviations. In the next section we present a small example, to show how learning can result from such deviations.

3. Example

When students first learn to use dataflow diagrams, they make a number of conceptual errors. For example, they may fail to distinguish between physical dataflow and logical dataflow, because they confuse the abstract notion of *process* with the concrete notions of *place* or *person*. Partly, this is because software engineering students take a while to become comfortable with the use of abstraction.

This leads to a number of typical mistakes, of which we will consider just one: a failure to appreciate that a dataflow diagram is concerned with *transformation* of data.

Figure 1 shows a portion of a dataflow diagram illustrating a typical mistake: the data item 'user records' is shown as both an input to and an output from the process 'validate user records', without any apparent transformation. This is a typical naive attempt to model an observed system in which (say) paper files are passed around an office. This diagram is inconsistent according the semantic rules for dataflow diagrams.

We can recognise this as an inconsistency, using any one of a number of techniques for detecting inconsistency. Indeed we would expect a specification tool to detect such problems. The detection of the inconsistency is not what we are interested in here, but rather, what the student then does. Imagine the student is using a CASE tool, and the tool reports the inconsistency in the above diagram. The tool may even provide some analysis of the problem, perhaps identifying the edit action that led to the inconsistency. However, the student still does not understand the problem, because he has not grasped the notion of data transformation. The student needs some guidance on what the options are from this position.

A brief analysis of the mistake leads us to suggest four likely options (see figure 2):

(a) fork: the same item of data should be passed to both processes 1.2 and 1.3;

(b) rename: process 1.2 does in fact transform the data before passing it on to 1.3;

(c) bypass: process 1.2 doesn't need this data item, and it

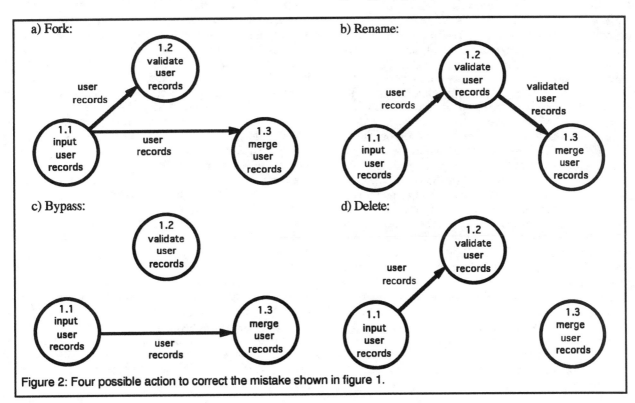

Figure 2: Four possible action to correct the mistake shown in figure 1.

should be passed straight to 1.3

(d) delete: process 1.3 doesn't need this data item, and the flow to 1.3 should be deleted.

We have given each of the actions a name for convenience: these could be offered as a menu of actions in a support tool. There are of course other actions that could also be taken that may resolve or ameliorate the inconsistency; we have merely selected the most likely.

Note at this point that the names of the processes suggest that the most likely choice is action (b). However, this is only an informal observation, available because the student has chosen particularly redundant names for the processes. In the general case, it is not possible to extract such semantic information to determine which action should be taken.

3.1. Prescribing Repair Actions:

Although the example and the four actions are relatively simple, we can imagine a large number of possible inconsistencies that can arise during software specification, and it is worth asking how feasible it is to generate a list of suggested actions for each possible inconsistency. There are three main sources of information from which the list of possible actions is constructed:

- Initial observations by the method designer - as each inconsistency rule must be explicitly defined, the designer may also be able to suggest some basic repair actions
- Analysis of the inconsistency rule - some actions can derived directed from the formal representation of the inconsistency rule. For example, any action that negates a precondition of the rule is a candidate for suggestion: actions (b) and (d) above have this effect, as they remove one of the items in the specification that caused the rule to fail.
- Past experience - each time the inconsistency occurs and is resolved, it provides data about possible actions. This is one of the learning outcomes we described below.

In addition to identifying possible actions, it is possible to reason about which to recommend. Such reasoning can take into account the context under which the inconsistency occurred. If we have available the development history of the specification, including the actions that led to the inconsistency, then some choices can be eliminated as they will be retrograde steps. Similarly, if the inconsistency occurs between parts of the specification developed by different people, and one has been updated more recently than another, then a transfer of information between the developers might be needed. Again, we expect to build up a set of heuristics to guide the selection as we gain more experience with the approach.

To explore these issues we have developed a framework for representing repair actions, in which each action has a name, for menu selection; pre- and post-conditions, to facilitate reasoning about its effects; and a rationale, to offer informal guidance about its applicability [3].

3.2. Learning Outcomes

There are five ways in which learning may occur in this example:

1) The developer learns what actions the method prescribes (or more often, proscribes). In this case the developers are students, making a rather basic mistake, and a tool that merely enforced the method *might* have induced this learning outcome. However, the lesson is reinforced by allowing the developer to explore the consequences of not obeying the rules.

2) The developer learns why it is that the method prescribes a particular way of working. In our example, this is a more important learning outcome that the first one, because it helps address the student's underlying conceptual confusion about data transformation in dataflow diagrams. It is unlikely that students would gain this learning outcome if they were prevented from making the mistake, unless a tutor observed their difficulty.

3) The method designer learns about whether the method needs updating. In our rather simple example, the method does not need changing, but one could equally well envisage an example in which the inconsistency turned out to be a new exceptional case, in which an alternative approach is needed. This is especially likely with experienced developers, who would normally have good reason to deviate from the method. One of the repair actions available in our framework is to disable the consistency rule. If the developer chooses this action, this is a strong indicator that there is a problem with method fit.

4) The method designer learns more information about how to guide subsequent developers. The resolution action chosen by the developers, and the context in which the choice was made, can be taken into account when reasoning about recommendations next time that inconsistency occurs. In this way a case library can be built up for various classes of inconsistency.

5) The developer learns more about the system being specified, because correction of the problem focuses attention on areas that are poorly understood. In our example, the student may need to go back to the domain and study further how data is passed around.

The first two of these outcomes are limited to the developers involved, and can play a useful role in training; however, as with most forms training it is impossible to observe the learning taking place directly. The next two outcomes form part of institutional learning, or process improvement. Both these types can be captured directly by the toolset, either as data for a process review activity, or as data for case-based approach to guiding development activities. The fifth outcome improves the quality of the specification, and can be seen as a validation activity.

There is one further learning outcome, not demonstrated in the example, but which we can expect to apply in team projects:

6) The developer learns more about how colleagues understand the system being specified. In cases where inconsistencies arise between portions of the specification developed by different people, they each may gain some insight into one another's view. In other cases the inconsistency may cause the developer to consult other members of the team.

It is unlikely that all six learning outcomes will apply at once, but we would expect at least one of them to apply each time an inconsistency occurs.

4. Empirical Experience

Having observed that exploration of inconsistency can lead to learning, we are currently investigating how to facilitate this learning process. We suspect that in many projects, the opportunity for this kind of learning is wasted. Our investigations are based on empirical work in conjunction with analysts currently working with NASA to assess the software requirements specifications for the International Space Station, as part of an Independent Verification and Validation (IV&V) contract.

We have been working on improvements to the methods used for performing traceability and completeness analysis on the Fault Detection, Isolation and Recovery (FDIR) requirements. At present, the development contractor produces failure models using the multigraph modelling method and associated tools. These models are then used to generate the FDIR requirements, which are currently represented in natural language, as part of a SRS conforming to DOD-STD-2167A. The IV&V team receives the SRS and validates it using their domain knowledge, and their own modelling tools. Our work concerns the introduction of a formal method that will allow the IV&V team to perform completeness analyses on these requirements. The method is based on SCR [6], and makes use of logic tables to represent state changes and the conditions under which they occur.

During the initial exploration of this new method, we have witnessed a number of inconsistencies occurring, and have used these as a way of learning more about how to fit the method to the project. We have also observed how investigation of inconsistency has helped us to develop a better understanding of the system being specified.

For example, one commonly occurring inconsistency in our initial trials with the method was that phrases expressing conditions in the SRS would be re-worded when they were placed in the tables. We had expected that a consistency check on the wording of these phrases could help with traceability and validation of the tables. In practice, the wording in the original phrases often did not make sense when removed from their original paragraphs. Forcing the two to be consistent is possible, but would reduce the readability of the tables. Hence, our preference is to allow the inconsistencies to stand for now, and to develop method guidance for certain kinds of re-wordings.

A second example arises when the requirements are analysed by different people. In some cases, the tabular representations produced by different people to represent the same requirement have differed in the number of conditions identified, and the ways in which conditions are combined. Literally, the tables had different numbers of both rows and columns. Investigation has demonstrated that the style used in the natural language specifications is inherently ambiguous. As a result we are exploring improvements in the way in which these original requirements are expressed, including introducing the tabular form earlier in the process.

Both of these examples show the method designer learning about how the method can be improved to fit the practice: learning outcomes (3) and (4) above. Whether we solve the problems by altering the method, or by evolving guidance on how to cope depends to some extent on the cost of changing the existing process. Most importantly, we have used the occurrence of inconsistencies to strengthen the argument for process change. Previous arguments about the ambiguity of natural language have foundered on the fact that replacing them completely with formal notations is prohibitively expensive. Now, however, we can show that certain kinds of ambiguity lead to specific inconsistencies. This allows us to identify smaller, incremental, changes to the process.

We have also observed how the occurrence of inconsistency leads to a better understanding of the system being specified. For example, one of the consistency checks we applied revealed that a particular mode was unreachable (Heitmeyer *et. al.* [6] describe this kind of consistency checking in more detail). Investigation revealed that the phrases "the current channel has not been reset within the last major [processing] frame" and "the current channel has not been reset within the major [processing] frame" had been interpreted as semantically equivalent. In fact the former refers to the *previous* processing frame, while the latter refers to the *current* processing frame. This distinction reveals an important aspect of the underlying model which had not been appreciated by our team: fault recovery actions can depend on events in both the previous and the current processing frames. We had assumed that only events in the previous processing frame were available for monitoring. Hence, the inconsistency allowed us to improve our understanding of the requirements.

The learning outcomes we have described in this section occurred only through careful (manual) analysis of particular inconsistencies. For learning associated with method improvement, this may be reasonable: this learning takes place outside the critical path of a project, and the time and effort needed may be reasonable. For other types of learning, scheduling deadlines may not permit the kind of reflection required. Hence our next step is to investigate how better to support the link between the actions taken to handle an inconsistency and the potential learning outcomes, so that the learning outcome is not lost. This will require further empirical work with the tools in place, to observe the conditions that help or hinder the learning effect.

5. Conclusions

A flexible approach to the application of methods allows designers the freedom to adopt development strategies that are appropriate to their particular needs. Rather than rigidly enforcing adherence to a method or process model, developers should be allowed to deviate, and to analyse the consequences. It is more important to be able to recognise that a deviation has occurred, than to prevent it. The ability to deviate from the prescribed method is important because:

- the method is never perfect
- every project is different
- developers have local expertise
- people learn best from trying things out
- deviations provide data on how to improve the method

This last point is particularly important. If changes to the method are inspired merely by stress points when the method is rigidly enforced, we will know where changes are needed, but not what those changes might be. If, on the other hand, changes are inspired by observed deviations from the method, the form and context of the deviation provides a great deal more data on how to improve the model.

This is not to say that every inconsistency would lead to an improvement in the method (or process model), but rather that every deviation has a potential learning outcome. Some inconsistencies may indicate that a method improvement is needed. Others may just provide a lesson about why the method is the way it is, and that it should be applied more rigidly in that respect in the future. Most importantly, it is not necessarily the case that the latter type of lesson is already known. Our example focused on apprentices, who are more in need of such lessons than experienced developers. However, even experienced developers and mature methods still need to learn. A commitment to continuous improvement implies a commitment to checking whether methods and process models are prescribing the right behaviour, if and when experienced developers have cause to doubt it.

5. Further Work

We are following up the ideas presented in this paper in a number of ways:

- further empirical observations of the types of inconsistency that occur in specification development, and the ways in which they induce learning.
- development of heuristics to improve the guidance offered for particular types of inconsistency, including reasoning about the development history (Eg. so that a recommended action does not take the developer back to a form that has already been considered and abandoned)
- case-based support for reasoning about which action is most likely by comparing the current situation with previous occurrences of the mistake.
- exploration of ways to alert developers to possible learning outcomes, using on our framework for inconsistency management.

6. Acknowledgements

Thanks to Bashar Nuseibeh, Jack Callahan, Chuck Neppach, Todd Montgomery, Jeff Morrison and Amer Al-Rawas for contributions to the ideas described here. This work is supported by NASA through cooperative agreement NCCW-0040.

7. References

[1] Balzer, R. (1991). Tolerating Inconsistency. In *Proceedings, 13th International Conference on Software Engineering (ICSE-13)*, Austin, Texas, USA, pp158-165.

[2] Cugola, G., Di Nitto, E., Ghezzi, C., & Mantione, M. (1995). How to Deal with Deviations During Process Model Enactment. In *Proceedings,17th International Conference on Software Engineering*, Seattle, Washington, pp265-273.

[3] Easterbrook, S. M., Finkelstein, A. C. W., Kramer, J., & Nuseibeh, B. A. (1994). Co-ordinating Distributed ViewPoints: the anatomy of a consistency check. *Concurrent Engineering: Research and Applications*, 2(3), 209-222.

[4] Easterbrook, S. M., & Nuseibeh, B. A. (1995). Managing Inconsistencies in an Evolving Specification. In *Second IEEE Symposium on Requirements Engineering*, York, UK, pp48-55.

[5] Gabbay, D., & Hunter, A. (1991). Making Inconsistency Respectable: A Logical Framework for Inconsistency in Reasoning, Part 1 - A Position Paper. In *Proceedings, Fundamentals of Artificial Intelligence Research '91,*, pp19-32.

[6] Heitmeyer, C. L., Labaw, B., & Kiskis, D. (1995). Consistency Checking of SCR-Style Requirements Specifications. In *Second IEEE Symposium on Requirements Engineering*, York, UK, pp56-63.

[7] Jamart, P., & van Lamsweerde, A. (1994). A Reflective Approach to Process Model Customisation, Enactment and Evolution. In *Third International Conference on the Software Process*, Reston, Virginia.

[8] Narayanaswamy, K., & Goldman, N. (1992). "Lazy" Consistency: A Basis for Cooperative Software Development. In *Proceedings, International Conference on Computer-Supported Cooperative Work (CSCW'92)*, Toronto, Canada, pp257-264.

[9] Nuseibeh, B., Finkelstein, A. C. W., & Kramer, J. (1993). Fine-Grain Process Modelling. In *Proceedings, Seventh International Workshop on Software Specification and Design (IWSSD-7)*, Redondo Beach, CA, USA, pp42-46.

[10] Schwanke, R. W., & Kaiser, G. E. (1988). Living With Inconsistency in Large Systems. In J. F. H. Winkler (Ed.), *Proceedings of the International Workshop on Software Version and Configuration Control*, Grassau, Germany, pp98-118.

Software Package Requirements & Procurement

Anthony Finkelstein & George Spanoudakis
Department of Computer Science, City University, UK
{acwf, gespan@cs.city.ac.uk}

Mark Ryan
School of Computer Science, University of Birmingham, UK
{m.d.ryan@cs.bham.ac.uk}

Abstract

This paper outlines the problems of specifying requirements and deploying these requirements in the procurement of software packages. Despite the fact that software construction de novo is the exception rather than the rule, little or no support for the task of formulating requirements to support assessment and selection among existing software packages has been developed. We analyse the problems arising in this process and review related work. We outline the key components of a programme of research in this area.

Motivation

It is increasingly being recognised that software construction de novo is the exception rather than the rule. The norm for most organisations (including defence procurement agencies, formerly the bastion of purpose-built software) is purchase of commercial off-the-shelf "package" software. In some cases this software is modified or extended, but in most cases the user organisations accept the software "as is". There is an observable trend in business and commerce in which purpose built software is replaced by software packages acquired, often on a pay-by-use basis, over a network and from a diverse supplier base.

Much attention has been given to providing methods and support tools for obtaining purpose built software - acquiring requirements from users, constructing specifications from the requirements, deriving properties of the specifications and ultimately, deriving programs which satisfy the specifications - little or no systematic (let alone soundly based) support exists to help the software user formulate their requirements and procure software packages that meet their requirements.

Our interest in this problem is drawn from experience gained in our work with a small specialist library, with an existing manual catalogue and accession system, who want to obtain software support for their activities - an application close to the heart of specification researchers!

Even from this crude sketch it should be immediately obvious that they will not be building their own "library system"; they have neither the skills nor resources to do so. They will undoubtedly purchase an existing library package. In this context how should the requirements document be organised and what guidelines can be provided to the "procurement team"? Existing requirements engineering practice provides little guidance, indeed a substantial field study reported by Edmunson & Jeffery (1984) casts significant doubt on the overall appropriateness of conventional requirements engineering approaches to the acquisition of packaged software.

Software Procurement

In the discussion below we identify four constituent "customer" activities within software procurement and outline some features of these activities that present problems for requirements specification. The activities are (1) acquisition and specification of requirements; (2) understanding the available packages (3) assessment of package compatibility (with respect to the requirements) (4) selection of the "best" available package.

Acquisition and Specification of Customer Requirements

The acquisition of requirements for purchasing software packages is an incremental and iterative process. Customers start from an initial perception of their requirements and the priority they attach to them, normally based on a detailed understanding of their domains (that is the application area of their concern), their existing manual systems and other aspects of their operational environment (for example hardware and other software systems in use). Initial requirements are revised on the basis of advertisements, package descriptions provided by suppliers, demonstrations, use of the packages and comparative studies provided by third parties (trade papers and the like).

At an early stage in this process a distinction has to be made between "core" requirements that is those requirements which we can safely assume are provided by all or most of the available packages (such as logging of borrowing transactions in a library) and those "peripheral" requirements which are very specific to the customer (such as a library containing books with titles having Hebrew or Cyrillic characters). The manner in which this distinction is made shapes the procurement process, core requirements are neglected, as they do not help to distinguish between packages, while peripheral requirements are emphasised.

In general, packages have some features which are relevant to customer's needs and others which are not (for example, the ability of a package to catalogue pictures in a library which only has documents). Of course customers may recognise new requirements in features, which become very attractive once demonstrated but were not perceived as requirements initially (an example might be the ability to add descriptors to the catalogue entries for photographs). Interdependencies between requirements are often only appreciated as the range of features available becomes apparent (in a library system the way in which foreign language text is stored is closely linked to the way in which the thesaurus is constructed).

Understanding Available Packages

Because packages are supplied by different vendors for different, though intersecting, markets they are described differently. The descriptions use a mixture of technical and application domain specific terms, dependent on the speciality or the emphasis of different vendors. Under such circumstances, extracting information about, and understanding the package is a very difficult task.

Understanding a package demands a translation between two types of vocabularies, the vocabularies of various package specifications (Pi) and the vocabulary of the customer's requirements specification (R). These translations may be thought of as morphisms from the vocabularies of Pis to the vocabulary of R, which may not be total, onto and isomorphic. In fact, there may be features of packages wholly irrelevant to customer's requirements, requirements not satisfied by some packages, requirements satisfied through a synergy of more than one package features and more than one requirements satisfied by the same package feature.

In certain cases, especially if the package to be bought is expensive, the translation may result from a cooperation among the customer and the vendors. In this setting the customer issues a request for proposal (RFP), which enables vendors to describe their packages in a uniform manner that is, in terms of the RFP. Of course

this process violates some of the "incrementality" discussed above. Further, experience suggests that the common response to an RFP is simply the standard package description! In most cases the onus for understanding packages rests with the prospective customer.

Assessment of Package Compatibility

Customers have to assess the extent to which different packages satisfy their requirements. Although in some cases the satisfaction of a requirement admits a binary answer (for example portability of a package onto a particular platform without alteration), for most requirements, different degrees of satisfiability may be distinguished. For example, the requirement for supporting foreign languages in a library catalogue is satisfied in various degrees by different library system.

Compatibility assessment demands some form of inexact matching between package and requirements specifications. This matching must cover both functional and non-functional requirements and cope with the feature dependencies and the incompleteness of both requirements and packages specifications. An additional complication is to distinguish cases where requirements cannot be satisfied by the package without substantial modification or rewriting and cases where requirements, although not satisfied by the default configuration of a package, could be met after some customisation, that is reconfiguration of the package within a predicted range.

Selection of Best Package

The selection of the "best" among the packages available depends on the assessment of their compatibility with the requirements specification and the prioritisation of these requirements. Selection is not static.

Customers may have to compromise on requirements not satisfied by any of the available packages, even if they had high initial priorities. In this situation, a common assumption underlying much work on specification for software development that "the customer is always right" is no longer valid. In this view the software always changes while the customers practices are fixed. In reality there is a "balance of mutability" customers may be prepared to change their practices in order to fit the best available package.

In many cases customers may decide to re-prioritise requirements. Such a re-prioritisation may be necessary in order to readjust the sensitivity of the selection process in the light of the merits and demerits of the different packages. This in turn requires the customer to have an accurate understanding of the impact of their priorities and the robustness of selection decisions to changes in those priorities.

Related Work

Though we have argued above that little or no support exists to help the software user formulate their requirements and procure software packages that meet their requirements some mention should be made of information system development methods such as Information Engineering and SSADM (Ashworth & Goodland, 1990) which recognise the make vs buy decision and its importance.

Conventionally software procurement has been viewed as a simple sequential process (Zviran, 1993; Conger, 1994), involving: (1) the identification of potential vendors; (2) the preparation of an RFP and selection of benchmarks for eventual validation; (3) the distribution of the RFP to vendors; (4) the evaluation of vendor's proposals and the selection of the best of them; and, (5) the validation of selected proposals and the final choice among remaining vendors.

The RFP plays a key role in the whole process, since (in principle) it compels vendors to describe their packages in a uniform way, which enables customers understand and compare them. The RFP is a structured form of requirements, response guidelines, contract terms and corporate information (such as vendor size and experience). By convention requirements are distinguished into technical (for example hardware, software and operating system requirements), managerial (for example delivery schedule) and financial (for example cost, payment schemes) as well as into measurable as against qualitative and mandatory as against mutable requirements. Some detailed typologies of requirements have been proposed as a basis for RFPs covering hardware, operating system, financial and managerial requirements.

Each of the requirements or bundles of requirements constitute a selection criterion, weighted by its importance. Weighting of criteria may be based on techniques such as an analytic hierarchy, fixed scale valuation or binary weighting. Packages are evaluated using overall scores, estimated as the weighted sums of their individual scores for each of the selection criteria. Such scores are assigned by the customer. Various refinements of this approach use sophisticated techniques drawn from economics and multi-criteria decision making in supporting the final selection.

In spite of their strength in supporting the evaluation of packages with respect to "non functional" (generally measurable) software requirements (such as security, reliability, performance), traditional approaches are weak

in treating qualitative and core functional requirements. In particular, they are weak in supporting multi-valued features, features valued in partially ordered sets and inexact-matching of features with requirements. The weighting techniques they employ generally require a total prioritisation ordering of requirements, an unjustified and misleading simplification, since commonly customers are only able to partially order requirements according to their significance. Finally, the view of procurement as a linear process fails to take into account revision, learning and iterative assessment.

Software selection and comprehension have been investigated as problems within the broader problem of software reuse (Biggerstaff & Richter, 1987; Krueger, 1992; Spanoudakis & Constantopoulos, 1994). However, it may be difficult to transfer the methods and techniques developed in this setting. In particular, the focus of concern in software reuse has either been fine-grain source code components (Diaz, 1991; Constantopoulos et al. 1995), algorithms and abstract data types (see software schemas in Katz, Richter & The, 1989) or software architectures, large grain global structures for software systems designs (Shaw, 1991; Neighbors, 1989). None are directly comparable with software packages. The reuse process generally entails significant further development, involving modification and integration into larger software frameworks as against the more limited customisation associated with software packages. In the case of reuse, research aims at creating a large, distributed and diverse market of software components while for software packages this market already exists and must be shaped, or at any rate, managed. Furthermore, since reuse is generally carried out by software developers knowledge and skills are required which cannot safely be presumed of those engaged in software package procurement.

A common, if misleading, way of fitting "the square peg" of software package procurement into "the round hole" of conventional software engineering practice is to view it as, in essence, a validation problem. Packages are validated against requirements, begging the question of what these requirements are, how they are acquired and structured. Suggestions have included the use of scenarios (Benner et al. 1992) though it is unclear where these scenarios come from and the extent of the assurance they deliver.

Research Programme Components

Some of the issues identified above are obviously not restricted to off-the-shelf software packages and apply to purpose-built software - though not with equal force. We might expect a research programme which looks at software package requirements and procurement to yield more general insight into the software specification process. Below we describe the key building blocks of such a programme whose objective is to develop a set of organising principles for the software package requirements and procurement process. In large part we believe that the issues we face are fundamental, and require us to pursue a theoretical-logical approach. By taking this approach we place software package requirements and procurement within the mainstream of specification research and establish clear targets in terms of the soundness of the guidelines and principles that may result.

• *Description*

Clearly there needs to be a coarse grain framework within which requirements can be described and to which compatibility assessment makes reference. To line up with package descriptions in terms of "features" we propose specification in terms of "services" with corresponding service descriptions which include the constraints on the provision of those services.

The description of a service is an abstract, independent specification of the services intended behaviour in isolation. It presents a theory whose terms and constraints are expressed in a formal language (Cohen, 1995). An important issue in a language for describing features is the need for feature specifications to make minimal assumptions about the specification they're over. This will allow features over one specification to be applied to another. For example, consider a basic library system package, and define for it the feature of being able to keep accounts of users' fines. We would like this feature to be specified in a way that makes as few as possible assumptions about the library system specification, so that it can be applied to any other library system specification.

• *Matching*

Questions of vocabulary matching have been addressed before in specification, and have given rise to the notion of signature. Much formal work addresses how to translate between signatures and compare specifications in different vocabularies (Goguen & Burstall, 1984; Fiadeiro & Maibaum, 1991; Turski & Maibaum, 1987). This work could potentially be recruited to our setting. The assumptions that a feature makes about a specification may be stated in terms of its signature. The users-fines feature assumes that the underlying signature has the notions of "users" and "overdue returns".

• *Compatibility*

The topic of ranking packages according to the degree to which they satisfy requirements is strongly related to

the topic of verisimilitude in logic (Brink, 1989 and Benthem, 1987), where theories are ordered according to how close they are to a notional "truth". But there are several ways in which the package requirements and procurement problem differs from the standard problem of verisimilitude. One difference is that the user is usually not concerned if a particular package extends the requirements in some way, as this is only an extra feature, the concern is only in the case that the package falls short of the requirements. Such a notion of verisimilitude is considered in Ryan & Schobbens, 1995. Another way in which our problem differs from the standard problem of verisimilitude is that there are priority relations among some of the requirements.

• *Revision*

In the case of revision, change and mutability, a theoretical approach could be expected to provide some insight too. The requirements could be represented as an ordered theory, where the ordering is used to specify the entrenchment, or priority, with which the user asserts the requirement. We could potentially exploit work in the topic of theory revision (Gardenfors, 1988; Ryan, 1994) to get a handle on the question of the degree of change required to the package.

The introduction of features on a specification involves specification revision. Returning to the library example, the library system augmented by the user-fines feature will manifest behaviours (such as blocking loans to users who have unpaid fines) which were not shown by the basic library system. Thus, a first approximation to the semantics of feature introduction might use the standard work on belief revision.

However, usually there are constraints within the original specification which should be considered immutable. In a state-based system such as the library, axioms constraining the notion of state should not be revised, but axioms describing the effects of actions should be.

We have worked on the idea that the models of the specification revised by a feature should be computed by taking those models of the feature which are "as close as possible" to the original specification. This requires the notion that interpretations are ordered according to closeness to the specification. Our results on simple specifications suggest that interpretations should be compared only if they agree on action occurrences.

Conclusion

This position paper has given an account of the problem of software package requirements and procurement and briefly reviewed related work. It has sketched the key components of an approach to this problem. In the final analysis however the purpose of this paper is to situate software package requirements and procurement within specification research and to argue that it is a problem worthy of serious consideration. Further, the issues it raises which if not wholly unfamiliar are differently configured and with significant change of emphasis. They are at any rate fundamental and we cannot expect to simply hand this problem on to management scientists or other research communities.

References

C. Ashworth and M. Goodland. (1990); SSADM: A Practical Approach, McGraw Hill.

K. Benner, M.S. Feather, W. L. Johnson & L. Zorman. (1992) ,Utilizing Scenarios in the Software Development Process; IFIP WG 8.1 Working Conference on Information Systems Development Process, 9 December 1992.

J.van Benthem. (1987); Verisimilitude and conditionals, What is Closer-to-the-Truth, (ed) T.Kuipers, pages 103-128, Rodopi, Amsterdam

T. Biggerstaff, C. Richter. (1987); Reusability Framework, Assessment and Directions, In Frontier Series: Software Reusability, Volume I: Concepts and Models, T. Biggerstaff and A. Perlis(eds), ACM Press, New York

C. Brink. (1989); Verisimilitude: Views and reviews. History and Philosophy of Logic , 10, pp. 181-201, 1989.

B. Cohen. (1995); The Description and Analysis of Services as Required and Provided by their Agents, Department of Computer Science, City University, London

S. Conger. (1994); The New Software Engineering, The Wadsworth Series in Management Information Systems, ISBN 0-534-17143-5, Belmont, California

P. Constantopoulos et al. (1995); The Software Information Base: A Server for Reuse, The VLDB Journal (to appear)

R.P. Diaz. (1991); Implementing Faceted Classification for Software Reuse, Communications of the ACM, 34(5), May 1991

R.H. Edmundson, D.R. Jeffery. (1984); The Impact of Requirements Analysis upon User Satisfaction with Packaged Software, Information & Management 7, Elsevier Science Publishers, North Holland

J. Fiadeiro , T. Maibaum. (1991); Describing, structuring and implementing objects, In Proceedings of REX Workshop on Foundations of Object-Oriented Languages, Springer-Verlag

P. Gardenfors. (1988); Knowledge in Flux: Modelling the Dynamics of Epistemic States, MIT Press

J.A. Goguen, R.M. Burstall. (1984); Introducing institutions, In Proceedings of Workshop on Logics of Programming, (eds) E.Clarke and D.Kozen, Lecture Notes in Computer Science 164, Springer-Verlag

S. Katz, C. Richter, K. The. (1989); PARIS: A System for Reusing Partially Interpreted Schemas, In Frontier Series: Software Reusability, Volume I: Concepts and Models, T. Biggerstaff and A. Perlis(eds), ACM Press, New York

C. Krueger. (1992); Software Reuse, ACM Computing Surveys, 24(2), June 1992

J. Neighbors. (1989); Draco: A Method for Engineering Reusable Software Systems, In Frontier Series: Software Reusability, Volume I: Concepts and Models, T. Biggerstaff and A. Perlis(eds), ACM Press, New York

M.D. Ryan. (1994); Belief revision and ordered theory presentations. In Logic, Action and Information, (eds) A.Fuhrmann and H.Rott, De Gruyter Publishers, 1994 (also in Proceedings of the 8th Amsterdam Colloquium on Logic, University of Amsterdam, 1991)

M. D. Ryan, P.-Y. Schobbens (1995); Belief revision and verisimilitude; Notre Dame Journal of Formal Logic, Vol. 36(1), 1995.

G. Spanoudakis, P. Constantopoulos. (1994); Similarity for Analogical Software Reuse: A Computational Model, In Proceedings of the 11th European Conference on Artificial Intelligence, Amsterdam, The Netherlands, August 1994

M. Shaw. (1991); Heterogeneous Design Idioms for Software Architerctures, In Proceedings of the 6th International Workshop on Software Specification and Design, Como, Italy, October 1991

W.M. Turski, T.S.E. Maibaum. (1987); The Specification of Computer Programs, Addison-Wesley, London

M. Zviran. (1993); A Comprehensive Methodology for Computer Family Selection. Journal of Systems and Software, 22(1), July 1993.

Supporting the Selection of Software Requirements

Joachim Karlsson[*]

SoftLab ab
Datalinjen 1
S-583 30 Linköping, Sweden
Internet: joachim@softlab.se

Kevin Ryan

College of Informatics and Electronics
University of Limerick
Limerick, Ireland
Internet: ryank@ul.ie

Abstract

The choice of candidate requirements for implementation is a primary determinant of customer satisfaction. It is argued that a set of requirements should be chosen which reflects both the importance and the estimated cost of each candidate requirements. A contribution-based method is proposed which determines importance and estimates cost and industrial experience in applying this method is reported. The results indicate that the contribution of candidate requirements can vary by orders of magnitude. By applying the method, software managers are in a position to select requirements for implementation based on each candidate requirement's contribution.

1. Introduction

One of the greatest risks commercial software development organizations face is that of developing systems that do not meet the customers' needs and expectations. The problem is common since most organizations are unable to measure the degree to which candidate features of a forthcoming software system are truly of value to the customers. Therefore, many software systems are developed with little knowledge about the probable customer acceptance of the software system. In the short run for the development organization this inability means time-consuming activities such as error correction, performance enhancements and adding functionality. In the long run it means a damaged reputation, lost orders and reduced profits.

This risk must be tackled early in the lifecycle by identifying the extent to which the customers' various requirements will contribute to the overall satisfaction with the software system. A requirement's ability to contribute to customer satisfaction can be operationally defined as the value it provides in relation to its cost.

In working with Ericsson Radio Systems AB we have studied this problem and developed a method, *the contribution-based method*, for determining the candidate requirements' contribution before any of them are selected for implementation [2]. By pair-wise comparisons of the candidate requirements each requirement's relative importance (value) and cost can be calculated using the analytic hierarchy process (AHP) [4]. Then, each requirement's contribution can be computed in terms of its importance in relation to its cost of implementation. By applying this method to commercial projects, we have observed that the contribution of requirements can vary by orders of magnitude. Thus, a primary determinant of customer satisfaction is which requirements are selected for implementation.

From a large-scale development project at Ericsson Radio Systems AB we found that selecting a "good" set of requirements means that we theoretically can implement 96% of the value at 76% of the cost. Conversely, implementing the other requirements would cost a fourth of the complete development budget and only marginally add value to the software system.

We have observed that without explicit knowledge about the requirements contribution, the probability of selecting a non-optimized set of requirements is high. Moreover, the negative effects of such a selection can be severe for all concerned, both in terms of development cost and development schedule. Our positive experience, on the other hand, is that the software engineers using the pair-wise comparison technique have found it easy to learn and use, and that it yields accurate and trustworthy results. The method is proposed as a replacement for selection strategies that are currently used, which are less systematic. The prototype tool for supporting the method is now being developed for more extensive use.

2. Motivation

Undertaking commercial large-scale software development is a challenging activity that involves numerous people and typically consumes several man-years. Such

---

[*]*Previous affiliation: Department of Computer and Information Science, Linköping University, S-581 83 Linköping, Sweden.*

146

challenges both include possible opportunities for the software organization, and possible risks. The planned software system may not be delivered on time, the available technology may fail, the personnel underperform, or probably worst of all, the software system may not sell.

Even though it must be kept in mind during the complete lifecycle, the question of meeting of customer needs is most crucial early in the lifecycle, in the requirements engineering process. Unfortunately, many software systems end up being developed without meeting their requirements, and thus cannot be used as initially expected [1]. In particular, when there are limited resources but an almost infinite range of candidate requirements, it is essential to choose those requirements that give the best return, in terms of customer satisfaction, on the investment involved.

We have developed and applied a novel approach to selecting the optimal set of requirements to implement when a project has limited resources. The remainder of this paper describes this approach, outlines our use of it and summarizes the lessons learned in the process.

3. Determining requirements contribution

In order to form a strategy for selecting requirements in order to maximizing customer satisfaction we applied and evaluated the notion of *requirements contribution*. To identify the requirements contribution we used a pair-wise comparison technique based on the analytic hierarchy process [4]. In this process the candidate requirements are compared pair-wise according to a predefined criterion (such as importance or cost). A pair of requirements have one the following relationships (for illustrative purposes, the criterion importance is used):

- Both requirements are of equal importance.
- One requirement is weakly more important.
- One requirement is strongly more important.
- One requirement is demonstrably or very strongly more important.
- One requirement is absolutely more important.

The AHP prescribes pair-wise comparisons of all candidate requirements, thus the required number of comparisons grows polynomally. For a software system with n candidate requirements, $n \cdot (n-1)/2$ pair-wise comparisons are required. When all requirements have been compared pair-wise the criterion distribution can be calculated using a method called averaging over normalized columns [4].

An important feature of the AHP is that the resulting requirements importances are relative and based on a ratio scale. That is, the importances always add up to 100%, and a requirement with an importance of 30% consequently represents 30% of the total importance. Moreover, a

requirement of importance 30% is three times as important as a requirement with an importance of 10%. The pair-wise comparison technique consequently provides a good means for discussing each candidate requirement's ability to achieve customer satisfaction.

Another interesting feature of the AHP is the redundancy of the pair-wise comparisons which makes them much less sensitive to judgement errors [3]. For example, assume requirement A is determined as being moderately more important than B, and requirement B is determined as being moderately more important than C. If, then, requirement C is determined as being moderately more important than A, a judgement error has definitely occurred. Such judgement errors of the pair-wise comparisons can be measured and thus identified using the AHP. This is accomplished by calculating the *consistency index* and subsequently by calculating the *consistency ratio* [4].

In the application of the pair-wise comparison technique at Ericsson Radio Systems AB we asked a senior developer to determine the relative importance (or value) of the candidate requirements, and then to estimate the relative cost of implementation for the candidate requirements. A simple prototype tool was developed which computes the resulting importance and cost distributions.

4. Case study

In order to evaluate the idea of requirements contribution, it was applied to the fourth release of a large-scale software development project at Ericsson Radio Systems AB, which had 11 candidate high-level requirements [2]. This project, Performance Management Traffic Recording (PMR) is a software system which enables recording and analysis of telecommunication traffic.

The candidate requirements in the PMR-project were of the type:

- Show only valid information in recording data report.
- Delete more than one recording at a time.
- Porting to Solaris 2.X.
- Previous/next in data reports.
- Quick buttons between reports.

The method was found to be very efficient in operation. A total of 35 minutes of effort was all that was required for the senior developer to perform the pair-wise comparisons using both the criteria of importance and cost.

We believe both criteria are necessary for the selection process. Merely focusing on the important requirements may lead to very costly software systems. Merely focusing on low cost may lead to systems lacking important functionality. Thus, a combined view of requirements importance and cost is required.

4.1 Requirements importance

The resulting importance distribution of the 11 candidate requirements is outlined in figure 1. It can be seen that the importance of the requirements varies by orders of magnitude.

Also, the Pareto Principle (named after the nineteenth-century Italian economist Vilfredo Pareto) seems to apply, i.e., 20% of the candidate requirements stands for 80% of the importance. The three most requirements, numbers 4, 5, and 6 stand for 63% of the importance of the requirements in the PMR-project.

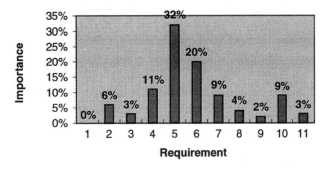

Figure 1. The importance distribution of the 11 candidate requirements.

4.2 Requirements cost

The resulting cost distribution of the 11 candidate requirements is outlined in figure 2. Here too, the Pareto principle seems to apply to the results. The three most expensive requirements, numbers 4, 5, and 9 stand for 57% of the estimated cost of implementation of the requirements in the PMR-project.

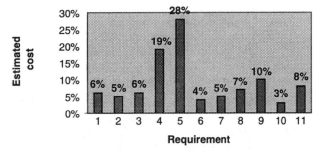

Figure 2. The cost distribution of the 11 candidate requirements.

When the importance is plotted against estimated cost of implementation as in figure 3, the candidate requirements' contribution to customer satisfaction becomes more clear.

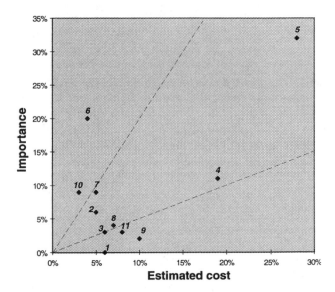

Figure 3. A cost-importance diagram of the 11 candidate requirements.

The requirements in figure 3 can be roughly divided into three categories; the requirements with *high* contribution, *medium* contribution and *low* contribution, respectively. A requirement with high contribution has an importance-cost ratio exceeding 2. A requirement with medium contribution has an importance-cost ratio between 0.5 and 2. Finally, a low contributing requirement has an importance-cost ratio lower than 0.5.

The individual requirement's contribution are very different according to the pair-wise comparisons. On the one hand, requirement number 1 accounts for 0% of the importance and still costs 6% to implement. At the other extreme, requirement number 6 accounts for 20% of the importance and only 4% of the implementation cost.

Selecting, for example, the high and medium contributing requirements for implementation (thus discarding requirements number 1, 9, and 11) implies that 95% of value can be given the customer, but at a cost of 76%. On the other hand, selecting requirements on an arbitrary basis is clearly a risk since the best set of requirements is unlikely to be chosen.

5. Lessons learned

The set of requirements selected for implementation is a primary determinant of customer satisfaction. Merely focusing on either the requirements importance or the cost of implementation would be a mistake in software development. The requirements with the highest relation of importance to estimated cost of implementation must be favored in the selection process in order to achieve customer satisfaction.

We have seen that requirements selection is a crucial step in software development. If information such as in figure 3 is not available the probability of selecting a wrong set of requirements is very high. Moreover, the negative impact of such a non-optimized selection is high on both development cost and schedule.

We have found the pair-wise comparison technique as described by the analytic hierarchy process useful and efficient in practice. Using this method, and the supporting prototype, we could determine more precisely the importance and cost distribution of the candidate requirements. We also found the notion of contribution useful in the requirements selection process. The people who have used this technique at Ericsson Radio Systems AB are very pleased with it, and are currently planning to extend its use.

For this reason, and to further explore the issues involved in requirements selection, we are currently developing an industrial strength support tool, which will support the method more fully, for example, by automatically generating the graphics shown in this paper. Also, we are investigating different strategies to reduce the number of required pair-wise comparisons so that our approach can more easily scale up.

6. Acknowledgments

This work has been supported by Ericsson Radio Systems AB and The Swedish National Board for Industrial and Technical Development, Dnr 93-3280.

7. References

[1] Davis, A. M. (1993). *Software Requirements. Objects, Functions and States*. Prentice-Hall International, Inc., Englewood Cliffs, New Jersey.

[2] Karlsson, J. (1995). Towards a Strategy for Software Requirements Selection. Licentiate Thesis 513, Department of Computer and Information Science, Linköping University, Sweden.

[3] Millet, I. and Harker, P. (1990). Globally effective questioning in the analytic hierarchy process. *European Journal of Operational Research*, 48(1):88–97.

[4] Saaty, T. L. (1980). *The Analytic Hierarchy Process*. McGraw-Hill, Inc.

Concern-Driven Design for a Specification Language Supporting Component-Based Software Engineering

W. (Voytek) Kozaczynski and Jim Q. Ning

Center for Strategic Technology Research (CSTaR)
Andersen Consulting Technology Park
3773 Willow Road, Northbrook, IL 60062-6212
{voytek, jning}@cstar.ac.com

Abstract

This paper concerns an approach to software development which is referred to as Component-Based Software Engineering (CBSE). The approach is based on the principle of extensive use of preexisting, standard or customizable components in building new systems. CBSE has received considerable attention recently since it promises to bring to software development the engineering discipline that has been long accepted in more mature engineering domains. In this paper we describe the design of a specification language intended for support of basic CBSE activities; the Architecture Specification Language (ASL). More specifically, we show how the language design choices have been driven by our understanding and prioritization of the concerns of the key stakeholders involved in the software development process.

1: Introduction

On large and very large Andersen Consulting jobs one role is always recognized and staffed. This is the role of an Architect. This role is usually split into two sub-roles: the *functional architect* (also called the *application architect*) and the *technical architect*. The latter role is usually "hidden" in a technical team and reports to the project architect, who assumes the role of the functional architect. We have also recognized a new role specific to the CBSE paradigm: the role of the *component producer*.

In the CBSE process the Architecture Specification Language (ASL) is intended for use by the functional and technical architects as well as the component producers. Here we take a closer look at the concerns of the three roles, as well as interactions between them, and try to use them to derive the specification language design guidelines and principles.

Component-Based Software Engineering (CBSE) is an approach to developing systems by assembling them from components. Central to the approach is the notion of a *component*, which we assume to mean the following:

- It is a large-grain system building block. Its granularity is larger than that of functional procedures or object-oriented classes. It corresponds closer to the concept of an *application* or an *executable*.

- It has meaningful functionality; it carries out a unique subset of a system's overall functional behavior.

- It is a unit of distribution and configuration; a component can be independently manufactured, packaged, and distributed for reuse without the consideration for other components.

- It can be a *subsystem* itself and may consist of other components.

Software components may be expensive to develop and difficult to maintain. On the other hand, they are inexpensive to reproduce and distribute. It is best to think of components as units of reuse. In fact, more and more software industry experts and researchers believe that the progress of the industry may depend on how fast it establishes a components market. Simple principles of this market are illustrated in Figure 1.

In this market, the *component brokers* obtain/buy and distribute/resell components. Object Management Group (OMG), for example, is attempting to play the role of a component broker.

150

Another role in this market is this of the *component producer*. There will always be companies like Microsoft, which manufacture and maintain commodity components. The third role in this market is that of the *component integrator*. Integrators add value by assembling components in unique ways to solve particular business problems of their clients. They are consumers of components.

Andersen Consulting primarily falls into the role of a component integrator; we are more interested in assembling components into large systems than fabricating them. However in the near future, before the component software market matures, Andersen also has to assume the role of a component producer for itself. This paper mainly addresses concerns of the component integrators and producers.

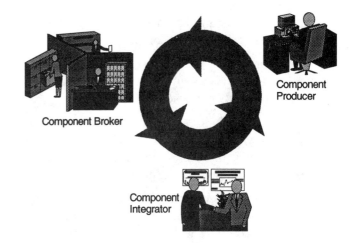

Figure 1. A component-based software market.

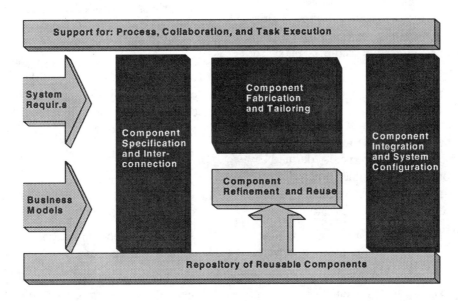

Figure 2. A CBSE-based development process.

2: Concerns of CBSE Process Roles

In a CBSE process (Figure 2), the role of component integrator is further classified into a *functional architect* and a *technical architect*. The functional architect is a pivotal role. We will, therefore, start from discussing this role.

2.1: Functional Architect

The high-level concern of the functional architect is to map the problem space into the solution space in a cost-effective manner. The problem is described by a set of system requirements. The solution is a decomposition of the system into a set of interacting components (see the left-most dark box in Figure 2) such that:

1. components are of manageable size and complexity and each encapsulates a meaningful subset of system functions

2. component functionality and properties can be easily understood at the interface level

3. reuse of existing components is taken into account in the system decomposition

4. interconnections between system components, how the interfaces of components should be plugged together, are well-defined

5. component definitions and interconnections can be used to evaluate the system against its original requirements without necessarily executing component implementations, and

6. component definitions are detailed enough to be used as purchasing orders for component brokers or design contracts with component producers.

In many cases, an architect cannot purchase all the required components off-the-shelf. The "distance" between what is available and the target solution requirements dictates what the architect needs to do. His options can range from putting simple "glue" between existing components, to defining tailoring requests, to generating new requirements for component producers.

2.2: Component Producer

The main concern of the component producer is how to deliver quality components that meet functional as well as extra-functional requirements defined by market standards or special customer orders (see the middle dark box in Figure 2). In order to do that, component producer must make sure that:

7. component definitions are precise and comprehensive enough to be used to develop new or tailor existing components

8. multiple versions/implementations of components are supported to meet different platform requirements

9. component definitions are sufficient to be used to test component implementations independent of the availability of other components.

2.3: Technical Architect

The functional architect defines a system's building "blueprint" -- what types of components are required and how the components should be interconnected.

The technical architect is concerned with the task of generating an executable version of a system according to a blueprint using component implementations provided by the producers (see

right-most dark box in Figure 2). In particular, technical architect is concerned with:

10. providing the right run-time environment for components to execute

11. handling potential heterogeneity of components

12. defining system distribution geometry

13. selecting compatible implementations of components

14. providing technical infrastructure for inter-component communication

15. assuring system performance and reliability.

3: Requirements for a Design Language

To support and capture the work products of the CBSE process we need a language. This language should address the concerns identified in the previous section and assist communication among component producers, brokers, and architects. We have taken these concerns and derived from them the following system properties that the language should describe (the numbers in the parentheses indicate mappings to the concerns):

I. component interfaces -- how the components can be used (2, 5, 6, 7, 9)

II. component semantics -- what the components are supposed to do functionally (2, 5, 6, 7, 9)

III. system decomposition -- hierarchical representation of a system in terms of components and nested components (1, 3, 12)

IV. component interconnection -- how to bind components together and how to handle differences between components (4, 5, 11, 14)

V. component implementations separate from interface specifications (8, 11, 13)

VI. system configuration -- how to map a functional architecture onto a technical platform (10, 12, 14, 15)

The above list forms a set of language requirements. Architecture specification has been a very active research area in recent years. We have seen a variety of proposed languages that meet some of these requirement. The following is an incomplete list that maps some of the representative languages to the above list:

- CORBA IDL [OMG91] -- component interface specification (I)

- Inscape [Perry89] -- component semantics and interconnection verification (II, III, IV)

- Darwin [MDK] -- functional architecture support (III, IV)

- Rapide [LKAVBM95] - functional architecture support (III, IV)

- UniCon [SDZ95] - component interconnection specification (IV)

- Polylith [Purtilo91] -- technical architecture support (V, VI)

4: Architecture Specification Language (ASL)

The CBSE project at the Center for Strategic Technology Research (CSTaR) of Andersen Consulting is aimed at developing enabling technologies for component integration. A central research focus of this project is the development of an Architecture Specification Language that meets all the design requirements identified in the previous section.

Although the design principles have been identified, ASL is still under development. It is not the intention of this short position paper to provide a precise definition of the language. Here we want to describe only the key features of the language and explain how ASL meets our design requirements.

Realizing the fact that the design requirements are so diversified, we have decided to separate ASL into three independent, but interrelated sublanguages:

(i) an *Interface Specification Language* (ISL),

(ii) a *Glue Specification Language* (GSL), and

(iii) a *Configuration Specification Language* (CSL).

The ISL is a pure semantic extension of the CORBA IDL. Specifically, the interface definitions in IDL are enhanced with *pre/postcondition*, *invariant*, and *protocol* specifications. The pre and postconditions specify what have to be true before and after execution of operations in an interface. The invariants specify what has to be true between operation invocations. The protocols are specified as part of pre/postconditions and describe order dependencies between operation invocations. The

short example below illustrates a protocol for standard operations in a File interface. It states that Open can only operate on a Closed file and Close can only operate on a file that is already opened for read or write:

```
interface File {
  states {OpenForR, OpenForW, Closed};
  void Open (in short mode)
    precondition { mode>=0; Closed; }
    postcondition {
      mode==0 --> OpenForR;
      mode>0 --> OpenForW; };
  void Close ()
    precondition {
      OpenForR || OpenForW; };
    postcondition { Closed; };
}
```

Obviously, ISL addresses the component interfaces (I) and semantics requirements (II).

The GSL introduces the concept of a component.

There are two types of components in GSL, *primitive components* and *composite components*. Primitive components consist of multiple interfaces, some of them *provided* and some *required*. Provided interfaces represent services that components offer to other components and required interfaces represent services that components have to acquire from other components. Composite components contain subcomponents and define interconnections between subcomponents. Below is a small example in which FileServer and FileClient are two primitive components and Application is a composite component:

```
component FileServer {
  provide File datafile;
}
component FileClient {
  require File db;
}
component Application {
  component FileServer fs;
  component FileClient fc;
  bind fs::datafile -- fc::db;
}
```

GSL is designed to support hierarchical system construction (III) and component interconnection (IV).

Finally, the CSL specifies implementation details for components (V) and configuration requirements (VI). It uses keywords such as **source**, **machine_type**, **operating_system**, **host**, etc., to specify technical architecture-related attributes of component implementations. The following are some partial examples:

```
implementation FS of FileServer {
  source "/tmp/examples/foo1.cc";
  machine_type SparcII;
}

implementation FC of FileClient {
  source "/tmp/examples/foo2.cc";
  operating_system WindowsNT;
}

implementation APP of Application {
  fs host @1;
  fc host @2;
}
```

CSL specifications are primarily used by a system packaging process to generate configuration procedures.

5: Conclusion

We started by recognizing concerns of component producers and integrators (functional and technical architects) in the CBSE process. We used these concerns to drive the requirements for a design language. We proposed a language, the ASL, and explained how its sublanguages (ISL, GSL, and CSL) meet the requirements:

- ISL will be mainly used by component producers to communicate with functional architects to express signatures and semantics of component interfaces,

- GSL will be mainly used by functional architects to communicate with technical architects to express composition and interconnection requirements,

- CSL will be mainly used by technical architects to express system platform, distribution, and other non-functional requirements to assist system packaging.

ASL is still under development and so are the tools that will support the CBSE process. It is reasonable to assume that the language will evolve, but we hope, that the requirements we derived from the design concerns will remain stable.

References

[AG94] Allen, R., and Garlan, D., "Formalizing Architectural Connection," *Proceedings of 16th International Conference on Software Engineering*, Sorrento, Italy, 1994.

[Callahan93] Callahan, J. R., "Software Packaging," *Technical Report CS-TR-3093*, U. of Maryland, 1993.

[Expersoft94] Expersoft Corporation, *XShell User's Manual*, Release 3.0, March 1994.

[KLNO95] Kozaczynski, W., Liongosari, E., Ning, J. Q., and Olafsson, A., "Architecture Specification Support for Component Integration," *Proceedings of the Seventh International Workshop on CASE*, Toronto, Ontario, Canada, July 1995.

[LKAVBM95] Luckham, D. C., Kenney, J. J., Augustin, L. M., Vera, J., Bryan, D., and Mann, W., "Specification and Analysis of System Architecture Using Rapide," *IEEE Transactions on Software Engineering*, Vol. 21, No. 4, April 1995.

[MDK94] Magee, J., Dulay, N., and Kramer, J., "A Constructive Development Environment for Parallel and Distributed Programs," *Proceedings of the Second International Workshop on Configurable Distributed Systems*, Pittsburgh, PA, March 1994.

[Microsoft93] Microsoft Corporation, "Object Linking and Embedding (OLE) Today and Tomorrow," *Technology Overview*, November 1993.

[ODMG93] Object Database Management Group, *The Object Database Standard: ODMG-93*, Cattell, R. G. G., ed., 1993.

[OMG91] Object Management Group, *The Common Object Request Broker: Architecture and Specification*, OMG Doc. Number 91.12.1., 1991.

[Perry89] Perry, D. E., "The Inscape Environment," *Proceedings of the 11th International Conference on Software Engineering*, Pittsburgh PA, May 1989.

[Purtilo91] Purtilo, J., "The Polylith Software Bus," *Technical Report TR-2469*, U. of Maryland, 1991.

[SDKRYZ95] Shaw, M., DeLine, R., Klein, D. V., Ross, T. L., Young, D. M., and Zelesnik, G., "Abstractions for Software Architecture and Tools to Support Them," *IEEE Transactions on Software Engineering*, Vol. 21, No. 4, April 1995.

[YS94] Yellin, D. M. and Strom, R. E., "Interfaces, Protocols, and the Semi-Automatic Construction of Software," *Proceedings of the OOPSLA'94*, Portland, Oregon, October 1994.

A "Coming and Going" Approach to Specification Construction: a Scenario

N. Levy and J. Souquières

CRIN-CNRS
BP. 239, 54506 Vandœuvre-les-Nancy Cedex, France
E-mail: {nlevy, souquier}@loria.fr

Abstract

The construction of a specification or a program is rarely done in one single step and in a linear way. "Coming and Going" among the different components of the specification are often performed, i.e., the specification needs to be frequently revisited. This paper illustrates this approach on the production cell case study by means of a scenario of development. It shows what could be automated and indicates which kind of help could be proposed to the specifier.

1 Introduction

Research on tool support for specifications design has been going on for years. In [1], formal methods are pointed out to develop systems of significant scale and importance. Among the recommendations, the authors encourage future research on developing notations more suitable to use by individuals not expert in formal methods or mathematical logic. Unfortunately notations will not solve all problems. The constructions offered by specification languages implicitly represent different specification styles or approaches. But representing a style does not mean supporting it.

Moreover, from a software developer's point of view [2], a software engineering environment should include common services to foster the high-quality software production. Formal specification tools essentially support the validation of specifications: types checkers, theorem provers, etc. Most of them do not address the construction itself. Methodologies exist to assist the software engineer in the production of specifications [3, 4, 5, 6]. Feather and Johnson propose a sizable library of evolution transformations [7] to change the meaning of specifications with a derivation model based on parallel development [8]. But they presuppose a linear construction process. For example, they encourage specifiers to define the structure of a type first and then its operations. But in fact, when defining the operations, some attributes appear to be forgotten. Then the structure has to be revisited in order to complete it. on formal account. These approaches have to be clarified and supported by tools for the construction of formal specifications.

Obtaining a formal text is a long process with much *"Coming and Going"*. Its mechanisation needs understanding and modelling the approach followed during the development [9]. Maintaining an agenda of what remains to be defined is a first idea of the kind of help that can be offered [10]. A second idea could be an agenda automatically fulfilled. The problem to be solved is to keep consistent the whole specification and to remember what is still to be introduced, defined and completed.

This paper illustrates this *"Coming and Going"* approach on the "Production Cell" case study [11] by means of a scenario of development. It shows what could be automated and indicates which kind of help could be proposed to a specifier.

2 Scenario of a specification construction by coming and going

We consider the "Production Cell" case study [11]. The system to be specified processes metal blanks which are conveyed to a press by a feed belt. A robot takes each blank from the feed belt and places it into the press. A table has to be introduced between the feed belt and the robot to bring the blanks into the right position for the robot to pick them up. A vertical movement is necessary for the table because the robot arm is located at a different level than the feed belt and because it cannot perform vertical translations. A rotation movement is also required because the robot arm's gripper is not rotary. The press forges the blank and the robot takes the metal plate from the press and puts it on a deposit belt. In this paper, we will concentrate on the feed belt and the rotary elevating table.

Our purpose is to present, step by step, the specification construction. The chosen specification language is Z [12]. During the construction, some decisions will bring us to navigate between the specification schemas, in order to maintain their consistency. New attributes will be introduced, schemas modified; those modifications will have to be propagated throughout the whole specification. The development steps presented in this paper will consist in defining the movement of a blank from the feed belt to the rotary elevating table.

2.1 Starting point

The starting point of our scenario is when a global view of the Production Cell system has been outlined. The system is composed at this point, due to lack of space, of two subsystems, the feed belt and the table; for each subsystem a first approximation has been given:

```
┌─ Prod_Cell ──────────────────
│ Feed_Belt
│ Table
└──────────────────────────────
```

```
┌─ Feed_Belt ──────────────────
│ State : Feed_Belt_State
└──────────────────────────────
```

```
┌─ Table ──────────────────────
│ Rot_Pos : ℝ
│ Vert_Pos : ℝ
└──────────────────────────────
```

$$Feed\_Belt\_State ::= on \mid off$$

where $\mathbb{R}$ stands for real numbers.

2.2 The *From_FB_To_Table* operation

The next step consists in defining the operation *From_FB_To_Table*, during which a blank moves from the feed-belt to the table. This operation can be performed when a blank has entered the final part of the belt and the table has got the right position, w.r.t. to its rotation and vertical movement. The operation is defined as follows:

```
┌─ From_FB_To_Table ───────────
│ Δ Feed_Belt
│ Δ Table
├──────────────────────────────
│ Feed_Belt.Blank_at_End
│ Feed_Belt.State = on
│ Table.Can_Receive
│ Table.Loaded'
│ Table.Rot_Pos' = Table.Rot_Pos
│ Table.Vert_Pos' = Table.Vert_Pos
│ ¬ Feed_Belt.Blank_at_End'
│ Feed_Belt.State ' = Feed_Belt.State
└──────────────────────────────
```

In this definition, several new attributes have been introduced: *Blank_at_End* related to the *Feed_Belt* subsystem, *Can_Receive* and *Loaded* related to the *Table* sub-system. To maintain the specification consistency, we have to go back to the definition of *Feed_Belt* and *Table* in order to add these new attributes.

It is to be noted that these attributes could be automatically introduced in the current specification state. In this special case, their type could also be deduced from their use in the *From_FB_To_Table* schema. Let us suppose it is not done automatically, so we have to do it by hand. In any case, a constraint can be added.

2.3 A new attribute for *Feed_Belt*

A new piece of information, namely *Blank_at_End*, has to be introduced and its type has to be given. It indicates whether a blank is currently in the final part of the belt or not. This piece of information will be deduced from a photoelectric cell indication and will have boolean type $\mathbb{B}$. No constraint between *State* and *Blank_at_End* has to be added for the moment.

```
┌─ Feed_Belt ──────────────────
│ State : Feed_Belt_State
│ Blank_at_End : 𝔹
└──────────────────────────────
```

As this abstract state is not used except in the definition of the operation *From_FB_To_Table*, no propagation of this modification is needed.

2.4 New attributes for *Table*

The two attributes *Loaded* and *Can_Receive* have to be added to the *Table* schema. *Loaded* indicates whether a blank is on the table or not. The table can receive a blank if it is in the right position and if it does not move. Both attributes will be of boolean type $\mathbb{B}$. It appears that *Can_Receive* is a constrained attribute, depending on *Rot_Pos*, *Vert_Pos* and on *Table* movement. To denote the right position, two constants are introduced, *FB_Rot* for the rotation and *FB_Vert* for the vertical position.

```
┌─ Table ──────────────────────
│ Rot_Pos : ℝ
│ Vert_Pos : ℝ
│ Loaded : 𝔹
│ Can_Receive : 𝔹
│ Movement : Movement_State
├──────────────────────────────
│ Can_Receive ⇔
│        (  Rot_Pos = FB_Rot
│        ∧  Vert_Pos = FB_Vert
│        ∧  ¬ Loaded
│        ∧  Movement = fix   )
└──────────────────────────────
```

The definition of *Loaded* and *Can_receive* has several effects: the introduction of the *Movement* attribute to be added to the table schema and the introduction of the constants *FB_Rot* and *FB_Vert*. The following actions could then be proposed to the specifier:

- define the basic type *Movement_State*,

- define the constants *FB_Rot* and *FB_Vert*,

- propagate the introduction of the attribute *Movement* throughout the whole specification: each operation using *Table* has to be revisited in order to indicate its precondition and postcondition in terms of the *Movement* attribute.

Once these actions have been outlined, the specifier will choose the order in which these parts will be defined. The final specification text will be reordered to be conform to the Z specification notation.

New type definition: A new basic type has been used for the *Movement* attribute. It is defined as an enumerated type with, for the moment, only one known value. It will be completed later when defining the other system operations.

$$Movement\_State ::= fix \mid \dots$$

New constraints: With *Can_Receive*, the right position of the table has been defined: the constants *FB_Rot* and *FB_Vert* have to be introduced. The next global definitions can be constructed, the types $\mathbb{R}$, being deduced. The values remain still to be given:

FB_Rot : $\mathbb{R}$		*FB_Vert* : $\mathbb{R}$
FB_Rot = ...		*FB_Vert* = ...

Propagation to the whole specification: Due to the introduction of the *Movement* attribute for the *Table* schema, we have to go back to the whole specification and to propagate this modification to every operation using the *Table* state. At this development stage, just the operation *From_FB_To_Table* has to be revisited. A tool could propose the following modifications:

```
__From_FB_To_Table_____
 Δ Feed_Belt
 Δ Table
 ─────────────────────────────
 Feed_Belt.Blank_at_End
 Table.Can_Receive
 ... Table.Movement ...
 Table.Loaded'
 Table.Rot_Pos' = Table.Rot_Pos
 Table.Vert_Pos' = Table.Vert_Pos
 ... Table.Movement' ...
 ¬ Feed_Belt.Blank_at_End'
 Feed_Belt.State ' = on
```

The specifier has now to give the precondition (*Table.Movement = fix*) and the postcondition (state unchanged *Table.Movement' = Table.Movement*).

2.5 New constraints for Prod_Cell

As the *From_FB_To_Table* operation modifies both the *Feed_Belt* and *Table* states, the question of introducing constraints between these two subsystems has to be answered. A tool could require the specifier to give such a constraint.

```
__Prod_Cell_____
 Feed_Belt
 Table
 ─────────────────────
 (Feed_Belt.Blank_at_End ∧
 ¬ Table.Can_Receive)
 ⇒ Feed_Belt.State = off
```

3 Conclusion

This scenario of specification development using the "Coming and Going" paradigm has shown that a formal text is rarely built in a linear way: parts of the current specification are often revisited. It has also shown a need for supporting tools to maintain consistency, and to keep information about what is still to be introduced, defined, completed and propagated.

A framework [13, 14] as well as a prototype tool [15] have been defined (partly within the Esprit 2 project ICARUS) to model developments. This model and its environment aims at providing the specifier with active tools. To do so, a development state is modelled by means of a tree of subtasks. The concept of *daemon* is currently investigated for triggering subtasks creation according to the constraints attached to the tasks.

Acknowledgements

We wish to thank to Robert Darimont for his most valuable comments and discussions.

References

[1] Dan Craigen, Susan Gerhart, and Ted Ralston. *An International Survey of Industrial Applications of Formal Methods*. NIST GCR 93-626-V1, 5285 Port Royal Road, Springfield, Virginia 22161, U.S.A., March 1993.

[2] Alan W. Brown, Anthony N. Earl, and John A. McDermid. *Software Engineering Environments: Automated Support for Software Engineering*. International Series in Software Engineering. McGraw-Hill, London, New York, Paris, 1992.

[3] M.A. Jackson. *System Development*. International Series in Computer Science. Prentice Hall, 1983.

[4] G. Booch. *Object-Oriented Design with Application*. Addison-Wesley, 1990.

[5] J. Rambaugh, M. Blaha, W. Premerlani, F. Eddy, and W. Lorensen. *Object-Oriented Modeling and Design*. Prentice-Hall International. Englewood Cliffs, New Jersey, 1991.

[6] J.B. Wordsworth. *Software Development with Z*. International Computer Science Series. Addison Wesley, 1992.

[7] WL. Johnson and MS. Feather. Building an evolution transformation library. In *Proceedings, 12th International Conference on Software Engineering*, pages 238–248, Nice, France, 1990.

[8] MS. Feather. Constructing specification by combining parallel elaboration. In *Transactions on Software engineering*, pages 198–208. I.E.E.E, 1989. 15(2).

[9] J. Souquières and N. Lévy. Description of Specification Developments. In *Proceedings IEEE International Symposium on Requirements Engineering*, San Diego (CA, USA), January 1993.

[10] R. Darimont and J. Souquières. A Development Model: Application to Z specifications. In *Proc. of the IFIP WG 8.1 Working Conference on Information System Development Process*, Como, Italy, 1993. North Holland. September 1993.

[11] Claus Lewerentz and Thomas Lindner. *Formal development of reactive systems: case study production cell.* Number 891 in Lecture Notes in Computer Science. Springer-Verlag, 1995.

[12] JM. Spivey. Understanding z, a specification language and its formal semantics. *Cambridge Tracts in Theorical Computer Science*, 3, 1988.

[13] N. Lévy and G. Smith. A language-independent approach to specification construction. In *Proceedings of the ACM SIGSOFT'94: Symposium on the Foundations of Software Engineering, New Orleans, USA.*, December 1994.

[14] J. Souquières and R. Darimont. La Description du Développement de Spécifications. *Technique et Science Informatiques*, 14(9), novembre 1995.

[15] G. Bosch and J. Souquières. Prototype Assistant: its function and its design. Esprit Project 2537 ICARUS, Deliverable #48, January 1994. Development Editor User Manual.

A Computational Mechanism For Parallel Problem Decomposition During Requirements Engineering

N.A.M. Maiden & A.G. Sutcliffe

Centre for Human-Computer Interface Design
City University, London, UK

Abstract

The earliest phases of requirements engineering capture large amounts of diverse facts about the problem domain. These facts must be structured according to useful decompositions of that problem domain. Existing goal-oriented decompositions methods do not address issues specific to such decomposition. This paper outlines a tentative model of parallel problem domain decomposition, and describes a computational mechanism for achieving it. The mechanism accesses a set of problem abstractions produced as part of the ESPRIT III 6353 'NATURE' basic research action.

1: Parallel goal and problem decompostion during requirements engineering

Requirements for software-intensive systems come from diverse sources and are expressed in different forms. However, there have been few methods for managing such requirements, although exceptions do exist (e.g. [13], [15]). More methods are needed. This paper argues for method guidance for integrated goal and problem decomposition, and proposes that computational mechanisms are needed to aid non-hierarchical problem decomposition for large and complex software-intensive systems.

Information about software-intensive systems tends to be in two basic forms. First, requirements for the desired system are expressed as functional goals and constraints (e.g. [1], [15]). Complexities are handled using hierarchical decomposition. Goals are divided into sub-goals which, together, achieve the higher-level goal. Second, facts describe diverse phenomena in the problem domain, such as behaviour, events, structure and states. The existence of powerful modelling languages (e.g. [3]) for describing such phenomena is testimony to this. However, hierarchical decomposition promoted by most structured methods is often inappropriate [4]. Such decomposition is too simplistic for complex problem domains. Structured methods also focus on separation of concerns into behaviour, process and data rather than into

coherent features of the problem domain. Such separation can hide complex patterns which are often critical for effective problem understanding. Rather, an alternative approach, known as parallel problem decomposition (Jackson 1995), is needed.

This paper argues for better methods for parallel problem decomposition, and integration of such methods with methods for hierarchical goal decomposition. The ESPRIT 6353 'NATURE' basic research action ([5]) has explored one such method. The goal decomposition approach is outlined in [15]. However, better computational mechanisms and methods are still needed for parallel problem decomposition. This paper describes one such mechanism. The next section defines the requirements for the mechanism, and describes results from NATURE which provide a basis for its design. This is followed by a brief description of the mechanism itself. The paper ends with future research directions.

2: Problem decomposition during requirements engineering

The requirements capturer is one tool in the AIR tool kit [7]. It acquires facts about a problem domain using a set of window-based frames for entering different types of fact into a data base. These facts make assertions about various problem domain phenomena such as objects and their properties and attributes, state transitions, states and events [15]. However, using this tool often results in a large and unstructured set of inconsistent facts.

2.1: Parallel decomposition of problem domains

Hierarchical decomposition has proved effective for decomposing system goals [1]. But as Jackson [4] points out, decomposition of a problem domain is different from functional decomposition in two ways. First, it is heterogeneous. Each of the decomposed problem parts will often be a different type. Second, the decomposition is not hierarchical. The decomposed problem parts fit together in a parallel structure. Each part has overlapping subsets of phenomena in the problem domain. This is demonstrated by the simple example shown in Figure 1.

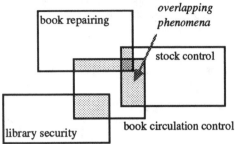

Figure 1. Parallel problem decomposition for a library domain. The overall problem is decomposed into four, overlapping parts. For example, loan and return behaviour overlaps in the book circulation control, repairing and stock control parts.

Furthermore, problem decomposition can drive goal decomposition. Examining the boundaries between the problem domain and software system implies the existence of goals. Indeed, it is events in these problem domain which often impose requirements on the software system [4]. Decomposing the problem into its parts reveals detailed interactions between the system and problem domain, thus aiding in the identification of goals. This kind of parallel problem structure is a powerful tool for reducing the complexities inherent in requirements engineering problems. Each decomposed problem part deals with one coherent aspect of the problem domain. Understanding these problem parts is critical for effective design, since requirements engineers must first understand what actual problems exist.

However, operationalising parallel problem decomposition is not trivial. The space of possible problem decompositions is large. Detecting the best-fit problem decomposition is also difficult. The entered set of facts will be incomplete, inaccurate and inconsistent, and different naming conventions will be used. Furthermore, there will often be no single, best-fit decomposition. Therefore, parallel problem decomposition warrants further research.

2.2: Prerequisites for problem domain decomposition

Three prerequisites for effective operationalisation of parallel problem decomposition have been identified: powerful domain semantics, problem domain categories and computational mechanisms.

Powerful domain semantics: problem phenomena are described using NATURE's problem modelling language. This language permits definition of complex problem descriptions as interrelated networks of different types of fact, rather than as the separation of concerns promoted by structured notations. This enables detection of coherent problem parts. It also enables more complex reasoning about problem domains, such as analogical reasoning for reuse [10]. The language is defined using the Telos knowledge representation language [11]. It enables description of objects, object properties and attributes, state transitions, states, events, goal states, preconditions on state transitions and functions.

Problem categories: effective decomposition should decompose a problem into parts which deal with coherent aspects of that domain. In essence, it should find problem parts which are natural categorisations of the whole problem. There has been research of both formal and informal categorisations of software engineering problems, however none has been extensive. In contrast NATURE has undertaken an extensive categorisation of requirements engineering problems. It has produced a set of over 200 object system models. Each model describes the fundamental objects, behaviour, states, goals, constraints and functions of all instances of one category of requirements engineering problem [15]. One of our key assertions is that problem decomposition will be more effective if problem parts instantiate these predefined object system models, as shown in Figure 2.

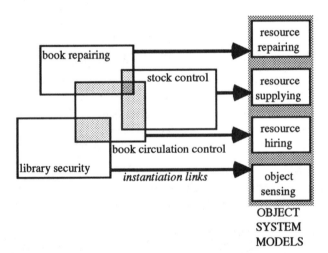

Figure 2. Mappings between problem domain parts and object system models for a library domain.

Computational mechanisms: computational mechanisms are needed to decompose large problem domains in a systematic manner. Descriptions of such large problems are unstructured and incomplete, so decomposition in such circumstances is difficult for people. Furthermore, a large problem description can lead to a combinatorial explosion in possible decompositions. To overcome these limitations, a mechanism is proposed which implements pattern matching algorithms to structure facts describing problem domain phenomena into parts which are the best-fit instantiations of different object system models. This mechanism works in parallel with another mechanism, called the domain matcher, which retrieves object system models for possible problem parts. The matcher uses internal problem structure rather than syntax to retrieve models, so it is independent of naming conventions.

NATURE has a model of parallel problem decomposition specific to its problem modelling language. Problem parts can share physical, observable phenomena (objects, some types of state, state transitions and events) which provide more recognisable shared features than non-physical ones. For example, most people can identify objects, agents (i.e. people) and tasks, whereas obtaining agreement on the existence on non-physical state or precondition is less reliable.

Such parallel decomposition has several advantages for requirements engineering. Overlapping phenomena can inform requirements engineers about the status of the problem. No overlapping phenomena with one problem part can indicate possible gaps in analysis since overlaps are often anticipated. On the other hand, too many overlapping phenomena indicates poor parts identification and hence decomposition. Once a problem is decomposed, more tools can be brought to bear. Within NATURE, the requirements critic tool matches object system models to descriptions of problem parts to check for incompleteness, contradictions and over specification [9]. It also provide a starting point for analogical reuse of requirement specifications [10]. In Figure 2, specification of the book circulation control system can be aided through analogical reuse of car rental or video hiring systems. Stock control can reuse analogical specifications for warehousing domains. Similar reuse is possible for the other problem parts. Reuse would be more difficult, if not impossible, without prior problem decomposition.

3: The domain decomposer

The domain decomposer is a computerised mechanism which identifies possible decompositions of large problems and presents them to users for acceptance or rejection. It is a general mechanism which can take problem descriptions for any application which instantiates some of NATURE's 200 object system models. It has been implemented using the ProLog language and ConceptBase data base [6]. As input, it receives a large set of facts which assert the existence of diverse problem domain phenomena. Output is one or more possible problem decompositions, ranked in order of goodness of fit with NATURE's object system models. The decomposition process first identifies all possible parts, then selects legal decompositions (combinations of these parts) from an exhaustive search of all possible combinations, and ends by determining the best-fit decomposition through matching to object system models. The decomposer has four main components. Each is examined in turn.

3.1: The problem part finder

First, the problem part finder uses simple pattern matching to detect possible problem parts from an input set of facts. It aims to find problem parts which can be matched to one object system model each. Twelve predefined fact patterns are hard-coded into the computational mechanism. These patterns describe relationships between events, state transitions, states and objects found in most object system models. The 4 problem parts in Figure 1 are each defined by a different pattern which is embedded in the part finder. The coverage of these patterns is wide, to maximise likelihood of finding problem parts, although this complicates subsequent selection of best-fit decompositions. An example of one pattern includes facts describing phenomena in which an object A moves from a container B to container C then back again. This indicates some form of resource returning object system model [15]. The result of pattern matching is a set of individual problem parts, see Figure 3.

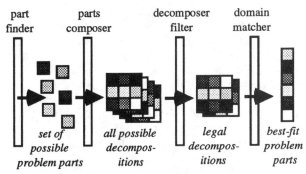

Figure 3. Schematic illustration of the parallel problem decomposition process

Consider the library domain outlined in Figure 1. The decomposer identifies problem parts for book repairing, circulation control, stock control, purchasing, statistical analyses, inter-library loans and library security.

3.2: The parts composer

This tool combines found problem parts into a large number of candidate problem decompositions. Each decomposition can contain one, several or all found problem parts. The composition is exhaustive in that it identifies all possible problem decompositions, see Figure 3. Due to the likelihood of incompleteness and over specification in the entered fact set, the final problem decomposition might exclude facts or even whole problem parts. This adds further complexities which are handled by the mechanism.

Returning to the library example, each decomposition will have a different combination of all or some of the facts describing circulation control, stock control, library security and so on. Each of these facts can be in one or more than one of these candidate decompositions. The mechanism generates all possible combinations of facts corresponding to patterns identified by the problem part finder.

Not all candidate problem decompositions will be legal. Indeed, due to the part finding algorithm, most decompositions will be illegal. For example, one problem part might be a subset of another problem part, or two problem parts might be inconsistent. Therefore a filter mechanism is needed to remove illegal decompositions.

3.3: The decomposition filter

The decomposition filter examines each candidate problem decomposition to determine whether it is legal. It utilises rules about permitted overlaps between problem phenomena. It filters out decompositions with too many and too little overlapping phenomena. Rules are applied to each pair of problem parts in the candidate decomposition. All part pairs must satisfy all rules for a decomposition to be legal. Illegal decompositions occur if, for example:

- one problem part is a complete subset of another part, or two problem parts are identical. This could result in retrieval of two object system models for the same area, whereas model should instantiate to a different area of the problem domain;
- one problem part shares more than 3 state transitions, states, objects and events with another part. This indicates too many overlapping phenomena, and is an artefact of poor problem part finding.

Filtering normally results in a much smaller set of legal problem decompositions.

3.4: The domain matcher

The aim of the domain matcher is to find problem parts which instantiate NATURE's object system models. For example, the matcher might retrieve resource returning models for circulation control, resource supplying models for stock control and object sensing models for library security. Candidate problem decompositions are ranked according to their degree of fit with these models. The decomposer first passes each part in each decomposition to the matcher to determine whether it matches with one or more object system models. A successful match increases the likelihood that the decomposition is a good decomposition of the problem domain. This occurs for all decompositions. The mechanism determines then explains the best-fit decomposition for the problem domain to the requirements engineer.

The domain decomposer and matcher have both been implemented. The decomposer is now undergoing evaluation. However, effective evaluation is difficult given the scale and complexities of its inputs and difficulties encountered when calculating what is the correct output of one input. One approach will be to observe and analyse the decomposition of real-world examples of problem domains. That said, this approach should be scaleable as long as the problem domain to be decomposed includes instantiations of NATURE's object system models. The range and completeness of these models is under constant review. The obvious downside of scaling is the efficiency of the computational mechanisms. However, complex problem decomposition is a long, error-prone human task. Any form of computational assistance is likely to be beneficial, even if this computation process itself takes some time and produces complex sets of results.

4: Benefits and conclusions

Real benefits for requirements engineers will be possible when parallel problem decomposition is integrated with hierarchical goal decomposition. This is our ultimate aim. For instance, problem domain phenomena provide important contextual information for interpreting and understanding functional goals. The goal "aircraft must not enter another aircraft's restricted air space" has little meaning for the reader unless accompanied by facts defining air spaces, algorithms for calculating these air spaces and background information describing the nature of mid-air collisions. Furthermore, goals can act as constraints which restrict acquisition to facts which are relevant to the purpose of the system. Domain modelling (e.g. [14]) has been bedevilled by the "stopping" problem of much domain detail to model. The answer to this question lies in purpose. For example, when defining requirements for an air traffic control system, facts about air traffic spacing, speed and direction are critical while facts about the aircraft owner and number of passengers onboard are not.

More direct assistance for requirements engineers is also possible. Object system models incorporate descriptions of functions and goal states. Therefore, retrieving a model for each problem part can indicate incompleteness in goal hierarchies. Indeed, all object system models have a specific notion of purpose, therefore mismatches between goal and problem decompositions can suggest incompleteness or over specification in both.

Decomposing problems into natural problem categories has other advantages:

- problem decomposition and viewpoint-oriented requirements engineering become two sides of the same coin (e.g. [8], [12]). This paper discusses problem decomposition whereas the viewpoints approach is often compositional. In practice requirements engineering, like most complex design tasks, is opportunistic and involves both problem decomposition and composition. In this context the domain decomposer can aid detection of new viewpoints and viewpoint hierarchies [2] which correspond to natural problem categories. This research direction is being explored;

- decomposition enables more effective generation of scenarios to assist requirements acquisition and validation (e.g. [13]). One idea is to generate scenarios from single object system models. A scenario generation mechanism uses the set of states and state transitions in each model to generate an exhaustive state space from which different combinations of states and transitions can be instantiated to form scenarios. Longer scenarios will then be generated using overlapping phenomena between problem parts.

At the theoretical level, the work outlined in this paper shares much with Jackson's work [4] on parallel problem decomposition and problem frames. However, theoretical definition and effective implementation are two separate issues. There is a need for operational tools to aid problem decomposition, if only to enable NATURE's reuse-oriented requirements engineering paradigm mentioned in this paper. However, we believe the tool described in this paper has wider importance. The next phase is to integrate tools enabling goal and problem decomposition. This will necessitate further process guidance for controlling interaction between the two decomposition activities.

Acknowledgements

The work reported in this paper was funded by the European Union as part of the ESPRIT III 6353 'NATURE' basic research action.

References

1. Dardenne A., Fickas S. & van Lamsweerde A., 1993, 'Goal-directed Concept Acquisition in Requirements Elicittion', Proceedings 6th International Workshop on System Specification and Design', IEEE Computer Society Press, 14-21.
2. Easterbrook S., 1993, 'Domain Modeling With Hierarchies of Alternative Viewpoints', Proceedings of IEEE Symposium on Requirements Engineering, IEEE Computer Society Press, 65-72.
3. Greenspan S., Borgida A. & Mylopoulos J., 1986, 'A Requirements Modeling Language And Its Logic', Information Systems 11(1), 9-23.
4. Jackson M., 1995, 'Software Requirements and Specifications', ACM Press/Addison-Wesley.
5. Jarke M., Bubenko Y., Rolland C., Sutcliffe A.G. & Vassiliou Y., 1993, 'Theories Underlying Requirements Engineering: An Overview of NATURE at Genesis', Proceedings of IEEE Symposium on Requirements Engineering, IEEE Computer Society Press, 19-31.
6. Jarke M., Eherer S., Gallersdörfer R., Jeusfeld M. & Staudt M., 1994, 'ConceptBase - A Deductive Object Manager for MetaData Bases', Journal of Intelligent Information Systems, 1994.
7. Maiden N.A.M., Mistry P. & Sutcliffe A.G., 1995, 'How People Categorise Requirements for Reuse: a Natural Approach', Proceedings 2nd IEEE Symposium on Requirements Engineering, IEEE Computer Society, 148-155.
8. Maiden N.A.M., Assenova P., Constantopoulos P., Jarke M., Johanneson P., Nissen P., Spanoudakis G & Sutcliffe A.G., 1995, 'Computational Mechanisms for Distributed Requirements Engineering', Proceedings 7th International Conference on Software Engineering and Knowledge Engineering, Knowledge Systems Institute, 8-16.
9. Maiden N.A.M. & Sutcliffe A.G., 1994, 'Requirements Critiquing Using Domain Abstractions', Proceedings of IEEE Conference on Requirements Engineering, IEEE Computer Society Press, 184-193.
10. Maiden N.A.M. & Sutcliffe A.G., 1992, 'Exploiting Reusable Specifications Through Analogy, Communications of the ACM. 34(5), 55-64.
11. Mylopopoulos J., Borgida A., Jarke M. & Koubarakis M, 1990, 'Telos: Representing Knowledge about Information Systems', ACM Transactions on Office Information Systems 8(4), 325.
12. Nuseibeh B., Kramer J. & Finkelstein A., 1994, 'A Framework for Expressing the Relationships Between Multiple Views in Requirements Specification', IEEE Transactions on Software Engineering 20(10), 760-773.
13. Potts C., Takahashi K. & Anton A.I., 1994, 'Inquiry-Based Requirements Analysis', IEEE Software 11(2), 21-32.
14. Prieto-Diaz R., 1990, 'Domain Analysis: An Introduction', ACM SIGSOFT Software Engineering Notes 15(2), April 1990, 47-54.
15. Sutcliffe A.G. & Maiden N.A.M., 1994, 'Domain Modeling for Reuse', Proceedings, 3rd International Conference on Software Reuse, IEEE Computer Society Press.
16. Sutcliffe A.G. & Maiden N.A.M., 1993, 'Bridging the Requirements Gap: Policies, Goals and Domains', Proceedings of 7th International Workshop on System Specification and Design, IEEE Computer Society Press, 52-55.

To Be *and* Not to Be: On Managing Inconsistency in Software Development

Bashar Nuseibeh

Department of Computing, Imperial College
180 Queen's Gate, London SW7 2BZ, UK
Email: ban@doc.ic.ac.uk

Abstract

The development of software systems involves the detection and handling of inconsistencies. These inconsistencies arise in system requirements, design specifications and, quite often, in the descriptions that form the final implemented software product. This paper presents a critical review of approaches that explicitly tolerate and manage inconsistencies, and explores different kinds of inconsistencies that arise during different stages of software development. Managing inconsistency refers not only to the detection and removal of inconsistencies, but also to activities that facilitate continued development in their presence. Such activities include procedures for controlled amelioration or avoidance of inconsistency, which in turn may require analysis and reasoning in the presence of inconsistency.

1. Introduction

The development of a software system inevitably involves the management of inconsistencies. Inconsistencies may arise in the early stages of development if, for example, contradictory requirements are specified. They may also arise in design specifications as developers explore alternative solutions; and in implementations if programmers fail, say, to consider particular exceptions. A large proportion of software engineering research has been devoted to consistency maintenance, or at the very least, has been geared towards eradicating inconsistencies as soon as they are detected.

In our previous work [12], we proposed an approach to software development that is tolerant of inconsistencies, and which provides rules for handling them explicitly. We also explored the consequences of taking a radically decentralised approach in which multiple development participants hold multiple - often inconsistent - views [14]. In this paper, we survey a range of approaches that tolerate inconsistency during software development, based on an analysis of the kinds of inconsistencies that arise and the ways in which they are handled. We then discuss the requirements for a framework for managing inconsistency.

The paper is organised as follows. We begin by outlining the origins and kinds of inconsistencies that arise in software development (section 2), and how they may be detected and identified (section 3). With reference to related work, we then discuss strategies for handling inconsistencies (section 4), and outline a framework for managing inconsistency in this setting (section 5). We conclude with a discussion of outstanding research issues, and propose an agenda for future work (section 6).

2. Causes of Inconsistencies (the why)

Inconsistency is an inevitable part of software development processes. Even in the most well-defined, managed and optimised development process, system requirements are often uncertain or contradictory, alternative design solutions exist, and errors in implementation arise.

The requirements engineering stage of development is particularly illustrative of such inconsistencies. During requirements acquisition, customer requirements are often sketchy and uncertain. For large projects in particular, a number of "client authorities" may exist who have conflicting, even contradictory requirements. In many instances customers may not even be certain of their own needs, and a requirements engineer's job is partly to elicit and clarify these needs. The requirements specification produced as a result of such a specification and analysis process however is not static: it continues to evolve as new requirements are added and conflicts identified are resolved.

Thus, there is a wide range of possible *causes* of inconsistencies in software development. Many of these are due to the heterogeneity of the products being developed (e.g., systems deploying different technologies) and the multiplicity of stakeholders and/or development participants involved in the development process. Inconsistencies arise between multiple development participants because of the:

- different views they hold,
- different languages they speak,
- different development strategies (methods) they deploy,
- different stages of development they address,
- partially, totally or non-overlapping areas of concern they have, and
- different technical, economic and/or political objectives they want to achieve.

Since inconsistencies can occur in software development processes and products for a variety of reasons, we adopt a single, simple definition of what actually constitutes an inconsistency:

An inconsistency occurs if and only if a (consistency) rule has been broken.

Such a rule explicitly describes some form of relationship or fact that is required to hold. In previous work, we examined three uses of such consistency rules.

They can describe syntactic relationships between development artefacts prescribed by a development method, which is also a way of describing semantic relationships between artefacts produced by that method [23]. They can also be used to prescribe relationships between the sub-processes in an overall development process, which is also a way of coordinating the activities of developers deploying different development strategies [7]. Finally, they can be used to describe user-defined relationships that emerge as development of a software specification proceeds [8, 9]. This is useful for capturing ontological relationships between the products of a development process (for example, two developers specifying a library system may use the term "user" and "borrower" to refer to the same person).

Reducing an inconsistency to the breaking of a rule facilitates the detection and subsequent identification ("diagnosis") of inconsistencies in specifications, and is a useful tool for managing other "problems" that arise during software development. For example, if we treat *conflict* as the interference of the goals of one party caused by the actions of another party [10], then we can use inconsistency as a tool for detecting many conflicts[1]. Similarly, if we define a *mistake* as an action that would be acknowledged as an error by its perpetrator (e.g., a typo), then we can detect mistakes that manifest themselves as inconsistencies.

Hagensen and Kristensen adopted a similar strategy in their explicit examination of the "consistency perspective" in software development [16]. They proposed a framework that focuses on structures for representing information ("descriptions") and the relations between these structures. Consistency of descriptions is defined as relations between interpretations of descriptions. Consistency handling techniques are modelled in terms of descriptions, interpretations and relations.

3. Detecting & Identifying Inconsistencies (the how)

Once consistency has been defined in terms of explicit rules, inconsistency may be detected automatically by checking these rules. For example, a type checker can check whether or not an instance or variable conforms to its type definition. Similarly, a parser can check whether or not a sentence conforms to the syntactic rules specified by its grammar. Simple inferences in classical logic can also be used to detect logical inconsistencies resulting from too much or too little information. For example, a *contradiction* (the simutaneous assertion, or deduction, of both X and ¬X) may be detected in this way.

Other kinds of inconsistency are more difficult to detect. A conflict between two development participants may not manifest itself as an inconsistency until further development has taken place (making the original source of the inconsistency difficult to identify). Furthermore,

---

1 Of course, not all conflicts will manifest themselves as inconsistencies, particularly if the conflict is caused by a "conceptual disagreement" such as a difference in personal values.

what actually constitutes an inconsistency from one participant's perspective may not be the case from another perspective. An example of this is an "inconsistency" in a person's tax return. Such an inconsistency may actually be a "desirable" piece of information from a tax inspector's point of view!

One of the difficulties in handling inconsistencies effectively, even after they have been successfully detected, is that the *kind* of inconsistency detected must also be identified. To address this difficulty, some form of classification of inconsistency may be helpful in diagnosing their source and cause. The CONMAN (*con*figuration *man*agement) system [26] for example, attempts to classify consistency in programs into one of six kinds in order to facilitate inconsistency handling later on. These are: *full consistency* - where a system satisfies the rules that a programming language specifies for legal programs (insofar as they can be checked prior to execution); *type consistency* - where a system satisfies the static type checking rules of the programming language; *version consistency* - where a system is built using exactly one version of each logical source code file; *derivation consistency* - where a system is operationally equivalent to some version consistent system; *link consistency* - where each compilation unit is free of static type errors, and each symbolic reference between compilation units is type safe according to the rules of the programming language; *reachable consistency* - where all code and data that could be accessed or executed by invoking the system through one of its entry points are safe. CONMAN checks for all six kinds of consistency automatically, and then reacts differently depending on the kind of inconsistency detected. The six kinds of inconsistency are very specific to configuration management applications, but their identification is fundamental to effective inconsistency handling in this setting.

4. Handling Inconsistencies

Identifying the cause and nature of an inconsistency may not be possible without further analysis and action in the presence of inconsistency. For this reason, approaches that tolerate inconsistency are needed. We now examine alternative approaches to inconsistency handling that tolerate inconsistency in a variety of ways. We then use this survey to suggest some general approaches for acting on, and reasoning in the presence of, inconsistency.

4.1. Related work (the who)

Schwanke and Kaiser suggest that during large systems development, programmers often circumvent strict consistency enforcement mechanisms in order to get their jobs done [26]. They propose an approach to "living with inconsistency", implemented in the CONMAN programming environment described in section 3. CONMAN handles inconsistency by: identifying and tracking the six different kinds of inconsistencies described above (without requiring them to be removed); reducing the cost of restoring type safety after a change (using a technique called "smarter recompilation"); and, protecting programmers from inconsistent code (by supplying debugging and testing tools with inconsistency information). CONMAN is somewhat restricted in kinds of handling strategies it supports, because of the small and fixed kinds of inconsistency it recognises.

Balzer proposes the notion of "tolerating inconsistency" by relaxing consistency constraints during development [1]. The approach suggests that inconsistent data be marked by guards ("pollution markers") that have two uses: (1) to identify the inconsistent data to code segments or human agents that may then help resolve the inconsistency, and (2) to screen the inconsistent data from other segments that are sensitive to the inconsistencies. The approach does not however provide any mechanism for specifying particular actions that need to be performed in order to handle these inconsistencies.

Gabbay and Hunter suggest "making inconsistency respectable" by proposing that inconsistencies be viewed as signals to take external actions (such as "asking the user" or "invoking a truth maintenance system"), or as signals for taking internal actions that activate or deactivate other rules [15]. Again, the suggestion is that "resolving" inconsistency is not necessarily done by eradicating it, but by supplying rules that specify how to act in the presence of such inconsistency. Gabbay and Hunter further propose the use of temporal logic to specify these meta-level rules. We have adapted this approach to multi-perspective software development [12], in which logical inconsistencies between partial specifications (ViewPoints) are detected by translating them into classical logic, and then using an action-based temporal logic to specify inconsistency handling rules. This approach however requires further development since classical logic does not allow reasoning in the presence of inconsistency.

Narayanaswamy and Goldman propose "lazy" consistency as the basis for cooperative software development [21]. This approach favours software development architectures where impending or proposed changes - as well as changes that have already occurred - are "announced". This allows the consistency requirements of a system to be "lazily" maintained as it evolves. The approach is a compromise between the optimistic view in which inconsistencies are assumed to occur infrequently and can thus be handled individually when they arise, and a pessimistic approach in which inconsistencies are prevented from ever occurring. Such a compromise is particularly realistic in a distributed development setting where conflicts or "collisions" of changes made by different developers may occur. Lazy consistency maintenance supports activities such as negotiation and other organisational protocols that support the resolution of conflicts and collisions.

Finally, work on programming languages which are

supported by exception handling mechanisms that deal with errors resulting from built-in operations (e.g., division by zero) is also relevant. Building on this work, Borgida proposed an approach to handling violations of assumptions in a database [3]. His approach provides for "blaming" violations on one or more database facts. In this way, either a program can be designed to detect and treat "unusual" facts, or a database can adjust its constraints to tolerate the violation in the data. Balzer's approach described above is based on Borgida's mechanisms.

Feather has recently also proposed an approach to modularised exception handling [11] in which programs accessing a shared database of information impose their own assumptions on the database, and treat exceptions to those assumptions differently. The assumptions made by each program together with their respective exception handlers are used to provide each program with its own individual view of the database. Alternative - possibly inconsistent - views of the same information can therefore be used to support different users or developers of a software system. Each program's view is derived from the shared data in such a way as to satisfy all the program's assumptions. This is achieved by a combination of ignoring facts that hold in the shared data and "feigning" facts that do not hold.

Table 1 summarises the various approaches to inconsistency handling described above.

4.2. Acting in the presence of inconsistency (the what)

The approaches described above handle inconsistencies in different ways. What they have in common, however, is the goal of allowing continued development in the presence of inconsistency. Such action may include:

- *Ignoring* the inconsistency completely and continuing development regardless. This may be appropriate in certain circumstances where the inconsistency is isolated and does not affect further development, or prevent it from taking place.

- *Circumventing* the inconsistency and continuing development. This may be achieved by marking inconsistent portions of the system (e.g., using Balzer's "pollution markers") or by continuing development in certain directions depending on the kind of inconsistency identified (e.g., as in CONMAN). It is appropriate in situations where it is desirable for the inconsistency to be avoided and/or its removal deferred.

- *Removing* the inconsistency altogether by correcting any mistakes or resolving conflicts. This depends on a clear identification of the inconsistency and assumes that the actions required to fix it are known. Restoring consistency completely can be difficult to achieve, and is quite often impossible to automate completely without human intervention.

- *Ameliorating* inconsistent situations by performing actions that "improve" these situations and increase

Approach	Mechanism	Scope
Living with inconsistency [26]	Smarter recompilation	Programming (Configuration Management)
Tolerating inconsistency [1]	Pollution markers	Programming
Making inconsistency respectable [15] *Application: Inconsistency handling between multiple perspectives [12]*	Meta-level temporal rules	(Logic) Databases *Multiple ViewPoints in software development*
Lazy inconsistency [21]	Announce proposed changes	Cooperative software development
Exception handling [3]	Run-time exception handlers	Database/Information systems
Modularised exception handling [11]	Multiple exception handlers	Programming views

Table 1: Some inconsistency handling approaches in software development.

the possibility of future resolution (this may involve ignoring or circumventing inconsistencies). This approach is attractive in situations where complete and immediate resolution is not possible (perhaps because further information is required from another development participant), but where some steps can be taken "fix" part or some of the inconsistent information. This approach however requires techniques for *analysis* and *reasoning* in the presence of inconsistency.

Logic-based approaches offer promising contributions to inconsistency handling by providing techniques that facilitate analysis and reasoning in the presence of inconsistency. For example, the proof rules of classical logic may be adapted to allow continued reasoning in the presence of inconsistency [2], and various labels and qualifications may be used to track and diagnose inconsistent information (e.g., by propagating labels during reasoning and computing maximally consistent subsets of inconsistent information) [17].

Promising contributions are also offered by work on fault-tolerant distributed systems [4] where continued operation of these systems is still possible in the presence of failure. Failure in this context is analogous to inconsistency in software development, and includes problems caused by omissions (e.g., server not responding to input), timing (e.g., server response is too early or too late), response (e.g., server response is incorrect) and crashes. What fault-tolerant systems have in common in such failure scenarios is their ability to react to these failures and continue operating. In fact, analysis of many such failures often produces information that identifies hitherto undetected errors which can then also be repaired.

Finally, it is worth noting that what we have been discussing thus far are inconsistencies that arise in the artefacts of software development (e.g., specifications, programs, systems, etc.). Inconsistencies can also arise in software development processes themselves. An interesting example of these is an inconsistency which occurs between a software development process definition and the actual (enacted) process instance [6]. Such an inconsistency between "enactment state" and "performance state" is often avoided by blocking further development activities until some precondition is made to hold. Since this policy is overly restrictive, many developers attempt to fake conformance to the process definition (for example, by fooling a tool into thinking that a certain task has been performed in order to continue development).

What is therefore needed is a software development process which is flexible enough to tolerate development that diverges from its definition, or a process that can be dynamically corrected, changed and/or improved as it is being enacted. Cugola *et al.* [5] have addressed exactly this problem in their temporal logic-based approach which is used to capture and tolerate some deviations from a process description during execution. Deviations are tolerated as long as they do not affect the correctness of the system (if they do, the incorrect data must be fixed, or the process model - or its active instance - must be changed). Otherwise, deviations are tolerated, recorded and propagated - and "pollution analysis" (based on logical reasoning) is performed to identify possible sources of inconsistency.

5. Towards a Framework for Managing Inconsistency (the where)

Clearly, managing inconsistency is a multi-faceted activity that is increasingly recognised as fundamental to the successful management of software development. In fact, one could argue that in reality software development practitioners live and work with inconsistent information on a daily basis. A framework is therefore needed within which a variety of inconsistency management activities may be performed. Such a framework should facilitate the interworking of a combination of, normally isolated, techniques, mechanisms and tools for *detecting, identifying (diagnosing/classifying) and handling inconsistencies.*

We are currently pursuing a logic-based approach to managing inconsistency, an elaboration of which is beyond the scope of this paper [17]. In summary however, we detect logical inconsistencies by translating different kinds of development knowledge (including specifications) into classical logic. We then use an adaptation of classical logic, called quasi-classical (QC) logic, that allows continued logical reasoning in the presence of inconsistency. We annotate the proof rules of the logic with labels which can then be used to diagnose the likely sources of inconsistency, and to track their consequences during development. Inconsistencies are handled (and ultimately managed) by specifying, in an action-based temporal logic, guiding actions that may be taken in the presence of particular kinds of inconsistency.

Providing automated tool support for the different activities involved in managing inconsistency is both crucial and in need of further work. For example, many commercial CASE tools provide specification consistency checkers, and process-centred environments check the processes by which these specifications are developed. However, most of these tools have limited inconsistency handling capabilities, concentrating instead on inconsistency detection and identification, and leaving handling to the users of these tools (this is similar to programming-support tools like debuggers which provide limited automated support for removing errors from programs). Some scope for conflict resolution is provided by negotiation-support tools [25], which can be useful for handling inconsistencies that occur between development participants. Finally, a class of research tools known as theorem provers [19] offer some scope for inconsistency handling in that they attempt to *prove* that a description (e.g., a specification) satisfies a set of properties or contains no contradictions. Therefore, these tools have the capability of reasoning about *why* an inconsistency exists when a proof cannot be produced.

6. Discussion, Conclusions & Future Work

We have argued that software development processes must explicitly support the evolving nature of software systems (specifications and programs), and must therefore be capable of managing the inevitable inconsistencies that arise in the descriptions of such systems. Managing inconsistencies in this setting does not necessarily mean removing them, although in many cases this may be desirable, rather, it involves: (a) detecting and identifying the kinds of inconsistencies, and possibly their source, and (b) continuing development in the presence of such inconsistencies, with a view to removing them later on down the line (or in some situations deferring resolution indefinitely). Often, intermediate steps that ameliorate the state of a specification, or simply make progress towards removing inconsistencies in it, are also useful.

Of course, depending on the application for which a software system is being developed, different "levels of reliability" may also be acceptable. For non-safety-critical systems for example, some degree of uncertainty or inconsistency may be tolerated - even in the final product. In such cases however, there is a need to *measure* (or at least estimate) both the likely consequences and frequency of failures, in order to assess system reliability, and then devise ways of handling such failures [20].

A clearer understanding of the nature of software development is also needed in order to help identify and prioritise inconsistencies. An illustrative example of this is the distinction between an inconsistency reflecting an error in development, and an inconsistency that only exists temporarily because certain development steps have not been performed yet. The latter inconsistency is a part of every development and, is less important than the former, which reflects a more fundamental failure in development. If at all, current process modelling technology [13] provides guidance for "normal" development (e.g., "what should I do next?"), whereas we are attempting to handle inconsistencies that are usually labelled as "undesirable" in such a development process (e.g., "how do I get out of the mess I'm now in?") [22]. Moreover, because some inconsistencies can only be identified as a development process unfolds, we have been exploring process-guided approaches to inconsistency handling that analyse explicitly recorded development actions, then act according to the context of any inconsistencies detected [18, 24].

Another interesting temporal consideration in this setting is what we might call the "age" of an unresolved inconsistency. This is a measure of, say, the number of development actions that were performed since the last time an inconsistency was introduced by an action. It may be useful to explore the correlation, if any, between the age of an unresolved inconsistency and the degree of difficulty by which it may be handled or resolved. Intuitively, one would expect that the greater the age of the last consistency check, the higher the risk becomes, and that there is a trade-off between the cost of consistency checking and the cost of resolution (we measure risk in this context as the likelihood of consistency failures multiplied by the cost of resolving them).

Finally, in this paper we have not explicitly addressed software development process considerations that determine *when* consistency checks should be performed, *how* these checks should be performed, and *what* should be done as result of performing these checks. Broadly speaking, deciding when to perform a consistency check should be determined by the process prescribed by a software development method. This should be designed to be "non-intrusive" since continuous reminders to perform checks are irritating and undesirable. The way in which checks are performed on the other hand, is an interaction issue and is determined by the context in which the check is applied. For example, in a cooperative development setting a negotiation protocol may be suitable, whereas in a distributed systems setting low-level communication protocols may be more appropriate. Finally, determining how to act once a consistency check has been performed is largely an inconsistency management issue which we have discussed in this paper.

We believe that many of the inconsistency management issues raised in this paper lie at the heart of software development. At all stages of a development life cycle, inconsistencies may arise and can be used to provide valuable input into a software development process. In fact, identifying and handling inconsistency in this context is a vehicle for monitoring and guiding development, and can be used as a tool for measuring many attributes of software development processes and products. We believe that there is a need to address issues of inconsistency management explicitly, and to provide computer-based tools that support this activity. These tools need to go beyond inconsistency avoidance or consistency maintenance, allow reasoning in the presence of inconsistency, and provide support for inconsistency handling which does not always involve immediate inconsistency resolution. Ultimately however, many inconsistencies can only be resolved by human intervention, and therefore there also is a need to provide tools that support human-centred inconsistency management.

7. Acknowledgements

The ideas presented in this paper have benefited from discussions with Steve Easterbrook, Martin Feather, Anthony Finkelstein, Michael Goedicke, Carlo Ghezzi, Tony Hunter, Jeff Kramer and Vic Stenning. Partial funding was provided by the UK EPSRC as part of the VOILA project, and the European Union as part of the Basic Research Action Promoter and the ISI project (ECAUS003).

8. References

[1] R. Balzer (1991); "Tolerating Inconsistency"; *Proc. of 13th Int. Conf. on Software Engineering (ICSE-13)*, Austin, Texas, USA, 13-17th May 91, 158-165; IEEE CS Press.

[2] P. Besnard and A. Hunter (1995); "Quasi-classical Logic: Non-trvializable classical reasoning from inconsistent information"; *(In) Symbolic and Quantitative Approaches to Uncertainty;* C. Froidevaux & J. Kohlas (Eds.); 44-51; LNCS 946, Springer-Verlag.

[3] A. Borgida (1985); "Language Features for Flexible Handling of Exceptions in Information Systems"; *Transactions on Database Systems*, 10(4): 565-603, December 85; ACM Press.

[4] F. Christian (1991); "Basic Concepts and Issues in Fault-Tolerant Distributed Systems"; *Proc. of Int. Workshop on Operating Systems of the 90s and Beyond*, Dagstuhl Castle, Germany, 8-12th July 1991, 119-149; LNCS 563, Springer-Verlag.

[5] G. Cugola, E. Di Nitto, C. Ghezzi and M. Mantione (1995); "How To Deal With Deviations During Process Model Enactment"; *Proc. of 17th Int. Conf. on Software Engineering (ICSE-17)*, Seattle, USA, 23-30 April 95, 265-273; ACM Press.

[6] M. Dowson (1993); "Consistency Maintenance in Process Sensitive Environments"; *Proc. of Workshop on Process Sensitive Environments Architectures*, Boulder, Colorado, USA, Rocky Mountain Institute of Software Engineering (RMISE).

[7] S. Easterbrook, A. Finkelstein, J. Kramer and B. Nuseibeh (1994); "Coordinating Distributed ViewPoints: The Anatomy of a Consistency Check"; *Concurrent Engineering: Research and Applications*, 2(3): 209-222, CERA Institute, West Bloomfield, USA.

[8] S. Easterbrook and B. Nuseibeh (1995); "Inconsistency Management in an Evolving Specification"; *Proc. of 2nd Int. Symposium on Requirements Engineering (RE 95)*, York, UK, 48-55; IEEE CS Press.

[9] S. Easterbrook and B. Nuseibeh (1996); "Using ViewPoints for Inconsistency Management"; *(to appear in) Software Engineering Journal*; IEE/BCS.

[10] S. M. Easterbrook, E. E. Beck, J. S. Goodlet, L. Plowman, M. Sharples and C. C. Wood (1993); "A Survey of Empirical Studies of Conflict"; *(In) CSCW: Cooperation or Conflict?;* S. M. Easterbrook (Ed.); 1-68; Springer-Verlag, London.

[11] M. Feather (1995); "Modularized Exception Handling"; *Draft technical report*, 9th February 1995; USC/Information Sciences Institute, Marina del Rey, California, USA.

[12] A. Finkelstein, D. Gabbay, A. Hunter, J. Kramer and B. Nuseibeh (1994); "Inconsistency Handling in Multi-Perspective Specifications"; *Transactions on Software Engineering*, 20(8): 569-578, August 1994; IEEE CS Press.

[13] A. Finkelstein, J. Kramer and B. Nuseibeh (Eds.) (1994); *Software Process Modelling and Technology*, Advanced Software Development Series, Research Studies Press Ltd. (Wiley), Somerset, UK.

[14] A. Finkelstein, J. Kramer, B. Nuseibeh, L. Finkelstein and M. Goedicke (1992); "Viewpoints: A Framework for Integrating Multiple Perspectives in System Development"; *Int. Journal of Software Engineering and Knowledge Engineering*, 2(1): 31-58, March 1992; World Scientific Publishing Co.

[15] D. Gabbay and A. Hunter (1992); "Making Inconsistency Respectable: A Logical Framework for Inconsistency in Reasoning: Part 2"; *(In) Symbolic and Quantitative Approaches to Reasoning and Uncertainty;* 129-136; LNCS, Springer-Verlag.

[16] T. M. Hagensen and B. B. Kristensen (1992); "Consistency in Software System Development: Framework, Model, Techniques & Tools"; *Software Engineering Notes (Proc. of ACM SIGSOFT Symposium on Software Development Environments)*, 17(5): 58-67, 9-11th December 1992; SIGSOFT & ACM Press.

[17] A. Hunter and B. Nuseibeh (1995); "Managing Inconsistent Specifications: Reasoning, Analysis and Action"; *Technical report*, DoC 95/15, June 1995; Department of Computing, Imperial College, London, UK.

[18] U. Leonhardt, A. Finkelstein, J. Kramer and B. Nuseibeh (1995); "Decentralised Process Enactment in a Multi-Perspective Development Environment"; *Proc. of 17th Int. Conf. of Software Engineering*, Seattle, Washington, USA, 23-30th April 1995, 255-264; ACM Press.

[19] P. A. Lindsay (1988); "A Survey of Mechanical Support for Formal Reasoning"; *Software Engineering Journal (special issue on mechanical support for formal reasoning)*, 3(1): 3-27, January 1988; IEE, UK.

[20] B. Littlewood (1994); "Learning to Live with Uncertainty in Our Software"; *Proc. of 2nd Int. Symposium on Software Metrics*, London, UK, 24-26th October 94, 2-8; IEEE CS Press.

[21] K. Narayanaswamy and N. Goldman (1992); ""Lazy" Consistency: A Basis for Cooperative Software Development"; *Proc. of Int. Conf. on Computer-Supported Cooperative Work (CSCW '92)*, Toronto, Ontario, Canada, 31st October - 4th November, 257-264; ACM SIGCHI & SIGOIS.

[22] B. Nuseibeh, A. Finkelstein and J. Kramer (1993); "Fine-Grain Process Modelling"; *Proc. of 7th Int. Workshop on Software Specification and Design (IWSSD-7)*, Redondo Beach, California, USA, 6-7 December 1993, 42-46; IEEE CS Press.

[23] B. Nuseibeh, J. Kramer and A. Finkelstein (1994); "A Framework for Expressing the Relationships Between Multiple Views in Requirements Specification"; *Transactions on Software Engineering*, 20(10): 760-773, October 1994; IEEE CS Press.

[24] B. Nuseibeh, J. Kramer, A. Finkelstein and U. Leonhardt (1995); "Decentralised Process Modelling"; *Proc. of 4th European Workshop on Software Process Technology (EWSPT '95)*, Noordwijkerhout, 185-188; Springer-Verlag.

[25] W. N. Robinson (1992); "Negotiation Behaviour During Requirements Specification: A need for automated conflict resolution"; *Proc. of 12th Int. Conf. on Software Engineering*, Nice, France, 26-30th March 1990, 268-276; IEEE CS Press.

[26] R. W. Schwanke and G. E. Kaiser (1988); "Living With Inconsistency in Large Systems"; *Proc. of the Int. Workshop on Software Version and Configuration Control*, Grassau, Germany, 27-29 January 1988, 98-118; B. G. Teubner, Stuttgart..

Assuring Accuracy and Impartiality in Software Design Methodology Comparison

Leon J. Osterweil

Department of Computer Science
University of Massachusetts
Amherst, MA 01003

Xiping Song

Siemens Corporate Research Center
755 College Road, East
Princeton, NJ 08540

Abstract

Software product and process modelling can be used as bases for more accurate, objective, and repeatable comparison of Software Design Methodologies (SDM's). In earlier work we have demonstrated the use of a fixed feature comparison process (called CDM), a fixed (but extensible) framework of design methodology features (the Base Framework, BF), and a fixed process/product modelling formalism (based upon HFSP) in supporting such comparisons. We have obtained both broad, general SDM comparison results, and sharp narrowly focussed SDM comparison results and have used them to confirm the power and validity of our approach. In the course of this work we have revised, modified, and extended the BF to improve its scope of applicability and its accuracy. We have also improved CDM by elaborating it down to lower levels of detail, and by being more specific about iteration conditions. In more recent work we have addressed the question of of how sensitive these comparisons and their results might be to the specific choice of process modelling formalism. We are learning that the comparison results remain surprisingly as the modelling formalism is changed.

1 Background

Suggestions for how to go about designing complex software systems continue to proliferate in the form of proposed software design methodologies (SDM's). The proposed SDM's have a variety of differences, ranging from superficial to fundamental, and it seems obvious that these differences make certain of these SDM's more suitable for some design projects than others. Designers face the daunting challenge of having to select from among this large, diverse, and growing collection of SDM's for the design projects that they undertake. To help with this challenge there have been a number of efforts to compare and contrast various of the SDM's. These comparison projects have largely been reports of anecdotal experience, however, and it is often difficult to decide what general conclusions and firm results can be safely inferred from these comparisons. We believe that a more scientific approach to categorizing, classifying, comparing, and evaluating SDM's can and should be taken.

2 Our Approach

We believe that design should be viewed as a process that can be developed using software development methods and formalisms. Thus, for example, we believe that design processes have goals and requirements that can and should be specified precisely (a design product specification is an example of a functional requirement for a design process). In addition, design processes should also have specifiable architectures and designs that are intended to demonstrate how the goals are to be met. We also believe that design processes can and should be implementable through actual executable code. We refer to the entire process of developing this whole family of software artifacts for processes as process programming. One of the key advantages of this notion is that it provides a strong semantic basis (namely the semantics of the programming formalisms) for categorization, classification, comparison, and evaluation of the various SDM's.

Over the past several years we have been evaluating these hypotheses by using process programming formalisms both to represent various SDM's and as the basis for hypothesizing comparison frameworks, and comparison processes. Our early work seems to support our basic hypotheses, in that it demonstrates that the use of programming formalisms does support both high level and low level comparisons of SDM's that have both major differences, and relatively minor differences. This work has also led to a sharpening of our proposed comparison frameworks and processes.

In our most recent work we have been exploring the extent to which the choice of process modelling formalism affects the nature and accuracy of SDM comparison results obtained.

2.1 Architecture of Our SDM Comparison Approach

Our classification and comparison approach is guided by the approach used in disciplines such as Biology and Geology that study and classify such natural artifacts as butterflies and rocks. Thus, we suggest that a standarized set of modelling formalisms should be used to model SDM's and that the models obtained should then be compared to each other by following a fixed standardized comparison process, based upon a fixed standardized framework of features that are understood to be critical differentiators.

2.2 CDM: The Process for Comparing Design Methodologies

In [3] and [6] we proposed and modeled CDM, a process for comparing SDM's. CDM was specified to a level of detail that we thought would be sufficient to enable others to repeat our comparisons. We believe it is crucial that others be able to use CDM to obtain useful comparison results of their own. Ideally they should also be able to reproduce the results we have obtained, as this sort of reproducibility is central to the establishment of scientific knowledge in other, more mature, disciplines. To date there have been some reports of success in using CDM to obtain useful SDM comparisons, although there have not yet been any reports of success in repeating our comparison results. This work has also indicated ways in which CDM needs to be altered and specified in more detail.

2.3 BF: The Base Framework for Comparison

In [6] we also proposed BF, a fixed framework to be used in classifying key features of SDM's. BF consists of two main component parts, one covering features of the design product, and one covering features of the process by which it is developed. In [5] we also suggested that BF was only an initial specification of this feature framework, and that BF would need to be evolved over time by the community as successive comparison efforts indicated omissions, inconsistencies, and other shortcomings. This paper even specified a process for migrating BF. Indeed there has been some migration of BF, and it is expected that that migration will continue.

2.4 MF: The Modelling Formalism

In [3, 6, 4] we also proposed the use of an enhanced version of HFSP [2] and a hierarchical data modelling formalism to model SDM's. These papers also include specifications of some of the models that we produced using those formalisms. The models proved to be sufficient basis for the development of a wealth of comparative information about a variety of SDM's. In one study we compared high level features of 12 SDM's, and in another low level specifics of two SDM's. This work has convinced us that our approach is valid and useful.

3 Current Work and Directions

While work to date convinces us that our approach does indeed support scientific comparison of SDM's, we also understand that this work leaves us far short of a scientific discipline, and an engineering practice, of SDM comparison and evaluation. Much further work is needed in indicating how best and most effectively to evaluate and compare SDM's.

Our current work is focusing on the choice of formalisms for modelling SDM's. The particuar question we are exploring is how sensitive the SDM comparison results obtained are to the specific choice of SDM modelling formalism. Our early work used a simple hierarchical data formalism to model the design product, and HFSP to model the activities of the design process. In order to study the sensitivity of the final comparison results to these modelling choices, we have experimented with the use of Petri Nets (specifically the Slang [1] formalism) to model design process activities, and will be using Object Formalisms to model the design product.

In our first experiments we used Slang as the basis for comparison of Booch Object Oriented Design and Jackson System Development. These experiments using Slang indicate that the comparison results obtained are strikingly similar to those obtained using HFSP. These results have encouraged us to use Slang for wider comparisons. In addition we are anticipating using Object-oriented data modelling to model SDM products, in an attempt to determine how closely our results follow the results obtained using a simpler product modelling approach.

Acknowledgements

This work is supported by the Advanced Research Projects Agency under Grant MDA972-91-J-1012 and Grant F30602-94-C-0137. The work on using Slang to model SDM's is being done by Rodion Podorozhny.

References

[1] S. Bandinelli, A. Fuggetta, and S. Grigolli. Process Modeling in-the-large with SLANG. In *Proceedings of the Second International Conference on the Software Process, Berlin, Germany*, pages 75–83, February 1993.

[2] T. Katayama. A Hierarchical and Functional Software Process Description and its Enaction. In *Proceedings of the Eleventh International Conference of Software Engineering*, pages 343–353, May 1989.

[3] X. Song. *Comparing Software Design Methodologies Through Process Modeling*. Technical report ics-92-48, Information and Computer Science Dept., University of California, Irvine, CA, 1992.

[4] X. Song and L. J. Osterweil. Using meta-modeling to systematically compare and integrate modeling techniques. Available from the authors upon request, March 1994.

[5] X. Song and L. J. Osterweil. Toward Objective, Systematic Design-Method Comparisons. *IEEE Software*, pages 43–53, May 1992.

[6] X. Song and L. J. Osterweil. Experience with an approach to comparing software design methodologies. *IEEE Transactions on Software Engineering*, 20(5):364–384, May 1994.

Design Decision Trees

Alexander Ran and Juha Kuusela
Nokia Research Center, Software Technology Laboratory,
P.O. Box 45, 00211 Helsinki, Finland
e-mail: [alexander.ran\juha.kuusela]@research.nokia.com

Abstract

This paper proposes a formalism to be used as a systematic approach to incrementally document, refine, organise and reuse the architectural knowledge for software design. The formalism is a hierarchical organisation of design patterns into a Design Decision Tree (DDT) that is a partial ordering of design decisions put in the context of the problem requirements and the constraints imposed by earlier decisions. Our model supports the representation of the essential problems that recur in the domain, knowledge of alternative solutions to these problems and the implications of the solutions. This model integrates architectural knowledge of software design into a software development process.

1 Introduction

Requirements for flexibility, openness, adaptability, and growing sophistication in functionality have lead to an explosion in the size and complexity of industrial software. Software development costs drive the development costs and development times of new products and many companies are looking for new approaches to build safe, usable, adaptable and extendible systems.

However, it is not always clear what part of the software development process (and the corresponding product) should be the primary target of improvement. Much effort is spent to improve the quality and in particular reusability of the source code. Significant attention is paid to design process and numerous software design methodologies are proposed and promoted. Instead, the effort should concentrate on the management of software design knowledge. We suggest a model and an approach to this end.

There is a definite relationship between the construction of a product, technology for planning and design, and the knowledge used for planning and design. It seems that as the complexity of the products increases, advances in productivity and quality may only be gained by concentrating the attention on the enabling factors: planning enables production and architectural knowledge enables planning (see Figure 1).

Thus, when looking for the ways to improve the productivity of the development teams or quality of the design products, the essential questions we must address are: How a software development team can elicit, represent, and share design expertise of its members? How this knowledge can be reused and refined in the process of evolution. How to reconcile the existence of alternative opinions within the development team regarding the best solution to what appears to be the same problem?

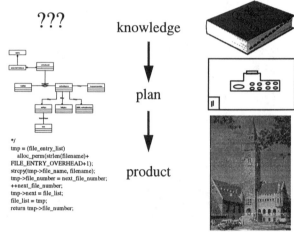

Figure 1. What constitutes architectural knowledge of software design?

Experienced software designers employ architectural knowledge to construct usable, flexible and gracefully evolving software. They know several alternative approaches towards a solutions and they are able to select a feasible approach based on its properties. However, in practice this knowledge based on experience is rarely shared or communicated. It stays implicit and may be only recognised by other experienced software designers examining the products of the design. Software architecture is often identified with the high level design because high level design may be the only tangible reflection of shared architectural knowledge in the entire system. And even the high-level structure of software gets eroded in long living systems that are shaped over time by many developers that do not share the knowledge and understanding of the problems addressed by and embodied in the software design.

Much work in computer science has been done exploring effective organisations of programs and processes, transient and persistent data, concurrency and distribution. An answer to almost any question may be found in one of the numerous textbooks on data structures and algorithms, operating systems, and data bases. Is this not sufficient as a tangible representation of shared knowledge on software design?

An important problem that is not addressed by this literature of answers is: What is the question? A software designer faced with the task of translating the requirements into an implementation must first of all recognise what are the essential problems that must be addressed by the design including the needs to test and later modify the program as requirements change. This task of identifying and understanding the problems must precede the search for the solution.

This gap is now being filled by a growing body of literature describing patterns of software design. A pattern analyses an essential problem recurring in a particular context and offers an experience-proven solution to the problem. Patterns serve as perceptual filters that help to understand the requirements in terms of the design problems they imply and offer a consistent set of effective solutions to these problems.

A complete collection of patterns for a specific domain could serve software designers as a repository of shared knowledge. But where would a complete collection of essential patterns for a specific domain come from? Is it possible to include pattern discovery and refinement in the normal software development process? Is it possible to incrementally analyse the problems and specify the corresponding solutions? How to relate and compare similar patterns?

All these questions can addressed by ordering design patterns into a decision tree. The resulting Design Decision Tree (DDT) is a partial ordering of design decisions put in the context of incrementally specified problem requirements and the constraints imposed by earlier decisions. We propose DDT as a systematic approach to express, refine, organise, and reuse architectural knowledge for software design.

In the next section we briefly introduce the ideas of design patterns and analyse some limitations of the basic approach. This serves as a motivation for using DDT. Section 3 describes the structure of DDT and section 4 explains the role of DDT in the process of software design. Section 5 provides discussion of related work and examines the contribution of our approach. Section 6 concludes the paper

2 Design Patterns

An approach to capture and communicate architectural knowledge in the form of design patterns [1,2,3,4] is rapidly gaining popularity with practising software developers. A design pattern specifies a solution to a problem recurring in a certain context; a solution that satisfies the requirements either explicit in the problem statement or implied by the context. An understanding of the problem context, intent, and trade-offs of the solution is important for appropriate application of the pattern and its preservation throughout system evolution. In particular the problem analysis must be such that a designer familiar with the pattern can readily recognise it and is capable to apply the suggested solution to the task at hand.

In a concrete application domain design patterns may be organised into pattern languages [5]. A design problem is a result of conflicting forces. A pattern proposes a solution that attempts to balance these forces. However, for most non-trivial problems application of a solution-pattern usually results in some residual imbalance. This is addressed by the succeeding pattern(s) of the pattern language. Application of the patterns from a pattern language should result in sufficiently balanced forces and thus provide an acceptable solution to the problem.

As an approach to capture and communicate architectural knowledge design patterns have several limitations. Even in the same context problems admit several solutions making different trade-offs. Varying contexts imply variation in solutions. Flat organisation of problem-solution pairs does not support exploration and evaluation of alternatives. If each alternative is specified as an independent pattern, there will be much replication in the specification of problems, contexts, solutions and reasoning. Patterns are expected to be complete and "correct" when expressed and thus do not support evolution and refinement of initially incomplete architectural knowledge.

3 Design Decision Tree

Design Decision Tree (DDT) is an approach to incrementally specify, and refine architectural knowledge in the course of evolution. To avoid replication when representing variations and alternatives DDT structures architectural knowledge hierarchically into fine-grain elements we call design decisions.

Each node of a DDT includes:

- partial specification of functional and quality requirements and constraints of the problem
- when requirements are sufficiently specified, an approach towards their satisfaction
- new requirements and constraints implied by this approach
- reference to further design decisions that refine the specification of the problem and the solution

Each design decision is explained in detail, using structured prose, common design notation, examples, and fragments of implementation.

A natural organisation of a DDT is from the more general design decisions to the more specific. This way a DDT allows incremental specialisation of context, requirements and constraints along with the corresponding specialisation of the design. Branching helps to explore the alternative designs and their differentiating qualities in the context of the problem requirements and the preceding design decisions.

Structure of a DDT should also reflect the dependency between the decisions. This supports understanding design by following the essential decisions (order, rationale, goals, alternatives), and re-design based on decision dependency information and traceability of the design to requirements.

At any level independent decisions may be ordered based on the tightness of constraints they impose on the design space. Decisions that introduce fewer constraints may be take first as they less likely to be reversed.

It is important to preserve the traceability of requirements and the corresponding design choices, as well as to know the source of the requirements. It is also important to be able to evaluate to what degree a particular design decision satisfies the requirements and what are its implications.

DDT offers a simple mechanism that supports tracing design decisions to requirements and exploring the alternative solutions. Design rationale in the form of a "logical" explanation may be convincing but is often misleading. A justification of a particular design decision is of a limited value unless the alternatives are presented and analysed using the same criteria.

Despite of its name, DDT is not a tree. Partial architectural knowledge is represented as a forest of several DDTs. Since the ordering rule of taking the least restricting decision first provides only partial ordering, a natural organisation for a DDT is a directed acyclic graph (DAG), where several branches shared same subtree.

Closer examination will also reveal that it is often beneficial to show also those solution alternatives to a problem that would violate the properties established by some earlier decision. These "illegal" branches would create cycles into the DAG, that would force the designer to reconsider earlier decisions. Since DDT aims to remove the need to revert earlier decisions we use these branches into the other direction to document the constraints placed by the decisions to following solutions alternatives.

DDT is designed to be an evolving organisation of architectural knowledge. When DDT reaches stability it represents a family of related design patterns. Each pattern is a collection of design decisions that correspond to a path on the DDT.

4 DDT in the Process of Software Design

Essential architectural knowledge is gained with practice. This knowledge may be refined and reused only if explicitly represented in a tangible form, accessible to and used by a group of people. To achieve this goal software designers are required to reflect on their decision-making process. They should explain and document their design

decisions in terms of problems they solve, constraints they satisfy, qualities they achieve, and consequences they imply.

A development team has to take special care in order to produce a coherent software design. A usable design guidance should strike a fine balance between offering the information that is sufficiently generic and sufficiently specific at the same time. The advice must be sufficiently generic to be useful in a wider range of situations and sufficiently specific to be applicable "as is" to a real problem. DDT addresses this problem by incremental refinement of the requirements and the corresponding design decisions. The direction of the refinement is determined by the specific problems faced by the development team.

DDT is developed by and for the software development team itself. Reuse of a generic element in the form of method, process, architecture, etc. commonly requires significant amount of work from the developer to make it applicable to the problem domain and then to the specific problem. DDT increases the probability of a larger part of the problem being explored and documented.

Strict rules and methods often have a negative effect on programmers productivity and the quality of the produced software. On the other hand, software development organisations cannot afford to repeatedly do everything from-scratch. DDT creates a balance between following the established practice and creating new solutions. Design decisions specified by the relevant DDT should be followed as long as they cover the requirements. If new requirements are introduced they must be specified and the appropriate branch added to the DDT.

When requirements change some design decisions must be reconsidered. To safely undo a design decision, a software designer must know what requirements and constraints this decision addressed, what other decisions depend on it, and what other design decisions were made to address the requirements and constraints that were consequences of the decision being undone.

5 Discussion and Related Work

Issue Based Information System (IBIS) [7] is a hypertext argumentation system, developed to handle system analysis problems that are hard for traditional approaches. IBIS has three types of nodes: issues, positions and arguments, and different types of relations between these nodes. The relations include: responds-to, question, supports, objects-to, specialises, generalises, refers-to, and replace. Unlike IBIS which generic, and rather formal, DDT is specific to software design and does not impose much formalism on the user.

Potts and Bruns [8] describe an interesting experiment of recording reasons for software design decisions. They structure the information as a network of design artefacts and deliberations that lead to these artefacts. While in the form their approach is very close to DDT there are some important differences. Potts and Bruns concentrate on justifying solutions, while DDT concentrates much on problem analysis. Deliberation network of Potts and Bruns captures the history of the design process. DDT also shows alternative solutions of the same or similar problems in varying context and provides information useful for reuse and refinement of represented design knowledge.

Skuce [9] describes a versatile knowledge management tool and an experiment in application of this tool to management of design knowledge involved in the design of a complex commercial software system. We believe that such a tool could also be used for management of design knowledge represented with DDT however, this is beyond the concerns of our work at this point.

We see the main contribution of our work in proposing a simple and concrete model to express and incrementally refine domain-specific architectural knowledge of software design as an integral part of software product development. Our model is based on understanding of the essential problems that recur in the domain and knowledge of alternative solutions to this problems and their implications.

Our ideas are not based on any theory or invention but are rather a report of concrete solutions we used to address the problems we faced when eliciting and documenting software design knowledge with design patterns [6]. We are currently testing these ideas in the context of telecommunication equipment software. A primary motivation for these publication is to better define the essence of our approach in order to encourage its application by software designers, and to welcome the feedback and advice of other software engineering professionals.

6 Conclusions

We see the essence of practical software architecture in shared knowledge and common culture of software design, based on well-understood problems recurring in a specific domain and experience-proven solutions to these problems that are developed incrementally and refined in the course of evolution as a part of the normal software development process. We do not believe that purely technological solutions can play significant role in improving the productivity and quality of industrial software. We emphasise the social aspects of software architecture that deal with establishing a common culture and sharing the knowledge required for software design in a development team. We also do not believe in the "technology transfer", when a would-be solution comes from outside the specific domain and the development team. We emphasise the need for integration of research and development and incremental improvement and refinement of domain-

specific problem understanding and effective solutions to these problems.

The approach based on Design Decision Trees offers an effective framework for co-operative software design for and with reuse of architectural knowledge. Use of DDT in the process of software design makes the designers to:

- consciously consider the choices they make
- explicitly specify their goals and assumptions
- evaluate their solutions against the specified goals
- consider and specify alternative solutions

DDT is a flexible and a versatile approach to express architectural knowledge for software design as families of design patterns. DDT may also be used to guide and document software design of specific products. DDT supports evolution of software by explicitly documenting the dependencies between various design decisions made during the construction of the product. When a certain design decision must be reconsidered DDT specifies what other design decisions depend on it. DDT may offer an effective mechanism to tie together the process and product of software design.

7 References

[1] R. Johnson, *Documenting Frameworks using Patterns*, Proceedings of OOPSLA'92, ACM SIGPLAN Notices, vol. 27, no. 10, pp. 63-76, ACM Press, 1992

[2] B.Anderson, *Towards an Architecture Handbook (Workshop)*, OOPS Messenger, vol. 4, no 2, pp. 109-114, OOPSLA'92 Addendum to the Proceedings, ACM Press, 1993

[3] Peter Coad, *Object-Oriented Patterns*, Communications of the ACM, 1993, September vol. 35, no. 9, pp 153-159.

[4] E.Gamma, R.Helm, R.Johnson, and J.Vlissides. *Design Patterns: Elements of Reusable Object-Oriented Software* Addison-Wesley, 1994.

[5] James O. Coplien and Douglas C. Schmidt (eds.), *Pattern Languages of Program Design*, Addison-Wesley, 1995

[6] Alexander Ran, *MOODS: Models for Object-Oriented Design with State*, in Proceedings of Pattern Languages of Programs PLoP'95 conference, Illinois, September 95. To be published in John Vlissides, James O. Coplien and Norm Kerth (eds.), *Pattern Languages of Program Design 2*, Addison-Wesley, 1996

[7] Begeman, M. L., and Conklin, J., *gIBIS: A hypertext tool for exploratory policy discussion*, ACM Transactions on Office Information Systems, vol. 6 no. 4, October 1988, pp. 303-331

[8] Colin Potts and Glenn Bruns, *Recording the Reasons for Design Decisions*, Proc. of the ICSE-10, 1988, pp.418 - 427

[9] Douglas Skuce, *Knowledge Management in software design: a tool and a trial*, Software Engineering Journal, September 1995.

Industrial Software Architecture with Gestalt

Robert W. Schwanke, Veronika A. Strack, Thomas Werthmann-Auzinger
Siemens Corporate Research, Inc.

Abstract

The architecture of a software system specifies, among other things, its decomposition into parts and the communication between those parts. The structure of this decomposition and interconnection is separable from the protocols (types and sequencing) of communication. A language for specifying this structure and a toolset for checking consistency between structure specifications and code would provide substantial benefits to practicing industrial software architects. Gestalt is an architecture language for specifying structure, with separate, partial support for protocol specifications. The Gestalt toolset checks structural consistency between the architecture and the code. It specifies and checks protocol type compatibility at the interfaces, using the implementation language and tools (e.g. compiler). It provides annotation support for sequencing and other architectural information.

1. Motivation

Practicing architects at Siemens tell us that their most pressing architectural concern is maintaining consistency between the architecture and the code. Whereas it takes a team up to a year to design an architecture, they must then live with it for up to 15 years of development and maintenance. They also tell us that, by the time an architecture specification is published, it is already wrong. There are two main causes for this. The first is that an architecture document is so hard to maintain that its publication is delayed until most of the decisions are final. The second is that the implementation phase begins before the architecture is finally published, and the structure of the system immediately begins to evolve in response to implementation experience. Consequently, the architecture specification is not a living document, but an historical record of what the architecture was supposed to be.

To our customers, "consistency" means structural, or topological, consistency. Intuitively, (a) the code should be broken into parts that correspond to the parts of the architecture, and (b) the paths of communication between parts of the code should correspond to the paths of communication specified in the architecture.

To fill this need for maintainable architectures, the Gestalt project seeks to develop a module architecture language that

- captures the structure of large, complex systems,
- supports those kinds of abstraction that are most needed by current practitioners,
- supports most types of communication mechanisms that are used in industrial software,
- is suitable for reverse engineering and re-engineering, as well as forward engineering, and
- can be rigorously, automatically checked for consistency with the code.

In keeping with our customers' priorities, the Gestalt project has de-emphasized more sophisticated kinds of architecture specification analysis, such as protocol specification and compatibility analysis [1]. Whatever deep reasoning must be done about the architecture, our customers are willing to do it in their heads. What they find difficult is dealing with the volumes of detail necessary to assure that the system being built conforms to the architecture, and that the architecture continues to describe the structure of the system throughout its lifetime.

Therefore, Gestalt emphasizes bridging the gap between the detail needed for automated consistency checking against the code and the abstraction needed for concise yet accurate overviews of the system structure. The principal features of the Gestalt language, most of which are introduced in this report, are:

- Multi-level decomposition into components, where each leaf component represents a set of code modules, as in Ada, C++, or Chill.
- Multiple ports on components, representing different interfaces to other components.
- Connectors between ports of components, representing paths of communication.
- Composite connectors, made out of components and connectors, to selectively conceal/reveal implemen-

176

tation details of complex communication mechanisms.

- A model of connection which generalizes definition/use and is compatible with Shaw's and Garlan's ideas on roles and players [2].
- Attributes to distinguish "implementation" from "interaction" connections (cf. Allen and Garlan [1]).
- Mechanisms to support virtual machine layering, structural exceptions, incompleteness, and multiple architectures.

An additional capability currently under design is user-definable port and connector types, to support architectural styles [4].

This paper introduces the language by using it to describe a well-known toy example architecture. For expository purposes, the example is presented top-down, as a forward engineering exercise. We then sketch a methodology for reverse-engineering the structure of an existing system.

2. Introduction to Gestalt

In figure 1 we see a diagram showing a simple system, previously described by Allen and Garlan [1]. Each directed edge in the graph represents a flow of data in the direction indicated. That flow is implemented by a *pipe*, for which Allen and Garlan give a formal definition.

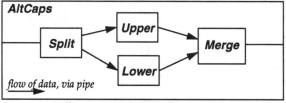

fig. 1: "AltCaps" Example

The same system is shown in figures 2 - 5 as a Gestalt architecture specification in different degrees of detail and completeness. Whereas figure 2 is approximately at the same overview level as figure 1, each subsequent figure adds detail that brings the description closer to the code. Each figure is a view of the design extracted from a common underlying design database. The toolset also maintains rigorous information about correspondences between more abstract and less abstract design entities. For example, figures 2 and 5 both describe the entire system, but figure 5 contains implementation details that are abstracted away in figure 2. The designer can be confident the Gestalt toolset takes care of consistency checking, both within the design and between the design and the code.

We now introduce the Gestalt language using the AltCaps example. Figure 2 shows the AltCaps system as a Gestalt architecture specification. Gestalt has a graphical syntax that gives the diagrams a precise meaning. Each of the four *modules*, named **Split**, **Upper**, **Lower**, and **Merge**, has two or more *ports* on it, with names attached for explanation purposes. Separate ports are used to distinguish different logical interfaces. Each of the flows of data is represented by an *abstract connector*, named **A**, **B**, **C**, or **D**. Connector **A**, for example, connects **Split.hi** to **Upper.in**. An abstract connector represents a tuple in a given relation. In this case **<Split.hi, Upper.in>** is an element of the relation *PipesTo*. The direction of the arrow gives the

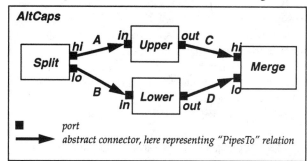

fig. 2: Architecture, showing ports and abstract connectors

ordering of the corresponding tuple. The two ends of **A** are called *plugs*. Their names, not shown, are **A.input** and **A.output**. **A.input** is said to *occupy* **Split.hi**, and **A.output** occupies **Upper.in**. Plugs on connectors are the duals of ports on components. The typical user need not be aware of the distinction between plugs and ports.

Next, we introduce *composite connectors*, *primitive connectors*, and *exposure*. In figure 3 we see a more detailed view of **A** and its two neighbors. Here, we see that

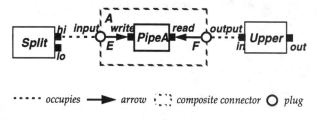

fig. 3: Composite connector

A is implemented as a *composite connector*, consisting of two plugs, **input** and **output**, a component, **PipeA**, and two connectors, **E** and **F**. These two connectors are examples of a kind of *primitive connector*, called an *arrow*, that represents definition/use[*], the most common and basic form of structural connection. An arrow has exactly two plugs, named **head** and **tail**, with the obvious correspondence to the ends of the arrow's graphical depiction. The port occupied by the head of an arrow exports a set of identifiers, which the port occupied by the tail may then import. In this case, **E.head** occupies the port **PipeA.write**. **E.tail**, however, does not directly occupy anything. Instead, it is *exposed* by **A.input**, which in turn occupies port **Split.hi**

Gestalt's model of connection is based on Shaw's model of roles and connection points [2]. A connector has some number of plugs (roles), each of which is intended to occupy a port (connection point) on some component. The connector represents an agreement among the ports as to the syntax of communication among them. There is a *spec* associated with each plug and port, representing an obligation imposed on the software to define[†] certain identifiers and use others. The declarations of a spec's identifiers do not necessarily belong to any of the modules being connected, but may be imposed externally or brought in from some other part of the system. In contrast to module interconnection languages, Gestalt has no syntax for the type signatures of interfaces. Instead, it associates each spec with a set of declarations appearing in the source code.

Next, we consider how pipes are implemented. Often, they are managed by a shared resource manager, which handles buffer allocation and synchronization. This situation is depicted in figure 4. In this view, we see a third plug on **A** and a third port on **PipeA**, both marked "impl". This attribute indicates that the communication going on through this path is an implementation secret of the connector. Communication paths so marked can then be highlighted or suppressed in any given view of the system.

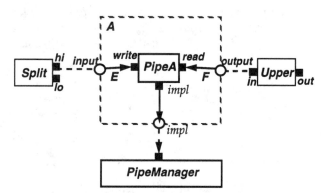

fig. 4: Impl ports and plugs

In general, attributes such as "impl" or element types such as "module" or "port" may be used in database queries and in construction of individual views, as in figure 5.

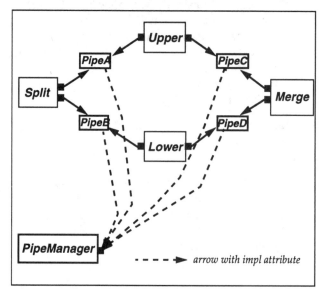

fig. 5: Impl connectors

Here, the boundaries, ports, and plugs of the composite connectors are suppressed, showing all four pipes connected to their common class manager, **PipeManager**.

Now that enough design detail has been introduced, it should be straightforward to develop code from this design. Suppose we wanted to create a system in which the components are independent of the topology of the connections between them. So, let TplSplit, TplUpper, TplLower, and TplMerge each be written as C++ class templates, with template parameters for establishing connections. The system could be programmed (in pseudo-C++) as follows:

```
Pipe PipeA,PipeB,PipeC,PipeD;
TplSplit<PipeA.write,PipeB.write> Split;
TplUpper<PipeA.read,PipeC.write> Upper;
```

and so on.

The system just described is so simple as to, perhaps, put the kind reader to sleep. The point, however, is that one (in particular: a tool) can now almost trivially assess structural consistency between the architecture and the code, by extracting cross-reference information from the code and matching it against the primitive arrows in the architecture. In this example, the cross-reference information is listed in the table below, and in fact match the primitive arrows in the architecture.[‡]

Having filled in the necessary design detail once, the designer may use any more abstract view of the system

178

Def	Use
PipeA.write	Split
PipeB.write	Split
PipeA.read	Upper
PipeC.write	Upper
PipeB.read	Lower
PipeD.write	Lower
PipeC.read	Merge
PipeD.read	Merge
Pipe	PipeA, PipeB, PipeC, PipeD

structure, e.g. for re-engineering purposes, with confidence that the view correctly represents the actual underlying code.

3.   Reality check

Large scale industrial software systems, particularly pre-existing ones, are much messier than the example described in Section 2. In order to be able to introduce the Gestalt methodology into such systems, and use it to maintain their architectures over the long term, the language must be robust enough to describe the structure of arbitrarily ill-structured code. In this section we describe the basic correspondence and consistency relationship between Gestalt and an implementation language, C. We then outline a re-engineering process by which one can capture the actual structure of a large, complex C program in an initial Gestalt architecture, then revise that architecture and the corresponding code.

Although cross-reference extraction tools can tell us about all the individual identifiers in a C program, in practice most developers think primarily in terms of communication and dependency between files. Studying inter-module structure at the granularity of whole files is an important pragmatic strategy, because it relieves the programmers of the burden of learning a structure that competes with the internal structure of files. Therefore, in this re-engineering process, we use Gestalt to specify the decomposition and communication structure of systems at the granularity of whole files. (C is also sufficiently flexible to allow for very small files, so this is not a serious restriction.)

---

‡   The last table entry appears because methods on class instances are implemented as calls to procedures defined by the class. For example, *A.write(X)* is implemented as *Pipe::write(A,X)*. If one chose not to treat such relationships as cross-references, one might still find cross-references from, say, *A.Write* to *Pipe::bufferpool*, in the case where *Pipe* maintains shared representation information on behalf of the pipe instances.

Consider the simple case depicted in figure 6 where a program consisting of two body files and one header file is described in a Gestalt architecture as two modules and one arrow. *Y* is the spec associated with the arrow, and corresponds to the set of identifiers declared in Y.h. *X* and *Z* correspond to body files X.c and Z.c, respectively. The presence of the connector in the architecture implies that X.c and Z.c communicate via a syntax defined in Y.h. The direction of the arrow indicates that X.c should only use the shared identifiers, whereas Z.c should define them.

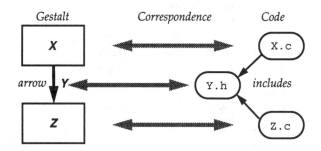

fig. 6: Correspondence to C files

Based on this concept of correspondence and consistency, constructing an initial architecture is straightforward, and can be entirely automated. The result is very similar, in content, to an import/export tree, except that those modules that need to communicate are explicitly connected, rather than having to infer connections by matching imports with exports. Although the details are specific to C, the process can be easily generalized to a broad class of languages and systems.

Given:

1.   A set of C files.
2.   A tool that can extract the INCLUDE graph from them.
3.   A tool that can determine whether a body file defines any of the identifiers in a file that it includes.
4.   A decomposition of the system into subsystems and files. This is typically available in the project documentation, or from the maintainers' heads.
5.   Assumption: Every communication path of interest between components is represented in the code by at least one shared identifier, declared in a header file.

To construct an initial Gestalt architecture,

1.   Define the architecture decomposition to be congruent to the given code decomposition, except that the architecture decomposition need not be as fine-grained as the code decomposition. This establishes

a many-to-one mapping from code module bodies to leaf modules in the architecture.

2. Give each component (module or subsystem) two ports: one for using identifiers defined elsewhere (the *im* port), and one for defining identifiers used elsewhere (the *ex* port).

3. Create one spec in the architecture for each header file in the code.

4. For each triple <*X*, *Y*, *Z*> such that *X* includes but does not define *Y*, and *Z* includes and defines *Y*, establish a path in the architecture from X to Z by the obvious method, illustrated in Figure 7. Each intervening *im* or *ex* port must obey the spec *Y*, either using or defining it, respectively. Where multiple spec names are attached to a port, the port obeys a spec defined as the union of those specs.

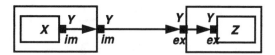

fig. 7: Constructing initial Gestalt architectures

Although these steps produce a valid Gestalt architecture, consistent with the code, it would not necessarily be a very good architecture. Therefore, the re-architects would follow up with any or all of the following kinds of actions:

- Define a separate port on each component for each distinct type of communication between that component and others. Clustering algorithms can be useful for finding groups of related header files. Reconnect the arrows and exposures involved to reflect the different types of communication.

- Attach implementation ports to modules, as appropriate, and reconnect arrows and exposures to distinguish implementation from communication relationships.

- Identify the modules that implement communications infrastructure, and devise composite and abstract connectors to describe how they are used. This may require breaking up the code into smaller pieces so that separate connector instances are declared in separate header files.

- Evaluate the modularity of the architecture and the code, both in body files (.c files) and header files, perhaps using a tool like Arch [5]. Revise both the code and the architecture to improve the structure.

After each incremental change to the code and/or architecture, the two can be automatically checked for consistency. Carrying out the re-engineering process in small,

manageable steps like these makes it much easier for an ongoing project to adopt the technology.

4. Case studies

To complement the language design, we have been studying the communication structure of two large industrial systems. Unfortunately, the Gestalt toolset was not ready in time to support the studies, which instead ran concurrently with tool prototyping.

In one 10 MLOC system, designed with a sophisticated distribution-transparent architectural style, we successfully extracted the client-server graph. We learned that, indeed, the code for a spec was often located in a different subsystem than either the clients or servers for that interface. We also learned that detailed cross-reference information was needed to recognize clients and servers.

In the other system, designed a decade ago and the victim of undisciplined maintenance, we were able nonetheless to find statically-declared mailboxes and semaphores, encapsulate them in composite connectors, connect them to the tasks that use them, and thus present the inter-task communication structure of the system.

5. Acknowledgment

We would like to thank Christine Hofmeister for many helpful suggestions for the organization of this paper.

References

[1] Allen, Robert, and Garlan, David. "Beyond Definition/Use: Architectural Interconnection." *Workshop on Interface Definition Languages*, Portland, OR, Jan 1994.

[2] Shaw, Mary. "Procedure Calls are the Assembly Language of Software Interconnection: Connectors Deserve First-Class Status." *Proceedings of the Workshop on Studies of Software Design*, Baltimore, Maryland, May 1993.

[3] Shaw, Mary. "Heterogeneous Design Idioms for Software Architecture." *Proceedings of the Sixth International Workshop on Software Specification and Design*. Washington, DC: IEEE Computer Society Press, Oct 1991. (Como, Italy).

[4] Perry, Dewayne E., and Wolf, Alexander L. "Software Architecture". *SIGPLAN Notices*.

[5] Schwanke, Robert W. "An Intelligent Tool for Re-Engineering Software Modularity", *Proceedings of the 13th International Conference on Software Engineering*. Washington, DC: IEEE Computer Society Press, May 1991.

Truth vs Knowledge:
The Difference Between What a Component Does and What We *Know* It Does

Mary Shaw
School of Computer Science
Carnegie Mellon University
Pittsburgh PA 15213

Abstract

Conventional doctrine holds that specifications are sufficient, complete, static, and homogeneous. For system-level specifications, especially for software architectures, conventional doctrine often fails to hold. This can happen when properties other than functionality are critical, when not all properties of interest can be identified in advance, or when the specifications are expensive to create. That is, the conventional doctrine often fails for practical software components. Specifications for real software must be incremental, extensible, and heterogeneous. To support such specifications, our notations and tools must be able to extend and manipulate structured specifications. In the UniCon architecture description language, we introduce **credentials**, *a property-list form of specification that supports evolving heterogeneous specifications and their use with system-building and analysis tools.*

Conventional software doctrine calls for component specifications that are:

- *Sufficient and complete:* the specification of a component says everything a user needs to know or is permitted to rely on about how to use the component,

- *Static:* the specification can be written once and frozen, and

- *Homogeneous:* the specification is written in a single notation.

For example, a typical discussion of the promise of reuse [Ben95] is introduced,[1]

> Three prerequisites must be met for a component to be used in more than one system: com-

plete, opaque enclosure; complete specification of its external interface; and design consistency across all sites of reuse. Without these, reuse will remain an empty promise.

It may be possible to adhere to the conventional doctrine for algorithms and data structures, or when functionality is the only property of interest. However, architectural, or system-level, components cannot in practice satisfy these criteria. Indeed, they inevitably will not, and it is impractical to try.

This paper is about what this implies and how to cope with it: why architectural specifications are insufficient, incomplete, incremental, and heterogeneous -- and how software development methods and tools must adapt in response.

Section 1 describes architectural components and explains why they cannot adhere to the conventional doctrine. Section 2 considers many of the properties that need to be specified. Section 3 sets out requirements for architectural specifications. Section 4 introduces an approach to a solution, *credentials* for those properties that have been specified to date.

1. Architectural components and their specifications

Software architecture deals with the overall structure and properties of software systems. The most common architecture description languages (ADLs) support components, connectors, and other aspects of the system such as styles, constraints, or design rationale [ShawGar96, PerWolf92]. Although the issues raised here apply to all architectural elements, this discussion focuses on specifications of the components, which may be either primitive (i.e., written in a programming language) or composite (i.e., defined in the ADL).

---

[1]Note that this description comes from the applications community, not the formal methods community.

The information required to use an architectural component goes beyond computational functionality to include *structural* properties that affect how the component can be composed with other components; *extra-functional* properties that describe performance, capacity, environmental assumptions, and global properties; and *family* properties that assert relations among similar or related components. Software development environments should accommodate an open-ended collection of tools for construction and analysis. Different tools may depend on different properties, and some tools may generate new specification information [ICSE95].

Specifications of architectural components are *intrinsically incomplete* because system correctness depends not only on computational functionality but on other properties as noted above [Shaw85, GAO95]. It's impractical to expect full specifications of all these properties because of the prohibitive effort required to specify a wide variety of properties, whether or not anyone will use the information. Worse, it's impossible: the developer cannot anticipate all the aspects of the component that its users might care about. As an added complication, the degree of precision in the specification may be influenced by the tradeoff between the costs and benefits of improved precision [Shaw81]. Although completeness is impractical, it is still appropriate to expect specifications for a common core of properties, and it is reasonable for a tool to require certain properties. Reasoning with partial specifications has already received some attention [Jac94, Per95].

Specifications of architectural components must be *extensible*, because developers discover new kinds of dependencies as they attempt to reuse independently-developed components together. Even with the best of good faith, component developers cannot describe all the incidental ways their components may interact with the entire environment. Garlan and colleagues analyze the implicit assumptions that interfered with one instance of attempted reuse [GAO95]. Not only is much important information implicit, but users have no effective way to capture information they discover for future reference. As the specifications are extended, information about a property may be received from multiple sources; these must be reconciled [BarWing90].

Specifications of architectural components must be *heterogeneous*, because of the diversity of significant properties, as described in Section 2. It is unreason-

able to expect a single notation to serve for all of them.

Thus the drivers of specification incompleteness, extensibility, and heterogeneity are

- *Open-ended needs:* The designer cannot anticipate all properties that may ever be of interest to some user. Further, future users may find new ways to take advantage of old properties. Interesting properties are of many different kinds.

- *Cost of information:* Even for common properties, it is not practical to produce a complete specification. Further, the precision of a specification may be selected to balance the cost of getting a tight bound against how badly it's needed. The cost of understanding a specification also affects its utility.

- *Evolution:* As time passes, new properties may be added to a specification because someone (not necessarily the developer) discovers new information or new dependencies. Developers can often make progress with partial information but take advantage of additional information.

2. Architectural properties

The main reason why architectural components require incomplete, extensible, and heterogeneous specifications is the diversity of facts about a component that may affect a designer's ability to compose it with other components and achieve a correct and consistent result. This section describes three major classes of properties that augment the conventional functional properties of type, signature, and pre/post conditions.

2.1 Structural properties

The most significant properties for architectural design deal with the ways components interact, and hence with the ways those components can be combined into systems. Especially important is the *packaging* of a component, which includes the type of component and the types of interactions it is prepared to support. The choice of packaging is often largely independent of the underlying functionality, but components must be packaged in compatible ways if they are to work together smoothly. For example, unix provides both a sort system call and a sort filter; although they have the same functionality, they are far from interchangeable. Some common packagings for components and the ways they interact are:

Component type	Common types of interactions
Module	Procedure call, data sharing
Object	Method invocation (dynamically bound procedure call)
Filter	Data flow
Process	Message passing, remote procedure call, other communication protocols, synchronization
Data file	Read, write
Database	Schema, query language
Document	Shared representation assumptions

Distinctions of this kind are now made informally, often implicitly. If the distinctions were more precise and more explicit, it would be easier to detect and eventually correct incompatibilities by analyzing the system configuration description. Such checking must address not only local compatibility (e.g., do two components expect the same kinds of interactions) but also global properties (e.g., are there loops in a data flow system?).

2.2 Extra-functional properties

In addition to functionality and structure, architectural specifications must be capable of expressing extra-functional properties related to performance, capacity, environmental assumptions, and global properties such as reliability and security [MCN92, Shaw85, CBKA95]. Many of these additional properties are qualitative, so they may require different kinds of support from more formal specifications. These other properties include:

time requirements

precision and accuracy

timing variability

reliability

real-time response

robustness

latency

security

bandwidth and throughput

service capacity (e.g. # of clients/server)

space requirements

dependence on specific libraries, services

space variability

conformance to an interface standard

possession of main thread of control

conformance to implementation standard

minimum hardware configuration

intended profile of operation usage

Some of these properties require periodic updates, especially those that assert conformance to external standards (e.g., Windows 95) that may themselves change.

The formal specifications familiar to the IWSSD community are not the most common kind. More prevalent are product descriptions such as the following, which specifies the interface between a software product and the environment required to run it [DeL95]. This specification deals with space and conformance to established standards. The functionality of the product is described (imprecisely) in associated prose and pictures.

IBM or 100% IBM-compatible microcomputer with Intel 80386 microprocessor or higher or 100%-compatible processor.

Minimum 4 MB RAM., 3 MB of available space on a hard disk.

ISO 9660-compatible CD-ROM drive with 640+ MB read capacity and Microsoft® CD-ROM extensions.

Microsoft®Windows˙-compatible printer (not plotter) recommended, with 1.5 MB printer memory for 300 dpi laser printing, 6 MB for 600 dpi.

Microsoft®Windows˙-compatible mouse (recommended).

Microsoft®Windows˙-compatible VGA card and monitor.

Microsoft®Windows˙ version 3.1 and MS-DOS® version 4.01 or later.

2.3 Family properties

Components are often designed in families, sharing assumptions about such things as division of responsibilities, data encoding and protocols. A large family of systems may have constraints on collections of components that must be used together. It may also be important for a specification to express not only the properties of the instance at hand, but also a larger envelope of capability that could be achieved by, for example, modifying setup parameters of changing inheritance relations.

3. Requirements for Practical Architectural Specifications

Component specifications play two roles:

- *Implementation:* giving information about "as-built" capabilities of individual existing components ("How do I *use this component*?")

- *Requirement:* setting out the requirements that a component that has not yet been selected or constructed must satisfy ("What component is needed to *fill this hole*?")

These roles are roughly analogous to the formal and actual parameters of procedures--they serve both to define the capability envelope of a required component and the actual capability of an instance. Just as actual and formal parameters of procedures differ in detail, so do the requirement and implementation specifications of components.

Given the setting described in Section 1, specifications require more support than they get at present (static text files in a given formal syntax). Let us consider, then, the requirements for models, methods, and associated tools that support specifications of the sorts of architectural components that appear in Real Life™. That is, what happens if you force the models to adapt to real-world elements rather than vice-versa? Some of the capabilities that must be supported for practical specifications are

- *Tolerate incompleteness.* Analysis tools must be able to indicate which properties they depend on; if information is missing, they must either explain why analysis can't proceed or warn about the limitations of the results. It should be possible to prohibit dependence on a property -- to be "actively silent"

- *Collect specifications incrementally.* Not only developers, but also users, must be able to add information to specifications. The source, and hence the credibility/validity of the information must be preserved.

- *Support specifications of many properties* in different notations. Add new properties as they turn out to be interesting.

- *Propagate new information.* When new information is supplied, it must be propagated to places where it might improve prior analyses. Further, some properties may be derived analytically rather than declared by the designer.

These can often be improved with new information.

- *Invalidate specifications* when appropriate. Modifications to a system definition or to the sources of derived information may render individual parts of a specification invalid.

- *Search* for components that partially match a partial specification, with an indication of the goodness of fit. [ZarWing95]

- *Support checking,* both that a component specification and its associated implementation are consistent and that a configuration of components is well-formed. Support tools to make minor adaptations when minor mismatches are detected. Support incremental checking for incremental specification.

- *Support flexibility.* Define limits on actual values of properties; describe the envelope of allowable behavior (retaining information about both the envelope and the current instance); separate policy from mechanism.

- *Yield partial value for partial information,* incremental value for incremental information.

4. Credentials for What We Know Is True

To address this problem, we propose the notion of *credentials*: incremental, evolving specifications. Credentials may be viewed as property lists, or lists of <attribute, value> pairs. Credentials must include

- *registered attribute names* and provisions for adding new names (including private ones); a means of indicating which ones are required or optional under certain circumstances

- *multiple notations* for values of attributes

- *credibility,* or sources for the values of attributes. They might, for example, include

asserted:	given by designer, taken on faith
verified:	proposed by designer, verified by tool
derived:	derived (preferably automatically) from other specifications
default:	provided as part of component definition
forced:	determined by nature of definition (for example as part of subtyping definition)

Credentials must be an integral part of the software definition, so that they are supported by the CASE environment and updated in tandem with the code. The associated tools must support operations including

184

- compatibility checks similar to type checking but involving a richer set of properties

- access to externally-defined tools, including extraction of relevant attributes for use by the tool and incorporation of results from the tools as new attribute values

- rules for resolving values for a given attribute that are proffered by multiple sources

- invocation of analysis for checking credentials after code is modified, including invalidation of properties whose values can no longer be confirmed

The UniCon architecture description language [SDKRYZ95] supports the bare bones of this proposal. UniCon specifications are given in the form of property lists; the set of attributes is open-ended; and particular attributes are required for certain checks and tools. Current development will add credibility values for attributes and make explicit the set of notations (including "uninterpreted") for values of attributes.

Research Support

The work reported here has been heavily influenced by an ongoing collaboration with the Composable Systems Group at Carnegie Mellon University, particularly on discussions with David Garlan, Greg Zelesnik, and Rob DeLine. It draws on material presented at the 1995 Dagstuhl in Software Architecture and in a special volume of Lecture Notes in Computer Science. It was improved during discussions in the Software Architecture Reading Group at CMU. It was sponsored by the Wright Laboratory, Aeronautical Systems Center, Air Force Materiel Command, USAF, and the Advanced Research Projects Agency, under grant F33615-93-1-1330 and by a grant from Siemens Corporation. It represents the views of the author and not of Carnegie Mellon University or any of the sponsoring institutions.

References

[BarWing90] Mario R. Barbacci and Jeannette M. Wing. A language for distributed applications. *Proc 1990 Int'l Conf on Computer Languages*, pp. 59-68.

[Ben95] Douglas W. Bennett. The promise of reuse. *Object Magazine*, vol 4, no 8, January 1995, pp. 32-40.

[CBKA95] Paul Clements, Len Bass, Rick Kazman, and Gregory Abowd. Predicting software Quality by architecture-level evaluation. In *Proc Fifth International Conf on Software Quality*, October 1995

[DeL95] DeLorme Mapping Company. WWW page describing MapExpert product. URL: http://www.delorme.com/catalog/mex.htm, 1995.

[GAO95] David Garlan, Robert Allen, and John Ockerbloom. Architectural Mismatch, or Why it's hard to build systems out existing parts. *Proc 17th International Conf on Software Engineering (ICSE-17)*, April 1995.

[ICSE95] David Garlan. *Report of ICSE-17 Software Architecture Workshop*, to appear ACM SIGSOFT Software Engineering Notes, 1995.

[Jac94] Daniel Jackson. *Structuring Z Specifications with Views*. Carnegie Mellon University Technical Report CMU-CS-94-126.

[MCN92] John Mylopoulos, Lawrence Chung, and Brian Nixon. "Representing and Using Nonfunctional Requirements: A Process-Oriented Approach. *IEEE Transactions on Software Engineering*, vol 18, no 6, June 1992.

[Per95] Dewayne E. Perry. System Compositions and Shared Dependencies. Unpublished manuscript, January 1995.

[PerWolf92] Dewayne E. Perry and Alexander L. Wolf, Foundations for the study of software architecture. *ACM SIGSOFT Software Engineering Notes*, vol 17, no 4, pp. 40-52, October 1992.

[Shaw81] Mary Shaw. When Is 'Good' Enough?: Evaluating and Selecting Software Metrics. In *Software Metrics: An Analysis and Evaluation*, A. Perlis, F. Sayward, and M. Shaw (eds), MIT Press, 1981, pp. 251-262.

[Shaw 85] Mary Shaw. What Can We Specify? Questions in the domains of software specifications. In *Proc Third International Workshop on Software Specification and Design*, pp. 214-215, August 1985.

[ShawGar96] Mary Shaw and David Garlan. *Software Architecture: Perspectives on an Emerging Discipline*. Prentice Hall, 1996.

[SDKRYZ95] Mary Shaw, Robert DeLine, Daniel V. Klein, Theodore L. Ross, David M. Young, Gregory Zelesnik. Abstractions for Software Architecture and Tools to Support Them. *IEEE Tr on Software Engineering*, May 1995.

[ZarWing95] A.M. Zaremski and J.M. Wing, "Specification Matching of Software Components." *Proc. of SIGSOFT Foundations of Software Engineering*, October 1995.

PDP: Programming a Programmable Design Process

Stanley M. Sutton, Jr. and Leon J. Osterweil
Department of Computer Science
University of Massachusetts
Amherst, MA 01003-4610

Abstract

We have been developing PDP, a system for programming the process of designing software that is based on Booch Object-Oriented Design. Because PDP allows tailoring and adaptation by participants, we consider it a programmable process. We believe that process programming can help in capturing and managing the inherent complexities of design processes and products, while programmability is necessary to accommodate the dynamic and creative aspects of design.

PDP views the design process as comprising process steps, product artifacts, and execution resources. The process is multi-user and multi-role. The control model includes both proactive and reactive elements. Explicit consistency conditions interrelate product state and process control. Issues that arise in the programming of PDP include the integration of proactive and reactive control, the capturing of interrelations among steps, artifacts, and constraints, the identification of consistency conditions for design products and their implications for process control, and the accommodation of inconsistency and indeterminacy in evaluating design product state.

Programmability is intended to provide organizations, managers, and developers with degrees of structured flexibility that are appropriate for their roles in the design process. PDP will make available variants of the design process; these will be tailorable through static and dynamic mechanisms. A number of issues arise with the introduction of programmability. For example, what distinguishes different design processes and their variants? What is a legal design process or product and to what extent can it be varied? What controls should be available to process managers and to design engineers?

1 Introduction

PDP is a programmable software-design process based on Booch Object-Oriented Design (BOOD) [1]. The PDP project has two major goals. The first is to demonstrate the benefits of process programming for a fundamentally creative discipline like software design, the second is to demonstrate the benefits of putting process programmability into the hands of designers and design-process managers.

With respect to the former objective, we expect the benefits to accrue from the formalization of the design process and products, including especially their interrelationships. We expect that benefits will also accrue

from the ability of the system to drive the process forward towards increasing completeness and consistency of design products. Together, these will contribute to the capture of design complexities and maintenance of design consistency, helping to free designers to concentrate on the more-essentially human aspects of the design process. With respect to the latter objective, we expect the benefits to accrue from a combination of specific features for process tailoring and adaptation, leading towards increasing process fitness, fidelity, and precision. This will help to make design processes more tractable, to keep them focused toward their objectives, and to assure that design products adequately address system requirements.

To realize the benefits we hope to obtain from PDP, we must resolve issues related to both the programming and programmability of design processes. To begin to address these issues, we have formulated a number of hypotheses about design processes and process programs. Development and use of PDP will allow us to test these hypotheses. For example, PDP will be a tool for helping us to discover the degree to which we can and should guide and direct design activities, and the degree to which we can and should offer tailoring support and flexibility. In this paper we describe significant aspects of our approach and indicate the sorts of issues that we have encountered.

2 Design-Process Programming

Although PDP is based on a described design method, the descriptions of that method are vague and lack specific details. For example, two different variants of the method are distinguished in [4]. One of these, the class-diagram oriented process, is illustrated in Figure 1. Even within this variant there are many possible versions of the process depending on the sequencing or concurrency of steps, the number and synchronization of iterations of cycles, and so on. Consequently, the programming of PDP requires many particular decisions about which variants and versions of the process will be supported and how programmability of these processes will be realized.

2.1 Approach

One of our fundamental hypotheses is that the design process must be represented as a coordinated set of perspectives, integrating various views of design activities, detailed representations of design products, and complete specifications of the necessary resources.

Proceedings of IWSSD-8

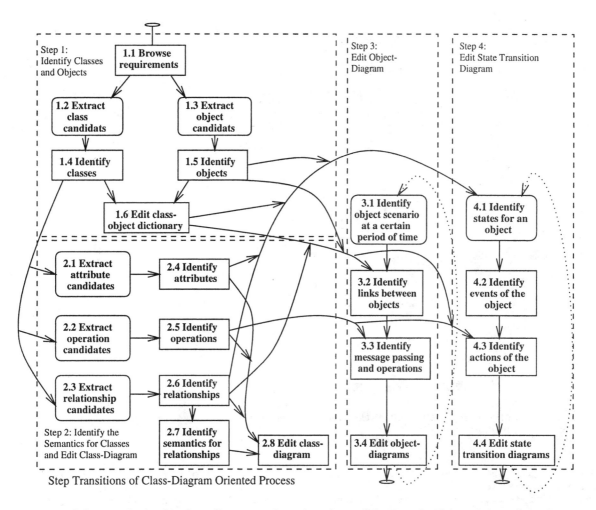

Figure 1: Control flow paths in the class-diagram oriented variant of the Booch Object-Oriented Design process.

Capturing the details of a completed design, and the activities needed to construct it, is crucial. A considerable part of the difficulty in doing this is attributable to the complex interconnections of the various design activities and artifacts. A good illustration of this is provided by our definition of a schema for the Booch Object Oriented Design product (Figure 2). This schema currently incorporates the class, object, and state diagrams of the Booch model. These include 13 types of entity (e.g., class diagram, class, object, state transition), of which 7 types are repeated in the schema, some several times. These repetitions of types correspond to shared objects or inter-object references at the instance level. For example, a given Booch object may be accessed through as many as five points in the schema, including various parts of both the object and class diagrams. Interconnections also occur within the process specification, where steps may subsume, precede or follow, and trigger other steps, and in the resource specification, where physical resources may map to multiple logical resources, and where active resources may use other (active or passive) resources.

Interconnections between steps, artifacts, and resources are also abundant. Process steps and product artifacts are interrelated by definition and use relationships. Process steps also rely on resources, and artifacts are viewed as resources in some contexts. Process steps and product artifacts are further interrelated by an extensive set of wide-ranging consistency conditions. These conditions characterize various states of artifacts, and they provide the basis for conditional control of steps, as preconditions and postconditions, as well as for constraints on steps during their execution. Additionally, as process and product state evolve over the life of the process, so does the enforcement of consistency conditions and their use in process control. In specifying the details of these complex interconnections we believe we have contributed to a more detailed and specific understanding of what makes design so complex and difficult. Moreover, by capturing these details through a programming language idiom, we have also rendered these complexities amenable to the use of computing power to help people deal with them. This computing power is supplied through the PDP control elements.

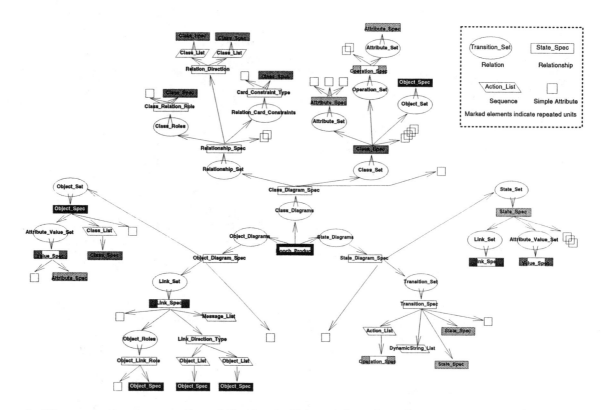

Figure 2: Diagrammatic representation of the Booch Object-Oriented Design product schema (for class, object, and state-transition diagrams).

We believe that the main stream of the design process is best represented through proactive control elements, which drive the process forward. However, these must be balanced and supplemented by reactive control elements, which assure that the evolving design product retains its internal consistency and is able to evolve in new directions as the process progresses. We further believe that proactive elements should control reactive elements. This is important to assure that the number, extent, and effect of reactions remains manageable and that the design process remains generally on course. Both proactive and reactive actions are viewed as recursively definable subprocesses, any of which may be composed (at least in part) from a common set of steps combined to an arbitrary degree of complexity.

Finally, as PDP is intended to support a realistic design process, it must be multi-user and multi-role. At a minimum it should accommodate a design-process manager and multiple design engineers, and these users should be able to participate in the process with a high-degree of concurrency.

2.2 Issues

The programming of a software-design process according to the premises outlined above leads naturally into a variety of issues. For example, it is not enough to simply represent steps, artifacts, and resources; these must be integrated into a meaningful execution model. This model must further accommo-

date the role of consistency conditions in constraining product changes and controlling process execution. The development of an execution-engine that addresses these needs is a project of the Arcadia Process Working Group. PDP represents a driving function to help identify and articulate the requirements for such an execution engine.

Several questions pertain to process execution and in particular the relationships between proactive and reactive control. How much of the process is represented in proactive steps versus reactive steps? What should be the run-time balance of these activities? What kinds of activities are suited for reactive control? (Within PDP we have so far planned repair actions as reactive, but we expect that additional sorts of actions will also be reactive.) In what characteristics are proactive and reactive steps similar, and in what characteristics different? (In PDP it so far seems that many proactive and reactive steps perform the same sorts of activities, but that they may access artifacts to different extents, and that the consistency conditions under which they operate may often be different.)

Another set of questions applies to consistency management. Process steps, product artifacts, and consistency conditions are all highly interrelated; we are still working out the implications of these interrelationships and attempting to determine how best to derive, represent, and make use of this information. A particular application of these interrelationships is in determining opportunities for parallelism in the PDP process definition and for dynamic concurrency control at run-time. Parallelism is needed to help support multiple concurrent users. It is also useful for the efficient evaluation of preconditions, postconditions, and constraints. However, the variety and breadth of consistency conditions implies a high potential for concurrency conflicts with process activities, making concurrency control an especially important and delicate issue. Our expectation is that it will not always be possible to evaluate consistency conditions, even those that are intended to control process execution. That means we face the prospect of having to accommodate not only inconsistency but also indeterminacy.

3 Design-Process Programmability

Software process research is predicated on the belief that process is important for successful software engineering. Processes appear to have utility at the levels of organizations, groups, and individuals. At the same time, there has been a recurrent criticism that specified processes are too inflexible or non-adaptable to be widely effective. This may be especially relevant to design processes, where human experience and intuition have an important role to play. We believe that the resolution of this dilemma is to put programmability into the hands of process users and participants. Programmability does not mean "writing code"; as used here, it means the ability to provide parameters and exercise controls that determine how a programmed process behaves. Programmability should allow organizations to tailor processes to organizational parameters, and it should allow managers and engineers to adapt the process to project requirements and individual needs. The goal is to allow the maximum benefit to be obtained from process control and support.

3.1 Approach

If PDP is to be useful to a range of different design participants, then we believe it must be adaptable and programmable. Our hypothesis is that this is best accomplished by adopting a layered approach. At the top layer we are going to offer users the ability to choose any of a range of variants of BOOD (such as those defined in [4]). It is our hope to eventually incorporate design processes that have proven successful and popular in actual practice. Initially we expect to simply provide a small number of variants, such as the template-oriented and diagram-oriented variants of the Booch process identified in [4].

PDP will give the design-process manager a variety of kinds of control over particulars of a given design process. These may include, for example the ability to select from among given steps in the design process, to orchestrate their sequencing and concurrency, to set the level and strictness of constraint enforcement, to tailor the preconditions and postconditions that control step execution, and to make run-time adjustments in these areas. PDP will also support project-management functions such as the scheduling of tasks and assignment of personnel and resources.

Engineers will have other areas of control available to them. These will include the ability to select from and switch between an agenda of current task assignments, the possibility of selecting from or recommending alternative successor steps, the ability to assess design process and product state as needed to facilitate task completion and control, and options in exercising the specific functionality required for each step. Additionally, engineers should have the ability to provide feedback to the manager on the efficacy of higher-level controls and the need for systematic or contingent adjustments at that level.

3.2 Issues

Programmability of processes raises a number of issues ranging from the philosophical to the practical. A fundamental issue for programmability concerns the identity of processes and the relationships among process variants. What are the properties that are identified with a process and that are essential to any of its variants, and what are the properties that may differ between variants and serve to distinguish them? This is already the subject of research into software design. These questions have practical implications for PDP because we must be able to define the common and variant parts of our alternative processes. The questions also have implications for process discovery, analysis, comparison, and validation, especially among process specifications and definitions from separate sources. What does it mean to support a Booch Object-Oriented Design process? What measures can be taken to validate such a process? And how does one version of the process compare to another?

A related set of issues applies to variants within a process. If variants are rigidly defined they can be kept clearly differentiable. However, if a selected variant is subject to further tailoring, the nature of the variant may be changable to a significant degree. What properties are deemed essential to variant, and what limits should be placed on the tailorability of the variant to preserve the properties required of it?

Many specific questions as to what forms of control should be provided for a design process. For example, we have made the initial decision that a PDP process may be modified by omitting or reordering steps but not by adding new steps. One reason for this is a concern over constraining the semantics of new steps to be consistent with the intended semantics of the PDP process (or, conversely, to avoid arbitrary changes to the process). Another reason is to gain experience in the specification of semantics for process steps that are complexly interconnected to other steps, artifacts, resources. In other words, until we have a more complete understanding of what is required to integrate the existing steps into the process, we cannot adequately determine what must be specified to integrate a new step.

A further example arises with respect to control over the enforcement of preconditions and postconditions for process steps. Must these conditions be adhered to strictly or can they be relaxed? If so, under what conditions? Allowing exceptions in condition enforcement increases the variability and uncertainty of process semantics, with concomitant implications for design quality, but it provides a potentially valuable dimension of flexibility in process control.

A related set of questions concerns who should be able to exercise what forms of control. For example, is it the prerogative of the organization or design-process manager to determine what steps may be omitted from a process? (Or do they both have some say?) Is it up to the manager to determine when preconditions and postconditions may be ignored, or should the design engineers also be able to make such determinations? (Perhaps if the manager is notified?)

Additional issue arise concerning potential conflicts between human perrogatives and inherent constraints on the integrity and feasibility of process and product structures. For example, should processes be designed to preclude patterns of execution that may lead to deadlock between steps, or should these patterns be allowed subject to dynamic managerial control? Alternatively, should a manager be able to direct a process into patterns of behavior that may lead to deadlock between steps? Or should it be possible to violate product integrity constraints that will compromise the subsequent evaluation of conditions that are important for process control?

A major technical concern is the feasibility of accommodating dynamic changes during process execution. These changes might include, for example, adding steps, deleting steps, or modifying step preconditions and postconditions. What are the implications of such dynamic changes for ongoing activities, the products they are producing, and the consistency conditions they are to fulfill? What are the implications for past executions of affected activities and the products of those past executions? In general, the introduction of dynamic changes into the process is complicated because of the implications for both ongoing activities and for historical artifacts and executions. Because of questions like these, rationale should become as important for design processes and process modifications as it is for design products.

4 Status

A PDP prototype is under development as part of the Arcadia project at the University of Massachusetts. A product schema has been defined using Pleiades [6] as the basis for a prospective product-state server. This schema includes types for the Booch Class, Object, and State diagrams, as well as example constraints, which will be further elaborated. A Pleiades schema for a resource-state server is also under development. Descriptions of process steps have been abstracted using template-based and graphical representations. Analyses of interrelationships between process steps, constraints, and product components are being performed. A simulator for the process, which we will use as a vehicle for testing and validation, is also under construction. PDP is also expected to incorporate external services including AI scheduling [3], reactive-control mechanisms from APPL/A [5], and the ProcessWall [2] for process-state representation.

5 Summary

PDP represents a software-design process based on Booch Object-Oriented Design. PDP emphasizes the formal representation of the design process, including process steps, product artifacts, and run-time resources. An important aspect of process representation is capturing the interrelationships among these different process perspectives, especially consistency interrelationships. PDP also emphasizes programmability of the design process, in the form of static and dynamic controls over process execution. These controls are designed to allow managers and engineers to extract the greatest benefits from process support and control. The PDP project allows us to test a number of hypotheses about process programming and programmability, and it has already raised many additional issues that we plan to explore.

Acknowledgements

This work is supported by the Advanced Research Projects Agency under Grant F30602-94-C-0137. Jin Huang has been responsible for development of the product schema, constraints, and step simulator, and Figure 1 is taken from her work. Rodion Podorozhny has been responsible for development of the resource schema. Many of the basic hypotheses and early architectural notions arose from consideration of the work performed in part by Xiping Song.

References

[1] Grady Booch. *Object-Oriented Analysis and Design with Applications.* The Benjamin/Cummings Publishing Company, Inc., second edition, 1994.

[2] Dennis Heimbigner. The ProcessWall: A Process State Server Approach to Process Programming. In *Proc. Fifth ACM SIGSOFT/SIGPLAN Symposium on Software Development Environments*, Washington, D.C., 9-11 December 1992.

[3] David W. Hildum. *Flexibility in a Knowledge-Based System for Solving Dynamic Resource-Constrained Scheduling Problems.* PhD thesis, University of Massachusetts, September 1994.

[4] Xiping Song and Leon J. Osterweil. Engineering software design processes to guide process execution. In *Proc. of the Third International Conference on the Software Process*, pages 135 – 152, 1994.

[5] Stanley M. Sutton, Jr., Dennis Heimbigner, and Leon J. Osterweil. APPL/A: A language for software-process programming. *ACM Trans. on Software Engineering and Methodology*, 4(3), July 1995. to appear.

[6] Peri L. Tarr and Lori A. Clarke. PLEIADES: An Object Management System for Software Engineering Environments. In *Proceedings of the First ACM SIGSOFT Symposium on the Foundations of Software Engineering*, pages 56–70, December 1993.

Author Index

The IEEE Computer Society's coordinating body for software engineering programs and services now includes over 25,000 participants!

Technical Council on Software Engineering

In July 1994, the Technical Council on Software Engineering (TCSE) was chartered by the Technical Activities Board of the IEEE Computer Society as the coordinating body for innovative programs and services in software engineering.

TCSE is the world's fastest growing software engineering association with over 25,000 participants worldwide. As successor to the technical committee of the same name, the Technical Council on Software Engineering continues the growth in member involvement and new topical programs that have been the hallmark of TCSE activities. TCSE is at the forefront of information exchange and support for both practitioners and researchers throughout the software engineering field. TCSE membership now includes the subscribers of IEEE Software and the Transactions on Software Engineering, bringing information and coordination on activities to the entire CS software engineering interest community.

TCSE serves as both a coordinating entity for existing programs and as a wellspring for new initiatives and activities. The key to the Technical Council approach is economy of scale. We provide both resource sharing and extra resources for developing and continuing programs. These activities cooperate in scheduling, awareness, and encouragement for new programs and services. This forms a new critical mass to foster innovation and the expansion of software engineering offerings for the international members of the IEEE Computer Society.

TCSE Coordination

TCSE Chair:
Elliot Chikofsky, DMR Group & Northeastern University

Exec Vice Chair & Vice Chair Conferences:
Gene Hoffnagle, IBM Systems Journal

Secretary:
James Cross II, Auburn University

Vice Chair (new appt):
Shawn Bohner, MITRE Corporation

Vice Chair Standards:
Peter Eirich, Eirich Consulting

Vice Chair Program Planning:
(open)

IEEE Software Editor-in-Chief:
Alan Davis, University of Colorado

IEEE Transactions on SE Editor-in-Chief:
Richard Kemmerer, UC Santa Barbara

Secretary Emeritus:
H. Jack Barnard, AT&T Bell Laboratories

TCSE is managed by an Operations Committee, including the chairs of all participating entities. In addition, a board of industrial, research, and academic leaders provides advice and guidance on the direction of TCSE programs.

TCSE Newsletter

Editor:
Sam Redwine Jr., consultant

Published 3 times a year, the TCSE Newsletter provides news and "where to find" information on programs throughout the software engineering field, including topical newsletters of the TCSE groups.

tcse@computer.org
http://www.tcse.org
http://www.computer.org

Software Engineering Standards Committee

Chair:
Leonard L. Tripp, Boeing Commercial Airplane

Management Board:
John Chihorek, Loral
James Moore, MITRE Corporation
Norman Schneidewind, Naval Postgraduate School

SESC is the principal entity for the development and refinement of software engineering standards within IEEE and coordination with other international standards bodies. SESC sponsors many standards working groups, as well as conferences such as the International Software Engineering Standards Symposium (ISESS).

Committee on Software Reliability Engineering

Chair:
Bill Everett, AT&T Bell Laboratories

Newsletter Editors:
Paul Franklin, AT&T Bell Laboratories
David Rentschler, Tandem Computers

As sponsor of the International Symposium on Software Reliability Engineering (ISSRE), this committee is at the center of research and practice for this emerging discipline. Efforts include comparison of methods, standards development, and support for moving reliability techniques into active use.

Committee on Reverse Engineering

Chair:
Linda Wills, Georgia Tech

Newsletter Editor:
Mike Olsem, SAIC

This committee promotes technologies for the examination of existing systems and approaches for reengineering of software systems. It co-sponsors the Working Conference on Reverse Engineering and has prompted significant growth in both research papers and industrial exchange on these topics.

TCSE Europe

Vice Chair European Programs:
(open)

To better support our significant European membership, a regional TCSE leadership structure is being formed in Europe to coordinate TCSE and CS activities in cooperation with national societies.

Committee on Software Reuse

Chair & Newsletter Editor:
Bill Frakes, Virginia Tech

The Software Reuse Committee publishes the electronic newsletter ReNews and sponsors meetings such as the International Conference on Software Reusability (ICSR).

Committee on Technology Transfer

Chair:
Jim Withey, Software Engineering Institute

Newsletter Editor:
(open)

This committee's objectives are to identify a body of knowledge in software engineering technology transfer, build an active community of professionals, and evolve a profession of transfer specialists.

Committee on Software Process

Chair:
Nazim H. Madhavji, McGill University

Newsletter Editor:
Khaled El Emam, McGill University

The Software Process Committee's purpose is to help structure and improve communication within the software process community. Its newsletter is intended as a vehicle for rapid dissemination of process research results and experience.

Emerging Programs

Members have suggested new initiatives in areas such as continuing education, software management and software maintenance, and research management. Ideas and enthusiasm for new projects and programs are always welcome. Leadership positions available.

Task Force on Software Engineering Profession

Chair:
Chuck Howell, The MITRE Corporation

This Task Force coordinates with the IEEE-CS/ACM initiative on the state of software engineering as a profession to support the dissemination of information and the involvement of members in on-going discussions.

Committee on Quantitative Methods

Chair:
James Bieman, Colorado State University

Newsletter Editor:
Linda Ott, Michigan Tech. University

This committee publishes the Q-Methods Newsletter and sponsors the Software Metrics Symposium as part of a growing series of programs to understand and promote quantitative approaches in software engineering.

Committee on Software Engineering Education

Chairs:
Laurie Werth & John Werth, Univ. of Texas at Austin

Newsletter Editors:
Keith Pierce, Univ. of Minnesota Duluth

The Software Engineering Education Committee has sponsored meetings and workshops at various conferences and has established a newsletter on education issues.

Coordination with CS Publications

IEEE Software

IEEE Transactions on Software Engineering

Representative Conferences and Technical Meetings

International Conference on Software Engineering (ICSE)

International Conference on Software Maintenance (ICSM)

International Workshop on Computer-Aided Software Engr (CASE)

International Symposium on Software Reliability Engineering (ISSRE)

Software Metrics Symposium

International Software Engineering Standards Symposium (ISESS)

Software Configuration Management

International Conference on Software Reusability (ICSR)

Requirements Engineering Symposium (RE)

Working Conference on Reverse Engineering (WCRE)

International Workshop on Software Specification and Design (IWSSD)

IEEE Intl Conference on Requirements Engineering (ICRE)

Symposium on Assessment of Software Development Tools

International Workshop on Software Engineering Education

International Workshop on Hardware/Software Co-Design

Conference on Software Engineering Environments

Workshop on Program Comprehension (WPC)

Joining TCSE

TCSE is an international membership body of IEEE-CS members and others interested in promoting software engineering. Membership is free for Computer Society members, included in your CS dues or subscription to IEEE Software or Trans on SE. Joining any committee listed above makes you a member of TCSE.

For membership information, contact:

Technical Council on Software Engineering
tcse@computer.org
fax +1-202-728-9614
IEEE Computer Society TCSE
1730 Massachusetts Ave NW
Washington DC 20036-1992 USA

updated 1 January 1996

 **IEEE Computer Society**
Technical Council on Software Engineering (TCSE)

developing innovative programs in software engineering for the next century...

Proceedings of the 8th International

NOTES

Workshop on Software Specification and Design

NOTES

Proceedings of the 8th International

NOTES

Workshop on Software Specification and Design

Revised 2/2/96